Oral History in Latin America

This field guide to oral history in Latin America addresses methodological, ethical, and interpretive issues arising from the region's unique milieu. With careful consideration of the challenges of working in Latin America—including those of language, culture, performance, translation, and political instability—David Carey Jr. provides guidance for those conducting oral history research in the postcolonial world. In regions such as Latin America, where nations that have been subjected to violent colonial and neocolonial forces continue to strive for just and peaceful societies, decolonizing research and analysis is imperative. Carey deploys case studies and examples in ways that will resonate with anyone who is interested in oral history.

David Carey Jr. holds the Doehler Chair in History at Loyola University Maryland. He is the author of *Engendering Mayan History: Kaqchikel Women as Agents and Conduits of the Past, 1875–1970* (Routledge, 2005).

Oral History in Latin America
Unlocking the Spoken Archive

David Carey Jr.

NEW YORK AND LONDON

First published 2017
by Routledge
711 Third Avenue, New York, NY 10017

and by Routledge
2 Park Square, Milton Park, Abingdon, Oxon OX14 4RN

Routledge is an imprint of the Taylor & Francis Group, an informa business

© 2017 Taylor & Francis

The right of David Carey Jr. to be identified as the author of this work has been asserted by him in accordance with sections 77 and 78 of the Copyright, Designs and Patents Act 1988.

All rights reserved. No part of this book may be reprinted or reproduced or utilised in any form or by any electronic, mechanical, or other means, now known or hereafter invented, including photocopying and recording, or in any information storage or retrieval system, without permission in writing from the publishers.

Trademark notice: Product or corporate names may be trademarks or registered trademarks, and are used only for identification and explanation without intent to infringe.

Library of Congress Cataloging-in-Publication Data
A catalog record for this book has been requested

ISBN: 978-0-415-71758-8 (hbk)
ISBN: 978-0-415-71759-5 (pbk)
ISBN: 978-1-315-87125-7 (ebk)

Typeset in Bembo
by Apex CoVantage, LLC

For Ava and Kate
May your love for stories continue to grow with you.

Contents

List of Figures viii
Acknowledgments ix
Foreword by Alessandro Portelli xi

Introduction: Oral History in Latin America 1

1 Techniques of Oral History 17

2 Archiving and Dissemination 56

3 Ethics, Power, and Activism 75

4 Language, Translation, and Performance 90

5 Interpretation and Memory 105

6 Topical Oral History 136

7 Oral Life History and *Testimonios* 169

Conclusion: Oral History in Twenty-First-Century Latin America 192

Bibliography 204
Index 231

Figures

0.1	Map of Latin American countries and cities	7
1.1	"El ojo indiscreto: Aprendiendo buenas costumbres" (Candid camera: Learning good customs)	18
1.2	Flyer inviting participation in the testimonial archive project in Famiallá, Argentina, ca. 2005	27
1.3	Mural scene of a massacre	40
1.4	Map of Aldea Agua Caliente, San Juan Comalapa, Guatemala	41
1.5	Wedding procession in San Juan Comalapa, Guatemala, ca. 1998	46
5.1	General Jorge Ubico with "representatives of the native race"	114
5.2	General Rafael Trujillo, Dominican Republic	116
5.3	Women preparing empanadas in Patagual, Chile, ca. 1991	129
6.1	A middle-class family, Cuernavaca, Mexico, 1990	145
6.2	Two couples in Calle Larga, Chile, ca. 1991	157
6.3	Japanese Peruvian men filing by armed military police	161
6.4	Transfer to US internment camps	163
7.1	Father Gerardo Papen in rural Chile, ca. 1991	178
7.2	Indigenous vendor in Cuzco, Peru, 1992	181

Acknowledgments

In some ways, I have been working on this book since I conducted my first oral history interview in highland Guatemala in 1995. Perhaps because of its breadth, this project has incurred a great number of debts. Even before the ink on my first book was dry, Walt Little encouraged me to write a book on oral histories in Latin America. Shortly after the publication of my second book, Kim Guinta replanted the seed. While I resisted their encouragement for years, I have been richly rewarded for ultimately embracing it. When the journey took me into unfamiliar territory, generous and gracious scholars almost invariably assisted my research. To any whom I inadvertently fail to mention, I apologize.

Although I have thanked them individually elsewhere for their contributions to previous projects, the Kaqchikel Maya interviewees, research assistants, families, and friends who shared their time, lives, and memories with me during my first forays into oral history continue to inspire and inform my research and scholarship. When motivation for the project ebbed, reflecting upon their energy, *joie de vivre*, and appreciation for storytelling buoyed me.

As I began to craft the framework, three anonymous reviewers of my book proposal at Routledge helped me to rethink its organization and content. A number of people read earlier versions of the chapters including Bill Taylor, Betsy Schmidt, Allen Wells, Rob Alegre, Renata Keller, Rod Camp, Judie Maxwell, Ben Fallaw, Deborah Estrada, Tom Pegram, Ardis Cameron, Matt Mulcahy, Jeremy Greene, Michael Hillard, Alison Bruey, Steve Stern, Seth Garfield, Rosanna Dent, Lydia Crafts, Dan Castillo, and Chriss Sutherland. Their insights, efforts, and critiques vastly improved the manuscript. Geoffrey Jones promptly responded to my questions about Harvard University's Creating Emerging Markets project. In presentations and discussions in their classes, students at Bowdoin College, Colby College, the University of Southern Maine (USM), and Loyola University asked questions and pushed me to clarify points that contributed to the coherence of the book. Criticisms and suggestions from Daphne Patai, Jim Wilkie, and the other (anonymous) reviewer of the manuscript for Routledge helped me to sharpen my arguments, broaden my conceptualizations, and rethink my emphases.

Although moving from USM to Loyola University undoubtedly slowed the progress of this manuscript, both institutions supported my scholarship and nurtured intellectual communities from which I gained knowledge, inspiration, and friendship. Crystal Wilder provided valuable research assistance. First conceived and organized by Brian Norman, Loyola University's Writing Retreats afforded me time and support to write and revise the manuscript and facilitated companionship in what is an otherwise solitary exercise. Among the many other wonderful Loyola colleagues who contributed to the project, Nick Triggs tracked down obscure sources, Patrick Brugh drafted the map, Ashley Buzzanca scanned a number of the images, and Rachael Martines prepared the bibliography.

In what I fear is a testament to either my tortuously slow pace or taxing personality (or both), I burned through three editors at Routledge before the book came to light. With their sage advice, Mary Dougherty and Bill Taylor helped me to make sense of these transitions and their implications. As the manuscript neared completion, assistant editor Dan Finaldi adeptly guided it through production. From afar, Eve Setch oversaw the process with aplomb.

Anita Jemio facilitated permission to reproduce the flyer from her research in Chapter 1. Parts of Chapter 4 appeared in *Words and Silences: The Journal of the International Oral History Association*. Excerpts from the Introduction and chapters five and six appeared in the *Oral History Australia Journal*. I appreciate the editors' permission to reproduce them here. Stephanie Moore and Grace Shimizu, the director of the Japanese Peruvian Oral History Project, pointed me to the photographs of Japanese Peruvians.

I especially want to thank my daughters, Ava and Kate (ages ten and seven as this volume was going to press). As some of the accounts in this book made it into our bedtime rituals, their unquenchable thirst for stories compelled my search for oral histories that both entertained and informed. With reactions that ranged from laughter to yawns, they were the toughest critics of this manuscript.

As my mother struggled with memory loss, this project took on a new sense of urgency and meaning. She could no longer recall our time together in Mexico, Chile, Guatemala, or Belize. Already indelibly informed by highland Mayas' resilience in the face of poverty, racism, violence, and genocide, my appreciation for the power of storytelling and nostalgia took a more personal turn as I noticed that some of the exchanges that most animated Mom were sharing stories from her childhood. With love, compassion, and commitment that was nothing short of heroic, my father was quick to stimulate such memories and create new ones despite their increasingly ephemeral nature in her mind. Highlighting our shared experiences and our individuality, stories have been a lifeline in our family.

Subjected to innumerable oral histories from Latin America over the years, my brother, Bob, and sister-in-law, Lisa, graciously listened with interest to each one. With her steadfast support and sense of adventure, my wife, Sarah, is central to all that I do and am. Both tangible and imperceptible, her contributions to this monograph have been invaluable.

Foreword

In 1987, Paulo Freire and Myles Horton had a fascinating conversation about participatory education, the culture of the oppressed, and practices of liberation. The dialogue became a "talk book," and the title they chose was derived from a line by Antonio Machado: *We Make the Road by Walking* [*Se hace el camino al andar*]. It was an apt title for a written book based on an oral exchange between a North American educator and a Latin American educator, which comes to mind while reading this book written by a North American scholar on Latin American orality and oral history.

Oral history has always been a path made by walking. When it began to take shape in its contemporary form, in the 1970s and 1980s, not only was there no ready methodology or theory, but it suffered from an excess of empiricism that exposed it to the justified criticism and perplexity of more seasoned historians. So we had to learn by doing, inductively—discovering the questions even before we started thinking of the answers. Oral history was always a learning experience at all levels, from listening to the narrators to trying to figure out the meanings of what they told us and from collecting the stories to finding ways of disseminating them.

That is where this book comes in. Because the questions raised by the interviews and the oral narratives we hear are not the same everywhere, doing oral history in Latin America is not the same as doing oral history in the United States or in Europe (and in fact, as this book suggests, it is not the same throughout Latin America, either, in Guatemala or in Chile, in urban Buenos Aires or among the indigenous peoples in the Andes). So the implicit story that David Carey Jr. writes in these pages is a story of learning—learning a new language; learning different epistemologies; a different sense of time and place; a different relationship between history, tradition, folklore, myth; and a different way of establishing dialogue and communication (in which cultures is it OK to make eye contact during the interview?). As this book shows, Latin American oral historians are fully conversant with the work done in North America and Europe and often display a nuanced theoretical sophistication, yet these experiences cannot be dumped wholesale on a whole other context. Each of our concepts needs to be redefined by the Latin American experience: a useful lesson for North Atlantic ethnocentrism.

Indeed, one of the great contributions of Latin American oral history has been the multilayered dimension of its cultures, including advanced scholarly research in fine academic institutions, thriving oral cultures in rural and indigenous communities (as well as among urban rural and indigenous migrants). Too often, in North American and Europe, orality has been perceived as a relic of a premodern past, as if each new "technology of the word" (to quote W. J. Ong) surpassed previous ones and made them obsolete. Latin America—as well as India or South Africa—teaches us instead that it is a vibrant part of our own multiform modernity in which orality, writing, visuals, and electronics coexist and interact in ways that we have only begun to explore. No wonder Spanish has become the other language in all Oral History Association publications and events, and major conferences have been held in Rio de Janeiro, Guadalajara, and Buenos Aires. (When I organized the XII International Oral History conference in Rome in 2004, the largest national contingent after the United States came from Brazil; some of the workshops were held in Portuguese.)

Oral history, then, has always been a learning experience. As the practice of oral history grew, ideas and methods were shared, theories were constructed, and, while field experience remains the primary learning tool, some of the basic approaches can be outlined and taught. Newcomers to the field now start with a little more background than in the past. This book, therefore, also functions in many aspects as a teaching manual. I especially like the way in which its impressive array of stories, ideas, and bibliographic sources is organized not so much in terms of thematic subjects or geographical areas as in terms of methodological discussions of "techniques," or the steps in which oral history work takes place, from interviewing to interpretation, and the problems oral historians face, from ethics to language. I am reminded of how Paulo Freire and Myles Horton started from the experience of listening and learning from the bottom up but then "talked" their book as educators, as people who not only listened but also spoke and taught. And I am thinking of my mentor Gianni Bosio, who urged us to be "upside-down intellectuals," capable not only of listening to the masses but also of using our intellectual tools to elaborate critically on what we heard and return it to our sources with an enhanced degree of clarity and self-awareness. By telling us what it is like to do oral history in Latin America, David Carey Jr. also helps teach how to do it. Yet unlike traditional manuals and books of theory, the implicit and explicit advice in these pages is not intended for all contexts and all seasons; rather, true to the nature of oral history, general principles are bent and nuanced in accord with what is learned from a specific social and historical experience.

Myles Horton was once charged with the crime of going to the site of a miners' strike (Davidson and Wilder, Tennessee) and "gathering information and spreading it." This is essentially what oral history is about, especially in places—like much of Latin America—where the flow of information and the right to free speech have been as threatened as in those Appalachian hills in the 1930s. In these contexts, as Carey alerts us, oral history is both a means and an end, a democratic way of gathering and spreading information to make democracy grow. This is especially evident in the chapters dedicated to political and topical research projects, but it invests oral history work as a whole, inasmuch as it validates the experience, culture, and language of nonhegemonic subjects and in turn challenges researchers' ethnocentric assumptions.

In this sense, one interesting aspect that seems more developed in Latin America than elsewhere, according to this book, is the oral history of the perpetrators. Too often, the work on memory has been used to reinforce preexisting assumptions, to make us feel good about what "we" did, to fan the flames of resentment about what "we" suffered. All this is necessary. Yet my experiences in interviewing fascists—both leaders and rank and file—have been important educational experiences for me. They did not change my values and my beliefs (nor did I change theirs; this is not what we're in this business for), but they gave me a different sense of the "enemy" as an intelligent human being—to be respected but also to be even more feared for this.

The price paid for higher sophistication and more respectability may have been the blunting of some of oral history's early radicalism and passion. Yet the broad political implications are still as powerful as ever, especially where freedom is more endangered, as is true in parts of Latin America (and elsewhere; it's not as though there were no shackles on freedom in Europe, in the United States, in the so-called developed world). Each interview is, for the researcher and the narrator, an encounter with otherness, an experiment in equality that enhances in both the capacity for confronting difference and questioning their preconceptions. Carey's book is full of such narratives in contexts in which the cultural difference between researcher and community was extreme. In all cases, oral historians had to make recourse not only to their knowledge of history, linguistics, anthropology, and literature, but also to a deeper, humbler form of cultural respect that is, ultimately, political.

Over the past few years, I have had the privilege of giving oral history seminars at the University of La Plata, Argentina. I learned a lot more than I taught. Reporting on the experience back home, I wrote, "This apparently anonymous town, where the streets have no names but numbers, is not unlike my historical hometown of Rome: you can't take a step without feeling history under your feet. And it's a history of a recent, still bleeding past." I met Estela Carloto two days after her grandson had been found at last. I met Chicha Mariani, indomitable in the search for her granddaughter Clara Anahí, stolen by the military the day they massacred her family. And I met Adelina Dematti Alaye. Her son Carlos Esteban, a student, was murdered in May 1977. She told me her family history, beginning with the ancestors who migrated from Italy in the 1870s. And she told how, as she was looking for traces of her murdered son, she met carpenters who were ordered by the police to make coffins for the victims they killed faster than they could bury them, and how the graveyard of La Plata was full of mass graves filled with nameless victims.

I was reminded of Adelina's story in a thoroughly different context: listening to Bruce Springsteen's song "We Are Alive." It, too, is about a cemetery, but as you go near the graves, you can hear the voices crying, "We are alive," and they are voices of the little children murdered in Birmingham, Alabama, in 1963, of the migrants who keep dying in the California and Arizona deserts, of the railroad workers massacred in the general strike of 1877. This is what oral history is about: unearthing the buried memory and the forgotten presence of the unnamed and the silenced, listening to their voices, finding our own voice thanks to theirs, and trying—as Bruce Springsteen sings— "To carry the fire and light the spark / To fight shoulder to shoulder and heart to heart."

Adelina Dematti Alaye passed away a year ago. But her teaching and her example are still part of us.

Alessandro Portelli

Introduction
Oral History in Latin America

In a region in which military regimes tortured, murdered, and massacred people in the last third of the twentieth century, violent pasts often cast a dark hue over oral history research and scholarship. A nineteen-year-old activist when she was arrested in 1970, Brazilian historian Jessie Jane Vieira de Souza recalls being transported in a police vehicle when she went into labor, giving birth to her daughter in the hospital, and waking up to "armed guards in my room, around my bed."[1] She called some friends, who had the guards removed from her room that day. But she later awoke to shouts of "'Let's kill her,' 'Let's kidnap her.' I woke up frightened, grabbed the phone, but it was dead. I yelled for the nurse, but she did not come. That continued for the rest of the night." Still terrified, Vieira was transferred back to prison shortly thereafter. Her account reveals how oral history can access profound understandings of political prisoners' plights.

It also can frame the broader structures of control and intimidation that guards and the prison system deployed to dehumanize inmates. Imprisoned in Uruguay for her activism against the military regime, another Brazilian professor, Flávia Schilling, recalls how Uruguayan authorities coerced her to lie about her treatment and condition before being released: "I had a myoma in my uterus at the time. It was a dramatic situation, because I was 25, and obviously I wanted to leave and have a child. They blackmailed me in the sense that I would only be operated on if I gave a statement . . . It was impossible for you to say that you are great when you only weighed 50 kilograms . . . we were not great."[2] In an indication of how femininity and biology influenced imprisonment, reproduction figured prominently in young female prisoners' incarceration. Considering their ability to access the emotional content of the past, oral histories are one of the best ways to tease out how gender, sexuality, ethnicity, race, and class affect people's lives. Instead of merely recounting facts, interviewees fashion narratives that make sense of the past, position themselves in the present, suggest strategies for the future, and perhaps call upon memory's healing powers.

The same methodology that reveals marginalized perspectives also can give voice to oppressors. A study of twenty-three police officers involved in torturing alleged subversives during Brazil's military dictatorship (1964–1985) demonstrates that violence takes a toll on perpetrators as well as victims. In addition to psychosomatic complaints, executioners describe the toll their work took on their marriages and other relationships. Analyzing those accounts, Martha Huggins and her coauthors show how changes in the Brazilian state affected how torturers justified violence. In light of the effects suffered by victims and perpetrators alike, the authors frame torture as a public health threat and reveal "how organizational systems . . . foster and excuse police atrocities."[3]

As much as reckoning with right-wing regimes has transformed oral history in Latin America, the field is broader than that in scope and practice. Deployable for almost any political purpose in any part of the world, oral history need not be tethered to politics. Adept at denouncing human rights abuses through oral history, Mexican scholars Eugenia Meyer and Elena Poniatowska also have used the method to capture survivors' perspectives of the 1985 earthquake that devastated Mexico City.[4] Their compatriot and the former vice president of the International Oral History Association Gerardo Necoechea Gracia similarly has deployed oral history to plumb the depths of Mexico's middle class from such seemingly mundane topics as state-subsidized housing.[5] Ranging from studies of elites to society's most marginalized members and characterized by topics as diverse as the environment, science, religion, labor, slavery, immigration, foreign relations, and bureaucracy, scholars have used oral history to revise the study of Latin America's past and present.[6] No matter the topic, target population, or individual, oral history is a valuable research tool and technique in Latin America.

My goal in writing this book has been to provide a synthesis of the impressive range of oral history scholarship in Latin America that also serves as a practical guide to conducting oral history research in the region in light of its unique linguistic, cultural, political, and social milieu. By addressing methodological and interpretive issues, I examine the interdisciplinary practice and scholarship of oral history in Latin America. Far from a universal approach to the field or its findings, within Latin America distinct national and ethnic contexts inspire different types of oral history. Rather than staking out new methodological or theoretical ground, I explore approaches to doing oral history research in Latin America.

Broadly defined, oral history is the practice of interviewing eyewitnesses or other people with knowledge of particular events or topics that occurred within their lifetimes. Deployed by historians, political and social scientists, organic intellectuals (to borrow Antonio Gramsci's concept), local leaders, and others, oral history provides both a set of primary sources and a process for reconstructing the past and understanding the present from them. While topical oral history generally seeks to understand a theme or particular event, oral life history is intended to understand how individuals influenced and were influenced by events over the course of their lifetimes. Social scientists often use oral history techniques to access another variant of oral history called oral testimony. Most valuable when contextualized and cross-checked with other sources such as archival documents, images, architecture, and secondary literature, individual interviews rarely stand on their own. What distinguishes those forms of oral history from oral tradition is the latter's pursuit of information beyond the interviewee's lifetime. In addition to interviews and narratives, oral tradition can take the form of epic poems, songs, legends, rituals, myths, folktales, and other creative customs. Those sources too provide insight into the past and present.

Despite its imperfect nature, the field of oral history continues to produce innovative scholarship. Borrowing from subaltern studies, cultural anthropology, and psychoanalytic concepts within literary criticism, scholars recently have used oral histories to explore the complexities of personal and national identities and to rethink the Latin American literature of *testimonio* or bearing witness to injustice.[7] Engaging oral sources offers one way of challenging conventional approaches and official histories that tend to be based on archival sources.

One of the most exciting aspects of oral history research is the insight it offers into how people reconstruct the past. While few historians can interrogate the scribes who produced archival documents, scholars can ask interviewees about their motives, inspirations, aspirations, objectives, and ideals to better understand why aspects of the past transpired as they did and why people recollect them as they do. Rich with historical information, oral histories contain worldviews, epistemologies, and systems of thought. Methods and theories gleaned from oral history research, particularly those in contradiction to European and US approaches such as Maya conceptualizations of time that are both linear and cyclical or Brazilian Kalapalo peoples' lack of concern with resolving ambiguities in their narratives, can challenge dominant paradigms and radically reinterpret the past and present.[8]

Oral history research affords access to history that is otherwise unrecorded. A clandestine meeting at the National Palace in Mexico between a select group of oil workers and top presidential advisers in 1987 offers an example of historical revelations through oral history. With tensions rising between the oil workers' union and foreign oil companies, authorities hoped to position workers sympathetic to the state in different sections of the union to advance the "interests of the national executive."[9] Absent a paper trail, interviews were among the only sources of information about the secret meeting and confidential plan.

The Politics of Oral History in Latin America

Oral history often reflects the complex relations between scholarship and activism. In a helpful distinction, historian Iván Jaksíc associates the former with a method that provides "both the context and the opportunity for individuals to develop their own stories fully" and the latter with a tool that uses interviews to condemn atrocities or advance particular political or social views.[10] Many Latin American scholars consider decrying human rights abuses and political corruption a cornerstone of their work. "Probably owing to the nature of our Latin American realities, the comings and goings of caudillos, military coups, dictatorships and constant violations of human rights, the work and products of oral history acquire a fundamental dimension, its character of denunciation," suggests Meyer.[11] The recent past makes recovering some histories inherently political, as well as extremely sensitive and often dangerous. In nations where victims continue to run into their torturers or family members' and friends' murderers, impunity reinvokes traumatic memories and forces victims to relive past horrors. As in other geographic areas, politics and history influence the practice and scholarship of oral history in Latin America.

For many scholars from the region, Latin America's radical political context offers a broader purpose to oral history—one reminiscent of the oral history projects in the United States in the 1960s involving African Americans, Native Americans, and women in general.[12] Shared techniques and methods are but one manifestation of the way social histories of ethnic groups, immigrants, prisoners, and others at the peripheries of power in the United States and Europe influenced Latin American scholars, who increasingly have used oral history to understand the participation and perspectives of those traditionally absent from the historical record.[13] At the same time, characteristics that Latin America shares with other developing regions differentiate it from the United States and western Europe. In addition to a long history of colonialism and imperialism, Latin America has been deeply marked by late-twentieth-century military regimes that deposed civilian governments and ruled ruthlessly. Argentine historian Pablo Pozzi insists, "It is notable how oral history manuals and guides written by First World colleagues have few uses, at least in Argentina, since they are based on practices and experiences of studying developed societies."[14] In turn, eminent oral historian Alessandro Portelli laments that in the United States and Europe, "little is known of the sophisticated contributions of Latin American oral historians."[15] Recognizing distinctions in the practice of oral history in Latin America that such scholars as Pozzi, Meyer, and Necoechea point out does not discount the many similarities in oral history as a methodology and research technique wherever it is practiced; it merely calls for careful consideration of regional differences to optimize the practice of oral history in discrete settings.

Similarly to how scholars and activists have deployed oral history techniques to denounce communist atrocities in the former USSR, Cambodia, and other parts of the world, oral history research has apprised truth and reconciliation commissions (TRCs) and judicial proceedings against Latin American architects of civil war and genocide. Among other precedents, the Leipzig war crimes trials after World War I and the more effectual Nuremberg trials after World War II established the importance of oral testimony in the pursuit of justice. Although they constitute a different type of oral source and are mediated by judges and lawyers instead of scholars, courtroom testimonies have been particularly powerful in Latin America too.

The 2013 trial of Guatemalan dictator José Efraín Ríos Montt offers an example of how oral testimonies affect outcomes. During his seventeen-month rule in 1982–83, Ríos Montt orchestrated attacks that razed hundreds of indigenous communities and killed tens of thousands of mostly Maya people. With 103 K'iche' Mayas testifying against him, survivors' traumatic recollections directly informed the judicial proceedings and Judge Yassmín Barrios' May 10, 2013, verdict that found Ríos Montt guilty of genocide and crimes against humanity. Even though Guatemala's Constitutional Court overturned the ruling ten days later, impunity is increasingly eroding in Latin America. By excavating the past, confronting the many truths of what happened, and filling in lacuna left by archival materials or a lack thereof, oral history research can facilitate transitions to more just, transparent, and democratic societies.

Therein lies oral history's tremendous potential in Latin America to assist in the rebuilding of postconflict or, as Guatemala and El Salvador have come to be known, postpeace nations. Collaboration between governments and universities is one of the ways academic research has political implications. The partnership between Brazil's Amnesty Committee of Justice Department and three federal universities—in Pernambuco, Rio de Janeiro, and Rio Grande do Sul—offers an example of how approaching the past "from an amnesty perspective" transforms how states and societies address particularly vexing aspects of their pasts to forge more fruitful futures.[16] Brazilian political scientist Maria Paula Araújo asserts, "Oral history is playing an effective role in the democratic transition of Latin America."[17]

The twin aspects of historicity—acting in and narrating the past—enjoy a synergy through oral history. As the actors become the tellers, they at once represent and appropriate their own agency and subjectivity. In contrast to portrayals of indigenous people as "mute and terrified cannon fodder" in Central America's civil wars,[18] oral histories reveal that many rural indigenous people in El Salvador embraced armed rebellion as a means to regain their land and assert their labor rights.[19] Communities can harness oral history to carve out their autonomy from dominant society even as they articulate their relations to it.[20] Exchanges between organizers and indigenous participants in oral history workshops in Oaxaca, Mexico helped the latter to understand "how they have shaped and been shaped by . . . events."[21]

In understanding how others have altered the past through their actions, people can recognize their own ability to improve the conditions in which they live. Local groups like some in Recife, Brazil, have used oral history to win the right to public services like water and electricity.[22] Against the backdrop of cities where everyday life was marked by violence and a lack of basic infrastructure and services, working-class people have realized they had to be self-reliant. Their sense of empowerment encouraged them to create their own history. One Guatemalan activist explains, "Trade unionism presented a possibility for change, for talking about the exploitation you experienced in flesh and blood and for becoming what we called 'the integral man,' the historical subject, through the transformation of oneself—not drinking, not accepting injustice."[23] Narrating and making history have intertwined in ways that allowed union members to forge their own paths and then validate their accomplishments by emphasizing them in their life histories.

A Brief History of Oral History in Latin America

With oral traditions dating back hundreds if not thousands of years, Latin America is a rich region in which to study and practice oral history. Orality has long been a cornerstone of communication in indigenous, Afro-Latin American, and other ethnic groups. Although a concerted effort to professionalize oral history research in Latin America began in the 1970s, not until Rio de Janeiro hosted the 1998 International Oral History Association conference were Latin American approaches to oral history disseminated throughout the field more broadly.

The archaeological record provides evidence of oral history and oral tradition in the Americas. Although sculpted stelae generally do not refer to oral texts, they are historic in nature, and the mythological references contained therein suppose a canon of shared beliefs and stories. Suggesting the orality of much history and other information, the word for "read" in some modern Maya languages is homophonous with "yell," perhaps dating back to public ceremonies in which theocratic readers would read texts on stelae or in codices aloud to assembled groups.[24] Many of the first-known written indigenous accounts after the Spanish invasions, such as the *Popol Wuj* from Mesoamerica and *Huarochiri Manuscript* from the Andes, were records of oral histories and oral traditions passed down through generations.[25] As evidence that the *Popol Wuj* was known for centuries and likely passed on orally, scenes from it appear on ceramic vessels from the sixth century. Traveling around Mesoamerica in the mid-sixteenth century, Franciscan friar Bernadino de Sahagún collected oral accounts from Nahuatl speakers for his *Historia general de las cosas de Nueva España* (1577). In the Andes, Pedro Cieza de León similarly consulted Andean oral histories and traditions to write his *Parte primera de la crónica del Perú* (1553). Some sixteenth-century Spanish chroniclers privileged spoken accounts over written records. In their studies of miraculous shrines and images in colonial Mexico, the chroniclers Francisco de Florencia and Cayetano Cabrera y Quintero considered popular opinion and reputation "the best proof of historical truth."[26] As Inquisition records in the Andes attest, during much of the colonial era, oral testimony was connected to surveillance and control of people.

In a reflection of their colonial predecessors, nineteenth-century intellectuals and elites used oral histories to justify social hierarchies that privileged those of European descent over indigenous and African peoples and their descendants. To write histories of independence and early nation building, historians like Bartolomé Mitre from Argentina and Diego Barros Arana from Chile interviewed "prominent actors and policy makers."[27]

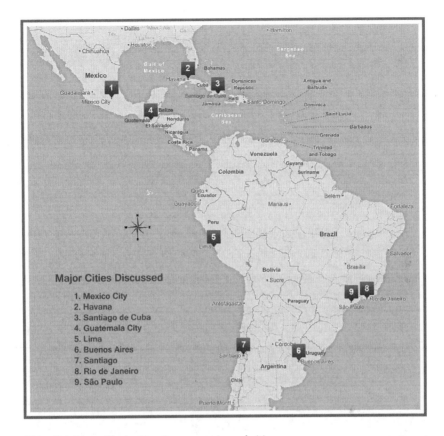

Figure 0.1 Map of Latin American countries and cities
License courtesy of Scribble Maps, created by Loyola University Maryland Language Learning Center

Throughout the colonial and national eras, oral history frequently served political and social agendas.

Even as Latin America broke free from European colonialism, independence did not necessarily set the region on a course of autonomy. Oral history was no exception. As an academic discipline, it developed in the shadow of US and European efforts to professionalize the practice. Such nineteenth-century endeavors as an attempt to write Hawai'i's history based on oral histories in the 1830s and Jonas Bergen's recordings of elders' memories in the 1880s notwithstanding, oral history in the United States became increasingly institutionalized after 1948 when Columbia University professor Allan Nevins began collecting oral histories of prominent individuals, mostly white, elite men. Eight years later, the University of California, Berkeley, founded the Regional Oral History Center; its existence can be traced back to the historian Hubert Howe Bancroft, who traveled the western United States,

Mexico, and Central America from 1874 to 1896 interviewing people to collect their "living memories" about exploration and settlement processes.[28] Precipitated by the US government's sponsorship of oral life histories during the Great Depression and through the Work Projects Administration,[29] oral history's focus on social, artistic, and political personalities was transformed when radio made it possible for a broader public to create, access, and analyze oral histories.

Before universities began supporting oral history research, popular educators and other scholar-activists deployed interviews to mitigate marginalization and empower disenfranchised people.[30] Beginning in the 1930s, the founder of the Highlander Folk School in Tennessee, Myles Horton, facilitated processes whereby people used their personal narratives "to analyze their own experience."[31] At Highlander workshops, miners and other industrial workers framed their memories in broader contexts of economic and political structures of oppression. Similarly pursuing progressive pedagogy, Brazilian educator Paulo Freire encouraged literacy among poor people through dialogue focused on themes of local significance. Ironically, Brazil's military government fast-tracked his influence abroad by exiling him in 1964. After living in Bolivia and Chile, he accepted a visiting professorship at Harvard in 1969. The next year, his book *Pedagogy of the Oppressed* was published in Spanish and English. While Horton's and Freire's ideas and practices have influenced oral history practitioners, the popular educators Alice Lynd and Staughton Lynd expanded the application of oral history research by using a portable cassette recorder—first available in 1963—to preserve working-class oral accounts.[32]

By the 1950s in England and 1960s and 1970s in the United States, historians began reconstructing the past around the perspectives of nonelites.[33] This shift in the academy correlated with broader civil rights and student movements of the 1960s. Inspired by the mantra "The personal is political," feminist scholars introduced new types of questions to explore ordinary people's everyday lives. With close links to labor and other social movements, the early British history workshops offered a model for Latin Americans who sought to write histories from below based on the historical perspectives of workers, peasants, women, indigenous peoples, and other marginalized populations. At a time when memory was enjoying a renaissance in many academic circles and social scientists encouraged the interview as a valuable source, the Oral History Association was founded in the United States in 1967 despite many historians' skepticism about using memory as a historical source. Whether in studies of rural people in Mexico, Ecuador, and Costa Rica, indigenous people in Guatemala, Bolivia, and Peru, political movements in Puerto Rico, or urban laborers, women, and migrants in Argentina and Uruguay, an emphasis on popular sectors continues to characterize many oral history projects in Latin America.[34]

Lively debates about the uses and goals of oral history in Latin America enriched the field. Sponsored by the Ford Foundation and the Getúlio Vargas

Foundation, an oral history training course for twelve Brazilian scholars offers one example of competing perspectives. As Meyer, James Wilkie, and Edna Wilkie led the course in Río de Janeiro in July 1975, they disagreed about the best focus for the regional oral history centers that the Brazilian scholars were charged with opening. Based on the model she had developed by interviewing often illiterate participants of the Mexican Revolution, Meyer encouraged participants to conduct topical oral history interviews with poor people to develop a "history from below."[35] In contrast, the Wilkies insisted scholars should focus their attention on recording accounts from leaders at various levels of society to shed light on the way modernization was shaping the nation. In the process, the workshop participants gained a rich sense of the issues, challenges, and choices involved in oral history research. At the federal universities that had sent scholars to the course, oral history research related to urban development, political exile, and foreign diplomacy soon came to life.[36]

Illuminating as the Río de Janeiro workshop example is, it suggests a false dichotomy between popular and elite history that belies the work of the many Latin American scholars who approach the field as a continuum. From early-twentieth-century Maya leaders who charted a course for the "improvement of indigenous people" in highland Guatemala to the Tarascan judges, community leaders, gunmen, and other leaders who directed daily life in the village of Naranja in Mexico, indigenous elites have formed the subject of oral history studies.[37] Pioneers in the study of marginalized peoples broadened their research to include wider swaths of the population. After earning international acclaim for his research among poor Mexicans and Puerto Ricans, the anthropologist Oscar Lewis conducted oral life histories with Cubans across different socioeconomic sectors in rural and urban areas.[38]

Based on interviewing people whose personal experience of injustice is reflective of that of a larger group, *testimonio* literature emerged around the time oral history research was taking off in Latin America. Throughout the last third of the twentieth century and into the twenty-first century, *testimonios* came of age in Bolivia, Peru, Honduras, Nicaragua, Guatemala, and elsewhere.[39] Often those sources inspired oral history projects. Although a thorough examination of the field is beyond the scope of this book, *testimonio* scholars, unlike oral historians, generally are less concerned with learning about the past more broadly than with using the interviewee's experience or perspectives of particular events—often related to exploitation and abuse—to craft narratives about social justice. Jaksić's description of two types of oral history in Latin America is helpful for understanding the distinction between *testimonios* and oral history. The former is akin to "an instrument that extracts impressionistic testimony to illustrate a view of history, rather than to explain history," and the latter is "a participatory method that weaves a person's knowledge, interpretation, and experience of events with those of the historian."[40] The divergent goals of oral historians, human rights workers, and *testimonio* scholars often result in distinct processes and products. Despite methodological and other differences, the fields often overlap.

Oral history as a field began to find fertile ground in Latin America around the same time the military in Brazil, Chile (1973–88), Argentina (1976–83), and elsewhere overthrew democratically elected governments and introduced repressive rule. Institutions in Chile, Argentina, and Colombia launched oral history projects to investigate human rights abuses and other subjects. In 1971, Argentina's Instituto Di Tella initiated an oral history program to collect memories about economic, social, and political conditions. During its few years of activity, it shared transcripts with Columbia University's Oral History Research Office, which had offered advice, guidelines, and funding. The research office's influence is evident in Argentine researchers' focus on politicians. With at least six active oral history archives, four journals dedicated to the study of oral history (most notably *Voces Recobradas*), and an annual oral history national conference, Argentina enjoys an active community of oral history practitioners. On the other side of the Andes mountain range, Chilean and foreign-led oral history projects emerged. Plying their trade cautiously under the Augusto Pinochet dictatorship (1974–90), Chilean scholars used oral histories to explore urban and mine workers' lives and organizational capacity as well as the plight of the Popular Unity coalition overthrown by the military.[41]

For projects in Peru, where a more benign military government seized power in 1968, and in Brazil, scholars developed oral history courses to train researchers in oral history techniques, methodology, and project planning. Although a few oral history projects such as Hélio Silva's study of the Getúlio Vargas regime (1930–45) predated the aforementioned 1975 Rio de Janeiro course, many other workshops developed as a result of that exposure to oral history's potential. In light of the failure of some large-scale projects during the military dictatorship, Brazil's recent renaissance in oral history can be attributed partly to grassroots initiatives and the democratic opening in the 1990s.[42]

Led largely by Meyer at the Instituto Nacional de Antropología e Historia (INAH, National Institute of Anthropology and History), Mexico too enjoyed a fluorescence of oral history projects. In 1971, Meyer founded the Programa de Historia Oral (PHO, Oral History Program) in the basement of INAH. Shortly thereafter, she organized the first formal project and opened the Archivo de la Palabra (Word Archive). Founded in 1956 by INAH, the Fonoteca (Sound Archive) preceded the Archivo de la Palabra. Focusing on historical perspectives of the "disinherited," Meyer considered Mexico's low education rates an advantage since illiterate interviewees' "information was fresh, unsophisticated, and uncontaminated by study."[43] With projects that ranged from interviews with Spanish and Latin American exiles to studies of cinema, education, medicine, tradition, and culture, the PHO has shed light on the extraordinary and ordinary aspects of life in Mexico. Concepción Millán describes her plight as an eight-year-old girl during the Mexican Revolution.

One night in 1914 as her family was preparing for bed, they heard a knock on the door. "My father got up and I slipped between his legs and put my feet on his feet and he walked with me holding his legs tight," she recalls.[44] When soldiers burst into the home and raided the kitchen, she clung to her father. When the troops left and conscripted her father, she again held on tight and thereby climbed onto the horse with him. There she stayed until her uncle negotiated her father's release. Such poignant accounts of large historical forces speak to the richness of oral history. An interest in working-class history and urbanization propelled many Mexican oral historians.[45] Almost immediately, PHO scholars began publishing catalogues, analytical essays, and methodological articles based on their projects.[46] As was true in Argentina, early collaborative efforts in Mexico with US institutions and scholars bore rich fruit.[47]

As much as Latin American scholars appreciated collaboration with US and European counterparts, as early as 1978, Meyer and others argued that Latin America's unique conditions and circumstances demanded distinct methodologies. As research in Peru, Colombia, Mexico, and other countries progressed, oral history practitioners crafted new approaches and analyses.[48] Workshops in Brazil and Venezuela in the late 1970s facilitated collaboration across borders. The distinct topics, styles, and theories that developed in different national contexts notwithstanding, the political instability and state violence that marked many Latin American countries altered the trajectory of oral history throughout the region. In the same way the Mexican government's 1968 student massacre precipitated an era when oral history research was decidedly political, many professional and popular intellectuals pursued questions of human rights and social justice because military governments in South and Central America tortured and murdered dissidents. Of course, those questions were not unique to Latin America.

Given the nature of its revolution, the prevalence of oral history projects in Cuba is not surprising, particularly in light of the Casa de las Américas International Testimony award. While the regime endorsed progovernment *testimonios*, scholarly oral historiography was largely absent. When interviewees critiqued the socialist government, Cuban authorities shut down oral history projects.[49] Memoirs like Reinaldo Arenas' *Antes que anochezca* (1992), films like Tomás Gutiérrez Alea and Juan Carlos Tabio's *Fresa y chocolate* (1993), novels, short stories, and other media offered incisive critiques of the Cuban Revolution, but even at the dawn of the twenty-first century, authorities only tentatively endorsed independent oral history research.[50]

Although Brazil, Argentina, and Mexico continue to dominate the field in Latin America, burgeoning efforts have coalesced in other countries, among them Colombia, Panama, and Nicaragua, each of which has hosted an International Oral History Association conference (in 2005, 2007, and 2009, respectively).[51] By 1984, scholars from Bolivia, Cuba, Guatemala, and Nicaragua had completed oral history projects. Shortly thereafter, new works emerged in Honduras, El Salvador, Costa Rica, Colombia, and Uruguay. In 1988, Mexico City hosted the first conference for oral historians from Latin

America and Spain. About 150 Spanish-speaking attendees came from eleven countries and Puerto Rico to advance debates and knowledge about oral history methodology, practice, and uses. Instead of setting oral history apart, they explored the complementary relation between oral and written sources, particularly as a means to make history accessible to and inclusive of people at the margins.[52] Even as the United States and Europe overshadowed the field.

Latin American scholars enjoyed a linguistic opening in 1989 when the journal *Historia y Fuente Oral* was launched in Spain. The International Oral History Association also helped to bring attention to the remarkable work being done in Latin America. In an indication of how the practice of oral history in English- and Spanish-speaking countries began converging, in 2002, the journal of the International Oral History Association, *Words & Silences/Palabras & Silencios*, published an integrated bilingual edition.[53] By that time, Mexico, Brazil, Argentina, Chile, and Nicaragua all boasted vibrant national oral history associations. To facilitate the exchange of ideas and scholarship among oral historians, Latin American institutions, universities, and oral history associations formed the Red Latinoamericana de Historia Oral (Latin American Oral History Network) in 2010.[54] The following year, it produced an anthology of Latin American oral history scholarship.[55]

Synergies around common ground and goals are especially evident in transnational collaborative endeavors. In a project that speaks to their geographies, the Asociación de Historia Oral de la República Argentina (AHORA, Oral History Association of the Republic of Argentina) and the Federal University of Paraná in Brazil have jointly studied migration and borders. The State University of Pelotas in Brazil, Autonomous University in Guanajuato, Mexico, and AHORA also have worked together to study "the world of work" through oral history research.

In an unintended consequence of the growing success and professionalization of oral history in Latin America, at times the field has become exclusionary. Even with regional gatherings and collaborations, Panamanian historian Marcela Camargo Ríos laments, "Blocks are formed according to regions and continents, creating invisible—but nonetheless real—walls."[56] The 2009 Associação Brasileira de História Oral (Brazilian Oral History Association) Southern Region's Fifth Biennial Conference marked two firsts: substantial federal funding and the exclusion of presenters who did not have or were not studying for graduate degrees. Such prerequisites discount the organic intellectuals, amateur historians, and others who have conducted oral history research. Such distance between academic and popular approaches to studying the past helps explain why indigenous theorizing about history and oral narratives is only recently making inroads among scholars. Restrictions are not necessarily the norm, however. AHORA attracts professional and amateur oral historians from universities, cultural institutions, municipal programs, secondary schools, and research institutions. Despite being isolated and resource poor, groups in nations with no oral history centers or archives have recorded and disseminated oral histories.[57]

The Interdisciplinary Nature of Oral History

Anthropology, ethnography, linguistics, biography, literary analysis, political science, folklore, oral tradition, sociology, psychoanalysis, journalism, and life stories (whereby the interviewer guides the storyteller in recounting "all the stories and associated discourses . . . and the connections between them") have enriched oral history.[58] By the mid-nineteenth century, journalists frequently used interviews to ply their craft; by the early twentieth century, anthropologists and other social scientists, too, used oral evidence. From sociology, oral history has borrowed methods of representative sampling. With its attention to how individuals craft narratives to make sense of their experiences, life-story methods have contributed to oral history practices. Oral history analysis has benefited from literary and cultural studies' focus on how emotion affects first-person accounts. As much as these disciplines overlap, they also maintain their distinct historical roots, trajectories, methods, and uses.

Enhanced by their analysis of the relation between life stories and social context, anthropologists have struck rich veins of historical data through their interviews and ethnographic fieldwork. Generally focused on the present, participant observation and other ethnographic methodologies frequently facilitate interpretations of the past. When Argentine sociologist Javier Auyero used participant observation to understand the relations between local politicians and their constituencies, he revealed how poor Argentines constructed memories of Eva Perón.[59] By casting a wide net and incorporating nontraditional historical sources, ethnographic studies have revealed myriad places where history resides: in myths, standardized prayers, clothing, topography, architecture, lineage and kinship conceptions, dance, song.[60]

Psychology's and anthropology's methods for critically analyzing oral sources and techniques for identifying how bias, fabulation, retrospection, repression, contemporary realities, and the interviewer alter interviewees' memories have helped scholars interpret oral histories as well.[61] By the 1970s, the usefulness of memory as a source was so hotly contested among scholars that it became a subject of study. Literary and biographical studies that explore how personal identity, memory, and narrative are intertwined have illuminated the many factors that shape how the past is remembered.

Feminist scholars, postmodern anthropologists, and qualitative sociologists who questioned the notion of researchers' objectivity in the 1980s encouraged scholars to reflect on their transformation through the research process.[62] Although many researchers stop short of the postmodern methodological turn of writing themselves into their scholarship, most explore how both the interviewer and interviewee affect the relationship, oral evidence, and interpretations.

As much as insights from other disciplines have sharpened oral history, the field maintains its own methodology and principles. Even as historians have borrowed the literary tools of discourse analysis to great ends, Ann Farnsworth-Alvear asserts, "For the work of a historian, discourse analysis is necessarily incomplete. Reconstructing a fictional character such as *la mujer obrera* [the working woman] is a first step, but our understanding of her place—even her place within the world of discourse—requires asking questions of her nonfictional sisters."[63] In his effort to distinguish the work of oral historians from that of geographers, journalists, sociologists, anthropologists, and ethnographers, Brazilian historian José Carlos Sebe Bom Meihy argues that oral history's interdisciplinary nature has hindered its full recognition as a methodology. He points to two ways whereby oral historians can stake their own ground: "Oral history, because it can capture half-meanings, silences, lies, forgetfulness and distortions, would occupy the privileged position of a discipline capable of dealing with subjectivity. From the last point follows another: fostering the political actions that stem from acquiring consciousness of identity."[64] Though oral history is not the only field that assumes those charges (anthropology, too, springs to mind), many Latin American scholars insist that their scholarship and activism are symbiotic.

Although I focus on Latin America in this book, I have endeavored to use case studies and examples in ways that resonate with anyone who is interested in oral history. Some of the challenges, benefits, and uses of oral history are specific by region and even community, but commonalities abound between Latin America, Africa, Asia, and other regions outside the literature's focus on the United States and Western Europe. Many nations share histories of colonialism and imperialism punctuated by violent rule. Throughout its history, the field of oral history has continued to expand access to and comprehension of the past through exploring interviewees' ideas, memories, conceptions, and other spoken reflections of events that occurred during their lifetimes. With multimedia approaches involving photographs, film, archival documents, biographies, sound, art, transcripts, and analysis, scholars attract a wide audience and facilitate opportunities for people to reconstruct the past and understand the present. Just as oral history recognizes ordinary people's contributions, it also acknowledges that amateur historians, diligent students, and curious citizens enrich the field. As it feeds a growing interest in oral narratives and memoirs, the Internet can attract new practitioners of oral history who, to get the most out of their pursuits, will need training in oral history theory and methodology. In Latin America, where technology is leapfrogging infrastructure—many Latin Americans who never had landline telephones in their homes own cell phones, for example—oral history has tremendous potential to grow.

Notes

1 In Araújo, "História oral, memória e reparação," 1. The special issue is published on line without consecutive page numbers; the numbers of cited pages pertain to the article, not the entire issue. Unless otherwise indicated, all translations are my own.
2 Ibid., 17.
3 Huggins, Haritos-Fatouros, and Zimbardo, *Violence Workers*, xviii (quote), 1–2.
4 Meyer, "Documenting the Earthquake"; Poniatowska, "Earthquake"; see also Salgado Andrade, "Epilogue."
5 Necoechea Gracia, "From Favour to Right."
6 See Winn, *Weavers of Revolution*; Price, *First-Time*; Forster, *Time of Freedom*.

7 See James, *Doña María's Story*; Reuque Paillalef, *When a Flower Is Reborn*; Tinsman, "Paradigm of Our Own," 1372.
8 E. Basso, *Last Cannibals*, 21; D. Carey, *Our Elders Teach Us*.
9 Adleson, Camarena, and Iparraguirre, "Historia social," 39.
10 Jaksíc, "Oral History in the Americas," 599.
11 Meyer, "Recuperando, recordando," 140.
12 Sebe Bom Meihy, "Radicalization of Oral History."
13 Meyer and Olivera de Bonfil, "La historia oral"; Wilkie, "Postulates"; Winn, "Oral History and the Factory Study."
14 Pozzi, "Oral History in Latin America," 3.
15 Portelli, "Apresentação," 10.
16 Araújo, "História oral, memória e reparação," 2.
17 Ibid., 18.
18 McAlister, "Headlong Rush, into the Future" 276.
19 Gould and Lauria-Santiago, *To Rise in Darkness*.
20 Rappaport, *Politics of Memory*, 26.
21 Necoechea Gracia, "Custom and History," 124.
22 Slim and Thompson, *Listening for a Change*, 106–15; Thompson, *Voice of the Past*, 65.
23 In Levenson-Estrada, *Trade Unionists against Terror*, 91.
24 Judith Maxwell, email correspondence with author, February 15, 2015. For the heterogeneity of the word "read" across Maya languages, see C. Brown, "Hieroglyphic Literacy."
25 See Tedlock's translation, *Popol Vuh*, and Solomon and Urioste's translation, *The Huarochiri Manuscript*.
26 W. Taylor, *Theater of a Thousand Wonders*.
27 Jaksíc, "Oral History in the Americas," 591.
28 Bancroft Library, "About the Oral History Center," http://www.lib.berkeley.edu/libraries/bancroft-library/oral-history-center/about-the-oral-history-center.
29 The government-commissioned audio recordings are archived at American Life Histories, Manuscripts from the Federal Writers' Projects, 1936–40 collection, at https://www.loc.gov/collection/federal-writers-project/.
30 Kerr, "Allan Nevins Is Not My Grandfather."
31 Horton, *The Long Haul*, 57.
32 Lynd and Lynd, *Rank and File*, 6.
33 Gluck, "What's So Special about Women?"; Bodnar, Simon, and Weber, *Lives of Their Own*; Evans, *Tools of Their Trade*; Zinn, *SNCC*.
34 Schwarzstein, "Oral History in Latin America," 419–20; Meyer, "Oral History in Mexico and the Caribbean."
35 I am indebted to James Wilkie for sharing his recollections of the course with me.
36 G. Brown, "Oral History in Brazil."
37 Esquit, *La superación del indígena* (quote); Friedrich, *Princes of Naranja*.
38 Lewis, Lewis, and Rigdon, *Living the Revolution*.
39 Examples of testimonial literature include Celiberti and Garrido, *Mi habitación*; Coiolarro, *Pájaros sin luz*; Gelman and La Madrid, *Ni el flaco perdón de Dios*; Gutiérrez, *Se necesita muchacha*; Neira Samarez, *Huillca*; Burgos-Debray, *Me llamo Rigoberta Menchú*; Barrios de Chungara, *Let Me Speak*; Alvarado, *Don't Be Afraid Gringo*; Tula, *Hear My Testimony*. For analysis of testimonial literature, see also Detwiler and Breckenridge, *Pushing the Boundaries of Latin American Testimony*; Sklodowska, *Testimonio hispanoamericano*; Kurasaw, "Message in a Bottle."
40 Jaksíc, "Oral History in the Americas," 591.
41 Cáceres Q., "¿Historia oral o fuentes orales?"; Pozzi, "Oral History in Latin America."

42 G. Brown, "Oral History in Brazil."
43 Meyer, "Oral History in Mexico and Latin America," 56; Olivera de Bonfil, "Treinta años de historia oral en México."
44 In Necoechea Gracia, "From Favour to Right," 10–1.
45 Necoechea Gracia, *Después de vivir un siglo*.
46 Meyer, "Oral History in Mexico and Latin America"; Meyer, ed., *Testimonios para la historia del cine mexicano*.
47 Necoechea Gracia, *Después de vivir un siglo*; Wilkie and Wilkie, *México*.
48 Meyer, "El Archivo de la Palabra."
49 Hamilton, *Sexual Revolutions in Cuba*, 3; Lewis, Lewis, and Rigdon, *Living the Revolution*; Wilkie, "Introduction."
50 Dore, "Foreword."
51 Torres Montenegro, "Dominación cultural y memoria," 156.
52 Meyer, "Oral History in Mexico and the Caribbean," 347–9.
53 By that point, Portelli lauded "the cosmopolitan theoretical formation of Brazilian oral historians . . . [who] are capable of being less provincial and more eclectic" than their counterparts in the United States and Europe; "Apresentação," 10.
54 Pozzi, "Oral History in Latin America"; Red Latinoamericana de Historia Oral, http://www.relaho.org/.
55 Necoechea Gracia and Torres Montenegro, *Caminos de historia*.
56 Camargo Ríos, "Past Conferences," n.p.
57 See, for example, AVANCSO, *Se cambió el tiempo*; Hostnig and Vásquez Vicente, *Nab'ab'l Qtanam*; Petrich, *Memoria de mi pueblo*.
58 Linde, *Life Stories*, 21 (quote); Atkinson, *Gift of Stories*; Atkinson, *Life Story Interview*.
59 Auyero, *Poor People's Politics*.
60 Carlsen, *War for the Heart and Soul*, 4; Hendrickson, *Weaving Identities*, 197–8.
61 Warren, *Symbolism of Subordination*, 144–55.
62 See, for example, Behar, *Translated Woman*.
63 Farnsworth-Alvear, *Dulcinea in the Factory*, 74.
64 Sebe Bom Meihy, "Radicalization of Oral History," 35. Sebe Bom Meihy does not discount the importance of interdisciplinary work. On the contrary, he encourages it; "(Re)Introduzindo a história oral no Brasil," 6, and "História oral."

Suggested Readings

Charlton, Thomas L., Lois E. Myers, and Rebecca Sharpless, eds. *Handbook of Oral History*. London: AltaMira Press, 2008.

Dunaway, David, and Willa Baum, eds. *Oral History: An Interdisciplinary Anthology*. 2nd edition. London: AltaMira Press, 1996.

Lins Caldas, Alberto. *Oralidade, texto e historia. Para ler a historia oral*. São Paulo: Loyola, 1999.

Necochea Gracia, Gerardo, and Pablo Pozzi, eds. *Cuéntame cómo fue. Introducción a la historia oral*. Buenos Aires: Imago Mundi, 2008.

Perks, Robert, and Alistair Thomson, eds. *The Oral History Reader*. 2nd edition. New York: Routledge, 2006.

Schwarzstein, Dora, ed. *La historia oral*. Buenos Aires: Editorial de America Latina, 1991.

Shopes, Linda. "'Insights and Oversights': Reflections on the Documentary Tradition and the Theoretical Turn in Oral History." *Oral History Review* 41, no. 2 (2014): 257–68.

Thompson, Paul. *The Voice of the Past: Oral History*. 3rd edition. Oxford: Oxford University Press, 2000.

1 Techniques of Oral History

While oral historians generally conduct formal interviews, many oral history projects lend themselves to impromptu interviews and ethnographic fieldwork. As my language skills and network of friends expanded during my oral history research in highland Guatemala in the 1990s, opportunities to learn about the past in less formal structures abounded. When the winner of the San Juan Comalapa Rumi'al Tinamit (Maya Queen, literally Town Daughter) contest invited me to accompany her to the regional competition, I readily accepted. So unusual was the presence of a gringo at this Maya ceremony that a Guatemalan tabloid picked up the story and ran a photograph of us performing the traditional *son* dance with this caption: "The gringo . . . became so excited watching the traditional dances . . . that he too danced with . . . traditional clothing."[1] With each contestant delivering a speech about the history of her pueblo and elders in attendance spontaneously sharing historical narratives throughout the evening and into the early hours of the morning, the event was rich with historical perspectives. References to the past were also woven into the clothes female contestants and audience members wore. In a testament to the contested and competing interpretations of historical references, the red stripe along the shoulders of the Comalapa *po't* (traditional hand-woven blouse) symbolized either the flames Spaniards used to burn Comalapa or the Maya blood they spilled thereafter to colonize it.[2] At times, opportunities to learn about the past emerge in unusual and surprising venues.

Oral history has evolved from experimental methodologies to a well-developed method of historical and social science research, yet interviewing remains culturally specific and contingent upon different contexts. Less formal settings (such as impromptu narratives) and sources (such as local mnemonic devices, topography, music, gossip, and prayers) offer rich troves of historical data. At the same time, recounting the past is not necessarily something that can be arbitrarily elicited; certain times, venues, conditions, and circumstances constitute valid conditions for reconstructing history.

In exploring the techniques of oral history, distinctions emerge between the approaches of topical oral history and oral life history. While the objective of both is to understand how interviewees reconstruct the past and

Figure 1.1 "El ojo indiscreto: Aprendiendo buenas costumbres" (Candid camera: Learning good customs). *Al Día*, September 2, 1998. The caption reads, "The gringo in the photograph became so excited watching the traditional dances in Sumpango, Sacatepéquez, that he too danced with everything including traditional clothing."

understand their positions in the present, topical oral history generally is an attempt to clarify interviewees' roles as participants in or observers of certain events or processes over time, and oral life history is meant to reconstruct how interviewees' lives have impacted the past and vice versa. Oral history techniques may differ depending on the study's focus. Scholars working with ordinary participants or observers may ask general questions about particular events or processes, while researchers interested in specific behaviors of elite decision makers may ask precise questions about how they pursued their careers, why and how they made particular decisions, and why they advanced certain policies and not others.

The first step in oral history research is defining the project, informant group, and interviewees. Through this process, scholars pin down their research questions and develop their theoretical and methodological approaches. Enhanced by good relationships with local research assistants and interviewees, successful interviews are contingent upon thorough preparation prior to and flexibility while conducting them as well as active listening. From identifying potential interviewees to recording, transcribing, and disseminating interviews, technology has facilitated oral history research. My objective here is to provide an adaptable guide with insights and techniques that can be tailored to specific research projects.

Defining a Project, an Informant Group, and Individual Interviewees

A crucial component that guides the project throughout, the research design lays out the subject and historical period, hypotheses, objectives, theoretical framework, type of oral history, and target population. Research projects can be topical (centered around events, social problems, movements), biographical (using life history), community based (defined by geography, culture, language, ethnicity, or another commonality), or a combination of these and other genres. Most are intended to collect and analyze information not available elsewhere and to provide new interpretations.

In general, oral history is carried out to inform specific research projects (whether they be for individuals, communities, or institutions) or to create a collection. Although this book deals primarily with the former, the latter merits brief discussion, particularly as it pertains to dissemination and archiving. Despite some common elements, research projects and the creation of oral history collections differ in significant ways. Since the goal is to inform future scholars, citizens, and journalists who may have dramatically different interests, creating an oral history collection is a complex task. Perhaps the most challenging aspect is formulating questions for projects as yet undefined. As the director of the Programa de Historia Oral at the Universidad de Buenos Aires, Dora Schwarzstein and her colleagues founded the Open Memory Oral Collection in 2001 "to collect testimonies on State terrorism in Argentina."[3] With their overarching goal of documenting the "historical process of extreme characteristics" for future generations, they sought to capture broad ranges of experiences and perspectives without creating redundancies. That archive serves as a model of how to create oral history collections for future users.

To a large extent, the research objectives and available informants determine the temporal and topical parameters of a project. Immediately after Mexico City's devastating earthquake in 1985, Poniatowska interviewed residents. To create a record of how their thinking changed during the year after the quake, Mexican researchers interviewed survivors again in 1986.[4] As Poniatowska explained it, the goal was not to interpret people's perspectives but rather to capture them so others could analyze them.[5]

Although their full exploration is beyond the scope of this book, theoretical approaches for analyzing oral histories abound. Concerned with understanding disenfranchised peoples and expanding their inclusion in the historical record, critical theory related to gender, class, race, ethnicity, and sexuality offers one lens through which to interpret oral histories. Although those approaches often target marginalized groups, the interviewees are not a priori nonelites.

Beginning with a clear subject and developing a theory based on their findings as the corpus of interviews grows, some scholars approach theory organically. In his quest to solve empirical problems, Portelli prefers an "inductive approach: starting from a specific riddle, creating a method, and discovering new principles to make sense of it."[6] Depending on the strategy and genre, adopting this approach may preclude preparing specific questions in advance to encourage interviewees to speak freely about a topic and researchers to develop questions dialectically from their observations. In addition to allowing interviewees to adjust the research process, an informant-influenced approach resonates with local activists. Keenly aware of a long history of colonialism and exploitation, the Nasa (Colombia) linguist Abelardo Ramos Pacho insists, "Indigenous priorities must provide the general framework for research" in indigenous communities.[7] Since indigenous people's different socioeconomic positions produce distinct and at times competing priorities, abiding by Ramos's stricture is difficult. Given the fractures and problems that often mark communities, whose priorities are best representative of a larger whole? When applied to powerful people, such preconditions become even more problematic. Had her subjects' priorities determined her project framework, sociologist Kathleen Blee might never have interviewed women of the Ku Klux Klan.[8] In turn, collaboration is not always welcomed; some communities and individuals prefer to limit or avoid involvement in research projects.[9]

With great care and patience, many scholars strive to develop their projects in conjunction and dialogue with local communities to avoid suppressing "local originality and autonomy."[10] Working through the protocols of local communities and politics often facilitates collaborative research. Some scholars have used community-organizing techniques to conduct local history projects.[11] Researchers who respect local cultures, buttress individuals' integrity, and strive to understand the goals, priorities, processes, and desired products of the people at the center of oral history projects enhance their experience and scholarship. By balancing local inclinations with research integrity, scholars who approach projects collaboratively often produce results that resonate with interviewees and with colleagues.

With its emphasis on leveling hierarchical relationships through a shared research process and product, collaboration almost invariably creates tension between participants and researchers, whose expectations about the purposes of oral history may differ.[12] If each party embraces negotiation and respects differences, tensions and contradictions between scholars and local collaborators can be productive instead of destructive. Joanne Rappaport and Ramos point out that decentering academic notions of research "may enable new interpretations of reality consonant with the epistemologies and political priorities of indigenous organizations."[13] Maintaining a broad theoretical and methodological agenda allows local methods and theories to inform projects. As is true in all aspects of research, transparency helps readers assess the extent to which collaboration has guided the methods, techniques, and analysis.

The importance of this process and the way it generates interview questions is underscored by how the research plan and strategy shape findings. Since he focused his research and questions on laborers' experience as communists rather than their experience as workers, for example, Costa Rican historian Víctor Hugo Acuña Ortega learned more about their public and work lives than he did about their home and family lives.[14] With as clear an idea as possible of what they hope to learn, researchers strive to avoid the danger of overdetermining interviews by remaining open to unintended directions, some of which may upend initial assumptions. Chance results frequently enrich data.

To limit their preconceived notions about subjects, some practitioners who develop theory organically do not engage in documentary research fully until after they have conducted interviews. The topics that arise in interviews then guide archival and other primary source research. In her study of rural Chile, historian Florencia Mallon used the Mapuche community's "memory of an event . . . to search the written record."[15] Informant-influenced approaches can lead to surprising results. As I was collecting oral histories in Kaqchikel-Maya (henceforth Kaqchikel) communities, several collaborators recalled the horror of the infirm during the 1918 influenza epidemic being buried alive by Guatemalan officials who feared contagion. Archival evidence of a survivor being disinterred when gravediggers heard noises from inside the coffin corroborated those macabre accounts.[16] As my research with Kaqchikel speakers grew, epidemics emerged as a central topic in oral histories and so became a subject of my archival research.

As the project unfolds, the conditions and resources available on the ground will temper the theoretical and methodological approaches laid out in the research design. A multiplicity of theories and methods often marks scholars' circuitous journeys from research to scholarship. Visiting the country and specific target locations is an important part of developing the research design, especially if researchers are seeking external grants to support their projects. From the outset of fieldwork, flexibility and a sense of humor are invaluable characteristics for handling the surprises, setbacks, and vagaries that accompany research projects. Interviewees may be indisposed or absent at the appointed time of an interview; research assistants may choose other priorities over the project; heavy rains may make getting to remote interviews impossible. Persistence and perseverance, too, are crucial attributes for researchers.

Vetting Research Projects

In many Latin American communities, local permission precedes research. Depending on the research objectives, researchers often first approach municipal or other officials or nongovernmental organization staff members for consent, endorsement, or input related to their oral history projects. For topics regarding the role of religion or labor, for example, researchers have approached *cofradías* (Catholic lay brotherhoods) or cooperatives, respectively.

Some national institutions insist on vetting projects before they proceed. One of four institutions that have to review and authorize any research in indigenous territory in Brazil (in addition to the local indigenous leadership), the Brazilian Indian agency, Fundação Nacional do Índio, requires foreign researchers to obtain its official authorization to gain access to indigenous reservations. Since the approval process can take a long time, creative researchers have found ways around it such as interviewing indigenous people in nearby towns or cities where they come for social services, shopping, or errands. If their projects are approved, researchers can build on these interviews as they engage indigenous communities directly. Barring approval, researchers have some material for their scholarship.

Before conducting interviews, most researchers consult their campus institutional review boards (IRBs). Institutional review of oral history projects has been hotly debated. Drafted to protect people from unethical practices particularly in medical and psychological experiments, federal regulations (Title 45 Public Welfare, part 46, Protection of Human Subjects, or 45 DFR 46) require researchers working with human subjects to submit their projects for IRB approval. Based on quantitative and questionnaire-based methodologies, some of the requirements—such as destroying any record of interviews after the project ends, refusing to allow interviewees to forgo anonymity, and submitting and adhering to detailed questionnaires—contradict fundamental principles of oral history research. In 1998, the Oral History Association, American Historical Association, and American Association of University Professors argued that oral history research should be exempt from the IRB process. After discussions with the appropriate offices within the federal Department of Health and Human Services, in August 2003, the Office of

Human Research Protections concurred by asserting that oral history projects do not produce "generalizable knowledge." Although some historians interpreted that distinction as a slight on oral history research, it was intended to reflect historical research's goal to capture and articulate unique perspectives. Partly because the Office of Human Research Protections subsequently contradicted its own language in communication with IRBs that suggested some oral history research should be subject to review, most IRBs continue to vet oral history projects. Even as the American Association of University Professors argued in June 2006 that conducting interviews should be exempt from IRB approval, confusion and conflicts between IRBs and researchers continue on college campuses.[17]

Since oral history research can be expedited and often exempted through the IRB process, careful attention to a few key elements can facilitate approval. Researchers must establish informed consent for their interviewees to demonstrate that the interviews are voluntary and can be terminated by the interviewee at any point. Informed consent verifies that respondents understand the possible benefits and risks from participating in the project, how and for what purpose the data will be disseminated, and where it will be housed. In nations where illiterate and semiliterate peasants were duped into forfeiting their land rights when they signed their names on documents provided by unscrupulous speculators, requiring signatures can be problematic. Late-twentieth-century military dictatorships in Latin America made asking for signatures thorny for other reasons. Pozzi explains:

> To ask an interviewee for their written authorization automatically implies that you enter into . . . doubts as to what the historian is going to do with the interview. Self censorship on both sides, as survival techniques when faced by cruel repressive governments, has become deeply ingrained in the testimonies, the memory, and the subjectivity of the participants.[18]

If informants are illiterate and/or addressing topics that may put them at risk, informed consent may be acquired orally to buttress their anonymity.

In contrast to the position of most IRBs that dissuade researchers from asking questions that may evoke trauma or put people in embarrassing or vulnerable positions, such questions can be an important part of scholarly inquiry and potentially cathartic or therapeutic for interviewees. Researchers must convince IRBs of the importance of such inquiries and their ability to refer people to the relevant professionals should the need or desire arise. Cumbersome and time consuming as it can be, the IRB process can also be an opportunity for researchers to hone their project designs, informed-consent forms, and objectives based on IRB reviewers' feedback.

Since most foundations and agencies will want to see a budget before funding a project, no matter the scale, oral history research designs generally include a breakdown of the costs of equipment, travel, personnel, dissemination, and other expenses. Donated and in-kind items should be included in the budget. To keep track of their projects, researchers create logs to record the name of each interviewee, interviewer, translator (if needed), and transcriptionist, the date when each interview, informed consent and release form, and transcription were completed, any additional materials such as artifacts or photographs obtained during an interview, and the date each interview was placed in a repository.

Working with Research Assistants and Interviewees

Identifying the right personnel is a crucial aspect of an oral history project. Because a researcher's gender, sexuality, nationality, ethnicity, and socioeconomic status and very presence can lead to omissions, enlisting local research assistants to conduct interviews can open up less accessible topics. Research assistants can provide social entrees into the society, facilitate introductions, help to establish a researcher's trustworthiness, and endorse the project. Some of the most poignant and insightful testimonies dealing with Argentina's Dirty War came from Mothers of the Plaza de Mayo who were interviewed by other mothers whose children had been "disappeared" by the military dictatorship.[19] Even the most sensitive and committed foreign scholars cannot communicate with Latin American interviewees the way locals who share the same experience can. Local interviewers introduce their own biases to the interview process, but they also hold the potential to elicit narratives to which outsiders would not have access.

An interviewer's relationship to the informant group pervades the interview process. Insiders may enjoy a rapport with interviewees and local knowledge of the broader social, cultural, and historical contexts and insights that outsiders may lack. Historian Jeffrey Gould noticed that his Salvadoran research assistant Reynaldo Patriz "picked up on locally specific clues and codes."[20] At the same time, insiders may avoid difficult questions or overlook questions that to them seem obvious. Interviewed by two female Cuban researchers, Josefa, a *mestiza* born in Santiago de Cuba, frequently responded to their questions about gender and sexuality with the phrase "You know what men are like."[21] Her assumption of a shared experience limited her narrative.

Although not privy to privileged information, researchers may hear stories precisely because they are outsiders. Anthropologist Orin Starn learned as much when Peruvian peasant women told him stories they insisted they would never tell men in their Andean community.[22] In the same way my command of the Kaqchikel language granted me a level of acceptance afforded locals even as my height and phenotype immediately identified me as an outsider, many researchers try to balance their positionality as outsiders and insiders. While he recognized the advantages his affiliation with the University of British Columbia afforded him in Colombia, Jan Boesten insisted his connection to the Universidad de los Andes was important too.[23] An interviewer's positionality is not necessarily obvious. Although they share the same language and culture, an illiterate, monolingual, indigenous, male elder may consider a young, university-educated, bilingual, indigenous female an outsider.

To minimize such insider–outsider partialities, Gould triangulated interviews between Patriz, the informant, and himself. Gould's presence ensured that questions central to his research would be covered, and Patriz's presence helped to establish trust and confidence between the interviewee and interviewers.[24] When Gould remained silent and Patriz posed his own questions, the interview often became more organic and intimate. Interviewees explored themes such as the shame and resentment associated with rejecting indigenous identities that they may not have explored with Gould alone.

Taking this approach a step further, some scholars hire research assistants to conduct interviews alone. As a man researching women's history in traditional indigenous communities, I was compelled to do just that. While my questions guided the interview, indigenous female research assistants directed the narratives in ways that emulated informal conversations among Maya women.[25]

Whether they come from inside or outside the informant group, research assistants need the right language skills. Ideally, they also would be experts in the research topic and in interviewing techniques. Even those without that background can be good interviewers, transcribers, and translators with some guidance from the researcher. In recognition of the co-constitution and joint authorship of the interview, researchers often request that interviewers sign legal releases so the project or public domain maintains the right to the interview.

Identifying and Developing Relationships with Interviewees

Since the informant group emanates from people most knowledgeable about the research topic, especially those with direct experience, the project design offers the first guide toward identifying interviewees. Background and archival research can yield valuable storytellers. To understand how the short-lived 1952 agrarian reform played out on the Caribbean coast of Guatemala, Ingrid Castaneda used land petitions to identify surviving participants whom she could interview about their experiences with the reform and political turmoil of the 1940s and 1950s more broadly.[26] Researchers do not choose people simply because of their ages or direct participation but rather because of their knowledge and perspectives specific to the topic. Informants must be able to recall relevant events and articulate their memories and perspectives clearly.

Because studies based on a very small number of interviews can undermine the validity of the findings, scholars pursuing topical oral history try to interview representative samples of people. Although people at the margins of society like the very rich and the very poor are the hardest to reach, the sample should account for as diverse a representation as possible across gender, race, class, religion, sexuality, occupation, location, and other factors to facilitate a broad range of perspectives. While particular studies may preclude some types of diversity, scholars seek to balance qualitative and quantitative criteria. By interviewing people at all levels of an organization, from dignitaries, board members, and superiors to unskilled and itinerant laborers, scholars gain a sophisticated understanding of an entity. With less to lose and being more engaged in daily operations than their bosses, subordinates often are better equipped to share complex details of an organization or business. Mid-level bureaucrats who resent their superiors tend to be forthcoming.[27] Although the quantity varies depending on the complexity of the topic and diversity of interviewees, generally after a few dozen interviews, scholars begin to develop analysis that rings true to each new account.[28] As interviewers hear the same story dozens of times from distinct narrators, they become confident they have acquired sufficient information on that topic.

Some researchers use sampling such as snowball, random, stratified, purposive, or quota techniques to develop a list of interviewees. Valerie Yow deployed purposive sampling to tap into the knowledge of particularly well-informed individuals and to fill in gaps left by her stratified sampling across all levels of a hospital workforce.[29] To avoid predetermining interviewees, oral historian Paul Thompson used quota sampling, whereby researchers develop a list of census categories—occupation, gender, class, race, location—to select participants in proportion to their representation in the broader population.[30] Argentine sociologists Alejandra Pisani and Ana Jemio designed and circulated a flyer to invite individuals to learn more about and participate in their research.[31] If target interviewees or their family members are literate and have access to the Internet, researchers can post inquiries online. Oral history archives and memory museums are also rich founts where researchers can listen to interviews or read their transcripts and follow up with particular interviewees to address specific topics. While conducting research at the Fundación de Documentatión y Archivo de la Vicaría de la Solidaridad in Santiago, Chile, historian Steve Stern used the "social location" method by keeping an eye out for former political prisoners who also were consulting archival documents there so he could interview them. He attended forums that targeted groups he hoped to meet as well. Stern also deployed what he called proactive opportunism, "which involved a state of hyperalterness . . . that enables one to notice and 'seize' any opening that emerges at any moment and to create verbal lures to observe reactions and actively create openings."[32]

When the topic or target population affords fewer than one hundred potential participants, scholars can use universal sampling by contacting each potential interviewee to set up interviews with those willing and able to participate.[33] For her research on cybernetics in Chile during Salvador Allende's truncated presidency (1970–73), the historian of science and technology

Figure 1.2 Flyer inviting participation in the testimonial archive project in Famiallá, Argentina, ca. 2005

Reproduced courtesy of Grupo de Investigación sobre el Genocidio en Tucumán

Eden Medina was limited to the few engineers and politicians who founded and participated in Project Cybersyn (1971–73). Her research pointed to the major players, who readily agreed to be interviewed and suggested others who would be informative. While her advertisements for informants in a popular leftist newspaper yielded nary a factory worker who was involved in Project Cybersyn, Medina posits that the press coverage of Project Cybersyn while she was conducting her research encouraged some interviewees to meet with her.[34] While such a specific topic narrowed the field of potential contributors, its parameters also facilitated Medina's ability to identify and contact interviewees by limiting the scope of her search. While visiting small Mexican communities where almost "everyone of a certain age had at some point gathered, bought, or sold barbasco," historian Gabriela Soto Laveaga approached everyone she saw to ask about the tuber that was so crucial to the development of oral contraceptives.[35]

For scholars pursuing transnational topics, a combination of strategies can be deployed in each national setting, including publicizing the project through public invitations, queries on the Internet, advertising in newspapers or other venues, searching for potential interviewees through archival research, and networking with national experts and local informants who are familiar with the target populations. Giving public talks about the subject offers another way of establishing contact with people knowledgeable about the topic, though it would be a very self-selected group.

As projects unfold, researchers strive to strike a balance between an assertive approach that identifies key informants and a willingness to follow leads from research assistants, acquaintances, and other sources. Potential interviewees also can be developed through formal networks as established in the project design and informal networks, friendships, family, and other relationships. Since communities are groups of people acting on a wide variety of agendas, not all of which are necessarily admirable, engaging locals in the selection of raconteurs guards against the creation of collections that merely mirror researchers' perceptions and interests. As my network of friends expanded and Kaqchikels became increasingly aware of my research, I received referrals regarding individuals who were known for their historical expertise or knowledge of individual events.

Some communities have designated storytellers and keepers of the past who have extensive preparation and practice and are recognized as local historians. In her study of the indigenous community of Cumbal, Colombia, Rappaport notes, "The tellers of these tales are local intellectuals, people who enjoy access to varied forms of oral and written historical documentation, but who are also skilled at interpreting evidence and are good at spinning yarns."[36] As in many other communities, men tended to dominate those positions of knowledge and power. The same social mores that have privileged men's storytelling have discouraged women from believing they had something to offer. In part due to women's humble self-perceptions, excessive demands on their time, and traditional gender norms, scholars—especially males—face significant hurdles in accessing this fount of knowledge. Thompson observes, "Women tend to be more diffident, and less often believe that their own memories might be of interest. It is also because men are much more often recommended as informants by others."[37] Although regionally recognized raconteurs offer great starting points, researchers are wise not to limit their interviews to them.

As researchers become more familiar with collaborators, they can delicately break from local conventions. Accessing female interviewees provides one example of this process. When I explained my research on Maya oral histories to community leaders, teachers, and friends, they invariably advised me to speak with elder males, for they were the sanctioned keepers of community history. Ixaq', a twenty-nine-year-old computer teacher, explains how structural components buttressed this division of labor: "In the past they valued men more than women because the man studied and the woman did not. That has stayed with the women so they say they do not know history and say you should not interview them."[38] Other women acted out their habit of deflection designed to shield their communities, families, and memories.

By interviewing women I knew well and hiring female Kaqchikel research assistants to interview others, I went against the grain of community counsel. Often female research assistants and I had to explain the project in great detail to help Maya female elders appreciate how important their perceptions of the past were. In her study of women from different social classes in São Paulo, Brazilian scholar Maria Christina Siqueira de Souza Campos similarly has noted their reluctance to participate. Attributing their reticence to a "rigid family education and more timid temperament," Siqueira overcame those obstacles by prolonging explanations about the study's objectives and fomenting an open and informal conversational style with those interviewees.[39] Echoing feminist oral historians' innovative interviewing and listening methods attuned to women's particular patterns of communication, Mexican historians Concepción Ruiz-Funes and Enriqueta Tuñón listened for "the specifics of feminine language."[40] Determining the best way to access female knowledge takes keen observation. Particularly among the working classes, husbands often accompany their wives during interviews, thereby shaping their responses with interjections, body language, and other influences. When present, Mexican wild yam gatherers answered questions posed to their wives. In addition to interrupting their spouses' interviews, Mexican railroad retirees insisted that their wives did not know anything about politics and so were not worth interviewing.[41] In such contexts, it is crucial to talk to women in settings devoid of males.

Indicating how gender and labor often determine where interviewees are most comfortable speaking, I found it easier to interview women in their homes or courtyards, where they could attend to such domestic tasks as making tortillas or weaving. Those places afforded them greater confidence in holding forth even if men were present. In turn, while men shared detailed oral histories in their courtyards, farms, and public places such as community halls and municipal buildings, few suggested being interviewed in the kitchen. Those circumstances also suggest the way local economic and social structures generally favor male raconteurs. Interviewing women while they were performing other tasks instead of enjoying their undivided attention speaks to the reality of rural poor and working-class women, who are working during most of their waking hours. "Women's workloads leave little room for meetings and public discussion, whereas male cultures often set aside time and space for communal debate," note Hugo Slim and Thompson.[42]

As feminist scholars have long demonstrated, gendered discourse tends to discount or downplay women's historical roles. Recounting his community's response to theft, one Peruvian peasant betrayed gendered omissions in his account: "The danger of assault and robbery was horrible. To save our animals, we slept inside with them, the cows and sheep bleating, snorting, and farting in the bedroom. . . . With the *rondas* [rounds], we rose like a single man to master the thieves."[43] As Starn points out, humor is part of what made this man such a great storyteller, but he also perpetuates distortions; women, not just men, played a crucial role in combating thieves. Only by interviewing women could Starn learn of their contributions and perspectives.

Since not all potential interviewees are good communicators or have relevant expertise or experience, before committing to an interview, researchers should meet or at least communicate with prospective interviewees to determine whether a formal interview will be worth the time and effort of both parties. Some people identified as key informants may decline to be interviewed. In the process of introducing themselves and the project and setting up where and when the interview will take place, scholars often ask for personal materials—diaries, documents, photographs, letters—or other sources that may shed light on an individual's past. Such materials help researchers optimize the interview.

At times, an interview can be conducted when the interviewee and interviewer first meet, especially if it is arranged through a trusted third party. Often, however, researchers must ingratiate themselves and establish reciprocal relations with potential interviewees before they will agree to be interviewed. In his study of railroad workers in Mexico, historian Robert Alegre had to dispel rumors about his being in the Central Intelligence Agency or too young to be an academic, so he arranged informal outings with individuals for them to get to know him. Since the workers were inclined toward socialism, he played up his Chilean background and accent and introduced conversations about Allende.[44] Although such strategies can take months, while getting to know interviewees, the researcher can inquire about their lifestyles and habits such as when they work, eat, and rest to arrange an interview time for when they are most attentive and lucid.[45] Given people's busy lives, ideal times can be elusive.

Influenced by linguistic, cultural, ethnic, class, national, and gender nuances, the interview is a social relationship between the interviewer and interviewee. Anthropologist Winifred Tate deployed gender to gain access to military officials who welcomed the opportunity to explain the complex issues of "the male world of security matters" to a "lovely" and naive woman. Still, she concluded that her privileged "Americanness" secured her access to generals and bureaucrats.[46] As a US citizen, she was considered to be above partisan politics associated with Colombians. An interviewee's perceptions of the interviewer are as important as the latter's sense of self.

Establishing good rapport between the two parties is a crucial determinant of an interview's success. For the interviewer, empathy, preparation, respect, and humor—a good-natured approach to adversity and an inclination to laugh—go a long way in establishing trust and confidence with interviewees. At the same time, feminist scholar Judith Stacey warns against developing such a close connection that the narrator drops all defenses and reveals information, assuming it will remain confidential.[47] Marcela Camargo Ríos faced both overfamiliarity and inhibition when she interviewed Perseverando Bernal, who before he became a union leader had protected and nurtured her as a child while he worked for her family. Her personal knowledge of his life allowed her to fill lapses in his memories during their interviews, but their close relationship may have discouraged him from being too forthcoming on certain topics, particularly working for her family and labor relations more broadly.[48] A comfortable relationship that becomes too intimate risks slipping toward social conformity and restricts the information conveyed. Rather than a conversation between friends, the interview is an exchange with specific goals.

One of the murkiest issues in oral history research is whether to pay interviewees. Research assistants are often the best guides in this gray area. If the relationship between interviewer and interviewee becomes more financial than social, they risk distorting narratives.[49] At the very least, researchers strive to avoid patron–client relations in which they exercise an advantaged position—whether based on money, status, or authority—over informants who come to depend on their largesse. Nonetheless, when working with impoverished or working-class people, payment may be appropriate, though it need not be money; food, a donation to a cause or group the interviewee is committed to, or another gesture to recognize the value of their time and knowledge may be preferred. In contrast to Puerto Rico, where payment for knowledge is often inconsistent with rural values, in rural Guatemala, Maya female research assistants have explained that women should be paid for their time since interviews distract them from their daily tasks.[50] The fee may affect the relationship between interviewee and interviewer and thus the information conveyed, but under the circumstances it often is not only just but pragmatic.

While conducting interviews in quite isolated places enhances sound quality, such venues can be elusive, particularly in impoverished conditions, and counterproductive. Asking people to go to places outside their comfort zones may inhibit their responses. Social and physical spaces that allow people to perform cultural practices put them at ease and facilitate access to memories. When Pisani and Jemio asked interviewees where in their homes they wanted to be interviewed, rather than choosing intimate, quiet places for sharing their stories, they tended to choose central areas where they could maintain symbolic or material connections to their daily lives.[51] Family members, neighbors, or friends within earshot may limit what interviewees are willing to share, but those conditions also emulate social interactions more broadly and thereby may put them at ease and encourage more in-depth explorations. Whatever the influence, dismissing interlocutors is often problematic, particularly when it contradicts local norms. Under such circumstances, interviewers focus on keeping the interview on track. When others present at their interviews interjected, Pisani and Jemio redirected the attention, questions, and narrative back to the interviewees.[52] Homes are not necessarily the best places to interview people, however. Still struggling with a housing crisis that compelled many extended families to live together in cramped and at times decrepit housing conditions, many Cuban interviewees insisted they not be interviewed at home where they did not have quiet, private places to talk.[53]

By allowing informants to determine where interviews should take place, researchers facilitate conditions that are conducive to eliciting interviewees' stories. In her research in Quintana Roo, Mexico, Ramsey Tracy learned that certain places nourish oral history; for accounts of the Mexican Caste War, one such place was where elders cared for the communal cross. Conducting interviews in their homes would have limited the scope of their historical reconstructions of the Caste War.[54] Social spaces including during rituals, festivals, and other ceremonies can trigger interviewees' access to deep memory.[55]

In different acoustic environments, background noise can be both distracting and enlightening. In her ethnographic study of Guatemala's Histórico de la Policía Nacional (National Police Archive), historian Kirsten Weld notes, "The sounds of gunshots from the adjacent police firing range or barking dogs from the nearby canine unit are heard throughout my recordings, yet another testament to the tensions of the Project's workplace."[56] In less-than-ideal acoustic settings and when interviewees prefer not to be recorded, careful note taking is crucial.

Interviewing Techniques

By adhering to appropriate dress, comportment, social codes, gender dynamics, class positions, and other norms, interviewers can facilitate a more relaxed and open exchange with interviewees. To do so, interviewers must be familiar with the local culture of communication. Many working-class people customarily begin a meeting with inquiries about each other's families, health, and work and oftentimes share a drink or food prior to commencing the purpose of the visit. Such socializing before and informal conversation after the interview are "constitutive parts of it."[57] Failing to adhere to local customs by beginning work abruptly without making social inquiries as well as refusing food or drink can result in interviewees feeling disinclined to reveal much to a disrespectful guest.

After the initial exchange, the interviewer can explain the interviewee's rights, including ending the interview at any time or withholding its release to the public, the purpose and anticipated outcomes of the research, and how the process will unfold, from recording the interview to returning a transcript to the interviewee and ideally securing an archive where the recording and transcript will be housed. Frank explanation of the goals, motives, and intended outcomes of the research will put most interviewees at ease and encourage their trust.[58]

Researchers who plan to make oral histories available online inform interviewees and indicate it on the consent form to allow them to opt out of that condition. When working with people who do not have regular access to the Internet, interviewers should explain how extensive such access is in places like the United States, Canada, and Europe, where the explosion of personal computers and online services in public schools and libraries enables hundreds of millions of people to see and hear what appears there. Interviewees' awareness of this potentially enormous audience might discourage discussion of controversial topics or encourage hyperbole.

Before asking any questions, interviewers generally introduce the interview by stating the people involved, place, date, and title of the project and then going over the informed consent so it is recorded. Beginning the interview with background questions about birthdate, education, work experience, marital status, and family life, many scholars start with small topics and work up to larger ones. To cultivate good rapport, most researchers defer difficult or sensitive questions for the latter part of the interview and intersperse thorny questions with less confrontational ones.

Interviewers can play passive or active roles that range from guiding a monologue to encouraging interviewees to expand upon certain themes. When narrative ruptures and continuities suggest rich veins of information and insight, interviewers can produce in-depth interviews by finding appropriate moments to ask follow-up questions.[59] Such interventionist interviewing techniques may create tensions. When Laura Pasquali and her colleagues asked men and women who struggled against Argentina's military dictatorship (1976–83) to clarify points or pursue them further, their questions were met "with a certain hostility because they diverted the course of the account, initiating a (generally silent) conflict in the flow of the interview but also in the interpretation of events."[60] In nations still struggling with the ghosts of genocide and civil war, asking pointed questions can be counterproductive. Manifesting how oral histories are co-created and malleable, questions may compel interviewees to rethink their historical perspectives and accounts. Finding a balance between an engaged dialogue and leading the interviewee is difficult. Interviewers who limit their reactions guard against informants distorting their narratives according to interviewers' perceived interests.

Interview structures differ depending on the project goals. Unlike topical oral history projects that work with a broad spectrum of interviewees, historian Daniel James's seminal study was informed by numerous interviews with one woman. For this and other reasons, he used life history interview methodology whereby the interviewer and the interviewee cooperate to produce a full-scale autobiographical account from childhood through adulthood.[61] When interviewing Argentine union members, intellectuals, and politicians about their efforts to return Juan Perón to power in 1972, Liliana Garulli and her colleagues found that semistructured interviews allowed interviewees to guide the interviews depending on their involvement in the resistance movement. Thanks to interviewers' flexibility and adaptability, the process unearthed topics researchers had not thought to pursue, such as how militants perceived their path to *peronismo* and why they chose confrontation as opposed to accommodation to reestablish the powerful working-class movement.[62] To capture the worldviews, epistemologies, and "systems of meaning" of victims and violators alike, anthropologist Jennifer Schirmer combined a "testimonial and structured interview" approach in her study with military officers.[63] Researchers interested in a particular event are more likely to conduct single-issue testimony interviews. Topics and interviewees also dictate interviewing styles. When studying housework, feminist sociologist Ann Oakley followed a formal interview schedule, but with her project on childbirth, she found that her presence at births and repeated interviews necessitated a more personal, reciprocal, and adaptable approach.[64] By listening to other oral histories, becoming familiar with the literature, and being attuned to local modes of communication, researchers develop their own interviewing styles.

In a manifestation of the way oral history resonates with court proceedings, interviewers may subtly cross-examine interviewees. While interviewers ask for elaboration, clarification, or explanations, they generally resist the urge to argue even when confronted by brazen or offensive comments. Armed with background research, they listen for and ask follow-up questions about areas of knowledge respondents have for which there are few if any other sources. If interviewees start to lose the thread of the interview, instead of interrupting them, researchers do better to ask follow-up questions based on interviewees' responses. After rereading the transcript of his interview with Argentine worker María Roldán, James criticized his penchant for interrupting her to press for "historical information" and chronological specificity; he feared such aggressive interventions did "symbolic violence" to her narrative.[65] "I found myself amazed at my own deafness, my own lack of judgment, as I read myself cutting off a promising story or failing to encourage a tentatively offered line of response," he lamented.[66]

Although too much interference can ruin a story, Uruguayan historian Silvia Dutrénit Bielous points out the risks inherent in an interviewer's flexibility, especially when working with political elites, "because excessive discourse is always present in politics."[67] To combat political elites' evangelizing tendencies, she suggests maintaining focus on the interviewees' memories rather than their "proselytizing work."[68] Redirecting respondents' thinking from the present to the relevant historical period can minimize nostalgia's influence on their narratives. To mitigate the extent to which the civil war (1960–96) influences how Guatemalans remember General Jorge Ubico's reign (1931–44), I asked raconteurs, "During Ubico's rule, how did you view [insert topic]?"

After developing a comfortable connection with interviewees, some researchers take an assertive stance. When the Wilkies interviewed Victor Paz Estenssoro, who was elected president of Bolivia four times, they pressed him to reconsider his economic policies. Conducted after the military overthrew his third administration in 1964, their interviews during the 1960s and 1970s may have encouraged Paz to reconsider his approach. During his final term (1985–90), he implemented very different economic policies to counteract Bolivia's problems with inflation and bankruptcy.[69] Such an interventionist approach is best suited for life history interviews or instances when the interviewer has developed a close relationship with the interviewee over the course of frequent interactions.

Technology is rapidly opening new methodological opportunities and improving others. Until recently, most oral historians shied away from telephone interviews unless absolutely necessary because rapport is hard to build over the phone and visual communication is lost. The advent of video telecommunication that captures nonverbal communication has facilitated international and remote interviews. Formerly limited to upper and middle classes, those technologies' increasing accessibility and affordability are slowly putting them within the reach of working-class people.

Although most interviews are conducted with one individual, in some contexts, group interviews can elicit rich historical data. Less common in Latin America than Africa, some cultures eschew individual interviews in favor of group remembering. Many oral historians avoid group interviews because they tend to exaggerate perspectives of the past and elicit only knowledge all interviewees share. Yet researchers in Latin America commonly conduct group interviews because they evoke the natural flow of storytelling in social settings and can elicit collective memories that otherwise would remain obscure or incomplete. They also facilitate dialogue that allows participants to both articulate and learn about the past.[70] When couples are interviewed together, they often help each other remember or offer gentle corrections, though certain topics such as domestic relations may be tempered by a spouse's presence. Many couples deploy body language and facial expressions to encourage deeper discussion or to avoid taboo topics.[71] Ideally, group interviews would include three to five people. In larger groups, the dynamic begins to resemble a town meeting, with one or two interviewers asking questions of the audience. In an exception to that tendency, historian Alison Bruey's interviews with as many as eleven to fifteen Chileans prompted wide-ranging discussions among participants.[72] Since the primary exchanges in these settings should be between participants, interviewers fade into the background and ensure that all participants have the opportunity to contribute. To learn how Chileans remember Pinochet's dictatorship, Stern organized focus group discussions around central topics such as memory.[73] Although video recording is ideal for group interviews, if only an audio recording is possible, the interviewer must determine how different narrators will be distinguished on the recording. As examples, people can restate their names before they speak, or the interviewer can keep a running tab of the order in which people speak.[74]

As central topics lend themselves to supplementary questions based on narrative threads, the questioning methods for group interviews may differ from those deployed in individual interviews. By affirming or contradicting historical narratives, participants corroborate collective memories even if the scope of topics is limited. The back and forth between participants can also stimulate memories. Although loquacious individuals can dominate these settings, others who might decline an individual interview may open up. When possible, researchers can follow up group sessions with individual interviews to understand how personal fates deviated from collective memories.

Innovatively combining individual life history and group interview formats, the Wilkies carried messages between Manuel Gómez Morín, who founded the center-right Partido Accion Nacional (National Action Party) in 1937, and Vicente Lombardo Toledano, who founded the Partido Popular Socialista (Popular Socialist Party) in 1948. Since these two Mexican opposition leaders seldom interacted after 1920, the exchanges in the 1960s represented their first significant contact in decades and helped each to think about how to frame his contributions within the broader context of Mexican history.[75] By introducing the narratives of a former rival, the Wilkies expanded each interviewee's audience, which in turn extended their life history interviews. Similarly, political scientist Rod Camp often invoked one Mexican elite's interpretation of a particular event to evoke a response from another.[76]

Being flexible in the amount of time afforded each interview allows interviewees to exhaust the subject to the best of their abilities. Interviewees who have more to say, broader historical knowledge, sharper memories, more perceptive accounts, or a cooperative nature are worth devoting more time to in the initial interview and returning to for subsequent interviews. If an interviewee begins to appear tired, lose interest, or respond with short answers, the researcher can end the interview and save remaining questions for a later date. Colombian novelist Juan Gabriel Vásquez reminds us, "Remembering tires a person out . . . [as] exercising one's memory is an exhaustive activity, it drains our energy and wears down our muscles."[77]

Given Latin America's diverse cultures and people, scholars seek to become familiar with local conceptual, cultural, and customary codes surrounding communication, speech, and interviewing. Physical contact, eye contact, gestures, silences, humor, and other means of communication vary among and within cultures. Adhering to those norms helps interviewers avoid offending narrators and facilitates more detailed accounts. In Guatemala, the *ladino* (nonindigenous Guatemalan) custom of a man and woman greeting each other with a kiss on the cheek was inappropriate among highland Mayas, who initiated greetings by grasping each other's arms. An attempt to kiss an indigenous woman upon arriving could cast an awkward hue over, if not preclude the interview, not to mention put the interviewer at odds with her male kin.

Within reason, adhering to individual requests facilitates interviews. When I arrived early one morning at a bootlegger's home to interview her, she insisted I first try some moonshine to gain firsthand knowledge of its flavor and potency. In addition to demonstrating my commitment to and knowledge about the topic, my complicity may have provided some assurance that my goal was not to denounce her. Intended to test my mettle, the ritual of drinking moonshine was crucial to gaining access to bootleggers' perspectives.[78]

In addition to an easygoing attitude, preparation is paramount. Local research assistants can offer insights into relevant historical questions, but researchers need to know something of national, regional, and community history and even the individual before beginning an interview. Some informants insist on it. Before consenting to be interviewed, an eighty-year-old Mexico City resident asked Alegre to read three books. When Alegre explained he had already read them, the informant proceeded to quiz him on Mexican railroad history and corrected inaccurate details.[79] For elites who are unlikely to grant an interview unless the interviewer is extremely well prepared, mastering background information is critical.[80]

Maintaining the ability to check for accuracy and consistency, researchers generally craft neutral, open-ended questions rather than abstract ones. If questions do not elicit the intended information, scholars experiment with them. Historian Justin Wolfe set out to learn about the urban geography of Nicaragua, but his direct questions seldom sparked memories. When he asked interviewees to describe their first dates in the city or favorite places to hang out, however, he unleashed descriptions of the physical environment seemingly lost to straightforward questions because interviewees' frame of memory was less overlaid with the present.[81] The desired results determine the types of questions to ask. To understand the way performative practices opened spaces for representation of sexual identities in Mexico and Brazil, Rafael de la Dehesa asked "how questions not just why questions."[82] The former offered him insight into the contested negotiations between authorities, the public, and sexual rights activists. In his collaborative research with homeless people in Cleveland, Ohio, historian Dan Kerr "moved away from asking questions that centered on life histories of narrators and asked them both what they felt the historical causes of homelessness were and what they thought could be done about the present situation."[83] Doing so allowed narrators to frame their own experience in the broader context of homelessness in ways that facilitated their analysis of the crisis. In some instances, hypothetical queries can elicit informative responses. To elicit indigenous perspectives of health and health care, Necoechea asked Zapotec and Mixtec speakers to imagine themselves severely ill and having to choose between indigenous and Western doctors.[84]

At times political context determines interviewing techniques and questions. Aware that the Cuban government disseminated, reified, and even enforced official histories about the nation's revolutionary past and present, historian Elizabeth Dore and her team followed a life history approach to allow interviewees to deviate from official histories by focusing on their personal experiences.[85] Creating broad parameters for oral histories may encourage interviewees to alter their narratives and reassess the past. In her second interview, a Cuban woman recrafted her story: "Ignore what I told you yesterday. Last night I couldn't sleep; I thought it all over, and today I want to tell you what really happened in my life."[86]

As their projects progress, researchers refine, drop, and develop questions. During the course of his interviews with Colombian Constitutional Court magistrates and clerks, Boesten discovered political processes that he had not thought to ask about. Recognizing the organic nature of research, he observes, "Even in the process of conducting the research itself, results in interviews alter the topics of questions or add new ones."[87] In his work with Mexican elites, Camp begins by asking each interviewee the same questions. When he has a consistent answer to a specific question across a small number of interviews, he adds a new question and thereby expands his research.[88] As new questions are incorporated and others discarded, maintaining some central questions will allow for comparisons across place and time.

Given that informants tend to give more reliable answers to questions that interest them, researchers often allow interviewees to guide interviews.[89] Although well-formulated questions are essential, in many cultural contexts, question guides work better than questionnaires. Formal interview techniques are not necessarily compatible with indigenous, Afro-Latin American, working-class, and other communication customs. In contrast to questionnaires, which can inhibit the natural flow of exchanges, unstructured spontaneous questioning often cultivates a relaxed dialogue that is more apt to provide revealing results. When narrators structure interviews, they can articulate their perspectives based on their particular ethnic, gender, and class positions. Specific topics in which interviewees have a vested interest may spark rich recollections. When interviewees make oblique references, scholars have the opportunity to ask follow-up questions. Some tangents are fruitful; at times the natural flow of the interview raises new topics.

By observing cultural cues about how the past is recounted, researchers can emulate local historical methods and theories and adapt questions accordingly. With their cyclical perceptions of time, Maya informants often eschew chronology in favor of thematic approaches to reconstructing the past. When recounting ritualized aspects of the past, they also tend to speak in couplets that lend an air of redundancy if researchers do not appreciate the poetic phrasing. A lack of understanding of cultural context can blind researchers. Outsiders who do not understand Brazilian and African religious and mythical tales often discard that aspect of Brazilian slave descendants' oral traditions.[90]

Given the politically charged context in some parts of Latin America, some of the Oral History Association guidelines regarding interviewing practices are difficult to maintain. For example, as the give and take between interviewer and interviewee develops, interviewers who refrain from expressing their own views about the topics at hand, particularly when prodded by interviewees, risk jeopardizing rapport with interviewees. Oakley encourages interviewers to delicately share their own ideas and experiences.[91] While conducting interviews with the Iron Guard, an extreme right-wing Peronist political organization in Argentina, Pozzi realized that he and his interviewees first had to clarify their political differences before he could productively interview them. Even then he had a difficult time "understanding their imagery" and appreciating that they would be willing to talk to someone from the left to get their story out. In light of those communication barriers, he considered it his "least successful . . . project."[92]

For left-leaning scholars, conducting oral history with elites can be complicated. After working with right-wing women in Chile, historian Margaret Power admits, "In order to talk to these women about their ideas and activities, I had to suspend many of my thoughts and emotions and concentrate on the information I hoped to obtain from them."[93] Doing so allowed her access to a little-understood but powerful movement. Similarly, Tate's experience as a human rights activist made her uneasy in the company of Colombian military officials who revealed the thought processes and strategies that perpetuated the civil war.[94] Some researchers refrain from engaging with interviewees because their politics or ideas do not jibe. James regrets that his inability to engage "in a discussion among equals about the intellectual underpinnings" of the life of one Peronist militant prevented him from accessing the deeper meanings of the narrator's story. Because James found the militant's "brand of religiously intense right-wing Peronism impossible to empathize with," the interview failed.[95]

When divides between interviewers and interviewees are too wide to bridge, some topics are left unearthed. Acuña Ortega laments that the stories of conformist laborers and anticommunist cobblers remain untold because of political differences between his team and interviewees: "Unfortunately, because of the interviewer's bias and the ideological position of the interviewee, we have left that type of human in the shadows. That silence, in which we have been complicit, the informant and the investigator, demonstrates the irremediably subjective and incomplete character that oral sources entail."[96]

With extremely sensitive topics or reticent narrators, projects can stall, as historian Deborah Levenson (formerly Levenson-Estrada) learned in her research on Guatemala City gangs. Conditioned to remain silent, one young man told her, "To talk is to die." Levenson admits, "It was impossible for me to conceptualize how to 'interview' anyone who did not want to talk." Her persistence paid off as "the difficulties of having conversations started to become its own topic."[97] Icebreakers can come in surprising guises. Generally reluctant to talk with outsiders about their experiences, some massacre survivors only did so after approaching anthropologist Victoria Sanford's dog; as their interactions with the dog put them at ease, many confided in Sanford and shared their testimonies of survival.[98]

Questions are not the only way to elicit oral histories. Participatory Rural Appraisal programs have illustrated that many people more effectively express themselves verbally when they can concurrently use visual aids.[99] Documents and material culture from ephemera to art can evoke memories and jump-start interviews. To provoke accounts of the past, Peruvian anthropologist and psychologist Olga González showed Sarhua community members a series of paintings created in the early 1990s by Sarhuino painters.[100] To understand one particularly conflictive period (1981–83), she analyzed both the nonverbal, particularly silence, and verbal responses to the images. Public art can play a similar role. Reflective of oral histories, a mural in Comalapa frequently evokes conversations about the past among passersby.

Figure 1.3 Mural scene of a massacre. An image from a mural in San Juan Comalapa, ca. 2000, depicts the thirty-six-year Guatemalan civil war. Often informed by and informing oral histories, public art such as this can evoke historical memories.

Photography by Walter Little

Photographs, too, counteract forgetting. In an Argentine union hall with former industrial laborers, James showed photographs of shuttered packinghouses and notes how the images catalyzed individual and collective memories.[101] After a veteran of the Mexican Revolution asked her to end the interview, Mexican scholar Beatriz Cano Sánchez inquired about the photographs he had on the wall of himself posing with other revolutionaries. The tone of the exchange completely changed as he went on for more than an hour with memories and anecdotes about those individuals and the revolution more broadly.[102] Other visual stimuli such as maps and time lines drawn on paper or on the ground can elicit rich historical memories. As the example of public murals demonstrates, environs both inform and evoke stories. On the bald face of a hillside carved out to make room for a road in highland Guatemala, a life-size carving of a donkey survives.

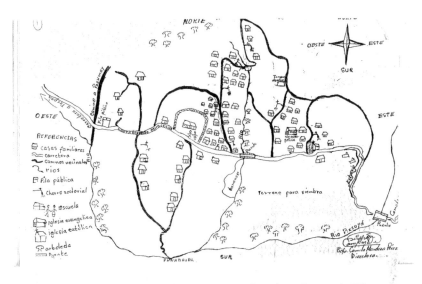

Figure 1.4 Map of Aldea Agua Caliente, San Juan Comalapa, Guatemala. The map was created by village teachers.

Personal Docente, Escuela Rural Mixta, Aldea Agua Caliente, "Mongrafia Aldea Agua Caliente, San Juan Comalapa, Chimaltenango," April 8, 1994

When I passed by it with Kaqchikels en route to their farms or homes, it often elicited stories about road construction, forced labor, and economic development. Before launching into those broader topics, raconteurs almost invariably began by clarifying that the donkey symbolized Mayas who historically used a tumpline to transport goods on their backs. They explained that Ubico's road-building program and the introduction of trucks to remote areas diminished that grueling manual labor. Visual and material culture provide segues into narratives.

Some scholars deploy archival research to elicit oral histories. If Andean interviewees did not recollect particular conditions or situations, historian Miguel La Serna countered with specific examples from the archives to stimulate their memories.[103] In a fascinating project, Kaqchikel scholars Edgar Esquit and Héctor Concoha bring copies of archival documents to highland Maya communities for their interpretation. In the process, participants have shared oral histories related to the documents and the past more broadly. Esquit and Concoha explain that the goal of creating a more democratic approach to studying the past is not simply to "break the paradigm of official history, but to broaden historical sources and construct new methodologies." The process has helped "to maintain memory."[104] Such innovative approaches to studying the past open up new mechanisms of participation.

Listening Skills and Tools

In oral history interviews, the primary goal is not to ask questions but to listen closely throughout the exchange to comprehend the meaning of what interviewees choose to share as well as their silences or omissions.[105] Over time, interviewers hone their skills from listening to what is said to listening for what is meant. As researchers increase their fluency in the interviewees' language, they more easily move from apparent to intended meanings. Feminist oral historians Kathryn Anderson and Dana C. Jack encourage researchers to "listen in stereo" to both facts and feelings because women often mute their own perspectives when they do not fit neatly into the dominant paradigm of men's narratives. For Anderson and Jack, learning to listen requires that researchers subordinate their own agendas, listen intently for perspectives that go "beyond prevailing concepts," and observe the narrator's vocal quality and body language.[106] Active listening helps researchers recognize when their questions may not be pertinent to local historical reconstructions. When one informant responded to Farnsworth-Alvear's question about unions in the 1950s by describing strikers who attacked workers with rocks in 1935, she indicated that the question was "wrong" and that Farnsworth-Alvear's sympathy for unions was "naïve."[107] Although it may compel researchers to jettison some of their prepared questions, careful listening allows them to ask new questions that will encourage narrators to reflect more deeply on their individual experiences.

Careful listening can open up new lines of thought as well. In the broader context of an indigenous community that emphasized continuity over change, a forty-year-old weaver explained how he taught his children the same trade he learned as a child. After listening to the recording several times, Necoechea and his colleagues noted that he mentioned using a ruler. When they asked him about that detail, he initially responded that rulers had always been used. After Necoechea followed up with a comment about how older people without a formal education may not have been able to use rulers, the weaver remembered that he measured with a stick when he first learned the trade. That realization prompted a flood of memories about weaving.[108] Follow-up questions and persistence can elicit memories interviewees may not otherwise readily access.

Since storytellers omit or obscure aspects of their accounts, an important part of oral history research involves listening for silences. At times, narrators do not have the language to describe their experiences, particularly if they do not see themselves as being part of dominant narratives. Literary critics call this the "presence of absence . . . where activity that one might expect is missing . . . or deceptively coded."[109] To access those absences, Meyer and her colleagues instilled in Mexican interviewees an appreciation "of their responsibility to history."[110] Informed by cultural and linguistic nuances, researchers can creatively stimulate communication with laconic locals.

Deployed sparingly, silence can serve the interviewer. By resisting the urge to move on to the next question and allowing for an occasional extended, even uncomfortable silence, researchers can create the space for raconteurs to share more information. Overused, this technique leaves an awkward sheen on the interview. It can be risky, too, particularly for survivors whose experience of trauma has rendered them incapable of articulating, if not recalling, their horrors. If a narrator is notably troubled or anxious, the interviewer should ask if she or he wants to continue. When recounting trauma, survivors' speech patterns often become monotonous and mechanical. This shift away from emotion and inflection is generally a manifestation of an attempt to distance themselves from the trauma. In their interviews with Argentines who had been incarcerated and tortured and whose friends were killed during the military dictatorship, Pasquali and her colleagues were "especially careful" when addressing those themes. Often interviewees asked that the recorder be turned off as they sat in silence or cried. Although that terminated some interviews, others continued.[111] Some topics are off limits. When asked about her work trying to locate people who disappeared during the civil war, a Colombian activist responded, "Don't ask me about those experiences, they are too painful."[112] Interviewees determine the extent to which they can share the past.

Talking through Trauma

Following the interviewee's lead with tact and delicacy is especially important when addressing traumatic topics. To avoid retraumatizing victims, researchers can limit interviews to a few broad questions that allow interviewees to craft their stories as they see fit.[113] Given the violent nature of the recent past—and in some cases present—in many Latin American nations that "has left very profound traces of terror," interviewers may unwittingly tap into interviewees' traumatic remembering even if the project is not explicitly about war or violence.[114] When it is, the act of granting an interview can be heroic. In their interviews with former Argentine activists, Pasquali and her colleagues note, "In some cases opening the door to someone they barely know with the objective of talking about events that happened some thirty years ago and that, in the majority of the interviewees, has left deep wounds is exceptionally courageous."[115]

Debilitating trauma is not limited to violence. Some Patagonian working-class women declined to be interviewed because evoking their unemployment and poverty was too traumatic for them.[116] Convinced she was injected with syphilis as an orphan when the US Public Health Service conducted sexually transmitted disease experiments in Guatemala from 1946 to 1948, Marta Lidia Orellana cried as she described such intimate details as doctors forcing her to remove her clothes and subjecting her to a gynecological examination. Recounting those violations some seventy years later was so traumatic that the interviewer, Lydia Crafts, took Orellana's testimony without asking any questions for fear of upsetting her further.[117]

Recounting the past can reaffirm as well as destabilize personal narratives. What can be liberating for some can be debilitating for others. While human rights reports and much scholarship on violence generally reject the notion that traumatic historical events are unknowable,[118] the work of Schwarzstein and other scholars suggests that certain experiences are so traumatic they cannot be recalled or communicated. When horror is incomprehensible, trauma destroys memory to the point that it may never be retrievable or only partially so after a long latent period. Omissions, alterations, and silences help victims reconstruct their lives and adapt. As memory heals, it also distorts; the greater the trauma, the more substantial the distortions.[119] In nations like Chile and Argentina where human rights victims and perpetrators share the same communities, buildings, and even homes, safe places to discuss trauma can be elusive. Seldom trained as therapists, social workers, or grief counselors, scholars respect the limits established by interviewees and refer them to therapeutic professionals if necessary. Aware of the risks involved in recounting the horrors of the Pinochet dictatorship, the Colectivo de Memoria Histórica José Domingo Cañas (José Domingo Cañas Historical Memory Collective) in Chile arranged for a psychiatrist or psychologist to be present at some interviews so they could follow up with interviewees as needed.[120] For some people, terror experienced later in life recalls trauma suffered decades earlier. When asked about the military rule of the 1980s, a Salvadoran survivor recalled an incident from the 1932 massacre: "A poor old *señor* was working when they decapitated him alive, and his body still stood upright about ten minutes or a little longer, until it collapsed. . . . They looked for people the way you hunt an animal."[121]

Some victims who recount their trauma can process and overcome its debilitating effects.[122] Likening it to "taking a dagger out of one's throat,"[123] many survivors of the Argentine Dirty War expressed relief after telling their stories and breaking the silence about government-sponsored human rights abuses. Recounting traumatic memories is not cathartic for everyone, however. "I haven't felt any sense of relief. . . . It's not like I go around talking about it and a weight is lifted off me, no, no," insists an Argentine woman whose father was kidnapped and killed by insurgents in 1974.[124]

The goal is not to relive trauma but rather to attribute some meaning to it. By incorporating specifics about perpetrators and victims in her stories, Chilean prison-camp survivor Nieves Ayress preserved evidence that could be used to try leaders and collaborators. To stave off the shame of rape, she deployed stories to build community among other victims; their capacity to articulate their ordeal and connect with others facilitated their survival and helped them to navigate their lives after incarceration.[125] Part of the therapeutic power of the stories is in their denunciatory nature. Argentine prison-camp survivor Pilar Calveiro felt buoyed because "someone [survived] to testify and tell the story; someone . . . preserved the memory of the concentration camps."[126]

Given the haunting nature of traumatic memories, listening to tales of trauma can psychologically affect interviewers. As interviewers "listen to the horror without reproducing its paralyzing affects," some experience acute emotional reactions. Upon hearing particularly tragic stories, Pisani and Jemio "literally went silent, unable to ask questions, redirect the story or, at the very least, propose a pause."[127] Survivors of the Guatemalan civil war who interviewed other victims for the United Nations' and Catholic Church's human rights reports were profoundly affected by stories that resonated with their own experiences; some interviewers were forced to address their own trauma anew.[128] Hearing traumatic material is almost invariably unsettling, but interviewers strive to listen carefully and resist the temptation to change the subject. Even as they maintain their composure during the interviews, some may seek therapeutic assistance thereafter to help them process what they learned.

Ethnography and Oral History

Prepared to listen attentively at inconvenient and inopportune moments, researchers benefit from being present at such local mnemonic devices as murals, hills, archeological sites, workplaces, dances, singing, churches, public works, and other evocative locations and events. By breaking down language and cultural barriers, these sites can help to formulate questions and engage storytellers.

Eminent oral historian Donald Ritchie asserts that little is gained from not recording an interview or from "hearing a story 'off the record,'"[129] yet in Latin America the art of oral history goes beyond formal recorded interviews. A colonel who served during Pinochet's dictatorship refused to be recorded, only allowing Stern to take notes.[130] To obtain "truly frank interviews," Camp took copious notes instead of recording his interviews with Mexican elites.[131] In some cases, concern for an interviewee's safety precludes recording interviews.[132]

Forgoing the contrived nature of a formal interview, scholars who gather histories in informal settings often approximate how communities share oral histories. As my network of friends expanded in Kaqchikel communities in Guatemala, I was increasingly invited to weddings, baptisms, and other celebratory gatherings. After the ceremonies, guests were invited to the hosts' homes to enjoy lunch and libations. As an outsider who spoke Kaqchikel, I frequently was afforded an honored seat with community elders. Once the alcohol began to flow, so too did historical memories. Unfortunately, there was an inverse relation between the richness of the stories that seemed to increase with each *copa* and my ability to remember them that seemed to decrease with each *copa*. As a result, I developed a strategy of excusing myself to the outhouse during lulls in the conversation to jot down notes about the context and content of the narratives. As an unintended consequence of capturing the richness of these historical reconstructions, I developed a reputation for having a weak stomach. Although data gathered in informal settings is less reliable, particularly in light of the tendency of some people to invent or exaggerate stories while drunk, it is also less adulterated, and information is often deeper and broader than narratives captured in more formal settings. When cross-checked against other accounts or with the same raconteurs

Figure 1.5 Wedding procession in San Juan Comalapa, Guatemala, ca. 1998. Such celebrations are good venues for hearing recollections about the past.

Photograph by David Carey Jr.

when they have not been drinking, stories gathered in these informal situations supplement conventional interviews.

Like celebrations, work offers venues into the past. Some of my keenest understandings of mandatory labor mechanisms and agricultural toil came from working alongside people. Even misdirected efforts can be fruitful. Unaware that communal labor was assigned by barrio, when I noticed men securing a road that ran alongside a ravine near my host family's home, I returned with a pick to lend a hand. As they talked about how communal labor had changed over time, the men joked that I would soon become more familiar with it, as the workday assigned to my neighborhood was fast approaching. Similarly using participant observation methods, Stern took part in workshops, demonstrations, and commemorations in Santiago to inform his understanding of memories of the Pinochet dictatorship.[133]

Place and landscapes influence and elicit historical memories. Living only five kilometers from the postclassic Kaqchikel capital of Iximche', residents of Tecpán maintain a more detailed narrative of the ancient Maya than their counterparts in communities farther removed from Iximche'. By serving as historical markers, topographical and geographical spaces can elicit historical recollections. Even the paths people walk can evoke narratives.

Doing fieldwork and documenting observations can be as valuable as conducting interviews. Farmers planting, weeding, and harvesting corn, women patting dough into tortillas, a priest presiding over a ceremony, and other quotidian settings are spaces in which people share their perceptions of the past and present. As researchers' time in the area of study, fluency in the language, and familiarity with the culture increases, their ability to listen for the past and its many meanings expands.

Technology's Tools

From wire recorders and reel-to-reel machines to digital devices and computer software, recording technology has changed dramatically over the past half century. Project budgets generally determine the choice of technology and equipment. Given the goal of posterity, researchers use the highest-quality equipment they can afford, particularly microphones, cables, and headphones. The key to capturing high-quality recordings is using a proper microphone. Although a review of technology falls beyond the scope of this work, researchers are increasingly using open-access formats for their recordings. Offering quality similar to or better than that of most closed formats, open formats are used by many recorders and players; they are not restricted to certain proprietary players, and thus they are unencumbered by software patents.[134]

Unobtrusive and easy to transport, digital audio recorders with built-in microphones are generally sufficient for recording interviews, as are laptop computers, smartphones, and other small portable devices. With the proper software, the recordings can be exported in almost any format and searched for specific information. Since interviews are original sources, the use of audio editing programs should be limited to reducing background noise and accentuating the clarity of voices.

Because it captures visual and physical communication that audio recordings miss, video is a particularly powerful tool. When the São Paulo–based Brazilian Film and TV Museum recorded artists' reflections about their own and Brazil's musical evolution, some interviewees initiated impromptu performances—the full richness of which would have been lost to an audio recording.

As much as it facilitates scholars' work, technology can inhibit rapport or preclude interviews altogether. In nations with long histories of human rights abuses, some people refuse to be recorded because they are concerned about reprisals. Others may decline because they are unfamiliar with the technology. Such reservations need not obviate interviews, however.

Wrapping Up an Interview

After the interview has ended, the interviewer can ask about unfamiliar terms, place names, acronyms, and people. She can go over the process moving forward such as the anticipated use of interviews and transcriptions, where they will be housed, and what will be produced based on them. At this point, the narrator should be asked to sign the informed consent form as explained at the beginning of the interview. If the narrator is illiterate, the interviewer can read the form aloud. Then the interviewee can mark it with a thumbprint, X, or other indication of agreement with the project. In some instances, oral consent may be preferred so no written record can connect the narrator to the recording or transcript. To ensure future access to the interview, the interviewee should sign a deed of gift or release form, which establishes who owns the rights to the interview, when or if it will be released to the public (as some interviewees may prefer to delay or deny public release), and what may be done with it. The interviewee's consent allows an archive to permit public access to the material and researchers to use it for their scholarship.

As part of the conversation after the interview, the researcher can query the interviewee for suggestions regarding who else to contact about the project. Impressed by his research and interviewing skills, Mexican elites frequently responded to that question from Camp by picking up the phone and arranging other interviews for him.[135] If the interviewee mentions he forgot to share something, the interviewer can ask to turn the recording device back on, assuming it was agreed upon for the interview.

Depending on how the interview went, a follow-up interview may be appropriate. Often more than one interview is necessary to break through niceties and superficial descriptions to reveal rich historical accounts and develop deeper confidence in one another. Photographing the interviewee and offering to furnish a copy provides one excuse to return; delivering a transcript or perhaps a recording of the interview offers another. Return visits provide opportunities to question narrators about any internal inconsistencies in their accounts. In addition to exploring new topics, follow-up interviews allow raconteurs to change their narratives. Interviewing people on multiple occasions over time is crucial to building the trusting relationship necessary for the most accurate conveyance of information. As is true of collaboration more broadly, researchers gauge interviewees' interest in continued contact. After two years of working with indigenous people in the Colombian rainforest, Elizabeth Kennedy turned her attention to lesbians in Buffalo, where she found that many interviewees did not want to be bothered with follow-up interviews, reading transcripts, or other demands on their time and energy.[136]

After the interview, the interviewer should write a summary of its major themes. As the corpus of interviews grows, these descriptions will help orient analysis. They are also crucial for cataloguing and archiving purposes. In describing the content and context of the interview for future users, the interviewer may include observations about the narrator's life and profession, ambient noise, and the venue, including why it was chosen. Further, the interviewer could note the narrator's health, mannerisms, and speech patterns, linguistic content such as more than one language spoken, and the source of any interruptions. An abstract of the interview that annotates the topics chronologically and indicates where they appear according to time elapsed in the recording facilitates future access. Since digital video and audio have time stamps, programs can locate particular passages and words and then play excerpts from time stamps where the reference terms appear.[137] With the archival process in mind, the researcher creates a log that records the interview date, brief biographical information about the interviewer and interviewee, where the interview took place and its duration, whether it was transcribed or accompanied by other materials, and whether there are any restrictions on its use.

Transcriptions

Original recordings are the most reliable and accurate accounts of an encounter; subject-indexed transcriptions are meant to supplement, not replace them. Although digitization and the Internet allow for backup, the transcript is crucial because it ensures that the interview will be accessible in the event the recording medium is not. The process is time consuming and expensive. Every hour of tape can take six to ten hours to transcribe. Since inaccurate transcriptions can lead to interpretive problems, the best transcribers are often native speakers who have a good understanding of regional accents, dialects, and idioms as well as cultural distinctions and linguistic subtleties. Since they have a memory of the exchange and its nuances, interviewers likewise can produce excellent transcriptions. Since transcribers' approaches vary widely, a transcription guide that addresses issues of format, style, standardization, and ethics is helpful. Throughout the text, transcribers note nonverbal cues in parentheses such as laughter, crying, pauses, silence, stuttering, and ambient sounds.[138] Transcription software is available for Spanish and Portuguese but not for many indigenous or creole languages. Constantly improving as technology grows, voice-recognition software is helpful, but those transcriptions must be corrected carefully. Although transcribing is time consuming, researchers benefit from the process because they can improve their interviewing techniques by listening for how their questions and reactions to the narrators sound, catching any unnecessary interruptions or failures to ask follow-up questions, and sharpening their sense of the flow of interviews.

After the researcher edits the transcription, it can be returned to the narrator for review. Transcripts can be read back to illiterate narrators. This process allows for clarification, particularly if any words or phrases on the recording are indecipherable, and correction may lead to further exploration of historical events. In consultation with the scholar, interviewees may want to remove certain information they deem inappropriate or harmful.[139] Except in extreme instances, the recorded interview should remain unedited. Information added or deleted after the original interview generally appears in brackets in the transcript with a footnote explaining the circumstances of the edit. Extensive explanations or additional stories should be recorded or at least noted separately. In addition to the electronic file of the transcript, a copy should be printed on acid-free paper.

If tight budgets or limited personnel preclude creating transcripts, each interview should at least have an abstract. Although researchers generally prefer to read transcripts rather than listen to recordings, a good abstract can point them directly to sections of the recording most relevant to their projects. If an arrangement can be worked out in advance, some repositories may cover the cost of transcribing recordings. Creating abstracts, logs, and transcriptions shortly after interviews are conducted maintains a manageable workload.

By identifying a few key informants and beginning with in-depth interviews, researchers can accomplish their objectives incrementally. As they conduct other interviews, scholars can be open to new questions emerging from their research. By working closely with interviewers, translators, and transcriptionists, researchers can learn from their research assistants' reactions to oral history accounts. Some may underscore the importance or accuracy of certain accounts or offer different takes on interviewees' assertions, perspectives, or emphases. With an eye toward flexibility, practitioners regularly reevaluate the project's goals and change course as needed.

Notes

1 "El ojo indiscreto: Aprendiendo buenas costumbres," *Al Día*, September 2, 1998.
2 Carlsen, *War for the Heart and Soul*, 4; Hendrickson, *Weaving Identities*, 197–8.
3 Schwarzstein, "Memorializing Effervescence," 18.
4 Salgado Andrade, "Epilogue," 22.
5 Poniatowska, "Earthquake," 16–17.
6 Portelli, *Death of Luigi Trastulli*, x.
7 Rappaport and Ramos Pacho, "Collaboration and Historical Writing," 131–2.
8 Blee, *Women of the Klan*.
9 Kennedy and Davis, *Boots of Leather*, 17, 24.
10 Sebe Bom Meihy, "Radicalization of Oral History," 40.
11 Brecher, "A Report on Doing History from Down Below."
12 Shopes, "Oral History and Community Involvement."
13 Rappaport and Ramos Pacho, "Collaboration and Historical Writing," 122.
14 Acuña Ortega, "Fuentes orales e historia obrera," 69.
15 Mallon, *Courage Tastes of Blood*, 15.
16 D. Carey, *Our Elders Teach Us*, 123–4.
17 American Association of University Professors (AAUP), "Research on Human Subjects."
18 Pozzi, "Oral History in Latin America."
19 Kaplan, *Taking Back the Streets*, 236n1.
20 Gould and Lauria-Santiago, *To Rise in Darkness*, xiii.
21 Hamilton, *Sexual Revolutions in Cuba*, 107.
22 Starn, *Nightwatch*.
23 Boesten, "When Tintos Break Ice," 5.
24 Gould and Lauria-Santiago, *To Rise in Darkness*, 281–2.
25 D. Carey, *Engendering Mayan History*.
26 Castaneda, "Fighting the 'Insatiable Octopus.'"

27 Thompson, *Voice of the Past*, 151–2, 212–14; Yow, *Recording Oral History*, 81–3.
28 Kennedy and Davis, *Boots of Leather*, 23.
29 Yow, *Recording Oral History*, 82.
30 Thompson, *Voice of the Past*, 146–8.
31 Pisani and Jemio, "El proceso de construcción del Archivo Testimonial," 4.
32 Stern, *Remembering Pinochet's Chile*, 229–30.
33 Quinney, "Childhood in a Southern Mill Village," 167–8.
34 Medina, *Cybernetic Revolutionaries*, xi–xii.
35 Soto Laveaga, *Jungle Laboratories*, 18.
36 Rappaport, *Cumbe Reborn*, 5.
37 Thompson, *Voice of the Past*, 213.
38 Ixaq', oral history interview by author, June 21, 2001, San Juan Comalapa, Guatemala.
39 Siqueira de Souza Campos, "Mulheres de diferentes classes sociais em São Paulo," 193.
40 Ruiz-Funes and Tuñón, "Historia oral," 194.
41 Soto Laveaga, *Jungle Laboratories*, 17; Alegre, *Railroad Radicals in Cold War Mexico*, 6.
42 Slim and Thompson, *Listening for a Change*, 6.
43 In Starn, *Nightwatch*, 80.
44 Robert Alegre, personal communication with the author, October 21, 2015.
45 Adleson, Camarena, and Iparraguirre, "Historia social," 42.
46 Tate, *Counting the Dead*, 19.
47 Stacey, "Can There Be a Feminist Ethnography?," 113.
48 Camargo Ríos, "Rebeldía y perseverancia," 29–34.
49 Crandon-Malamud, *From the Fat of Our Souls*, 40.
50 Mintz, *Worker in the Cane*, 6; D. Carey, *Engendering Mayan History*.
51 Pisani and Jemio, "El proceso de construcción del Archivo Testimonial," 14.
52 Ibid.
53 Hamilton, *Sexual Revolutions in Cuba*, 228, 230.
54 Tracy, "Mayan Interpretations of Time and History," n.p.
55 James, *Doña María's Story*, 149–56.
56 Weld, *Paper Cadavers*, 22.
57 Pisani and Jemio, "El proceso de construcción del Archivo Testimonial," 13.
58 Freire Montysuma, "Um encontro com as fontes."
59 Garay, "La entrevista de historia oral"; Camarena and Necoechea Gracia, "Continuidad, ruptura y ciclo," 61.
60 Pasquali, Ríos, and Viano, "Culturas militantes," 116.
61 James, *Doña María's Story*, 158. For more on life history, see Ritchie, *Doing Oral History*, 40–1; Johnstone, *Stories, Community, and Place*, 77.
62 Garulli, "Oral History and Peronista Resistance."
63 Schirmer, "Interviewing Military Officers," n.p.
64 Oakley, "Interviewing Women."
65 James, *Doña María's Story*, 135–6.
66 Ibid., 159.
67 Dutrénit Bielous, "La memoria de los políticos," 89.
68 Ibid.
69 I thank James Wilkie for sharing his experience of interviewing Victor Paz Estenssoro.
70 Cáceres Q., "¿Historia oral o fuentes orales?," 22.
71 See for example, Carey and Atkinson, *Latino Voices in New England*, 82–95, 137–53.
72 Bruey, "'I Don't Like to Ask Names.'"
73 Stern, *Remembering Pinochet's Chile*, 228, 230–1.

74 Garcés Durán, Ríos Etcheverry, and Suckel Ayala, *Voces de identidad*, 38–9; Garcés Durán and Leiva, *El golpe en La Legua*.
75 Wilkie and Wilkie, *Frente a la Revolución Mexicana*.
76 Roderic Ai Camp, email correspondence with the author, January 5, 2016.
77 Vásquez, *Sound of Things Falling*, 252.
78 D. Carey, *I Ask for Justice*, 56–89.
79 Alegre, *Railroad Radicals in Cold War Mexico*, 94.
80 Camp, email, January 5, 2016.
81 Justin Wolfe, personal conversation with author, January 7, 2011.
82 Dehesa, *Queering the Public Sphere in Mexico and Brazil*, xiii.
83 Kerr, "'We Know What the Problem Is,'" 34.
84 Necoechea Gracia, "Custom and History," 128.
85 Dore, "Foreword," ix.
86 Ibid.
87 Boesten, "When Tintos Break Ice," 4.
88 Camp, email, January 5, 2016.
89 Anderson and Jack, "Learning to Listen."
90 Frotscher and Freund, "Conference Report," 2.
91 Oakley, "Interviewing Women."
92 Pozzi, "Oral History in Latin America," 4.
93 Power, *Right-Wing Women in Chile*, xi. Compelling scholars to confront their own assumptions and biases, support for right-wing regimes can come from surprising sources. When survivors of the Dirty War supported victimizers and the military government's actions more broadly, Pisani and Jemio confide, "listening proved to be more complex than we had expected"; "El proceso de construcción del Archivo Testimonial," 7.
94 Tate, *Counting the Dead*.
95 James, *Doña María's Story*, 131, 133 (quotes, respectively). On the other hand, James developed excellent rapport with *Doña* Maria because she reminded him of his mother and his working-class background.
96 Acuña Ortega, "Fuentes orales e historia obrera," 67–8.
97 Levenson, *Adios Niño*, 89 (all quotes).
98 Sanford, *Buried Secrets*, 3.
99 Slim and Thompson, *Listening for a Change*, 57.
100 O. González, *Unveiling Secrets of War in the Peruvian Andes*.
101 James, *Doña María's Story*, 150.
102 Cano Sánchez, "El mensaje de los silencios," 178–9.
103 La Serna, *Corner of the Living*.
104 Esquit and Concoha, "Anthropologists in the Archives," n.p.
105 On the methodology of listening, see Myerhoff, *Remembered Lives*; Slim and Thompson, *Listening for a Change*.
106 Anderson and Jack, "Learning to Listen," 11, 26.
107 Farnsworth-Alvear, *Dulcinea in the Factory*, 124–5.
108 Necoechea Gracia, "Custom and History," 128.
109 Heilbrun and Stimpson, "Theories of Feminist Criticism," 62.
110 Meyer, "Oral History in Mexico and Latin America," 59.
111 Pasquali, Ríos, and Viano, "Culturas militantes," 116.
112 Van Isschot, "Heart of Activism in Colombia," 244.
113 Evaristo Wenceslau, "Afimação e resistência." The American Psychological Association's "Ethical Principles of Psychologists and Code of Conduct" provides guidelines for limiting researcher intrusiveness.

114 Dutrénit Bielous, "La memoria de los políticos," 86.
115 Pasquali, Ríos, and Viano, "Culturas militantes," 111.
116 Gatica, "Industrialización y proletarización," 138. Historian Dominick LaCapra has demonstrated that subsequent generations can be traumatized by something they did not experience personally; *History and Memory after Auschwitz*.
117 Lydia Crafts, personal conversation, Baltimore, MD, February 16, 2016.
118 See, for example, Scarry, *Body of Pain*.
119 Schwarzstein, "Historia oral, memoria," 8–10, 21.
120 Bruey, "'I Don't Like to Ask Names.'"
121 In Gould and Lauria-Santiago, *To Rise in Darkness*, 240.
122 Hook, "Awakening from War"; Jelin, *State Repression and the Labors of Memory*, 6–7; Felman and Laub, *Testimony*, 69; Millar, "Assessing Local Experience of Truth-Telling"; Gould and Lauria-Santiago, *To Rise in Darkness*, xi.
123 Pisani and Jemio, "El proceso de construcción del Archivo Testimonial," 7.
124 In Stockwell, "'Country That Doesn't Want to Heal Itself,'" 33–4.
125 Kaplan, "Reversing the Shame," 184, 191.
126 Calveiro, *Poder y desaparición*, 114.
127 Pisani and Jemio, "El proceso de construcción del Archivo Testimonial" (quotes 18, 17, respectively).
128 Oficina de Derechos Humanos del Arzobispado de Guatemala (ODHAG), *La memoria tiene la palabra*; Comisión para el Esclarecimiento Histórico (CEH), *Guatemala, memoria del silencio*.
129 Ritchie, *Doing Oral History*, 98.
130 Stern, *Remembering Pinochet's Chile*, 90.
131 Roderic Ai Camp, email correspondence with the author, March 29, 2015.
132 Stephen, *¡Zapata Lives!*
133 Stern, *Remembering Pinochet's Chile*, 228.
134 For more about what equipment to use and how technology aids oral history research, see Sommer and Quinlan, *Oral History Manual*, 33–43.
135 Camp, email, January 5, 2016.
136 Kennedy and Davis, *Boots of Leather*; Patai, "U.S. Academics and Third World Women," 147. See also Hale, "Feminist Method, Process, and Self-Criticism."
137 Frisch, "Oral History and the Digital Revolution," 104.
138 Cano Sánchez, "El mensaje de los silencios," 174–5.
139 Dutrénit Bielous, *El maremoto militar*, 21.

Suggested Readings

Aceves Lozano, Jorge. *Historia oral e historia de vida. Teoría, métodos y técnicas*. Mexico City: Centro de Investigaciones y Estudios Superiores en Antropología Social, 1991.

Alberti, Verena. *Manual de história oral*. Rio de Janeiro: Edita FGV, 2004.

Alterman Blay, Eva. "Histórias de vida: Problemas metodológicos de investigação e análise." *Cadernos* (Centro de Estudios Rurais e Urbanos, São Paulo) 19 (1984): 115–16.

Brown, Lyle. "Methods and Approaches in Oral History: Interviewing Latin American Elites." *Oral History Review* 1 (1973): 77–86.

Camarena, Mario, and Gerardo Necoechea Gracia. "Continuidad, ruptura y ciclo en la historia oral." In *Cuéntame cómo fue: Introducción a la historia oral*, edited by Gerardo Necoechea Gracia and Pablo Pozzi, 55–62. Buenos Aires: Imago Mundi, 2008.

Camarena Ocampo, Mario, Teresa Morales Lerch, and Gerardo Necoechea Gracia. *Metodos y técnicas de historia oral*. Mexico City/Oaxaca: Instituto Nacional de Antropología y Historia, Universidad Nacional Autónoma de México, 1990.

Carey, David Jr. "Methodology." In *Our Elders Teach Us: Maya-Kaqchikel Historical Perspectives. Xkib'ij kan qate' qatata'*, 1–21. Tuscaloosa: University of Alabama Press, 2001.

Dore, Elizabeth, Dayma Echevarria Leon, Julio González Páges, and Jorge Ramírez Calzadilla. *Documento de trabajo: Criterios teórico metodológicos*. Unpublished manuscript, ca. 2005, Havana and Southampton, England. http://www.southampton.ac.uk/cuban-oral-history/pub.html.

Dutrénit Bielous, Silvia. "La memoria de los políticos: Sobre la pérdida y la recuperación de su estelaridad." In *Cuéntame cómo fue: Introducción a la historia oral*, edited by Gerardo Necoechea Gracia and Pablo Pozzi, 113–20. Buenos Aires: Imago Mundi, 2008.

Freitas, Sónia Maria de. *Historia oral, possibilidades e procedimientos*. São Paulo: Humanitas/Imprensa Oficial SP, 2002.

Frisch, Michael. "Preparing the Interview Transcripts for Documentary Publication: A Line-by-Line Illustration of the Editing Process." In *A Shared Authority: Essays on the Craft and Meaning of Oral and Public History*, 81–146. Albany: State University of New York, 1990.

Garcés Durán, Mario. Chapter 3 of *Recreando el pasado: Guía metodológica para la memoria y la historia social*. Santiago, Chile: Educación y Comunicaciones, 2002. http://www.ongeco.cl/wp-content/uploads/2015/04/Guia_metodologica_Recreando_el_pasado.pdf.

Howarth, Ken. *Oral History*. Phoenix Mill, England: Sutton, 1999.

Lance, David. "Oral History Project Design." In *Oral History: An Interdisciplinary Anthology*, edited by David K. Dunaway and Willa K. Baum, 135–42. 2nd edition. Lanham, MD: Altamira Press, 1996.

Larson, Mary A. "Research Design and Strategies." In *Handbook of Oral History*, edited by Thomas L. Charlton, Lois E. Myers, and Rebecca Sharpless, 105–34. Lanham, MD: Altamira Press, 2008.

Oral History Association. "Principles and Best Practices: Principles for Oral History and Best Practices for Oral History." Carlisle, PA, 2009. http://www.oralhistory.org/about/principles-and-practices/.

Passerini, Luisa. *Fascism in Popular Memory*. Cambridge: Cambridge University Press, 1987.

Ritchie, Donald. Chapter 4 of *Doing Oral History: Using Interviews to Uncover the Past and Preserve It for the Future*. 2nd edition. Oxford, NY: Oxford University Press, 2003.

Schorzman, Terri A., ed. *A Practical Introduction to Videohistory: The Smithsonian Institution and Alfred P. Sloan Foundation Experiment*. Malabar, FL: Krieger, 1993.

Sebe Bom Meihy, José Carlos. "Tres alternativas metodológicas: Historia de vida, historia temática y tradición oral." In *Cuéntame cómo fue: Introducción a la historia oral*, edited by Gerardo Necoechea Gracia and Pablo Pozzi, 25–32. Buenos Aires: Imago Mundi, 2008.

Shopes, Linda. "Historians and Institutional Review Boards: A Brief Bibliography." American Historical Association, 2007. http://www.historians.org/press/2003-11-10-IRB-Bib.htm.

———. "Making Sense of Oral History." *History Matters: The U.S. Survey Course on the Web*, February 2002. http://historymatters.gmu.edu/mse/oral/.

———. "Transcribing Oral History in the Digital Age." In *Oral History in the Digital Age*, edited by Doug Boyd, Steve Cohen, Brad Rakerd, and Dean Rehberger. Washington, DC: Institute of Museum and Library Services, 2012. http://ohda.matrix.msu.edu/2012/06/transcribing-oral-history-in-the-digital-age/.

Sommer, Barbara W., and Mary Kay Quinlan. *The Oral History Manual.* 2nd edition. Lanham, MD: Altamira Press, 2009.
Thompson, Paul. Chapters 6–7 of *The Voice of the Past: Oral History.* 3rd edition. Oxford: Oxford University Press, 2000.
Yow, Valerie Raleigh. *Recording Oral History: A Guide for Humanities and Social Sciences.* 2nd edition. Lanham, MD: Altamira Press, 2005.

2   Archiving and Dissemination

Besides contributing to knowledge, oral history practitioners expand its building blocks by creating primary sources. Ensuring access to materials facilitates their use by scholars, students, and community members for their own purposes. It also allows findings to be verified. When Lewis's detractors insisted that poor Mexicans did not use the scatological language he attributed to them in *The Children of Sánchez*, two Mexican scholars reviewed the interview tapes to confirm that the quotations were accurate.[1] When oral history serves community interests, its producers and users frequently share goals. Some communities conduct oral history research and establish their own repositories for them. Since these projects are intended for immediate and open consumption, their approach to the distribution of and access to oral histories may differ from those of collections developed by scholars and archivists.

In a manifestation of the field's interdisciplinarity, scholars who practice oral history are increasingly acquiring archivists' skills. When Pisani and Jemio embarked on their oral history project in Famaillá, Tucumán, the site of the Argentine military's first detention and torture center, they decided to establish an archive to preserve the oral histories and to promote and disseminate them through workshops, seminars, homages, and other memory activities. As such, they went beyond collecting and analyzing oral histories to contributing to "the collective construction of knowledge."[2] Given that the goal was to uncover the history of the government's terror program dubbed Operativo Independencia, "building the archive was a political act."[3] In the context of postwar societies where people are hard pressed to avoid references to civil war and other forms of violence, the stakes and costs of establishing and preserving oral history collections can be high. Deciding to donate materials to an archive or help establish one demands careful consideration of political circumstances and financial resources. Whether or not projects are politically charged—and many are not—creating and preserving oral histories is a crucial first step to countering erasure. Discussions about potential collaborations with a repository should begin from the outset of the project.

Identifying Repositories

For posterity, practitioners prioritize the protection of oral histories. Concerns about the longevity of materials must be weighed against their accessibility and whether any particular population's access should be prioritized. In some cases, access may be restricted. To facilitate local access, copies of materials may be kept in local communities even if conditions are less than ideal and originals can be housed in better-resourced archives. Collaborative approaches facilitate inclusive outcomes, as researchers balance the needs and desires of local participants with historical preservation of materials. Often the two are compatible; decisions are more difficult when they are not. Although not a long-term solution, digital surrogates ameliorate the potential of damage or loss.

Many US universities will house oral history interviews conducted by their faculties and students. The Bancroft Library at the University of California, Berkeley, has more than 250 hours of interviews with Mexican, Bolivian, and Costa Rican elites. Thanks to an oral history project it sponsored, the University of Kansas, Lawrence, library holds interviews with Costa Ricans. With interviews exploring the Mexican Revolution and a focus on northern Mexico, the Institute of Oral History at the University of Texas, El Paso, has an excellent oral history collection.[4] The Latin American Library at Tulane University has hundreds of hours of Kaqchikel oral histories. As a result of its collaboration with the Instituto Torcuato Di Tella, Columbia University's Oral History Research Office has interviews with Argentines, particularly labor leaders, lawyers, and intellectuals.[5] Particularly rich in accounts of migration and Latin American heritage, a number of archives in the United States house oral histories of Latino/as.[6] Like the Hebrew University of Jerusalem's Institute of Contemporary Jewry, which houses a collection of interviews with people who migrated to Argentina, Brazil, Chile, Mexico, and other Latin American nations during the first half of the twentieth century,[7] a few archives outside the Americas have extensive oral history collections pertaining to Latin America.

Of course, institutions outside Latin America should not be the sole repositories of Latin American research. Interviews from the collaborative project between the Columbia University research office and the Instituto Torcuato Di Tella are available at the latter's archives. Even if university libraries and special collections make oral history interviews available on the Internet, they are of little use to people who do not have access to it. Ethical practices call for returning materials to their origination sources. Fortunately, recordings and transcripts are easily copied, and thus surrogates can be housed at another archive, library, or institution.

In countries including Mexico, Argentina, and Brazil where national oral history programs exist, every effort should be made to deposit oral history materials in their archives. Since 1959, Mexico's PHO has recorded interviews pertaining to politics, social movements, and culture and houses them at the INAH Archivo de la Palabra. Instead of resulting from specific research questions, most of the collections in the archive are products of efforts to capture the historical perspectives of participants in such broad phenomena as the Mexican Revolution and Spanish emigration to Mexico.[8] For oral histories pertaining to the revolution, the archive at the Instituto de Investigaciones Dr. José María Luis Mora in Mexico City also has a fine collection.[9] Encouraged by the growth of oral history in Mexico, the PHO established regional centers in Sonora, Jalisco, Veracruz, and other states so sources and findings from local and regional oral history projects would be available to the surrounding populations.[10]

Like the Famaillá archive, many Latin American archives offer outreach as well as repositories. The Instituto Histórico de la Ciudad de Buenos Aires promotes research, dissemination, and training in secondary schools, municipalities, social organizations, unions, and other entities. When the Universidad de Buenos Aires founded the Programa de Historia Oral, its goal, too, was to train practitioners as a way of promoting research.

In an indication of how oral history remained on the margins of academics, as the field of oral history grew, it seldom enjoyed close relations with higher education, partly because prior to 1980, many scholars in Latin America dismissed the value of oral sources. In an exception that proved that rule, the history department at the Universidad de Costa Rica established research projects with popular organizations and working classes in the 1980s.[11] One effect of the broader disassociation between oral history and universities was the mushrooming of specific research projects, foundations, and institutions that started their own archives. By the 1990s, oral history came to find firmer ground in Latin American universities. Argentina has experienced a flourishing of oral history archives and archives that include oral histories.[12] The Universidad Nacional de Mar del Plata, the Universidad Nacional de Cuyo, and la Universidad Nacional del Nordeste established oral history projects and archives to explore twentieth-century histories of their cities and provinces.[13] Emerging in the shadows of Brazil's military dictatorship, oral history programs in Rio de Janeiro and elsewhere have collected memories about twentieth-century political history.[14] The democratic opening in Brazil facilitated the foundation of its national Oral History Association in 1994.

Some archives develop directly from research projects. Housed at the Universidad de Buenos Aires, the Archivo de Palabras e Imágenes de Mujeres (Archive of Women's Words and Images) began as an interdisciplinary project intended "to recuperate women as historical subjects [and] . . . to find their mark under the androcentric frame of memory politics," explains Argentine historian Marta Zaida Lobato.[15] Support from the Universidad de Buenos Aires was crucial to the archive's establishment, maintenance, and success. To counteract the tendency of private archives in Argentina to restrict access to their holdings, Lobato was intent on making the archive's materials accessible to the public. Particularly interested in labor and migration since the 1930s, Lobato and her colleagues interviewed female labor leaders, professionals, artists, composers, actresses, feminists, and ordinary women. By accepting oral history interviews from individuals and other research projects, the archive expands its holdings and contributes to the "networks necessary to ward off amnesia."[16]

At times, governments take leading roles in oral history projects and their dissemination. Shortly after the Sandinistas' 1979 overthrow of the Somoza dictatorship, they established a literacy program that was accompanied by an oral history project aimed at capturing Nicaraguans' experiences of the dictatorship and the revolution. Within three years, they published a collection of the interviews.[17] Ultimately, they conducted more than five thousand interviews related to the Sandinista Revolution.[18]

The importance of established archives notwithstanding, leaving materials in cities alone may restrict access for many people involved in the project. The restrictions are not solely related to physical access, resources, or time. At times, racism, sexism, and classism discourage potential solicitors.

Given the uncertainty related to archival conditions and political unrest in parts of Latin America, deciding where and even whether to house interview materials is as much an ethical as a practical issue. The frequency with which some Latin American archives purge or destroy their materials for lack of resources, space, or desire to preserve them is cause for caution.[19] Since archives cannot house everything, archivists regularly make decisions about what materials to keep depending on whether they are copies, intended for long-term use, or historically important. Corruption poses a challenge to archival integrity as well. Wily Latin American directors and archivists have sold patrimonial materials. Of course, secure, safe, and accessible archives exist in Latin America. Researchers simply do their due diligence before committing their collections.

Resource-poor communities, climates that range from hot and humid to frigid temperatures, and remote locations can make establishing local archives difficult. Although conditions can be less than ideal for archiving materials, rural municipal buildings can house materials; some already have archives. Researchers can work with local entities to apply for historical preservation grants from such entities as the US National Endowment for the Humanities and the British Library's Endangered Archives Programme. Organizations associated with those participating in the study often can provide repositories. For example, research with indigenous people can be housed in governmental or nongovernmental agencies that work with them. Many lay organizations such as *cofradías* have closely guarded icons and documents dating from the colonial period; they could be trusted to house oral history materials, though negotiating access to them may be more complicated.

Involving locals in the process of cataloguing materials for an existing archive or establishing a new archive allows yet another point where the actors shape the telling. Preserving the past can have a profound impact on interviewees and archivists alike. Similar to the way recounting the past allows interviewees to shape historical narratives, archivists working with new collections determine how those materials will be studied. Intentionally or not, archivists' organizational and indexing decisions can just as easily obfuscate perspectives of the past as highlight them. Haitian anthropologist Michel-Rolph Trouillot calls the creation of archives—and by extension collections within archives—"the moment of fact assembly" and warns that silences almost invariably accompany that process.[20] Whatever their content, archives are venues of power.

Once the materials are housed in a secure and accessible location, researchers can publicize their existence. For academics, such dissemination is often best done through professional organizations and listservs such as the American Historical Association, Oral History Association, Latin American Studies Association, H-net, and H-Oralhist, or more country-specific organizations. In-country publicity can attract nationals to the collection.

Access

Access policies should be articulated from the outset. In communities that cannot afford a full-time staff person, let alone an archivist, how will arrangements be made for interested users to consult the materials? An agreement with members of the local municipal council or municipal employees could facilitate access to the materials and a space in which to consult them. If oral history research forms part of a new community archive, researchers and archivists should consider whether the community wants to make information available for a wider public, sell materials and products, provide teaching tools and resources, use the archive to express creativity, or some combination thereof. Dialogue with local community members is essential in developing procedures for Internet access. Some groups have expressed a desire to keep access local and thus forgo uploading recordings or transcripts to the Internet. While funding alone can greatly limit access to records, international copyright and other laws, donor agreements, licensing agreements, rights agreements, and privacy and safety concerns further complicate access.

For any archive, the two central goals of preserving materials and ensuring their access can be at odds. Since the lifespan of digital files is unknown and the software attached to them may no longer be supported as technology progresses, analog (open reel or cassette) tapes remain the gold standard for archival purposes. Copied from the original recording, an analog master tape should be rerun every two years to guard against the blurring of sound; a copy can be used for transcription and research. When limited resources preclude the creation of a master tape, users' preference for transcripts over recordings mitigates the challenges of maximizing preservation and access since recordings can be preserved while users consult transcripts, although that approach perversely perpetuates privileging written over oral sources.

Oral History Association guidelines call for open access to materials, but in communities and nations where violence often accompanies dissent, repositories may have good ethical arguments for restricting access. In the wake of Latin America's brutal military dictatorships, collecting oral histories can be dangerous. With the increasing frequency of prosecutions and convictions informed by oral testimonies, former leaders and supporters of authoritarian regimes have felt threatened by them. As such, serious thought must be devoted to the risks involved for those associated with archiving and disseminating potentially sensitive materials. In light of national insecurity and the politically charged nature of genocide survivors' testimonies, Pisani and Jemio restricted use to the archives they created to students, researchers, and human rights organizations. Through the release form, they also allowed interviewees to withhold their identities and partially or totally restrict access to their interviews.[21] High-profile incidents underscore the importance of safeguards. Among these are the 2006 kidnapping and disappearance of Dirty War survivor Jorge Julio López just prior to a public trial against impunity and the 2015 suspicious death of prosecutor Alberto Nisman one day prior to his testimony before lawmakers accusing Argentine President Cristina Fernández de Kirchner (2007–15) of conspiring to cover up Iranian involvement in a 1994 terrorist attack in Buenos Aires. Given the extensive judicial record of libel and defamation during the colonial and modern periods in Latin America, researchers are wise to restrict access to any aspect of the interview that mentions a person by name in ways that damage his or her reputation. Once the interviewee or individual mentioned dies, in most cases, the restriction can be released. Soto Laveaga uses a pseudonym to "discuss someone who was accused of graft or corruption in an interview."[22]

For projects in which narrators request or need anonymity, the selection of an archive must be contingent on its ability to maintain the security of the materials. Can materials that may jeopardize narrator's safety be secured? At times, violence, war, unstable governments, paramilitary forces, and other security threats preclude the return of oral history materials. In nations where *narcotraficantes* (drug traffickers) and other paramilitary forces control communities, will access be restricted? If so, how will it be enforced against an armed inquirer? While the archivist code of ethics ensures equal access (in theory) by prohibiting discrimination against any researcher, local realities may undermine that goal. In nations where racism continues to marginalize Afro-Latin American, indigenous, and other groups, can their access be guaranteed?

Although a few recordings are used for commercial purposes or otherwise generate profits, archives are not profitable ventures, so archivists do not monetize collections. Recognizing fair use and educational purposes, repositories generally waive fees for academic and other nonprofit uses. When film, television, or audio production companies are interested in materials, however, museums and other collections generally charge a fee for their use. Since most archival and oral history collections operate on a shoestring, the fees can offset the costs of smaller projects such as digitizing a collection. Narrators may take this into account and forgo any potential earnings, but such arrangements must be clearly articulated from the moment the materials are deposited.

Storage and Maintenance

The literature on processing and care of materials is thorough, so a few practical points for initiating the process of working with a repository suffice here. To protect their interviews, researchers make backup copies of all recordings and store them in a separate place. When labeling recordings, they use only acid-free markers.

Although climate-controlled archives are rare in Latin America, every effort should be made to keep collections in a secure, cool, dry place that is free from direct sunlight. To the extent possible, media should be protected from dust and dirt. Since technology's rapid progress quickly makes recording media obsolete, archivists plan for either regularly transferring data to new media or maintaining equipment that may no longer be in use elsewhere. Assuming people involved have access to the Internet, online archiving can temporarily extend the life of and access to the collection. With its commitment to "universal access to all knowledge," the Internet Archive digital library offers one such repository. If donors allow public access to their materials, the Internet Archive does not charge a fee for maintaining and upgrading them.[23]

The Internet should not be considered a storage solution, though. With websites vanishing or being neglected, web addresses changing, and the content on the Internet disappearing as websites are updated, Internet sources are often ephemeral and thus do not offer alternatives to archives. Despite these drawbacks, the Internet offers the possibility of sharing oral history recordings and transcripts with a worldwide audience. Technology allows for online archiving and sophisticated digital indexing, cataloguing, and search tools.[24] Audio and video recordings can be linked to written comments, photographs, maps, and other supplementary materials.

In many parts of the world, scholars and archivists are grappling with the complex issues involved in uploading full recordings to the Internet. Unlimited access and copying, intellectual property rights, protection of privacy, security, and the misuse and manipulation of materials have raised thorny ethical and legal issues. As a result, many researchers and repositories have opted to use the Internet to publicize their collections and to make finding guides available while withholding access to those who are physically present. Although a DVD can be loaned or sold, it offers digital solutions that have allayed some archivists' concerns about losing control over materials. As with the Internet, DVDs facilitate connecting text with sound by linking transcripts, interview setting information, maps, and other supporting documents to the audio.

Whether using the Internet or DVDs, converting to new technology is expensive and requires considerable time and energy. Uploading interviews to the Internet is a demanding process. For researchers and other users, downloading recordings consumes memory space and can be slow. Bypassing some limitations of speed and space, the cloud is a good repository, though storing interviews there has risks. Since not all websites use the same software, users may have to download a number of programs to listen to recordings from different archives. For that reason and to mitigate the extent to which recordings can be misused, some archives upload interviews that cannot be downloaded but only accessed directly from their website; others have put excerpts on the Internet to pique researchers' interests. For the same reasons the Internet lends itself to short articles and images, posting full-length recordings may not be fruitful. Given the limitations of reading online—few read entire books on the Internet; most users read screen-sized bits of information—most people who consult uploaded transcripts are researchers looking for specific information rather than casual users who will read an entire document.

Since it sharpens transparency and expands accessibility and usability, researchers and directors of repositories generally use the Internet as best befits their collections and circumstances. As the Internet attracts people to oral history research, archives will remain crucial for researchers who want to access interviews. Virtual visits may encourage physical ones. Ritchie concludes, "Given the democratic impulses of the oral history movement, it seems contradictory for oral historians not to avail themselves of the most universal and cost-effective means of mass communication and dissemination of information ever devised."[25]

Supporting Materials

Collection catalogues help users find the materials germane to their topics, and indexes help them locate relevant information within each source; for these reasons, researchers generally work with archivists to create them. While information can be drawn from the researcher's log and other sources, experts are exploring technological ways to combine those two tasks and thus facilitate creative research.[26] The process of categorizing interviewees may change as a collection grows. Many of the categories may overlap as interviewees' identities and experiences resonate with more than one category. For example, someone may be a trade unionist, Catholic lay leader, midwife, insurgent, and civil war survivor. For general guidelines, local archivists and researchers can consult the Society of American Archivists' oral history cataloguing manual.[27]

Supporting materials are essential to archival collections. Since the founding of the INAH Archivo de la Palabra, Meyer has sought to gather a transcript, photograph of the interviewee, summary and index for the interview, and any other complementary materials to accompany each recording.[28] When donated to a repository, transcripts, interview notes, abstracts, and other materials should be in order and organized. Any correspondence between the researcher and narrator also can accompany the recording. The complete package includes the recording, transcript and its index, complementary photographic and documentary materials, abstract, signed deed-of-gift form, and any notes pertaining to the interview.

Although the cost can be prohibitive for many Latin American collections, digital technology allows for searching transcripts and digital and audio recordings for terms. Technological tools that facilitate hands-on interaction with the materials are especially helpful for small, discrete collections. Well-funded archives in the United States and Europe have created searchable online collections that provide innovative access to the international community.[29] The National Gallery of the Spoken Word at Michigan State University and Project Jukebox at the University of Alaska, Fairbanks, offer models of how archives can transition to digital technology and integrate written and oral materials in multiple languages into a common database.

In a similar project with Latin American content, the University of New Mexico's Latin American and Iberian Institute launched its K'iche' Maya Oral History Project in 2013. Drawing from oral histories collected by James Mondloch from 1968 to 1973, the project features 149 audio recordings and bilingual K'iche' and Spanish transcripts accessible on the Internet. Two K'iche' speakers transcribed the recordings and then translated the transcriptions, which include their handwritten edits aimed at closely rendering the oral narratives. To guide researchers and other virtual visitors, the index links to each story's abstract.

Offering an equally impressive model for multilingual collections, the Harvard University Business School has been conducting oral history interviews with business leaders from Latin America, Africa, the Middle East, and Asia to understand how emerging markets developed over the past forty years. Initiated in a 2008 pilot project with nine Chilean and eleven Argentine executives, the Creating Emerging Markets Oral History Collection launched a website in 2014 that has photographs of interviewees, short translated excerpts, video clips, and most of the full transcripts.[30] With interviewees from Brazil, Mexico, Argentina, Chile, and Peru, the project offers in-depth access to the lives, perspectives, and worldviews of Latin American elites. Not all consented to have their interviews videotaped or to have their transcripts accessible on the Internet.[31] The transcripts and audiotapes are in the original languages. To increase the audience, video recordings have English subtitles. Posting some transcripts and video clips in their original languages on the Creating Emerging Markets website ensures that Latin Americans and other people living in emerging markets have immediate access to them, albeit with some restrictions.

The Voces oral history project at the University of Texas at Austin offers another model, with more than five hundred interviews with Latino and

Latina veterans of World War II, and the Korean and Vietnam Wars. As much for their wartime experiences as for their integration into US society, these recordings offer a window to experiences that ranged from combat to returning to segregated communities. Descriptions of the interviewees and the content of the interviews are available on the website along with other sources pertaining to the topics and methodology.[32]

Dissemination

Dissemination begins with interviewees. By giving each one a copy of the recording and/or transcript, researchers undergird collaborative efforts. Rather than attempting to control history or dictate interpretations of their interviews, raconteurs generally impart their recollections and perspectives so others can learn from them. "I am an optimist, and so I believe in the young people. We lived it, but they can interpret it in new ways," notes one Guatemalan interviewee.[33] As such, most interviewees welcome the opportunity to disseminate their knowledge beyond the interviewers.

Unless foreign researchers produce scholarship in relevant national and/or regional languages, their books and articles will be largely inaccessible to the people whose knowledge informed them.[34] In addition to fulfilling the ethical obligation of returning research findings and analyses to interviewees and their broader communities, publishing scholarship in interviewees' languages can facilitate future research. With the vast majority of his scholarship translated and published in Spanish, Camp realized that most of the Mexican elites with whom he worked read his work. Their willingness to continue granting him interviews was based on their perceptions of his objectivity, diligence, and thoroughness.[35] Publishing work in an informant's first language can be powerful symbolically too. When I first gave my Kaqchikel manuscript *Ojer taq tzijob'äl kichin ri Kaqchikela' Winaqi'* (A history of the Kaqchikel people) to interviewees whose oral histories—including accounts of *ladinos* and officials denigrating Kaqchikels and their language—informed the book, even those who could not read were pleased to have their words and analyses reproduced in their own language for generations to come. To reach a broad audience, Salvador Guzmán López and Jan Rus published a bilingual Tzotzil and Spanish volume of their collaborative oral history project about a Tzotzil community's purchase of a *finca*.[36]

In a manifestation of how public schools provide excellent venues for disseminating oral history research, Kaqchikel primary school teachers continue to use *Ojer taq tzijob'äl kichin ri Kaqchikela' Winaqi'*. To encourage indigenous integration in schools of Santa Fe Province, Argentina, Proyecto Aborigen collects memories about indigenous peoples' migrations. In a similar effort to inject regional history into local schools, Brazilian scholar Geni Rosa Duarte recorded and analyzed interviews about people who were forcibly removed from their homes to make way for a dam project. Students now learn about local refugees' responses to forced migration and resettlement.[37]

Researchers have deployed a broad range of venues and media to return materials and analyses to local collaborators in ways that are accessible and helpful. In addition to identifying the most appropriate means, deeper understandings of the role of oral history come from allowing community members to advise how best to disseminate findings: through writing, images, sound, or some combination thereof. Public presentations of interviews, including excerpts in local newspapers or on radio and television stations, may encourage interviewees to give or lend photographs, letters, and other items of material culture to enrich exhibits and collections.

As demonstrated in the São Paulo Museu da Pessoa's sophisticated multimedia program that showcased oral histories in the early 1990s, sound and video documentaries and exhibits are engaging and effective ways to disseminate oral history research. The state-sponsored mural program in Mexico and more recent nongovernmental mural programs in Guatemala and other Latin American nations demonstrate how public art expresses history.[38] To understand the motives, inspiration, and insights of such artists, the University of California, Los Angeles, film professor Jorge Prelorán and anthropologist Mabel Prelorán filmed interviews with self-trained indigenous artists from Latin America. Beginning in 1982, they interviewed Zulay Saravino over the course of six months in Ecuador and off and on for eight years in the United States. Hailing from Argentina and Ecuador, the Preloráns had experiences that resonated with Saravino's life story. The multilingual (Quechua, Spanish, and English) film conveys a complex tale of transnationalism, transculturation, and migration. Despite her entrepreneurship in Los Angeles and family in Otavalo, Saravino never felt fully at home in either place.[39] With his insistence that in his "ethnobiographies . . . [t]here is no mention of history," Jorge Prelorán attests to the interdisciplinary nature and wide applicability of oral history techniques.[40]

Like directors, film audiences can shape the production of videos. While watching the documentary film *Cicatriz de la memoria* about the 1932 massacre in El Salvador, tears of joy and rage poured from informants who saw themselves on film recounting the horrors of the past. As they offered critiques and comments after screenings that helped Gould and his codirector, the Venezuelan journalist Carlos Henríquez Consalvi, better understand the massacre and reconstructions of it, audience members related aspects of the film to contemporary oppression.[41]

In an indication of how appropriate means of local dissemination ensures that people at the heart of a project can interpret and ideally write their own history, indigenous activists have used *Cicatriz de la memoria* to spark discussions about the past and present in towns throughout El Salvador. The directors then had to live with activists' appropriations of the film, some of which contradicted or simplified analysis in the documentary. Gould in particular lamented how some meanings were marginalized because the fixed nature of a documentary demanded elisions that ultimately betrayed the complex nature of memories and competing narratives.[42] Historian Michael Frisch looks forward to the not-too-distant development of a "post documentary sensibility" that will allow for the inclusion of the very elisions Gould regretted by breaking down the distinction between oral history as a documentary source and oral history as a documentary product.[43]

Transmitting oral histories through writing, recording, film, or art and fossilizing them through publication or production inevitably imposes an inert quality that belies their organic nature. Thus scholarship countervails one of the most vibrant characterizations of oral histories. Even the most comprehensive medium of video freezes oral histories in a moment in time. Argentine sociologists Elizabeth Jelin and Pablo Vila offer another model for how to make research available to interviewees and facilitate its organic nature. Intended to continue a dialogue between urban popular-sector residents and social scientists, their book *Podría ser yo* was not the culmination of their research but rather its perpetuation. To capture "multiple, contradictory, and ambiguous realities" of working-class lives, Jelin and Vila present various themes with excerpts from interviews and photographs selected by their subjects.[44] They want readers to add their own comments and images to the book—an aim that speaks to their effort to break down the distinction between scholars and subjects.

While some researchers caution that marginalized people refrain from taking center stage or offering their own analysis until encouraged to do so by outsiders,[45] many disenfranchised Latin Americans have taken the lead on oral history research projects with little or no involvement of academics. Toward the end of *Cicatriz de la memoria*, an indigenous Salvadoran insists that indigenous people should be the creators of their own history. In places as different as Chile, Colombia, Brazil, Guatemala, and Mexico, indigenous people and other marginalized groups have assumed that role. Through community museums and exhibits, indigenous Oaxacans have articulated their participation in and perceptions of the past.[46] Afforded as much access to materials as professional historians, local leaders and intellectuals have built confidence in their capacity to construct their own history.

Their incisive analysis, publications, and creative works have helped unmoor oral history from university affiliation. Even absent professional oral history organizations and archives, Guatemalans like Juan Yool Gómez and Juan Kaqjay have used oral history to write historical narratives about themselves, their communities, and their nation.[47] The volume *Nab'ab'l Qtanam: La memoria colectiva del pueblo Mam de Quetzaltenango* explores, among other questions, how state power and responses to it that ranged from cooperation to confrontation shaped the lives of rural indigenous people. Hostig Rainer and Luis Vasquez Vicente proclaim, "With this work, we are finally producing a tribute to all Mam people, a marginalized and mistreated people . . . who know how, through oral tradition, to keep alive their collective memory and history—essential elements of their culture."[48] The Mam raconteurs' focus on famine, epidemics, forced labor, coastal migration, dictators, land titling, education, and the establishment of their communities resonates with the themes raised by other indigenous and Afro-Latin American groups.[49]

Such sources and insights are particularly important in light of the *historia patria* (the history of the fatherland) nature of so many national narratives written by Latin Americans—like the Mexican liberal intellectual Justo Sierra Méndez (1848–1912)—from the dominant male mestizo culture. In their tendency to promote a fraternal national bond and portray a homogeneous society around which citizens can identify with their nation, *historia patria* narratives often elide contributions to nation building by Afro–Latin Americans, Asian–Latin Americans, indigenous people, women and the poor in general, and other marginalized groups. Rather than recognizing their historical agency, Latin American authors of *historia patria* depict marginalized people as abject or absent. Liberal historians' portrayal of the Caste War in the Mexican Yucatán that continued intermittently from the mid-nineteenth into the twentieth century offers one example of *historia patria*. Mayas were fighting for autonomy to secure basic human rights denied to them by the Mexican government and regional landowners; mestizo authors portrayed them as savages bent on eliminating nonindigenous populations. When previously silenced voices contribute their knowledge and analysis of the past to national histories, they can influence national identities. In turn, inclusion often encourages people on the periphery to become more engaged in their nation.

Similarly highlighting the benefits of inclusivity, collaborative dissemination of research and scholarship has helped Latin American scholars overcome national barriers. Showcasing the potential of transnational oral history projects, researchers from Latin America have developed a broad framework for understanding leftist political militancy in Nicaragua, Brazil, Mexico, and Argentina. Edited by Necoechea and Pozzi, *Voltear el mundo de cabeza* is a scholarly collaboration that explores how the distinct lived experiences that led individuals to political and at times armed activism often intersected with liberation theology, labor unions, or social movements.

Given technology's capabilities and affordability, some scholars include recordings of their oral histories with their publications. Guatemalan anthropologist and activist Ricardo Falla's *Negreaba de zopilotes* includes a compact disk with audio recordings of his interviews and their transcripts. For anyone, listening to survivors recount the 1982 massacre of some 350 people is haunting, but the importance of such projects is underscored by younger generations of Guatemalans who have no knowledge, let alone memory, of the civil war. In another example of integrating technology with scholarship, the *Journal for Multimedia History* publishes articles with audio excerpts embedded in them online or on CD-ROM/DVD media, allowing the reader/listener access to the primary source material.[50]

Competing Interests of Truth, Reconciliation, and National Healing

In nations where the recent past is characterized by civil war and violence, dissemination of oral testimonies and oral histories is often political. First established in Chile in 1990, Latin American truth and reconciliation commissions (TRCs) have provided survivors and witnesses a forum to recount gruesome details of torture and murder. Moving trauma from private to public spaces in TRCs has had tremendous historical, legal, and social implications. "[We] collectively and responsibly took on the task of breaking the silence that thousands of war victims have kept for years. We opened up the possibility for them to speak and have their say, to tell their stories of suffering and pain, so they might feel liberated from the burden that has weighed them down for so many years," explained the Guatemalan bishop Juan José Gerardi Conedera when on April 24, 1998, he released the Catholic Church's study of human rights abuses.[51] Two days later, he was bludgeoned to death in his garage.

In Chile, the Catholic Church preceded the work of the TRC by interviewing family members whose loved ones had been kidnapped and killed by security forces.[52] After Pinochet was voted out of power in 1988, Raúl Rettig headed the TRC to study disappearances and other human rights abuses during the military dictatorship. Informed by victims' family members, cellmates, and friends who last saw them alive, the subsequent report documents how and why security forces targeted people and the ways people's jobs, locations, and political affiliations shaped their fates during the dictatorship.[53] Often offering the most definitive accounts of kidnappings and disappearances, reports such as the Rettig commission's invigorated national discourses about postwar politics and society.

For those and other reasons, TRCs were controversial. Besides marginalizing victims who pushed for justice rather than forgiveness, historians Greg Grandin and Thomas Klubock contend, "reconciliation imposes profound obstacles to the production of historical truth" and national healing.[54] Survivors whose supposedly forbidden, unutterable, or shameful memories contravene official history and reconciliation efforts face ostracism. Even within victims' groups, memories like these may disrupt dominant narratives.[55] Instead of transforming postwar societies through "social integration and solidarity," reconciliation frequently results in "mere coexistence" that does not address destroyed social fabrics.[56] Conversely, focusing on individual stories can undermine broader processes of restitution and retribution. Since many TRCs collected oral testimonies with an eye toward consensus, they privileged reconciliation and collective healing over prosecuting the engineers and perpetrators of human rights abuses. Some survivors were incensed by the failure to implement significant change and hold victimizers accountable, as an Argentine survivor affirms: "It angers me that justice in this country is not used in a way that finishes with the business, because the longer this goes on, the sicker Argentina becomes as a society. It's thirty-three years ago! Can you believe it? A country that doesn't want to heal itself; that doesn't want to begin anew."[57] Highlighting traumatic pasts without eradicating their root causes fails to set nations on a course of peace and stability.

As reminders of past horrors, survivors of torture and other human rights abuses assume controversial roles in postwar societies. "Survivors of atrocity become deeply uncomfortable signifiers for the post-atrocity societies within which they live, excessive to structures of normality that privilege forgetting, getting over and getting on with things," explains the philosopher Edith Wyschogrod.[58] Torture survivor and Chilean President Michelle Bachelet (2006–10, 2014–) asserts that an imposed consensus "does a disservice to the memories of thousands of victims of the Pinochet regime, to the many thousands more who were tortured and to their families—many of whom still do not know what actually happened to their relatives, spouses, and friends."[59] With its tendency to bury histories of nineteenth- and twentieth-century political violence so as not to undermine democracy, Chile has followed a firm path of reconciliation at the cost of historical oblivion.[60] Yet efforts to prevent future abuses by bearing witness to past ones complicate many survivors' attempts to forget.

One of the ways survivors of civil war and human rights abuses have refused to accept the status quo is by demanding exhumations and the proper burials of victims. In so doing, they compel a public recognition of traumatic pasts. Since the process can lead to the prosecution of powerful perpetrators who want secrets to remain buried, exhumations are often highly charged and contested; forensic anthropologists frequently work amid death threats. Informed by those involved with the process, scientific research, and survivors' testimonies, Sanford reveals "local attempts to make meaning of the experience of survival."[61] Relentless in her pursuit of suppressed information, or what she calls "truth telling," she insists talking about past atrocities is a critical component to transitional justice that helps survivors rebuild their lives and communities in the wake of unspeakable crimes.

To avoid the trap of trivializing suffering by focusing on acts of torture, victims and perpetrators alike articulate its long-term effects, particularly how they process and continue to live with their experiences.[62] In contrast to "social narratives of war [that] often reproduce overly simplistic interpretations of extremely complex issues," oral history allows people to demonstrate that authoritarian rule and violence do not preclude the articulation of complex critiques and insights about politics, society, and the economy.[63] The 1973 coup and subsequent oppression forever shaped many Chileans' lives; for others, the transition was less noteworthy.[64] By interpreting history in their accounts, interviewees influence the historical record.

The process of rebuilding postconflict societies in Latin America is most fruitful when survivors' stories are recognized as valid regardless of whether they adhere to official discourse. Dissemination can have distinct venues. With a program dubbed the Amnesty Caravan, the Brazilian government charged officials to hold public trials wherein each survivor had ten minutes to share their experience. If the amnesty committee considered the account compelling, on behalf of the Brazilian government it asked for forgiveness for the damage caused by the military dictatorship's abuses. In her testimonial to researchers, Brazilian historian Dulce Pandolfi describes her reaction after recounting the torture and incarceration she endured beginning in 1979:

> The government is now before me, bowing to me and treating me this way, how wonderful! . . . That was when I crumbled, I felt very compensated, it was a beautiful thing! . . . It does not erase the past, but we feel that finally citizenship has arrived in our country. . . . It was a very beautiful moment in my life.[65]

A number of Brazilians who participated in this official ritual identify it as a vital element in redressing the harm done to them and to the nation.[66]

For Brazilians in areas where the caravan did not arrive and for Latin Americans more broadly, forgiveness and healing are seldom so clear-cut. Throughout Latin America, relatives and offspring of victims and perpetrators live side by side. Even though Domitla's neighbors denounced her brother, which led to his murder, she refused to take action against them: "What for, if they and I know what happened. Moreover, time has passed and my grandchildren play with their grandchildren in the street and school patio."[67] Such cruel realities of fate both contribute to and countervail oblivion and erasure.

In some postwar instances, local leaders, mid-level participants, and the rank and file on both sides have recognized their shared subjectivities as they listened to each other's stories. Although they never forgave or empathized with the generals who engineered violence, former insurgents came to perceive police officers, soldiers, and other state agents who were their deadly enemies during wartime as victims of the same larger forces that marginalized Latin Americans more broadly.[68] Building peaceful societies is often contingent upon facilitating a process of dissemination whereby multiple competing and contradictory narratives can coexist.

The crucial complement to facilitating people's voices is ensuring that they can be heard. As such, preserving recordings and transcripts is as important as circulating excerpts from and analysis informed by interviews. The creativity with which scholars have approached the dissemination of their results speaks to the increasing accessibility of oral history processes and products in Latin America.

Notes

1 In Wilkie, "Introduction."
2 Pisani and Jemio, "El proceso de construcción del Archivo Testimonial," 4
3 Ibid., 24.
4 McCoy, "University of Kansas Oral History Project in Costa Rica"; Jaksíc, "Oral History in the Americas," 593–4. For the UTEP Oral History collection see http://digitalcommons.utep.edu/interviews/.
5 Mason and Starr, *Oral History Collection of Colombia University*. For other US archives with Latin American oral history collections, see Jaksíc, "Oral History in the Americas," 594–5.

Archiving and Dissemination

6. Jaksíc, "Oral History in the Americas," 592.
7. Bibliographic Center of the Institute of Contemporary Jewry, *Oral History of Contemporary Jewry*.
8. INAH, *Catálogo del Archivo de la Palabra*, 3–6; Olivera de Bonfil, "Treinta años de historia oral en México," 76–80; Pla Brugat, "Algo acerca de archivos," 98.
9. Jaksíc, "Oral History in the Americas," 594.
10. Meyer, "Oral History in Mexico and Latin America," 57.
11. Olivera de Bonfil, "Treinta años de historia oral en México," 82–3, 85. For an early assertion in Latin America that oral history was objective and scientific, see Reuda and Olivera, "La historia oral."
12. Schwarzstein, "Oral History in Latin America," 418–19.
13. Schwarzstein, "Tendencias y temáticas."
14. Lobato, "Recordar, recuperar, conservar," 9.
15. Lobato, "Introducción," 17.
16. Lobato, "Recordar, recuperar, conservar," 12.
17. Instituto de Estudio del Sandinismo, *Y se armó la runga*.
18. Pozzi, "Oral History in Latin America." 2.
19. Ibid., 4.
20. Trouillot, *Silencing the Past*, 26.
21. Pisani and Jemio, "El proceso de construcción del Archivo Testimonial," 20.
22. Soto Laveaga, *Jungle Laboratories*, 17.
23. Internet Archive, "About the Internet Archive," https://archive.org/about/.
24. See the Open Archives Initiative, particularly its Protocol for Metadata Harvesting, at https://www.openarchives.org.
25. Ritchie, "www.oralhistory.infinity," 14.
26. Frisch, "Oral History and the Digital Revolution," 107–8.
27. Matters, *Oral History Cataloging Manual*.
28. INAH, *Catálogo del Archivo de la Palabra*, 3–6.
29. Frisch, "Oral History and the Digital Revolution," 105.
30. *Creating Emerging Markets*, Harvard Business School, http://www.hbs.edu/businesshistory/emerging-markets/Pages/default.aspx.
31. Geoffrey Jones, email correspondence with the author, July 31 and August 1, 2014.
32. *Voces: Giving Voice to the American Latino Experience*. Oral history project, University of Texas, Austin. http://www.lib.utexas.edu/voces/index.html.
33. In Weld, *Paper Cadavers*, 183.
34. Such Latin America journals as *Secuencia* (Instituto Mora, Mexico), *Oralidad, Anuario para el rescate de la tradición oral de América* (UNESCO Latin American and Caribbean section, Havana), and *Entrepasados: Revista de historia* (Omega Laser, Buenos Aires) publish oral history scholarship for Latin American audiences.
35. Camp, email, January 5, 2016.
36. Los Socios de la Unión Tierra Tzotzil, *Lo'il sventa k'u cha'al la jmankutik jpinkatkutik Kipaltik*. Guzmán López and Rus translated and edited the volume.
37. Frotscher and Freund, "Conference Report," 4–5.
38. Coffee, *How a Revolutionary Art Became Official Culture*; Carey and Little, "Reclaiming the Nation through Public Murals."
39. Prelorán, Prelorán, and Saravino, *Zulay, Facing the Twenty-First Century*, film.
40. In Frank, "Woman's Journey: From Ecuador to L.A.," n.p.
41. Gould and Henríquez Consalvi, *1932: Cicatriz de la memoria* (Scars of Memory), film; Gould and Lauria-Santiago, *To Rise in Darkness*, 282.

42 Gould and Lauria-Santiago, *To Rise in Darkness*, 287.
43 Frisch, "Oral History and the Digital Revolution," 110–14.
44 Jelin and Vila, with D'Amico, *Podría ser yo*, 7. For a similar attempt to facilitate dialogue through publication, see Lynd and Lynd, *Rank and File*, 7–8.
45 Sebe Bom Meihy, "Radicalization of Oral History," 37.
46 Necoechea Gracia, "Custom and History," 119.
47 Yool Gómez and Kaqjay, *Tzijonik kan qate' qatata'*.
48 Hostnig and Vásquez Vicente, *Nab'ab'l Qtanam*, x.
49 See, for example, Iglesia Guatemalteca en el Exilio, *Nosotros conocemos nuestra historia*; AVANCSO, *Se cambió el tiempo*, 2 vols.
50 The journal and recordings are produced by the Department of History, University at Albany, SUNY, and are available at http://www.albany.edu/jmmh/.
51 In REMHI, *Guatemala Never Again!*
52 Vicaría de Solidaridad, *¿Donde están?*; Vicaría de Solidaridad, *Chile, la memoria prohibida*.
53 Comisión Nacional de Verdad y Reconciliación, *Informe de la Comisión*.
54 Grandin and Klubock, "Editors' Introduction," 6.
55 Araújo and Sepúlveda, "História, memoria e esquecimento."
56 Rigney, "Reconciliation and Remembering," 252 (quotes); Grandin and Klubock, "Editors' Introduction," 6; Weld, *Paper Cadavers*, 177.
57 In Stockwell, "'Country That Doesn't Want to Heal Itself,'" 31.
58 In Cubilié, *Women Witnessing Terror*, xii.
59 In Rieff, "After the Caudillo."
60 Loveman and Lira, "Truth, Justice."
61 Sanford, *Buried Secrets*, 26.
62 Jaksíc, "Oral History in the Americas," 599.
63 Grupo de Investigaciones Agrarias, *Vida y palabra campesina*; Van Isschot, "Heart of Activism in Colombia," 242 (quote).
64 Barrientos, "Texturas, políticas y fisuras," 44, 46, 48–9.
65 In Araújo, "História oral, memória e reparação," 18.
66 Ibid., 17–18.
67 In Barrientos, "'Y las enormes trilladoras vinieron,'" 141.
68 Weld, *Paper Cadavers*, 176–7, 247; Posocco, *Secrecy and Insurgency*, 141.

Suggested Readings

Brewster, Karen, "Internet Access to Oral Recordings: Finding the Issues." Elmer E. Rasmuson Library, University of Alaska, Fairbanks, 2000. http://library.uaf.edu/aprc/brewster1/.

Frisch, Michael. "Oral History and the Digital Revolution: Toward a Post-Documentary Sensibility." In *The Oral History Reader*, edited by Robert Perks and Alistair Thomson, 102–14. 2nd edition. New York: Routledge, 2006.

———. "A Shared Authority: Scholarship, Audience, and Public Presentation." In *A Shared Authority: Essays on the Craft and Meaning of Oral and Public History*, 179–263. Albany: State University of New York, 1990.

Gluck, Sherna Berger, Donald A. Ritchie, and Brett Eynon. "Reflections on Oral History in the New Millennium: Roundtable Comments." *Oral History Review* 26, no. 2 (1999): 1–27.

González Quintana, Antonio. "El archivero y las fuentes orales," *Historia y Fuente Oral* 5 (1991): 157–62.

Larson, Mary A. "Potential, Potential, Potential: The Marriage of Oral History and the World Wide Web." *Journal of American History* 88, no. 2 (2001): 596–603.

MacKay, Nancy. *Curating Oral Histories: From Interview to Archive*. Walnut Creek, CA: Left Coast Press, 2007.

Matters, Maron. *Oral History Cataloging Manual*. Chicago: Society of American Archivists, 1995.

Perks, Robert, and Jonnie Robinson. "'The Way We Speak': Web-Based Representations of Changing Communities in England." *Oral History* 33, no. 2 (2005): 79–90.

Pla Brugat, Dolores. "Algo acerca de archivos de historia oral." In *Historia y testimonios orales*, edited by Cuauhtémoc Velasco, 91–102. Mexico City: Instituto Nacional de Antropología e Historia, 1996.

Stein, Steve. "La historia oral y la creación de los documentos históricos." *Universitas Humanística* 15, no. 26 (July–December 1986): 135–40.

Swain, Ellen. "Oral History in the Archives: Its Documentary Role in the Twenty-First Century." In *The Oral History Reader*, edited by Robert Perks and Alistair Thomson, 343–61. 2nd edition. New York: Routledge, 2006.

3 Ethics, Power, and Activism

Returning from an interview with a monolingual Maya elder in Comalapa, I was startled to hear someone yelling at me from across the plaza. As I shifted my mind's language from Kaqchikel to Spanish, I realized he was accusing me of exploiting Mayas and their stories to make millions of dollars with a book I would publish in the United States.[1] Although I was writing a book in Kaqchikel for use in local schools and aware that publishing a monograph in English with an academic press would bring me little immediate financial gain, his accusation compelled me to rethink my project and very presence in highland Guatemala. Given the time, support, and resources Kaqchikels offered me, was I doing enough in return? I worked hard to ensure my personal and professional conduct was moral, but that hardly seemed sufficient. Though I did not profit from my publications, they facilitated my employment and career. Publishing and distributing a book written in Kaqchikel about their history hardly seemed fair compensation for the benefits I continue to derive from their oral histories. Still struggling with issues of inequity in my own research, I do not intend to allay but rather to raise ethical concerns involved in oral history research and some approaches to rectifying them.

Unless the project involves elites, foreign researchers working in Latin America generally enjoy privileges and power their interviewees do not. Researchers' very presence in Latin America conveys liberties and resources that elude most poor and working-class and many middle-class Latin Americans. Where equality is elusive, respect and reciprocity comprise the principal measures of ethical relationships; both are facilitated by transparency. Frisch's notion of "a shared authority" based on a "profound sharing of knowledge" and "dialogue from very different . . . bases of authority" is helpful for framing ethical research. That dialogue with interviewees, research assistants, other collaborators, and audiences can "inform the process of participation in design and development . . . [and] more deeply characterize the experience of finished products themselves."[2] Collaboration is a foundation upon which ethical relations can thrive.

Because research involving human subjects inevitably contains the possibility of exploitation,[3] stringent ethical standards are crucial to oral history projects. However clearly they may be articulated, ethics frequently become murky when applied. The Oral History Association and American Historical Association guidelines and codes of ethics are meant to balance a commitment to the well-being of the people being studied with truth in scholarship. Portelli characterizes that truth as "a utopian striving and urge to know 'how things really are' balanced by openness to the many variants of 'how things should be.'"[4] In research as in life, the dynamic interplay between caring and truth is more complex than principles and guidelines can anticipate. Contextually contingent and informed by personal values and professional knowledge, ethical decision making requires reflection.

Practicing Ethics

Before projects get under way, ethical questions arise for scholars. "*Others* are always the subject of *our* research, almost never the reverse,"[5] notes feminist scholar Daphne Patai. Although researchers increasingly consult and collaborate with communities, few ask locals if they want to be subjects of study in the first place. After anthropologist Nancy Scheper-Hughes published her book about Ballybran, Ireland, the local schoolmaster asked, "It's not your science I'm questioning, but this: don't we have the right to lead unexamined lives, the right *not* to be analyzed? Don't we have the right to hold on to an image of ourselves as different to be sure, but as innocent and unblemished all the same?"[6] Even among those who initially welcome the opportunity to collaborate, some ultimately may consider their portrayal a betrayal. A prominent labor lawyer in Guatemala City, Jorge Enrique Torres spent many hours talking with Levenson when he was a union leader in the 1980s; he later lamented that she had downplayed his role in the Coca-Cola labor movement and privileged the perspectives of others over his.[7]

Because research between US academics and marginalized people in developing nations is based on inequalities, hierarchies, and privileges that favor the former, Patai argues that ethical research in developing nations is not possible: "One cannot write about the oppressed without becoming one of the oppressors."[8] Regardless of an interviewee's socioeconomic status, the nature of research with humans, namely using someone for the scholar's purposes, makes oral history exploitative, she argues.

To shift from utilitarian to more reciprocal relations, some scholars adapt their methodologies. Frustrated by the futility of social science methods that discourage interviewers from engaging in personal exchanges and sharing their own insights and experiences with interviewees, Oakley advocates a collaborative, shared interview process, which, she asserts, produces better results.[9] Patai critiques that approach because it is based on female researchers identifying with female interviewees through their shared gender position but ignores the often stark ethnic, racial, class, and religious identities that separate them.[10] In a world comprised of unjust political, economic, and social structures that can only be changed with political action, Patai questions the utility of researchers' excessive self-reflection and ethical preoccupations.[11] Collaboration can mitigate exploitation, and invitations to conduct research can reverse them, but generally researchers advance their own agendas regardless of whether they advance those of their interviewees.

Paralleling the extractive practices of foreign companies and governments, some researchers have collected their data and returned home to analyze it and publish their findings in languages inaccessible to the people with whom they worked.[12] Such academic imperialism undermines the efforts of people who seek to learn from their past to guide their present. The indigenous intellectual Wankar (Ramiro Reynaga) argues, "The whites block our road toward the future by blocking our road to the past."[13] This conflict arises not only when locals are denied access to information about them but also when dominant discourses fail to incorporate indigenous, African, women's, and other marginalized groups' epistemologies and knowledge. It is no longer sufficient to serve "communities, movements, or individuals," as Portelli contends by "amplify[ing] their voices by taking them *outside*, to break their sense of isolation and powerlessness by allowing their discourse to reach other people and communities."[14] Providing participants feedback through recordings, transcripts, and analysis forms the core of ethical relations between researchers and interviewees. Taking subalterns' theories, methods, perspectives, and epistemologies seriously is another crucial step toward decolonizing research and scholarship.[15]

Since the late 1990s, collaborative research, methodology, analysis, and scholarship have become increasingly common in Latin America. By collaborating with local leaders, organic intellectuals, and other community members, researchers facilitate participants' shift from subjects to agents. When locals shape the research processes, goals, and methods, they have a vested interest in the projects' success. Through such models as participatory research or collaborative activist ethnographic research, scholars enable a shared research process. Anthropologist Lynn Stephen advocates "engaged, activist anthropology" that establishes "two-way relationships."[16] Developing a shared analytical language between researchers and community members through which they can debate theory, methodology, empirical evidence, and interpretation is a crucial collaborative component. Rappaport professes, "By acknowledging the value of historical information both to the Cumbales and myself, I could situate us in a common historical moment where we could share common evidence of the past, evidence we approached in similar, but also in different ways."[17]

A similar process unfolded in Kaqchikel communities where I worked and lived. Community leaders organized public presentations of my findings and distributed my Kaqchikel monograph. As local intellectuals took the initiative for future historical projects, I was poised to become a participant in their endeavors. During my oral presentations to highland audiences, I often heard in-depth analyses and detailed information regarding Kaqchikel perceptions of the past to which I was not previously privy. Intended to share my findings, those lively discussions and debates enriched my scholarship. Groups that have used oral history as a tool to reclaim their past and ground their activism in historical arguments are poised to be partners instead of subjects.

Even in collaborative settings, scholars struggle to reciprocate interviewees' time and generosity. Returning with transcripts, photographs, or finished products approximates reciprocal relations, but how can researchers fulfill other promises or expectations such as maintaining contact with interviewees? Unable to stay in touch with all sixty Brazilian women she interviewed, Patai struggled to justify a means for determining with whom, if anyone, she should continue to correspond.[18] When interviewees are forthcoming with intimate or traumatic accounts, such imbalances are all the more acute. Historian Temma Kaplan questions scholars' roles in recording and analyzing stories: "Like most oral historians, I worry about taking people's testimonies without giving them something in return."[19] Easing those concerns, torture survivor Nieves Ayress explained that she wanted her story to reach as many audiences as possible "as a way of creating communities of people committed to social justice."[20] However broadly defined and pursued, social justice holds the potential to chip away at the structural inequalities that overdetermine the relationships between Latin American interviewees and scholars. While researchers can pursue that goal, it may not address, let alone satisfy, the expectations of every interviewee.

At the very least, scholars can reconstitute democratic relationships through oral history research. The give and take of the interview process compels scholars to democratize their practices. Pozzi appreciates that oral history questions, "the feudal limits established by academe between disciplines and between the professional and the non professional, in that it recognizes that a historical study cannot be done without the active participation of the subjects."[21] He also celebrates how oral history research develops "practitioners who will influence the future while generating a democratic, plural, and fairer society."[22] Therein lie the goal and potential of oral history research. Although it cannot level unequal relations, it can contribute to more democratic processes that can address such injustices.

Authorial Relations

Despite the capacity of feminist methodology and indigenous theorizing to disrupt hierarchical relations between scholars and informants, researchers are wise to heed postmodern scholars' warnings about the complex authority relations inherent in the creation of oral texts and the struggle to democratize interviews.[23] Tackling those issues openly makes the interview "an experiment in equality."[24] If researchers create the conditions for as equal a relationship as possible in light of the socioeconomic, ethnic, gender, and other differences between the interviewer and interviewee, communication can be clearer and accounts less adulterated. Scholars who emphasize that they are there to learn from and not simply study interviewees lay the groundwork for bridging differences. Even in the field of testimonial literature, itself an attempt to redress power imbalances by allowing marginalized peoples to tell their stories, equality remains elusive. The spokesperson seldom enjoys equal status with the outsiders who provide or suggest this forum, yet they often have more power than those they represent. Alberto Moreiras posits that Latin American testimonial discourse can be likened to "a mask through which one's own voice is projected onto another, where that other is always suffering from a certain inability to speak. The relational mediation is then always unequal and hierarchical, even at its most redemptive."[25] Unequal power relations between interviewer and interviewee persist, even when scholars remove themselves completely from the interview.

By inviting input from local research assistants, interviewees, and informants on how they would frame a historical project about their people and communities, I tried to mitigate inequality. Some of the interview questions came from community members. In addition to oral presentations in highland communities, I wrote about Maya history in Kaqchikel, which allowed literate Kaqchikels to analyze the data and contribute to the final product. These interactions moved me closer toward presenting a written past that Mayas would recognize as their own since they were primary sources of historical data, research assistants, and critical readers rather than merely objects of research. Collaboration is not a panacea, however. Had I only followed the lead of Kaqchikel leaders and research assistants, who invariably steered me toward elder men as historical experts, I never would have conducted interviews with women. As researchers weigh the pros and cons of collaboration, they consider the project's goals and integrity of the research.

Bygone are the days when oral historians blithely asked questions to collect data. While the interviewer asks the questions, the interviewee controls what is and is not conveyed; interviews are co-constructed. To a large extent, what is spoken and what remains unspoken are contingent upon the identities of and relationship—which is in constant flux—between the interviewee and interviewer.[26] Identities of class, gender, race, religion, and sexual orientation are some of the dynamics that concurrently circulate through the interview and thus influence the oral account. Though his analysis is directed toward the hegemonic process between states and subordinates, political scientist James Scott's notion of "reciprocal manipulation" is helpful for thinking about how interviewers and interviewees shape oral history interviews.[27] The interviewer approaches the interviewee to learn from her, but that does not preclude the latter from studying the former throughout the interview. In her research with former insurgents in Guatemala, ethnographer Silvia Posocco realized that in many of her initial interviews, she was the interviewee, as ex-guerrillas asked her questions to determine how much they could trust and thus disclose to her.[28] Historian Luis van Isschot similarly noted in his interviews with political activists in Colombia, "More often than not, I was the one being tested."[29]

Just as questions lead informants and influence their responses, the investigator's presence and perspective affect which narratives are recounted and which bits of information are omitted. Interviewees often accommodate accounts to what they believe their audience wants to hear and the lessons they wish to convey.[30] Similar to the way an elderly black woman interviewed for the Federal Writers Project in the 1930s offered a harsh portrayal of slavery to a black man but painted a relatively benign picture when interviewed by a white woman, Mayas articulate more critical accounts of the past among community members in their own language than they do to outsiders in Spanish. Extolling the successes of the revolution when interviewed by two Cubans, a white, middle-class Cuban woman later critiqued the regime in an interview with a British scholar.[31] As K'iche' Maya Nobel Peace Prize laureate Rigoberta Menchú reminds us, omissions often are intentional: "Not even anthropologists or intellectuals, no matter how many books they have, can find out all our secrets."[32] Sacred or spiritual knowledge that is privileged within a group is often inaccessible to outsiders.

Often, interviews are cordial, yet they are still contested processes whereby the interviewee contests, however casually, the interviewer's conceptual framework for the interview, the questions asked, and the intended narrative. Interviewed by two Cuban women, a middle-age Cuban *mestiza* redirected their question about sexual orientation to draw them into a tale about her sexual liberation.[33] James insists that we should not underestimate the ability of informants to "negotiate the conditions under which communication takes place" and thereby to direct, influence, and even control not only the information conveyed but also the topics addressed.[34]

Distinctions in historical content, methods, and theory can mitigate marginalization. By maintaining their historical methods and epistemologies, Wakuénais have preserved their agency amid disempowering national politics in Brazil and Venezuela. Because they are only two-dimensional, books and writing are manifestations of white people's weakness and incompleteness in Wakuénais' eyes.[35] Many ethnic groups consider oral accounts more vibrant, malleable, and accessible than writing. The Afro-Cuban elder María de los Reyes Castillo Bueno hints at why black Cubans and other Afro-Latin Americans consider oral communication more accurate and truthful than writing: "Papers will back up whatever's put down on them. . . . [B]ooks don't really reflect reality that well."[36] Some indigenous peoples perceive the writings of historians to be more legendary than accurate.[37] Like Wakuénais, Colombian Cumbales dissociate history from writing. Rejecting a dependence on documents to articulate the past, they emphasize the power of history as they reconstruct it.[38] By asserting some control over how the past is reconstructed, marginalized groups shape their own history and reality.

Laying bare the partiality that characterizes historical sources, oral history research affords scholars the opportunity to challenge subjectivity. Interviewees represent and appropriate their own agency and marginalization. By crafting narratives in which they are in control, raconteurs articulate a vision of history that situates and often reformulates their roles, contributions, and tribulations in the past. That dominant discourses, ideologies, and structures influence interviewees should not blind scholars to interviewees' ability to inject their own meanings into past events.[39] Recognizing the interviewee's power, in his analysis of Menchú's *testimonio*, literary critic John Beverley avers, "We should worry less about how *we* appropriate Menchú, and . . . understand and appreciate more how she appropriates *us* for her purposes."[40]

The ability of interviewees to shape interviews notwithstanding, James finds that scholars have a tendency to misappropriate marginalized interviewees' lives, ideas, and histories. Foreign scholars' perspectives and the Western historical canon tend to permeate scholarship. With final control over the selection, editing, and framing of accounts, scholars cannot claim to enable subalterns to speak for themselves. As authors' and editors' voices dominate narratives, making hidden privileges apparent brings transparency into sharper focus. Striving not to arrogate interviewees' voices, scholars grapple with how to interpret their data in light of the asymmetrical power relations between interviewer and interviewee that introduce bias. To mediate their privileges, some foreign scholars coauthor publications with Latin American collaborators or provide forums for their single-authored scholarship. Yet these instances almost invariably involve local intellectuals rather than their more marginalized counterparts.

The co-constructed nature of oral history interviews complicates the rights to and ownership of them. Although Menchú and the Venezuelan anthropologist and journalist Elizabeth Burgos-Debray co-created *I, Rigoberta Menchú*, only Burgos-Debray claimed authorship. When Menchú questioned not being listed as an author, their relationship soured. "[T]he authorship of the book should be more precise, shared, right?" she notes in a 1991 interview.[41] Two years later, Menchú asked Burgos-Debray to sign over authorship rights "so she could make her own contracts."[42] Burgos-Debray refused the request and in September 1993 asked the publisher to stop sending Menchú her share of the royalties. While few *testimonios* or oral life histories earn such rich profits, some scholars insist on listing interviewees as contributors and reinvesting royalties in their communities.[43] Frisch claims that "what is most compelling about oral and public history is a capacity to redefine and redistribute intellectual authority, so that this might be shared more broadly in historical research and communication rather than continuing to serve as an instrument of power and hierarchy."[44] Some interviewees usurp control of interviews from researchers.[45] After the Brazilian military exiled senator Francisco Julião in 1965 for his efforts to implement land reform in Northeast Brazil, Wilkie conducted an extensive oral life history interview with him. When Wilkie sent the transcript to Julião for corrections, instead of returning it, Julião edited out Wilkie's questions and their debate and published the interview as his own account without Wilkie's knowledge or consent.[46] Shedding light on an ethics of ownership and authorship, the disparate fates of Menchú's and Julião's interviews highlight the need to clarify rights and intentions prior to commencing interviews; they also encourage embracing Frisch's notion of shared authority.

Interviewees' Identities and Information

Particularly in Latin America, oral history research raises thorny ethical questions about the protection of informants. Testimonies and oral histories that touch upon war crimes could be subpoenaed and ultimately put narrators' lives at risk. Scholars commonly use pseudonyms to protect sources; some have ensured this protection by keeping all identifying information in encrypted documents. In small communities where people and their histories are well known, identity protection is more complicated. Researchers may need to go beyond changing any identifying descriptions to suppressing or restricting parts of the interview that would readily identify interviewees. Where security is a concern, interviewers should ask interviewees not to provide their full names or edit them out if they are mentioned. At times the need for anonymity is immediately apparent. Conducting interviews with former insurgents at a police base where officers tortured and executed alleged subversives, Weld could hear the palpable tension in her recordings: "There are pauses in the tapes, or moments of hushed whispering, when interviewees would see an officer walk by or thought one was within earshot."[47] Some researchers use oral instead of written informed consent because the latter would have to be secured. Whether written or oral, informed consent should mention security concerns when appropriate.

For historians, anonymity is problematic. While some drawbacks can be mitigated, others cannot. Ensuring access to recordings and transcripts of anonymous narrators' interviews allows other historians to check sources and verify statements in publications. Little can be done, however, to assuage critics who contend that anonymity precludes narrators from taking full responsibility for their words and that maintaining anonymity often obfuscates a narrator's relation to specific events. Seldom do such professional costs outweigh the risks of revealing identities, though.

In light of the volatility of politics in Latin America, scholars can never guarantee collaborators' protection. Impressed by Lewis's concept of the "culture of poverty" in *The Children of Sánchez* (1961), Fidel Castro invited Lewis and his wife, Ruth, to conduct research in 1969. Having lived under Castro's regime (1959–2008) during its first ten years, interviewees shared their perceptions of how the revolution had succeeded and failed. Although he promised not to intervene, as scathing critiques of the revolution emerged, Castro assigned secret agents to infiltrate and spy on the Cuba Project. Increasingly aware of the threat to the project, Lewis had moved most of the oral history material to the United States by the time the government shut it down on June 24, 1970. Although that transfer facilitated project publications, it failed to safeguard participants whom the Castro regime arrested and harassed for being disloyal.[48] To protect human subjects, IRBs often request that recorded interviews be destroyed after the researcher has used them. Faced with such a mandate, researchers can make compelling arguments based on the American Historical Association and Oral History Association best practices that researchers protect the materials through encryption or physically secure holdings until they can be placed in an institutional archive. At that point, the archive's rules take precedence, but researchers can withhold the identifying information or release it after death or other agreement with the narrators. Archive rules are not inviolable, however; national courts could decide the fate of controversial or sensitive interviews. Since US courts have not given absolute protection to academic research, researchers should warn interviewees of the possibility that their recordings may be subpoenaed.

Legal and ethical obligations can compromise research confidentiality as well. For a Boston College oral history project on Ireland's civil war, researchers and archivists promised interviewees confidentiality until their deaths. When the Police Services of Northern Ireland learned of the project, they requested access to Irish Republican Army activists' oral history interviews through the US Justice Department for the criminal investigation of the 1972 kidnapping and murder of the alleged informant Jean McConville. In May 2013, the US Court of Appeals for the First Circuit ruled that Boston College had to turn over eleven interviews relevant to the investigation. When they learned of this breach of confidentiality, some interviewees asked for their recordings back. The legal proceedings and publicity effectively halted and sealed the project; researchers may never gain access to the collection. Emboldened by the interviews, on April 30, 2014, the police arrested Sinn Fein president and former Irish Republican Army leader Gerry Adams for the crime. Though he was released a few days later because of a lack of evidence, the arrest demonstrated the potentially dire consequences of participating in politically sensitive oral history projects. In another case that may resonate in Latin America, Mississippi prosecutors subpoenaed and were granted three sealed oral history interviews with an imperial wizard of the Ku Klux Klan who was accused of murdering a civil rights leader.

In Latin America, scholars have faced similarly sticky situations. Mexican scholar Graciela de Garay published parts of her interview with the architect Mario Pani, who implicated himself and the Mexican government for failing to ensure basic maintenance and perform structural repairs on the Tlatelolco housing unit that collapsed in the 1985 earthquake, killing hundreds of people and leaving many more homeless. A Supreme Court judge then demanded the entire manuscript. Pani had given Garay permission to publish the interview in weekly installments in *Excelsior*, one of Mexico's largest newspapers, and remained comfortable with that agreement. Arguing that the release agreement compelled her to respect Pani's confidentiality, Garay refused to release the transcription.[49] The judge desisted, but more persistent provocateurs may test the limits of the legality of such agreements.

Human rights abuses and other crimes associated with civil wars in the region during the last third of the twentieth century introduce vexing ethical issues, particularly regarding how oral history research can be solicited and deployed. On three different occasions, public prosecutors have cited Pozzi's interviews in trials against former guerrillas for crimes against humanity. To date, he has never been called upon to testify in court, but that prospect looms large over his scholarship. "The possibility that what a participant declares in an interview can be used towards ends never imagined by the historian is an ethical and practical problem," Pozzi cautions.[50] That risk is especially daunting in projects that depend on secrecy. Such was the case for the sociologist Martha Huggins and her colleagues when convincing Brazilian police officers who tortured prisoners to talk about their experiences: "Whether securing interviewees, getting their responses to potentially threatening questions, documenting their atrocities, or analyzing and writing about the horrors of state-sanctioned violence, secrecy had to be reckoned with in both the interviewer and interviewee, or else the study could not have proceeded."[51]

When oral histories are made available on the Internet, the potential for complicated ethical issues expands. Critical for researchers, finding guides can compromise informants. Based on a finding guide that listed "atomic bomb testing" as a category, Federal Bureau of Investigation (FBI) agents interrogated an Indian American narrator about his connection to atomic bomb testing in India in the 1990s even though he had been living in the United States since the 1960s. After the FBI called the narrator a second time, the repository administrator changed the subject heading in the finding guide from "atomic bomb testing" to "current events"—a more innocuous but less helpful term.[52]

In nations where the spoken word trumps documentation in some courts, oral historians can unwittingly find themselves collecting data that could be used in land disputes and other community conflicts. They must weigh how to share this information and, to the extent that it is possible to anticipate such requests, explain this risk to interviewees as part of the informed consent process.

Scholar-Activists

A keen awareness of power imbalances in research relationships and society more broadly compels some scholars to become activists. "Latin America continues to be a space for utopia, for thinking about the far-away relatively just society and fearing the fracture of the ever fragile present. Politics there jumps out at you as soon as you open your eyes," explains Necoechea.[53] When studying social movements or groups struggling to establish their rights and livelihoods, researchers frequently find themselves pulled into—or leading—efforts to counteract exploitation. Sebe Bom Meihy unabashedly advocates "a politically active oral history . . . [that] should serve social purposes; the intellectual effort it entails ceases to be alienated when it finds justification in politics."[54] Responding to military dictatorships, activists and academics alike have deployed orality to denounce human rights abuses. The interplay between knowledge and action "distances us from self-celebration and complacency," maintains Argentine historian Cristina Viano.[55] As an instrument for change, history does not merely comfort or conform; it challenges and provokes. It also can be used as a tool to mobilize people facing discrimination, extreme poverty, or forced relocation. The politics of nostalgia can be radical.

Even as Latin American scholar-activists embrace a synergy between politics and scholarship, researchers concerned about the conflicts that develop when the two overlap are careful to guard against activism undermining the legitimacy of research processes or results. Subordinating research methods and results to political aims paves the way for misunderstandings, distortions, and other problems. When advancing a cause overrides research protocols like those that assure accessing as diverse a group of interviewees as possible, the data gathered become biased. Equally problematic are attempts to shape the thinking of interviewees to adhere to a researcher's perspectives. Distinct from asking follow-up or probing questions, efforts to convince interviewees of a political perspective or how their circumstances should be understood betrays the interviewee's implicit trust that the researcher is there to learn, not proselytize. Pointing out that "imposing our own politically correct analyses requires an arrogance incompatible with a genuine respect for others," Patai criticizes feminist scholar-activist Marjorie Mbilinyi for making "consciousness raising" an explicit part of her oral history research in Tanzania.[56] Such restraint need not paralyze scholars, however. Stephen encourages "research that seeks to serve the communities it studies."[57] At the very least, as part of researchers' responsibility to disseminate the data they gather, communities and individuals should have access to and benefit from scholars' research. As demonstrated by scholar-activists in Latin America and elsewhere who carefully maintain the integrity of both roles, research and activism need not be antithetical. Confronted by the realization that many interviewees needed and qualified for psychological and financial assistance, Pisani and Jemio contacted Argentina's Secretaría de Derechos Humanos to connect torture survivors with that agency's resources without preaching about their importance.[58]

Some groups approach scholars as resources. When middle-class female residents of San Pedro de los Pinos in Mexico City learned that the Instituto Mora Programa de Historia Oral was writing a history of their neighborhood, they requested its assistance. Through oral history interviews, researchers empowered residents. By highlighting their heritage, the Instituto Mora's history legitimated neighborhood organizations and justified residents' attempts to defend and improve their lived spaces.[59] Historians in Mexico, Chile, and elsewhere have facilitated disenfranchised communities' capacity to research and analyze their own pasts.[60] Necoechea and his colleagues developed symbiotic research processes whereby their work with Zapotecs and Mixtecs gave the indigenous participants "a needed language to understand their own role as history makers. In this way they appropriate the history they have researched."[61]

Many groups use oral histories to guide and inspire them. Young gay men in Brazil developed oral narratives to help "forge new ways of living."[62] In his study of the Quechua-speaking Yuras in the Andean highlands, anthropologist Roger Rasnake notes,

> Myths serve not only to structure thought but also to structure action. They create an arena for construction of social identity that is very much at odds with the vision of the dominant urbanized elite, by defining a world in which Yura identity is integral to the very nature of things, in opposition to a wider context of power relations that negates that identity. In this sense myths are a strategic license for social action.[63]

When people's worldviews differ dramatically from those whose political and economic power constrains them, oral narratives legitimate their distinctions and inform their activism.[64] During Guatemala's civil war, K'iche's turned to the lessons of their elders in developing strategies to defend themselves from army incursions.[65] The Cumbales of Colombia continue to use historical knowledge to inform their political strategies and harness political action.[66] Suggesting how memory and activism influence each other, Mario Castañeda asserts, "Memory is actualized in struggle, in rebellion, in the negation of our society's status quo."[67]

Oral history helps to sustain social activism across generations. Concerned that their struggles for justice might die with them, former insurgents often welcome the opportunity to tell young people about their experiences. "We have the responsibility to tell them what we did, but also to tell them what we really think about it, in order to sustain it," contends a Guatemalan activist.[68] To elders' delight, some youth are eager to learn. One young activist observes, "We have to speak to people who lived these realities so that we can come to understand them . . . to build a more just, fair country."[69]

Some projects begin with advocacy in mind. Such was the case when the National Waters Commission and Regional Waters Management in the Valley of Mexico set out to promote clean waterways. The authorities deployed oral historians to learn local people's divergent perspectives of environmental issues, particularly as they related to water. María Concepción Martínez Omaña explains that the Instituto Mora gladly accepted the charge with an eye toward implementing public policies aimed at "furthering the preservation of the natural environment . . . especially when it concerns near extinct resources such as water."[70] Knowledge of local perceptions and concerns helped the regional management agency develop strategic approaches and prepare to defend those that might be met with resistance. Offering other examples of how oral history informs public policy, international development organizations use oral history to understand how history, social relations, and culture affect aid programs and issues like poverty and education.

Research products can become tools for advocacy. Shown in rural Salvadoran communities, the documentary film *Cicatriz de la memoria* helped indigenous activists initiate discussion among audiences about racism and the erasure of indigeneity. Providing a public forum for horrible histories and traumatized memories encouraged viewers to recognize the tremendous emotional and economic losses caused by state violence in 1932 and in the 1980s. At their best, such airings facilitate individual and national healing.

From the initial stages of the research design through the production of scholarship and other means of disseminating findings, transparency is crucial. Although it alone will not mitigate unequal relations or guarantee ethical practices, by allowing reviewers, readers, viewers, and listeners to assess the nature of the project and its products, transparency discourages exploitation. Given researchers' positions of privilege, ethical relations should go beyond not harming target populations to collaborating with them in ways they identify as fruitful and consequential. At the same time, facilitating collaboration and embracing local epistemologies should not infringe upon researchers' ability to critique assistants, interviewees, or other participants involved in the project and products.

Notes

1 Informed by a long history of colonialism and imperialism, such accusations are not uncommon in Latin America; see Crandon-Malamud, *From the Fat of Our Souls*, 36–7; D. Carey, "Symbiotic Research."
2 Frisch, *Shared Authority*, xxii.
3 Patai, "Ethical Problems," 16.
4 Portelli, *Battle of Valle Guilia*, 55.
5 Patai, "U.S. Academics and Third World Women," 149 (emphasis her own).
6 In Scheper-Hughes, *Saints, Scholars*, vii.
7 Gabriela Torres, personal conversation with author, November 8, 2013.
8 Patai, "U.S. Academics and Third World Women," 139.
9 Oakley, "Interviewing Women."
10 Patai, "U.S. Academics and Third World Women," 144.
11 Ibid., 139, 149–50.
12 Gluck and Patai, "Introduction," 2–3; Patai, "U.S. Academics and Third World Women," 149.
13 Wankar, *Tawantinsuyu*, 279.
14 Portelli, *Battle of Valle Guilia*, 69. Emphasis in original.
15 See, for example, Chakrabarty, "Postcoloniality and the Artifice of History"; Smith, *Decolonizing Methodologies*.
16 Stephen, *¡Zapata Lives!*, 343.
17 Rappaport, *Cumbe Reborn*, 22.
18 Patai, "U.S. Academics and Third World Women," 149.
19 Kaplan, "Reversing the Shame," 196.
20 Ibid., 197.
21 Pozzi, "Oral History in Latin America," 6–7.
22 Ibid., 6.

88 *Ethics, Power, and Activism*

23 Iacovetta, "Post-Modern Ethnography."
24 Portelli, *Death of Luigi Trastulli*, 32.
25 Moreiras, "Aura of Testimonio," 210.
26 Aguila and Viano, "Las voces del conflicto."
27 Scott, *Weapons of the Weak*, 309 (quote), 322–40.
28 Posocco, *Secrecy and Insurgency*, 95.
29 Van Isschot, "Heart of Activism in Colombia," 250.
30 Marcus and Fischer, *Anthropology as Cultural Critique*; Clifford and Marcus, *Writing Culture*; Finnegan, "Note on Oral Tradition"; Mallon, "Editor's Introduction," 17; James, *Doña María's Story*, 183; Hall "'You Must Remember This,'" 440; Trouillot, *Silencing the Past*, 146.
31 Hamilton, *Sexual Revolutions in Cuba*, 57.
32 In Burgos-Debray, *I, Rigoberta Menchú*, 247.
33 Hamilton, *Sexual Revolutions in Cuba*, 14–15.
34 James, *Doña María's Story*, 139.
35 Hill and Wright, "Time, Narrative, and Ritual."
36 Reyes Castillo Bueno, *Reyita*, 31.
37 Wankar, *Tawantinsuyu*, 279–81.
38 Rappaport, *Cumbe Reborn*, 176.
39 James, *Doña María's Story*, 139, 243.
40 Beverley, "The Real Thing," 272–3 (emphasis in original).
41 In Grandin, *Who Is Rigoberta Menchú?*, vii.
42 Ibid.
43 See, for example, Sexton and Rodríguez, *Dog Who Spoke*. After Florencia Mallon promised to reinvest all royalties from her book in the Mapuche communities that informed it, community members continued to press her on how they would benefit from the book; *Courage Tastes of Blood*, 22–3.
44 Frisch, *Shared Authority*, xx.
45 Ibid., xi.
46 Julião, *Cambão*. I am grateful to James Wilkie for sharing his side of this story with me.
47 Weld, *Paper Cadavers*, 22.
48 Lewis, Lewis, and Rigdon, *Living the Revolution*; Wilkie, "Introduction." For an erudite critique of Lewis' notion of a "culture of poverty" (and *La Vida*), see Briggs, Reproducing Empire, 163–4, 170, 177–88.
49 Garay, "Another Turn of Screw," 14–15.
50 Pozzi, "Oral History in Latin America," 3.
51 Huggins, Haritos-Fatouros, and Zimbardo, *Violence Workers*, 2.
52 Sommer and Quinlan, *Oral History Manual*, 29.
53 Necoechea Gracia, "Editorial," 2.
54 Sebe Bom Meihy, "Radicalization of Oral History," 36.
55 Viano, "Historia reciente e historia oral," 288.
56 Patai, "U.S. Academics and Third World Women," 148.
57 Stephen, *¡Zapata Lives!*, 13.
58 Pisani and Jemio, "El proceso de construcción del Archivo Testimonial," 10–1.
59 Pensado Leglise, "Reach of Oral History."
60 Garcés Durán and Leiva, *El golpe en La Legua*. To facilitate disenfranchised people's ability to conduct their own historical research, Garcés Durán also authored and coauthored oral history methodology guides aimed at popular sectors such as his *Recreando el pasado*, especially chapter 3, and Garcés Durán, Ríos Etcheverry, and Suckel Ayala, *Voces de identidad*.

61 Necoechea Gracia, "Custom and History," 129.
62 Laverdi, "Vivencias urbanos de jóvenes muchachos homosexuales," 121.
63 Rasnake, "Images of Resistance," 153.
64 Warren, *Symbolism of Subordination*; Landsman, *Sovereignty and Symbol*; Ramos, "Indian Voices."
65 Burgos-Debray, *I, Rigoberta Menchú*.
66 Rappaport, *Cumbe Reborn*, 18–19.
67 Castañeda, "De memoria y justicia," n.p.
68 In Weld, *Paper Cadavers*, 180.
69 Ibid., 191.
70 Martínez Omaña, "Oral History, a Political Resource for Public Action," 12.

Suggested Reading

American Historical Association. "Statement on Standards of Professional Conduct." http://www.historians.org/about-aha-and-membership/governance/policies-and-documents/statement-on-standards-of-professional-conduct.

Carey, David Jr. "Symbiotic Research in the Humanities and Social Sciences: A Utilitarian Argument for Ethical Scholarship." *Thought and Action* 19, no. 1 (Summer 2003): 99–114.

Grandin, Greg, and Thomas Miller Klubock, eds. *Truth Commissions: State Terror, History, and Memory*. Special issue of *Radical History Review* 97 (Winter 2007).

Groundswell: Oral History for Social Change. http://www.oralhistoryforsocialchange.org/about/.

Kerr, Daniel. "'We Know What the Problem Is': Using Oral History to Develop Collaborative Analysis of Homelessness from the Bottom Up." *Oral History Review* 30, no. 1 (Winter–Spring, 2003): 27–45.

Neuenschwander, John A. *A Guide to Oral History and the Law*. 2nd edition. New York: Oxford University Press, 2014.

Oral History Association. "Principles and Best Practices: Principles for Oral History and Best Practices for Oral History." Carlisle, PA, 2009. http://www.oralhistory.org/about/principles-and-practices/.

Riaño-Alcalá, Pilar. "Seeing the Past, Visions of the Future: Memory Workshops with Internally Displaced Persons in Colombia." In *Oral History and Public Memories*, edited by Paula Hamilton and Linda Shopes, 269–92. Philadelphia: Temple University Press, 2008.

Roque Ramírez, Horacio N. "Memory and Mourning: Living Oral History with Queer Latinos and Latinas in San Francisco." In *Oral History and Public Memories*, edited by Paula Hamilton and Linda Shopes, 165–86. Philadelphia: Temple University Press, 2008.

Stephen, Lynn. "Testimony in Truth Commissions and Social Movements in Latin America." In *Pushing the Boundaries of Latin American Testimony: Meta-Morphoses and Migrations*, edited by Louise Detwiler and Janis Breckenridge, 109–29. New York: Palgrave Macmillan, 2012.

4 Language, Translation, and Performance

Given the nuances of linguistic subtleties, nonverbal communication, and translation, communication across cultures requires mental acuity and focus. Only after living in Guatemala for some time could Daniel Wilkinson listen thoroughly to informants. When he asked a raconteur if his people were guerillas during the civil war, the man responded with a grin, "The only thing that made us *canches* [blonds, also a gloss for guerrillas] was the dust."[1] Later Wilkinson realized the man was not simply referring to dust literally lightening their skin; his double entendre also suggested that drought, as manifested in dust, and poverty had compelled them to resist the military government whose repression and economic development schemes marginalized poor and working-class Mayas. The playfulness and poetry of language demand close attention to the history and culture of the people with whom one is collaborating.

The diversity of languages and cultures in Latin America adds to the richness and complexity of conducting oral history research. To cite but one example, Japanese Peruvians whom the US government relocated to US internment camps spoke English, Japanese, Okinawan, Spanish, and Hawai'ian creole English.[2] As true for interviewers as for interviewees, the multiple meanings of linguistic turns, body language, and physical gestures are difficult to ascertain in a second language and new culture. Compelled to respond in European languages, indigenous and Afro-creole speakers may not convey the same information, sentiments, or perspectives that they would in their first languages. Essential for some research projects and crucial for disseminating results to multiple audiences, translation seldom transfers the entirety of meaning from one language to another. Even when translators capture the many meanings embedded in single phrases, rarely can they concisely communicate them, and thus the poignancy of the meanings suffers.

Imbued with worldviews and epistemologies, language is intricately related to power and empowerment. Various groups maintain their original or hybrid languages to stave off the effects of neocolonialism and assimilation. In her research with indigenous people's oral histories, Brazilian scholar Marina Evaristo Wenceslau asserts, "Maintaining the Guaraní language is the most important weapon for the self-defense of the group."[3] Such exceptions as the official recognition and widespread use of Guaraní in Paraguay notwithstanding, European languages generally enjoy privileged positions over indigenous, African, creole, sign, and other marginalized languages. Conducting interviews in such colonial languages as Spanish, Portuguese, or French rather than interviewees' first languages perpetuates marginalization, while performing interviews in nondominant languages emboldens interviewees' and their larger communities' voices by affirming their distinct cultures and epistemologies. Sowed by such past and present geopolitical relations as US imperialism and intervention in Mexico, Central America, and the Caribbean, foreign researchers face animosity in certain contexts. Learning national and local languages is a crucial first step to breaking down those barriers. In many ways, doing an oral history interview undercuts the colonial power of archives whereby textuality is considered superior to orality, which in turn discounts subjugated peoples' oral traditions and histories as inferior to European written knowledge. By legitimizing marginalized languages and contradicting the idea that orality is less valuable than writing, conducting interviews in subordinate languages upsets neocolonialism on two levels.

Historically, many Latin American elites, bureaucrats, teachers, and other authority figures have derided people who maintained their distinct languages. Haiti offers a particularly stark example where French-speaking elites consider the Haitian Creole spoken by the majority of people inferior and at times subversive. To denigrate indigenous languages in Chiapas, Mexico, Spanish-language representations of Maya languages often intentionally included grammatical errors and "backwoods Spanish . . . suggesting a sort of minstrel-speak."[4] Scholars struggle to balance respect for people's word choices and idioms with an awareness that the stigma of "improper speech" or "wrong" Spanish can belittle interviewees.[5] By conveying their commitment to the projects and people, researchers who learn the local languages can gain people's trust and confidence.

Since many bilingual indigenous peoples do not tell the same stories or relate the same concepts in Spanish that they do in their native languages, local fluency can lead to insights that remain elusive in colonial languages. "Our languages express our culture, and speaking and understanding them means learning about a new world, and thinking about things in a new way," explains Menchú.[6] According to Menchú, Spanish fails to capture the essence of Maya languages and, by extension, cultures and histories. Indicating a cognitive gap between Spanish and indigenous languages, Amerindians often omit or alter details when they are not speaking their native languages.[7] For some, entire topics are only accessible in their native languages. A Maya female elder explains, "I spoke about history to a man who was interested but I could not speak about it in Spanish. I only know history in Kaqchikel."[8]

Such cognitive variance may be related to the way language shapes memory; what people name things is one way in which they remember them. As a result, different languages elicit distinct memories even in one individual.

"Among Tzotzil-speakers speaking in Tzotzil there was an internal, indigenous conversation about history and politics that was not only different from, but also opposed to the ways those same themes were talked about in Spanish, even by the same people," observe scholar-activists Jan Rus and Diane Rus of their interviews in Chiapas.[9] Neocolonial social and political relations influence narratives specific to a language. Before they can analyze oral histories, scholars first become attuned to the multiple ways information, meaning, and emotion are conveyed by sharpening their listening and observation skills.

Body Language and Other Nonverbal Cues

Context is crucial for understanding communication. "Clothing, house décor, gestures, ritual movements, etc. communicate; in many cases, they tell us more than words can," Cano Sánchez notes.[10] Nonverbal cues communicated through the interview's material and emotional environment convey meaning.[11] Since words and phrases have multiple meanings and between 50 and 65 percent of communication is nonverbal,[12] tone and body language help listeners move from grasping the apparent to understanding the intended meaning. Louis Menand reminds us, "Speech is somatic, a bodily function, and it is accompanied by physical inflections—tone of voice, winks, smiles, raised eyebrows, hand gestures—that are not reproducible in writing."[13] For this reason, many researchers prefer videotaping interviews. As video recordings become more common, researchers can pursue nuanced analysis of interviews based on verbal (including sounds other than words) and visual communication cues. When videotaping is not possible, interviewers can make notes about interviewees' nonverbal behavior. Manifesting how facial expressions, gestures, and body language hint at deeper meanings and rival consciousness, "the pained expressions" on Ecuadoran peasants' faces while being interviewed conveyed their disappointment at not having established their economic and political autonomy.[14] Behavior such as finger tapping, dancing eyebrows, avoiding eye contact, nuanced nostril flares, body tilts such as sitting up straight or slouching, and changes in the velocity of speech also alert listeners that the events or circumstances being recounted have affected and continue to affect the narrator.

Nonverbal communication includes such vocalized puffs of air as sighs, exhalations, coughs, and moans. Whether short or extended, a pause accentuates the meanings of words. It also allows interviewees to rethink and perhaps reorder their narratives.[15] Some pauses correspond to a particular community's narrative style or trope. In chants about their history, the San Blas Kuna of Panama use pauses to create melody.[16] Often speech characteristics clue interviewers in to significant patterns. Increased velocity of speech may suggest an attempt to gloss over well-known information or controversial or otherwise problematic aspects. When interviewees articulate traumatic information, their speech may slow. Emotion, humor, sarcasm, sorrow, irony, and facetiousness can be communicated through combinations of body language and the pitch, speed, stress, intonation, volume, and inflection of speech. When raconteurs look away, pause, or change their voices in some way, they may be betraying that they have more to say about the topic or that it is particularly painful. Rather than prod, researchers generally ask follow-up questions later.

Some immediately obvious nonverbal cues can halt an interview. When recounting harrowing or tragic experiences, interviewees may cry. Such was the case for Ixq'anil when she first recounted how her young daughter answered a knock at the door of their highland home one night only to let in men who abducted and likely killed her father; Ixq'anil had to halt her account several times to control her tears, but she wanted to continue.[17] The pain of losing her husband and the sorrow she felt for her daughter who bore the cross of unwittingly aiding his murderers was a palpable manifestation of how the trauma of Guatemala's civil war continued to mark her life. Like Ixq'anil, interviewees often can regain their composure and continue on the same topic. In some cases, the interviewer may need to change the subject or halt the interview.

When recounting trauma, shifts in body language can be particularly pronounced. Interviewing Violeta, a member of the Comité de Cooperación para la Paz en Chile (Committee of Cooperation for Peace in Chile, later called the Vicaría de Solidaridad) about the discovery of human remains from a massacre that occurred during the Pinochet dictatorship, Stern noticed that "Violeta's body language took a restless almost writhing turn. She continually squeezed her hands hard and pulled at her nails. Perhaps this was because she recalled not only the impact of the news and the subsequent struggles to identify and bury the remains, but also what had happened *before* the discovery."[18] In addition to the trauma communicated through her body language, Stern observes that her speech was marked by "her difficulty of finding the right words."[19] Attuned to her anguish as it manifested in gestures, stutters, and words or lack thereof, Stern came to appreciate how traumatic it was for her and others in the group when they realized the remains were of the *desaparecidos* (disappeared ones) for whom the committee had been searching. Examined in all its nonverbal and verbal complexities, communication conveys emotions, memories, and meanings that transcriptions and translations alone fail to capture.

Like interviewees, interviewers influence the interview with their body language and nonverbal cues. If an interviewer does not maintain eye contact or looks elsewhere, the interviewee may interpret that as boredom and shorten their responses. Yet since not all cultures promote direct eye contact with those outside the family or people of different genders or status, avoiding eye contact may be appropriate. In many African cultures, eye-contact avoidance is viewed as a sign of respect.[20] To encourage a storyteller to continue a narrative thread, a nod or a smile is better than a verbal "yes," "ahuh," or other distracting placeholder that unnecessarily encumbers the recording.

Verbal and nonverbal forms of communication shape the cognitive and affective connection between the interviewer and interviewee. For these reasons, when returning to an interview to interpret it, viewing or listening to the original recording affords richer communication detail than reading the transcript. If only an audio recording is available, researchers can listen along while reading the interviewer's notes regarding nonverbal communication.

Language and Translation

Because they do not so much interpret words as meanings, translators have to understand and live in multiple worlds. To communicate across the different languages in which they research and publish, scholars have to make sense of and clearly convey disparate epistemologies, knowledge, and cultures. Language acquisition is an essential part of that process. Since speaking the national and oftentimes local language is imperative, most foreign scholars working in Latin America become fluent in at least one language other than English.

When researchers achieve fluency, translation remains challenging; it invariably adds a layer of complexity to analysis—offering another example in which insight and interpretation from local research assistants is invaluable. Often the exact meaning of a word or phrase is unclear or does not translate well. Many a turn of phrase in foreign languages cannot be literally rendered comprehensible in another language. Comprehension becomes more complicated when the language of communication is not native to either party. Unavoidably creating another filter through which listeners and readers must sift, translations generally are approximations of the content of statements that are intended to remain true to the meaning, rhythm, and flavor of the words. Some words are reserved for specific contexts and topics and thus only exist in one language; among Yukatek Maya speakers in Quintana Roo, Mexico, some Maya words are solely uttered when describing the Caste War. In highland Bolivia, the Aymara Kallawayas, a group of traditional healers, have their own language for their ancient medical practices, which fathers pass on to their sons.[21] Capturing linguistic subtleties is crucial for conveying the richness of oral histories and for pursuing potential leads from storytellers.

Speaking the same language does not guarantee clear communication between interviewers and interviewees, especially because idioms and dialects that vary by region can cloud comprehension. Steven Lief Adleson and his colleagues note, "Ignorance of linguistic turns, implicit understandings, and . . . puns can cause misinterpretations."[22] When Necoechea and his colleagues were offering oral history workshops in Oaxaca, Mexico, they realized that their understandings of some Spanish words were different than those of the Zapotec and Mixtec participants. Necoechea used the word *problema* (problem) to evoke an abstract process of understanding events and their nature, but Zapotecs and Mixtecs deployed it to refer to "practical problems that needed solutions."[23] As a result, when Necoechea and his team used the term *problema* to introduce topics such as education, emigration, and traditional medicine, the participants responded not with historical narratives about those topics but rather with how contemporary crises might be addressed. Their framework shifted from sharing oral histories to strategizing with planning developers. Once the project leaders replaced the phrase "research problem" with "aspects of their lives we wanted to know more about," the participants grounded their responses and queries in oral histories.[24]

As researchers' language proficiency expands, their projects and analyses become more sophisticated. Such was the case during the Zapotec and Mixtec oral history project. Neither the Zapotec nor the Mixtec language had a word for *artisan*. Instead, speakers described such specific labor as stonemasonry, wood carving, and weaving. As Zapotec and Mixtec speakers used the word, Necoechea notes, "they added their own meanings to it."[25] Exploring those conceptualizations, the project team learned how local labor was related to the environment and the past. As participants described intricate processes of weaving and stonemasonry learned from years of apprenticeship as well as objects made at home from reeds and wood, the researchers realized that their own concept of artisans as highly skilled laborers failed to capture local renderings. In the process, they "discovered a wider variety of feelings and attitudes toward work" than they expected.[26] They also came to appreciate how work connected people to the past. Whether they made goods at home or worked a trade outside it, Zapotecs and Mixtecs associated their activities with their parents and previous generations who had transmitted knowledge of those particular skills and crafts. Passing those techniques on to their children honored past generations. Working through the challenges of communication opened up the team's awareness of how Zapotecs and Mixtecs preserved the past.[27]

To develop a common language, Necoechea and his colleagues worked with Zapotec and Mixtec participants to define the meanings of key terms and concepts. Lengthy discussions about another word brought Zapotec and Mixtec conceptualizations into focus. Although they often used the word *costumbre* (custom), they did not have a literal translation for it in either language; they offered "norm," "duty," and "law" as approximations. Instead of tradition, *costumbre* meant continuity and was set against the threat of change represented by history in Zapotec and Mixtec worldviews. Associated with "the language of the conqueror," history constantly clashed with *costumbre*, which perpetuated practices, epistemologies, and rituals aimed at resisting outside transformational influences. Idealizing continuity and harmony over change and conflict, Zapotec and Mixtec narratives cast alterations in an unfavorable light.[28] When direct translations are elusive, rich meanings come forth that may provide windows into new conceptualizations and theories.

Even when words are readily available, their fluidity can lead to confusion. Conducting research in Cuba, Nadine Fernandez came across this problem when she asked people to state their racial identities.[29] In some cases, people of mixed races identified themselves as mulattos or mestizos, although their families identified them as black or white. Racial categorizations can change over time. Identified as black on her first government identification card, one woman was classified as *mestiza* on her second ID. Another woman was thrilled when her official card changed her classification from *mestiza* to white since that lighter-skinned identity advanced her social position in Cuba's pigmentocracy. Like skin color, hair can determine people's identities. Identifying race by phenotype is complex and contested in Latin America. The mutability of these categorizations complicates communication about race. Similarly, shifting terms and malleable meanings are deployed to classify or resist sexual identities. While younger Cubans tend to use the words "gay" and "lesbian," most older men who have sex with men define themselves as "homosexual." Many interviewees refrain from using any term at all when describing such relations.[30]

Depending on the project, scholars may be working on the frontiers of more than two worlds. When working with indigenous peoples, Afro-Latin Americans, Asian-Latin Americans, or other groups that maintain their own languages in addition to the colonial ones that dominate their nations, foreign scholars may need to translate across colonial as well as foreign frontiers. Differences between marginalized and dominant groups in Latin America are often stark.

Disparaging remarks about indigenous languages that accompanied pressure to discontinue them came from within as well as outside ethnic communities. In the 1970s, Salvadoran children made fun of their parents and grandparents who spoke Nahuate.[31] Often parents discontinued native language use to help their children avoid discrimination. For that reason, some Okinawan Peruvian parents only spoke Spanish at home.[32] Attributing it to education, migration, racism, and other forces of assimilation, many Latin American indigenous peoples lament the loss of their languages; conducting interviews in native languages can countervail that loss. As indigenous and other ethnic groups embrace collaboration, they increasingly are expecting foreign researchers to learn the local language. Some speakers cannot conceive of research without native languages. A Q'anjob'al Maya man asked geographer and historian George Lovell, "How is it possible to write a book about our people without knowing our language?"[33]

Aware of the way indigenous languages isolated and disenfranchised peoples, historians, sociologists, anthropologists, and linguists in Bolivia came together in the 1980s to form the Taller de Historia Oral Andina (THOA, Andean Oral History Workshop) to collect histories of Aymara and Quechua speakers. Although the focus on indigenous languages initially marginalized the organization, when the Bolivian government began recognizing the importance of indigenous cultures in the late 1980s, THOA enjoyed increased support. The election of Aymara-speaking President Evo Morales (2006–) underscored THOA's importance. Concerned as much with recovering indigenous knowledge, culture, and history as with empowering indigenous peoples, THOA investigators explore questions of indigenous people's relations to mestizos and authorities. Since many of the participants are illiterate and to reach as broad an audience as possible, THOA produces radio and video documentaries about indigenous history, culture, and rights. By creating a "counterpublic sphere" where Aymara activists and intellectuals can articulate indigenous-informed perspectives of the past and strategies for the present, THOA decolonizes discourse and methodology.[34]

Researchers and interviewees who move from one epistemology to another often reinterpret concepts and ideas. Generally less concerned about literal equivalents than conveying meaning, indigenous speakers who reconfigure their languages to explain concepts and terms in a second language often transform narratives and the ideas contained therein. When Nasa Yuwe speakers translated the Colombian constitution, they reconceptualized notions of justice and nation within the framework of their own epistemology and worldviews; from their perspective, they improved Spanish terms by injecting them "with a new Nasa significance."[35] To fully grasp the concepts laid bare in these processes, researchers must be fluent in both languages and willing to collaborate with native speakers. The window this cultural and linguistic translation affords into indigenous theorizing holds the potential to transform our understanding of the multivariate processes that reconstruct the past.

Languages' impact on narratives and their telling can be indiscernible. Ten years after I conducted my research in Kaqchikel, Esquit embarked on an oral history project in one of the Maya towns where I had lived. When he asked bilingual interviewees if they wanted to be interviewed in Spanish or Kaqchikel, the vast majority preferred Spanish. The more facile explanations for these distinct developments are that Esquit was an insider and thus did not need to prove himself the way I did or that male elders whose formal education rarely exceeded the sixth grade preferred to speak Kaqchikel with someone for whom it was a second language but preferred Spanish with a native Kaqchikel speaker who held a graduate degree. Beyond these possibilities, I am still at a loss for how to explain those different predilections. Between the time I conducted my research (1997–1998) in the shadow of the Acuerdos de Paz (Peace Accords, 1991–1996) and Esquit conducted his research during the second decade of the new millennium, Maya language use may have become less politicized because violence in postwar Guatemala was less clearly connected to ethnicity. I posed the question of indigenous interviewees' different language choices based on interviewers' nationality or ethnicity at a 2013 conference in Guatemala where Mayas dominated the audience, but I elicited no replies. Whether they were equally stumped, uninterested in the distinct responses, or the phenomenon was unknowable to foreigners is unclear. At the very least, Esquit's experience suggests the complex ways language, memory, identity, reconstructions of the past, and power are intertwined.

Particularly striking when considered in light of the histories of colonialism and exploitation that mark social relations in Latin American nations, intercultural negotiations between foreign scholars and national and/or local intellectuals and other collaborators can facilitate creative explorations of new ways of thinking about and deploying scholarship, activism, and history. With sophisticated studies of languages and narratives, scholars have come to recognize that marginalized peoples' histories are only local from dominant viewpoints. Despite their subordinate positions, disenfranchised people often shape as much as they are shaped by globalization.[36]

Gaps in communication and comprehension are not limited to language. Different cultures, epistemologies, and conceptions can impede communication. Paul Sullivan argues that Mayas and foreigners "were guided by very different motives; had different ideas about speaking and writing and the kinds of beings who can use language; had different senses of place, time, causality, and different knowledge of what had gone before. They could not share one set of answers to questions about their dialogues."[37] He characterizes that effect as a double monologue that impedes the effective exchange of ideas. With such distinct backgrounds and ways of knowing, approximating meaning and significance is often the best scholars can do.

Performance

Play on words and double meanings remind us that storytellers are performers, particularly in oral societies where specific individuals are recognized as keepers of history. Raconteurs often use history to teach, argue, or entertain. Such intentions and creative license can lead to distortions and fabrications through which researchers must sift. More animated when discussing the use of chemical fertilizers and military service, particularly his experience as a parachutist, than when he addressed education or migrant labor, the Kaqchikel merchant B'eleje' Imox underscored what he considered significant about the past with gestures as well as words. He also deployed humor to accentuate certain points.[38] As entertaining a storyteller as he was, his embellishments and eye for the sensational made interpreting his narratives difficult. For example, his account of transporting moonshine by hiding it in coffins was plausible but nearly impossible to corroborate. By eluding authorities, evasive moonshiners skirted clear of the archives. Such evidence is precisely what makes oral history indispensable, yet the performative aspects of his storytelling added another layer I had to scrutinize to get at the story's meaning, accuracy, and veracity.

To express emotion or simply animate the telling, some narrators wave their arms or act out the story to emphasize aspects of it. When Ruth Ramírez opened her arms to draw the interviewer's attention to her simple home, it was an expression of her disappointment: "When I married a railwayman, I expected something more. You expect something more than this."[39] In her study of sexuality in Cuba, historian Carrie Hamilton learned to listen not only for how speakers deployed sexuality as a metaphor for other forces and desires but also "how sexuality expresses itself through emotion."[40] Whether absent or accompanied by words, emotions communicate particularly passionate perspectives.

Verbal accounts, animated explanations, and ritual reenactments are crucial to many people's understandings of how the past is reconstructed and related to the present. Community conventions regarding oral transmission shape narrative styles and content. In many indigenous communities, storytellers can conflate similar or related historical events so as not to bore listeners as long as the core of the narrative remains representative and unchanged. To maintain audience attention, interviewees construct narratives that tap into what folklorist and anthropologist Richard Bauman calls the "essential artfulness" of oral accounts.[41] Recognizing the performative aspects of storytelling helps researchers understand the significance of certain events and the nuanced meanings involved in recounting them.

The motive and context of the performance, whether it be an oral history interview or another manifestation that reveals something about the past, are crucial for interpreting the information gathered. In his study of Chamulas in Mexico, ethnographer Gary Gossen identified three speech patterns, two of which were contingent upon the speaker repeating words and phrases and deploying parallel syntax and metaphors. Audiences evaluated raconteurs on the way they spoke and thus interpreted content through performance.[42] Among the Kuna, performative aspects of chants conveyed history and other information to assembled audiences.[43] The communicative efficacy of performance is as dependent on the audience's interest and goals as the speaker's competence.[44] To historian and anthropologist Jan Vansina, historical information gleaned from poems, prayers, songs, and storytelling is trustworthy precisely because it is unintentional.[45] Yet in light of the creative license inherent in those sources, the information articulated in them may not be true to past events. Such traits underscore the importance of approaching oral histories critically. Because it offers a window through which researchers can learn about the meanings of events, the performative nature of oral histories is precisely what Portelli finds most valuable about them.[46] In a 1999 interview twenty-five years after exhaustive hikes into rural Mexico, one administrative assistant broke into a ballad decrying transnational companies that she and her colleagues sang to steel themselves against their difficult working conditions.[47] Performance conveys meaning.

The more theatrical and intricate an enactment, the more significant its meaning. According to Rapa Nui oral tradition, when the Chilean navy captain Policarpo Toro Hurtado approached the Rapa Nui leader Atamu Tekena to annex Easter Island in the late 1800s, Tekena put soil in his own pocket while he handed grass to Toro to indicate that while Chileans were welcome to visit the island and exploit its resources, the Rapa Nui chief was not conceding his people's territorial rights. More than one hundred years later, Rapa Nui people continue to enact that scene whenever asked about the political relations between the island and Chile.[48]

Paying attention to performance is not solely an academic endeavor aimed at getting close to raconteurs' intended meanings. Identities such as gender, class, ethnicity, race, sexuality, religion, and generation shape how people tell stories and thus their content. Even as scholars deconstruct essentialist observations, some commonalities emerge in broad brushstrokes. The way public discourse and pressure encourage people to adhere to normative portrayals calls into question the extent to which men and women veer from accuracy or shroud details to abide by social expectations of gender. Women often reflect dominant narratives that portray women as weak, passive, and meek.[49] When María Elisa recounted her experience with labor movements and two incidents of rock throwing in Colombia, she distanced herself from the violence. "Throughout our long interviews, she negotiated a line between presenting herself as having been shy, almost over-modest, and slipping in stories that pointed to an earlier rebelliousness and a street-smart confidence gained from having come to the city as an orphan who had to fend for herself," observes Farnsworth-Alvear.[50] As an older, respectable woman, María Elisa may have worried about her reputation and not have wished to draw attention to some of the gender-bending activities in which she engaged while younger. Gender, class, humility, and a desire to evoke a pacifist personal past all shaped her narrative. Through their oral histories, interviewees tack between idealized and critical representations of themselves.

Many female narrators break from gender norms, often more so in their past behavior then in their present narratives, in ways that evoke a disconnect between society's expectations and women's experiences. Maya women's accounts of the midwife Germana Catu (1879–1966) offer one example of how women break from narrative disenfranchisement—whereby scholars less frequently interview them, and local men devalue and discount women's stories—to tell oral histories that capture their experiences with their own protagonists and resolutions.[51] At the center of the struggle between indigenous approaches to health care and the state's imposition of biomedicine, Catu not only maintained her traditional practices in the face of authorities' pressure to adhere to their regulations, she also convinced a few Guatemalan doctors that Maya midwifery had much to offer. That male raconteurs never mentioned Catu or the struggle between indigenous midwifery and biomedicine in their narratives about health, illness, and state intervention can be explained partly by indigenous men's ignorance of reproductive health. But it also can be attributed to their inability to fit such stories into their broader historical narratives because Catu's experience did not jibe well with conventional cultural forms or gendered discourse.[52] Public discourse and social pressure influence not only narrative performances but also the ability of audiences, researchers included, to listen to and comprehend their layered meanings.

Generally an absent audience in the interview, the community contributes to an interviewee's historical consciousness. Recording an interview makes the community's presence more pronounced since, barring any restrictions, anyone has access to the recording thereafter. This virtual public created for posterity represents another audience that influences the interview.[53] Understanding the relationships between interviewees and their communities helps researchers interpret the meaning and significance of narrative strands.

As the Rapa Nui example demonstrates, performance can facilitate community building. The politics of nostalgia become radicalized, and storytellers recount histories with organizational goals in mind as narratives with an activist bent are passed down over generations. After years of persecution by the military government and their employer, Coca-Cola union members in Guatemala produced their own history to inspire their demands for improved wages and working conditions, which culminated in a year-long occupation of the Guatemala City bottling plant in 1984. Based on survivors' memories, they wrote an anthem and commissioned its score, erected a Plaza de Mártires (Martyrs Plaza) with a mural of defiant workers, hung photographs of murdered union leaders, and wrote a brief history of their struggle. To buoy confidence that they could achieve their goals against great odds, the workers emphasized the heroic aspects of their past and downplayed international solidarity, state power, divisions among workers, and other forces that contributed to the union's development.[54]

The ability of language to empower speakers may distort narratives by encouraging raconteurs to deploy creative license when recounting events of oppression and resistance. In her analysis of the Coca-Cola union members' historical reconstructions, Levenson points out, "There was nothing irrational about this semimythmaking, which told as whole truths, important partial ones . . . [but] This image of . . . the union's past nevertheless denied workers access to many of their own problems."[55] Such distortions are part of the performative aspect of oral histories that researchers take into account in their analyses. Long explanations tend to describe circumstances or justify representations of what narrators wished had happened—what Portelli calls uchronic imagination—not what actually did happen.[56] Even as her analysis captures a more nuanced history, Levenson recognizes the redemptive powers and purposes of the union's version. Indeed, workers would not let her forget: "'You! You think we are poor,' a Coca Cola worker said to me. Pointing to his head, he continued, 'We are not poor, we are rich.'"[57]

Oral histories are only as good as the communication and exchanges that produce them. Articulating the narratives and perspectives gathered in a second language and culture can be incomplete and frustrating. The humbling experiences of interpretation and translation highlight that scholars seldom capture the truth of what happened but only converging and competing perspectives of it. The very process that limits scholars as they write is a microcosm of the larger struggle of understanding the past they seek to express.

One of the ways researchers can fine-tune cultural communication is by immersing themselves not only in the language and culture but also in the specific communities with which they engage. Familiarity is an antidote to miscommunication. Informed by local cultural, historical, and social knowledge, fluency facilitates a broad understanding of how and what people communicate. Passing time with interviewees outside formal interviews allows researchers to observe communicative nuances specific to individuals that can shed light on their intended meanings. Given that listeners bear as much responsibility as speakers for optimizing communication, ethnographic approaches to oral history research can deepen insights and analysis.[58] Establishing deep, respectful relationships also facilitates researchers' ability to build trust with interviewees and communities. As scholars move beyond ethnography to collaboration, communication becomes richer still. In light of the complex process of understanding interviewees' perspectives, oral history research benefits from local experts' insights.

Notes

1 Wilkinson, *Silence on the Mountain*, 356.
2 Iwao Ueunten, "Japanese Latin American Internment."
3 Evaristo Wenceslau, "Afimação e resistência," 220.
4 Rus and Rus, "Taller Tzotzil of Chiapas," 160.
5 Pisani and Jemio, "El proceso de construcción del Archivo Testimonial," 21.
6 Menchú, *Crossing Borders*, 207–8.
7 Petrich, *Memoria de mi pueblo*, 1–2; D. Carey, *Our Elders Teach Us*, 2; Maxwell, "Three Tales."
8 Ixkate', oral history interview by the author, June 6, 2001.
9 Rus and Rus, "Taller Tzotzil of Chiapas," 146.
10 Cano Sánchez, "El mensaje de los silencios," 171.
11 Hamilton, *Sexual Revolutions in Cuba*, 176.
12 Tedlock, *Spoken Word*; Cano Sánchez, "El mensaje de los silencios," 171.
13 Menand, "Bad Comma," 104.
14 Striffler, *In the Shadows of State and Capital*, 17.
15 Cano Sánchez, "El mensaje de los silencios," 174.
16 Sherzer, "Kuna and Columbus," 907–8; Sherzer, "Strategies in Text and Context." For pause patterns, see also Tedlock, *Spoken Word*, 16, 152; Hymes, *"In Vain I Tried to Tell You,"* 337–41.
17 Ixq'anil, oral history interview by the author, May 5, 1998, San Juan Comalapa, Guatemala.
18 Stern, *Remembering Pinochet's Chile*, 58.
19 Ibid.
20 Elizabeth Schmidt, email correspondence with the author, May 23, 2015.
21 Tracy, "Mayan Interpretations of Time and History"; Crandon-Malamud, *From the Fat of Our Souls*, 42.
22 Adleson, Camarena, and Iparraguirre, "Historia social y testimonios orales," 43.
23 Necoechea Gracia, "Custom and History," 124.
24 Ibid., 125.
25 Ibid., 126.
26 Ibid.
27 Camarena and Necoechea Gracia, "Continuidad, ruptura y ciclo," 59; Necoechea Gracia, "Custom and History."

28. Necoechea Gracia, "Custom and History," 127–8 (quote); Necoechea Gracia, *Después de vivir un siglo*, 109–28.
29. Fernandez, *Revolutionizing Romance*, 18–23.
30. Hamilton, *Sexual Revolutions in Cuba*, 11–2, 20–1.
31. Gould and Lauria-Santiago, *To Rise in Darkness*, 257.
32. Iwao Ueunten, "Japanese Latin American Internment," 113.
33. In Lovell, *Beauty That Hurts*, 3.
34. THOA, "Taller de Historia Oral Andina"; Stephenson, "Forging an Indigenous Counterpublic Sphere," 101 (quote); Schwarzstein, "Oral History in Latin America," 420.
35. Rappaport and Ramos Pacho, "Collaboration and Historical Writing," 125 (quote); Mallon, "Introduction," 8.
36. Mallon, "Conclusion," 220.
37. Sullivan, *Unfinished Conversations*, xxvi.
38. B'eleje' Imox, oral history interviews by the author, September 7 and November 30, 1997; January 11 and August 1, 1998. Whether they perform prominently or subtly, interviewers also affect the performative aspects of the interview.
39. In Alegre, *Railroad Radicals in Cold War Mexico*, 1–2.
40. Hamilton, *Sexual Revolutions in Cuba*, 11.
41. Bauman, *Story, Performance, and Event*, 8.
42. Gossen, "Chamula Genres of Verbal Behavior"; Gossen, "To Speak with a Heated Heart."
43. Sherzer, "*Namakke, Sunmakke, Kormakke*."
44. Bauman, "Verbal Art as Performance," 292, 296–8, 300–2.
45. Vansina, *Living with Africa*; Vansina, *Oral Tradition as History*, 92–3.
46. Portelli, *Death of Luigi Trastulli*.
47. Soto Laveaga, *Jungle Laboratories*, 138–9.
48. Desling, "Issues of Land and Sovereignty," 56–7.
49. James, *Doña María's Story*, 181.
50. Farnsworth-Alvear, *Dulcinea in the Factory*, 126.
51. Richardson, "Narrative and Sociology."
52. D. Carey, *Engendering Mayan History*, 31–60; James, *Doña María's Story*, 226.
53. Alberti, *Manual de história oral*, 112.
54. Levenson-Estrada, *Trade Unionists against Terror*.
55. Ibid., 210.
56. Portelli, *Death of Luigi Trastulli*, 99–100, 110.
57. Levenson-Estrada, *Trade Unionists against Terror*, 230.
58. See, for example, Abercrombie, *Pathways of Memory and Power*; D. Carey, *Our Elders Teach Us;* Rappaport, *Cumbe Reborn;* Rappaport and Ramos Pacho, "Collaboration and Historical Writing."

Suggested Readings

Bauman, Richard, and Charles L. Briggs. "Poetics and Performance as Critical Perspectives on Language and Social Life." *Annual Review of Anthropology* 19 (1990): 59–88.

Frisch, Michael. "Presenting and Receiving Oral History across Cultural Space: A Note on Responses to Chinese Students to the Documentary Trilogy *One Village in China*." In *A Shared Authority: Essays on the Craft and Meaning of Oral and Public History*, 147–57. Albany: State University of New York, 1990.

Hanks, William. *Converting Words: Maya in the Age of the Cross*. Berkeley: University of California Press, 2010.

———. *Language and Communicative Practices.* Boulder, CO: Westview Press, 1995.

Hymes, Dell. *"In Vain I Tried to Tell You": Essays in Native American Ethnopoetics.* 2nd edition. Lincoln: University of Nebraska Press, 2004.

Jones-Gailani, Nadia. "Third Parties in 'Third Spaces': Reflecting on the Role of the Translator in Oral History Interviews with Iraqi Diasporic Women." In *Oral History off the Record: Toward an Ethnography of Practice,* edited by Ann Sheftel and Stacey Zembrzycki, 169–83. New York: Palgrave Macmillan, 2013.

Swann, Brian, ed. *On the Translation of Native American Literatures.* Washington/London: Smithsonian Institution Press, 1992 (especially "Part Three: Central and South America," 311–469).

Tavárez, David. "Naming the Trinity: From Ideologies of Translation to Dialectics of Reception in Colonial Nahua Texts, 1547–1771." *Colonial Latin American Review* 9, no. 1 (2000): 21–47.

Tedlock, Dennis. *Spoken Word and the Work of Interpretation.* Philadelphia: University of Pennsylvania Press, 1983.

Wright, Ann. "The Interpretation of Translation, the Translation of Interpretation: Mediation in the Books of Rigoberta Menchú." *In Other Words: Journal of the Translators' Association* 15 (Autumn 2000): 13–26.

5 Interpretation and Memory

"Subjectivity is as much the business of history as are more visible 'facts.'"
Alessandro Portelli

Never simply a description of the past but rather a set of arguments that create knowledge about it, history is at its best when the interpretive process is transparent.[1] In light of the co-constructed nature of oral histories and the ways language, performance, translation, and memory can distort them, interpreting historical narratives is both exhilarating and daunting. Brazilian historians Olga Cabrera Garcia and Eliesse Scaramal note oral histories often defy rationality and linear organization.[2] As fragmentary mediated sources, they point to how people create their consciousness and subjectivity given the material, intellectual, and social resources at their disposal. Oral histories are vibrant social constructions, not static edicts. Interpreting them is a subjective task.

As empowering and revelatory as the first wave of oral history projects in Latin America was, scholars like Schwarzstein have lamented the "crude empiricism" and lack of interpretation that characterized them prior to the 1980s, when universities increasingly came to support and spearhead oral history projects. Conducted outside the confines of academic analysis, most of the early projects prioritized the collection and dissemination of oral histories.[3] For some practitioners, democratizing history was contingent upon "deprofessionalizing" it.[4] One of the strengths of oral history is its accessibility. Latin American popular historians were capable of interpreting their data—Colombian Cumbal indigenous leaders provide but one example of organic intellectuals' deft analysis—but they often lacked the resources and, at times, motivation to do so.

Informed by the international oral history movement and finding increasing support in Latin American universities, Latin American scholars have recognized oral history techniques as part of a historiographical field replete with theoretical and methodological debates. Because it is not enough to remember the past through testimonies, like many of her counterparts, Argentine intellectual Beatriz Sarlo underscores the importance of critically examining interviewees' perspectives in the context of history's broader forces.[5] Firmly grounded in sophisticated studies of memory, silence, subjectivity, and identity, Latin American oral history scholarship provides incisive interpretations. Acuña insists that oral history "only has one real interest . . . the production of new, more critical knowledge."[6]

Ever changing, oral histories say as much about contemporary events and influences as they do about the past. While their perceptions of the future shaped their narratives, women from Panguipulli, Chile, constructed oral histories that were as related to current conflicts as they were to the past.[7] Understanding the dynamic between the past, present, and future helps researchers make sense of historical narratives. When analyzing oral narratives, scholars distinguish between what can be taken as direct evidence and what should be mined to understand perspectives and meanings.

The nature of oral history research facilitates the crucial first step of interpreting data: considering how the source was created. As comfortable and natural as the relationship between the interviewer and interviewee may be, it casts a complex hue on the interview. In any oral exchange, social context shapes content, form, and meaning. The very ambiguity and flexibility that make oral histories adaptable to a broad array of situations and deployable as strategies for the future complicates analysis of them. Lacking the fixity and permanence of archival records and much material culture, oral histories demand analytical adeptness.

Interpretive Transparency

In addition to the dialectic between human experience and structural determination, the contemporary context within which scholars conduct research affects their sources and thus should be part of the analysis. Set in Latin America, one of the more heated debates among oral historians occurred when the United States invaded the Caribbean island of Grenada in 1983. The director of the US Marine Corps Oral History Program Benis Frank accompanied the troops and interviewed them as the invasion was taking place—a privilege denied journalists. In response to his sympathetic report, Frisch criticized the research and methodology as ideological tools that supported an imperialist military operation. Claiming Frisch only criticized the research because of his opposition to the invasion, Frank accused him of falling prey to his own ideological lens. The debate raised issues about the objectivity and neutrality of oral history research, particularly when conducting projects closely related to established institutions. It also preceded another debate taken up more recently about whether interviews conducted as events happen or shortly thereafter can be considered oral histories.

Although many historians resist the postmodern tendency of inserting themselves into the text, scholars are wise to articulate their sympathies so readers can assess how biases influence scholarship. Unlike Frank's report, much of the oral history research and scholarship coming out of

Latin America during the Cold War challenged US imperialist narratives about the region. Scholars' predispositions influence their methodologies, such as by not asking certain questions, and their analyses, for example by being less critical of some assertions. I noticed as much while living alongside Kaqchikels with whom I was collaborating. As I learned their language and history, my approach to studying Maya perspectives of the past became increasingly susceptible to advocacy. Aware of my sympathies, I sought to avoid romanticizing their past by explaining the effects of oppression on Mayas without becoming strident or exaggerated.[8]

Since oral history projects address topics within interviewees' lifetimes, their emotions and feelings can affect researchers' interpretations. On the bus to Chuschi, Peru, historian Miguel La Serna came face to face with the tricky task of interpreting the past in the midst of informants. Going over interview questions with two research assistants, La Serna described the landowner Humberto Azcara as a particularly abusive mestizo power holder, only to learn that the woman sitting across from him was Azcara's granddaughter. Embarrassed for having derided Azcara within her earshot, La Serna recovered by explaining his research project to her. She then shared that her father was Vicente Blanco, another powerful mestizo landowner, the sordid history of whom La Serna had researched in the archives, though he refrained from elaborating on his findings when she asked if he had heard of him.[9] Conducting research involving people who are still alive or whose children or neighbors are living, scholars try to tread lightly in their host communities. La Serna points out, "How I interpreted my data suddenly mattered in that it could affect my standing with my informants."[10] Ripe with the potential to disrupt his project, that tension facilitated a process whereby archival and oral history research informed each other. Among other insights, it revealed his subjects' reputations, status, and relative power in their communities.

Understanding how people reconstruct the past is crucial to interpreting oral histories. Products of but not confined by their past, many indigenous people deploy oral narratives to understand change and to chart life courses. As Rappaport learned with Nasa people in Colombia, "Nasa history is not a set of texts, but an expression of goals informed by the Nasa *habitus* . . . a complex of calls to action that orient members of society toward particular practices as opposed to others."[11] She and Ramos report that Nasa activists explore their oral narratives "to learn to live a new mode of life. . . . [T]heir objective is to take hold of cultural potentialities, not to textualize cultural differences."[12] In short, their goals are more practical than academic.

Armed with the knowledge of specific groups' distinct approaches to reconstructing and mobilizing the past, scholars can offer analysis that accounts for alternative epistemologies. Eschewing dates in favor of themes, Amerindians who convey history in both cyclical and chronological patterns compel scholars to rethink historical periodization. By identifying those themes instead of adhering to a strictly chronological framework, researchers can focus their analysis on indigenous peoples' perceptions of the past.[13] Rather than conveying a progressive narrative, many South American indigenous people conceived of history "in relation to a few 'peaks' or critical periods of rapid change."[14] Similarly disregarding chronology, Cuban interviewees seldom referred to specific dates when they moved back and forth through different generations to mark time; some narrators "telescope" time by merging events from different periods.[15] By focusing on events in and of themselves as opposed to when they occurred, memory disrupts chronological time. Absent the specifics of chronology, interviewees frequently use "before and after" or "before and now" frameworks to establish temporality.[16]

In addition to different temporal notions, unique spatial conceptions affect the way some people reconstruct the past. In the northwestern Brazilian Amazon, Wakuénai worldviews distinguish between the lived reality of human beings, the netherworld of the recently deceased, and the ancient celestial paradise of their gods.[17] Instead of trying to reconcile such conceptions with western notions of time and space, ethnohistorians and anthropologists analyze them to better understand indigenous epistemologies.

To align events with larger narratives, some narrators alter chronology. "Wrong" chronology, to paraphrase Portelli, offers insight into which events reinforce and which events upset people's and communities' identities and worldviews. By rearranging chronology, interviewees can articulate the cause and effect crucial to their perspective whether or not it is accurate. Doing just that, Kaqchikel women conveyed accounts of the iconic midwife Germana Catu that distinguished her leadership in Catholic Action from that movement's role in inciting deadly riots in 1967.[18] Wrong chronologies offer signposts for how the past and reconstructions of it influence people's lives.

Oral histories can decenter watershed events. Maya interviewees downplayed or ignored the 1954 CIA–engineered overthrow of Guatemalan President Jacobo Arbenz (1951–54). For Kaqchikels, a historical pattern of violent manifestations of racism—punctuated by a 1944 massacre in Patzicía on the eve of the nation's democratic transition—and the 1976 earthquake whose geological rumblings further disrupted political and social tensions go further in explaining Guatemala's recent past than the 1954 coup. One Kaqchikel intellectual notes, "My people do not talk about Arbenz much except for his land reform and that they no longer had to work on the *fincas*; that was good. But the politics is not as important. The Patzicía massacre was more important than the 1954 coup. . . . They associate Patzicía with being afraid of the state."[19] Because Guatemala's democracy was born in and begot violence, Kaqchikels' lived experiences encouraged them to support strong-armed, consistent, even harsh authoritarians who could maintain stability as opposed to more progressive leaders who in disrupting the status quo may not have been able to mitigate the deleterious effects of political transition and freedom. For many, 1954 simply marked the end of another failed government, an event that did not merit particular attention in their historical trajectory.[20] A similar process was apparent in Cuban and Chilean oral histories that articulated continuity and change before and after the 1959 Cuban

Revolution and 1973 military coup in Chile, respectively, without dwelling on them.[21] By shifting the focus from individual political ruptures to wider political conjunctures, oral histories disrupt accepted periodizations.

Without subordinating storytellers' perspectives, scholars seek to relate those reconstructions of the past to larger historical processes and contexts.[22] Since raconteurs may change details, characters, and even plot lines depending on the venue, audience, and moment in time in which stories are recounted, scholars stay attuned to the uses and contexts of oral accounts. After analyzing interviews in their entirety, scholars generally focus on the parts that speak most directly to their research goals.[23] In much the same way historians in general approach documents, oral historians critically assess each oral account and seek to corroborate evidence by comparing the account to various sources such as other oral histories, documents, images, and material culture. As similarities arise among oral history interviews, few individual accounts can be generalized as representing the larger groups' views. Each perspective is unique and contributes to nuanced analysis.

Researchers begin to recognize patterns of narrative organization that reveal individuals' and social groups' attempts to reconstruct their pasts and reconstitute their integrity across time as the corpus of interviews grows.[24] Such patterns "can suggest larger, collectively constructed notions of experience," observes folklorist Barbara Allen.[25] Labor historians have demonstrated that social justice and political activism are common themes in working-class oral narratives. As he moved from such topics as the devastating effects of epidemics, famine, and earthquakes to the challenges of life marked by dictatorial rule and mass migration, the Maya linguist Kab'lajuj Tijax (Martín Chacach) articulated an oral history that was similar to the more than one hundred interviews with Kaqchikels I had recorded up to that point.[26] Although his professional life compelled him to live and work outside his hometown, his community's narrative form left an indelible mark on his oral accounts. In addition to each individual's relationship with his or her community and its dominant discourses, such commonalties reflect the broader economic, political, and social models that circumscribe their lives.

Since stories are told within a larger master narrative, recognizing that framework is crucial to unpacking how historic, official, mythical, and other narratives create meaning. Interviewees' narrative patterns may vary by gender, class, sexuality, ethnicity, race, and religion. Discursive communities and dominant social models advance norms and expectations by which people live that in turn influence their stories. For example, Argentine working-class activists' emphases, use of images, and the way they crafted their explanations differed from that of their middle- and upper-class counterparts.[27] Crediting their religious convictions with buttressing their struggles in the face of death threats, Guatemala City labor activists revealed the factors that shaped their stories and lives. Associating their activism with Christian principles gave them the strength to press forward.[28] Within any narrative pattern, contradictory portrayals cast a dark hue on central themes, thereby complicating the telling and interpretation.[29]

Postmodern scholarship and participatory research models caution scholars against interpreting their findings alone. Sophisticated, authentic, and authoritative analysis demands collaboration. Acuña deepened his analysis of shoemakers by collaborating with the head of their union: "Our intuitions, hypothesis, and research questions owe much to the continuous dialogue that we maintained with the General Secretary of the union."[30] Although researchers generally strive to mitigate differences between themselves and interviewees, masking these distinctions is fraught with interpretive peril. James points out that in his interviews with Doña Maria, without having lived her life, he could never fully access her knowledge or experience.[31] By creating the conditions for interviewees, local research assistants, and locally recognized experts to analyze findings, scholars can push beyond their own paradigms and epistemologies.[32] When returning transcripts to interviewees, researchers can elicit such input. They also can invite interviewees to listen to the recordings and speak about the significance of their stories.

How scholars convey their findings affects how audiences interpret them. Whether the final products are texts, images, video or audio recordings, or some combination thereof, creators must weigh the advantages to presenting interviews in their entirety or highlighting excerpts to marshal their cases. While oral life histories tend toward the former, topical oral histories generally deploy the latter. In a style he developed in Mexico and Puerto Rico, Lewis reordered transcribed statements and eliminated his questions to facilitate narrative flow.[33] Some scholars include the questions to which interviewees responded to enrich readers' understanding of the context. Like Lewis, Burgos-Debray similarly reordered and edited her interview with Menchú.[34] Lewis considered his interview format an art form rather than social science, which he argued was limited in its approach.[35] In contrast, when Menchú's account was scrutinized first by anthropologist David Stoll and then a host of other scholars, some argued that Burgos-Debray's failure to adhere to rigorous social science methods undermined the text.[36]

Since the social context of oral histories alters memory's content and form, understanding that relationship helps researchers interpret narratives. Following the postmodern focus on reflexivity in the interview process, few scholars approach oral narratives or the memories that create them as transparent autochthonous texts. The shift from objectivity to subjectivity in understanding the creation of oral histories has highlighted how narratives and memories are constructed. The very existence of an interview "implies the confrontation of at least two different points of view," notes Mirta Zaida Lobato.[37] Reflecting on how their identities shape the interview and the practice of oral history more broadly, some scholars have heeded psychoanalysts' call to pay close attention to transference, countertransference, and collaboration in interviews. Anthropologist Ruth Behar offers one model for portraying those exchanges; in *Translated Woman*, she explores how her experience as a Cuban American framed her interviews with Esperanza Hernández, a sixty-year-old Mexican woman. Their differences and commonalities influenced the questions Behar asked, how Hernández understood and responded to them, and how Behar interpreted Hernández's responses and silences. As Behar shared her story with Hernández, their narratives began to reflect each other.[38]

Memory

With its biases and constructed nature, memory is both problematic and a crucial source for analyzing the past because it interprets and describes current and past realities. Stern reminds us, "Memory is the meaning we attach to experience, not simply the recall of events and emotions of experience."[39] In the same way archival materials are created through the lens of a scribe, so too are individual memories limited to the perspectives of one person even as larger communities influence them. Despite the vagaries and flaws of memory production, archival sources frequently substantiate historical memories.[40] After cross-checking their historical narratives against archival materials, anthropologist and historian Richard Price realized that Saramakas, descendants of African slaves in Suriname, "collectively preserved an uncannily accurate memory of these diverse events from more than two centuries ago."[41] Paying close attention to how narratives are produced, not just what they convey, illuminates the intentional and interrelated processes of remembering and forgetting.

The complex, contradictory, and faulty nature of memory complicates interpreting oral histories. According to the neuroscientist Gerald Edelman, "Every act of memory is to some degree an act of imagination."[42] As narrators revise memories to make sense of their lives, they forget, omit, and emphasize certain aspects to adapt their personal narratives to their audiences. Schwarzstein observes, "No memory is primary since it is always affected by elements not derived from experience."[43] Embodied in people, historical memories are organic archives that are constantly changing. As much as people seek to control memory, some memories manage people, particularly victims of trauma. So formative were the violence and police repression in the late 1940s and early 1950s that they eclipsed southern Chileans' memories of state terror in the 1970s.[44] At times such processes are intentional. Reflecting on his research during Colombia's civil war, anthropologist Michael Taussig warns of the "use of memory to change and dominate people."[45]

Memory's fault lines are both intentional and unintentional. "Because my memory, my mind is poor, because I've experienced so much hunger and so much need and so much suffering in love that there are things I forget," exclaims a Cuban mestizo born in 1963.[46] Related to age, education, and mental acuity, shifts in memory also can be attributed to memory's healing powers. Descriptions can be diminished, erased, amplified, or invented to contribute to mental health.[47] Like healing, mourning affects oral histories. In an indication of how generation sways memory, young Salvadorans with some schooling were better able to recall events from the 1980s than were their parents or grandparents, who more acutely remembered events from the 1930s.[48] It is not simply through death, trauma, or memory loss that information becomes irretrievable, however; even as repetitive storytelling helps individuals and communities to maintain certain meanings and narratives, shifts in memory obscure former recollections. Sometimes omissions are practical; time and narrative demand that some details be left out.

People misremember events to buttress their own and their stakeholders' dignity. Ethnohistorian Thomas Abercrombie calls such selectivity "structured forgetting," whereby interviewees elide certain aspects of the past in the interest of a more coherent narrative.[49] To avoid being associated with facilitating the downfall of their union, Mexican railroad workers frequently misrepresented their roles in the past.[50] Many narrators prefer to portray themselves as observers rather than participants when recounting violent incidents; fear of incrimination also discourages participants from revealing their roles in certain activities. Peasants from Alto Peru were particularly proud of their communities' lynching of five alleged cattle rustlers and intimidation of the police in April 1978, but no one interviewed more than ten years later admitted to being one of the thousands who participated in those acts. Conceding that "maybe the violence went too far," some raconteurs were shocked to learn that one of those killed was only sixteen years old.[51] That revelation complicated the story's moral undertones and claims to power. Since interviewees are not always aware of—or willing to admit—motives or interests that alter their perspectives and how they remember the past, scholars cross-check oral accounts with parties whose interests may differ.[52] Archives can expose omissions as well. Forcibly removed from Sonora to the Yucatán in the late nineteenth and early twentieth centuries, Yaqui elders remember the early twentieth century as a time of hunger, thirst, abuse, and even slavery, but the 1907–1908 yellow fever epidemic that devastated their population does not flourish in their social memory; in contrast, the archives teem with documentation about the epidemic's effect on Yaquis.[53]

Since oral histories and memories are simultaneously collective and individual, some scholars situate case studies of a few individuals within larger groups of oral histories to assess the ways individuals speak for the collective and the ways they are atypical.[54] Discerning the scope of narratives is a crucial aspect to interpreting them, particularly with groups that approach history collectively.[55] In his trilogy *The Memory Box of Pinochet's Chile*, Stern explores how people remember, understand, and address trauma collectively. His broadening idea of a collective memory box stands in sharp contrast to the Chilean documentary filmmaker Patricio Guzmán's use of memory and oral histories.[56] Guzmán selectively uses interviewees to inspire his understanding of the past; Stern examines the contentious processes of creating emblematic memories as struggles over legitimacy, primacy, and power.[57] Although they build their cases distinctly, both emphasize the importance of not forgetting what happened during Pinochet's repressive rule.

New information shifts memory's interpretations and recollections. In nations that have suffered widespread trauma, tensions and conflict often mark interpretations of the past. In light of the threat posed by communist insurgents known as Sendero Luminoso (Shining Path) during Peru's twenty-year civil war, some Peruvians have portrayed ex-president Alberto Fujimori (1990–2000) as a hero for defeating them; others have considered him a despot who violated human rights. Heated debate rekindled after the release of the TRC's final report in 2003. After reading it, some people reconsidered their accounts of the civil war depending on whether they thought it was necessary to suspend civil liberties to achieve security. Fujimori's subsequent trial, conviction, and sentence of twenty-five years in prison for crimes against humanity precipitated another round of discussions about how Peru's recent past should be reconstructed.[58] Changing narratives may have as much to do with mutable social and political contexts as with individuals' reassessments of the past.[59]

Because it allows narrators to think about the significance of the happenings, the time that elapses between events and their telling modifies interviewees' interpretations. "All history is retrospective. We're always looking at the past through the lens of later developments. How else could we see it?" Menand insists.[60] General Jorge Ubico's dictatorship (1931–44) offers insight into this process. His heavy-handed and at times harsh rule had different meanings for Guatemalans who lived through it than for historians assessing it through the archival record. Historians generally portray Ubico as one of Latin America's most brutal dictators, and some Mayas, particularly those living in the remote regions where Ubico exerted little control, maintain a certain antipathy toward his rule; however, many Mayas in the central highlands laud him for leveling race relations and maintaining security by applying his personalized Lone Ranger style of justice.[61] Conducted during the middle of Guatemala's civil war (1960–1996), Guatemalan anthropologist Claudia Dary's 1985 study of Kaqchikel oral histories reveals a critical assessment of Ubico. Referencing the government's excessive demands on their time and labor, informants described his dictatorship as "bitter." To ensure that citizens complied, his administration assigned cards to verify requirements ranging from road labor to vaccination control. "Through these papers, Ubico had the town well tied up," contends one interviewee.[62] In sharp contrast, shortly after the Acuerdos de Paz were finalized in 1996, Kaqchikel elders in the same town lauded Ubico because he brought peace, order, and justice to the region and respected Maya ethnicity. Compared to late-twentieth-century lethal, capricious military rule, Ubico's iron-fisted regime, which clearly articulated the rules of the game and spared and at times even aided people who abided by them, was benign.[63] Problematizing memory is crucial to scholars' contextualization and analysis of such dramatically different historical perspectives.

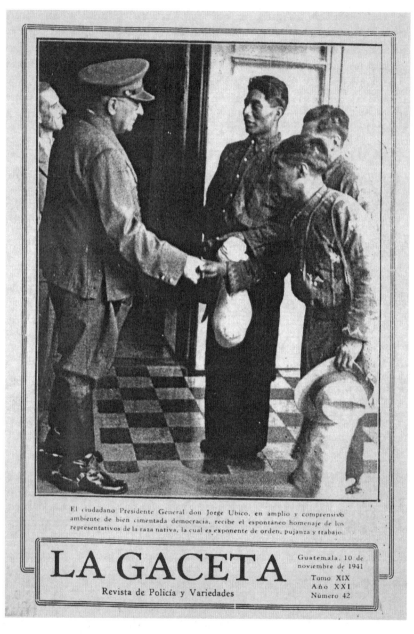

Figure 5.1 General Jorge Ubico with "representatives of the native race." *La Gaceta: Revista de Policía y Variedades*, November 10, 1941.

Image courtesy of The Latin American Library Rare Books Collection, Tulane University

In its broadest sense, history is most compelling when it seeks to balance competing and contradictory reconstructions of the past. Similarly positive memories of Ubico's counterpart Maximiliano Hernández Martínez (1931–44) are common among Salvadoran elders who survived a 1932 massacre over which he presided. Perceptions of Martínez's indigenous origins and sympathy for the rural poor before the massacre and pro-Indian actions after it buoyed his reputation among indigenous people.[64] These and other nuances of authoritarian regimes have reframed the way historians think about dictatorial rule in Latin America. More broadly, such memories are an example of what Taussig calls "contradictory images, dialectical images . . . [that] bring our own expectations and understandings to a momentary standstill."[65] Seemingly incongruous accounts remind us that oral histories do not advance a particular politics.

Although tempting to conclude that such accounts vindicate dictatorships, these sources demonstrate the complexity of memory and counternarratives that challenge hegemonic interpretations about the functioning of authoritarian regimes on the ground. Gould points out in his comparison of Guatemala and El Salvador, "This seemingly anomalous support for right-wing authoritarians whose hands were soaked in indigenous blood can only be understood in the context of a deep divide in the political culture of the two countries, dramatically exacerbated in Salvador by the legacy of 1932" and in Guatemala by the legacy of the 1944 Patzicía massacre.[66] Oral histories help to explain support for dictatorial regimes in some places. They also tease out how memories of authoritarian rule affect democratic institutions that emerged in Latin America by the 1980s and 1990s. Contested interpretations of state-sanctioned violence continue to mark politics in many Latin American nations.

The effect the present and past have on memory is multivariant. Seen through the lens of contemporary poverty, crime, and poor health care compounded by administrative corruption, bureaucratic morass, and ineptitude, Dominican peasants emphasize the material support and cultural affirmation afforded them by the otherwise brutal Rafael Trujillo regime (1930–61).[67] The capricious caudillos, banditry, and insecurity of the distant past have reinforced more benevolent portrayals of Trujillo. "To elderly peasants, Trujillo's rule came to represent a long parenthesis of public order within an overall history of violence, crime, and corruption before as well as after his regime," observes historian Richard Turits.[68] In truth, Trujillo's dictatorship was one of the most corrupt and violent in Latin America, though those machinations were not as visible to rural peasants as they were to other sectors of Dominican society. Even as they describe the fear, violence, silencing, and surveillance that characterized the dictatorship, many rural Dominicans selectively romanticize the past. By noting the consistency of favorable recollections across 130 interviews and corroborating his findings with documentary evidence, Turits demonstrates their historical accuracy and challenges conventional portrayals of the Trujillo regime. The way subsequent and prior

116 *Interpretation and Memory*

Figure 5.2 General Rafael Trujillo, Dominican Republic

From Lawrence de Besault, *President Trujillo: His Work and the Dominican Republic* (Washington Publishing Company, 1936).

realities condition memories and oral histories underscores the importance of critical analysis.

Oral histories often reveal as much about current appropriations of the past as they do the past itself. Kaplan has found that when narrators seek to establish a link between the people they were and the people they have become, oral histories may reveal "more about the intervening time than about the past or the present. . . . The past is reshaped . . . in relationship to the process of becoming."[69] When contemporary chaos and violence in Colombia made working-class exploitation and abuse fifty years earlier seem peaceful and orderly, Farnsworth-Alvear approached nostalgia as a style of remembering and used it to frame her questions so she could better understand how manufacturing technology changed notions of masculinity and femininity.[70] Given the irregular reliability of recollections, distinguishing between tangential truths and accurate accounts in oral testimonies is crucial to interpreting them.

Even as the present influences historical perspectives, it is not ahistorical.[71] "It was not simply 'the view from the present' that shaped her remembering. Any view from the present is already profoundly imbricated with influences from the past," observes James.[72] In some narratives, the past's influence on the present is intentional. Kalalapo of the Brazilian Amazon consciously connect their lives to those of their ancestors. By emboldening a sense that generations are connected across time, contemporary Kalalapo emphasize that the consequences of their decisions will resonate for future generations. As they establish the continuity of their lives with those of their forebears, they chart strategies for future generations.[73]

Memory formation has its own processes. Reflecting on her experience of collecting oral histories about Argentina's Dirty War, Schwarzstein notes, "Memorialist effervescence has its own rhythm of remembering: a time for silence, a time for bearing witness, a time for reconstruction and recognition."[74] By repealing laws that granted amnesty to Dirty War murderers and torturers, Argentina opened a space for historical reconstruction. Upholding the repeal two years later in 2005, Argentina's Supreme Court found the laws unconstitutional because they were "oriented toward '*forgetting*' grave violations of human rights."[75] According to the justices, amnesia threatened to make the nation susceptible to future horrors; memory was the antidote. By trying human rights crimes, the judicial system facilitated a public mourning process for those whose loved ones were "disappeared." At its best, oral history can counteract what historian Pierre Nora calls the "eradication of memory by history."[76]

As traumatic as many histories are, survivors and their descendants have worked hard to avoid a sense that sacrifices were in vain. In the context of state repression, memory can facilitate community cohesion and solidarity.[77] Although institutionally funded public monuments intended to evoke memories of Latin American military dictatorships are rare, a few states have reclaimed sites of violence to stave off historical amnesia.[78] Inaugurated by Chilean President Michelle Bachelet on January 11, 2010, the Museo de la Memoria y los Derechos Humanos (Museum of Memory and Human Rights) stands as a testament to the power of memory. In Argentina, civic action and performance invigorate memories of the Dirty War.[79] The state-controlled Cuban media preserve memories of the October 6, 1976 bombing on a Cubana Airlines flight. "The bombing of Cubana Airlines was the bloodiest act of terrorism against Cuba. It hurt the whole country," explains Carlos Manuel Permuy Diaz, whose father was on the flight. "It's constantly talked about in Cuba. Everyone knows and there is always something on the radio, on the television, some notice about it. You can never get away from it."[80] Traumatic events and experiences can define people and nations. In another public preservation of the past, the National Literacy Museum in Havana has moving accounts of young urban students who went into rural communities to teach literacy during the early years of the revolution. It is a powerful if unabashedly favorable portrayal of the revolution. With national historical narratives, monuments, museums, and public gestures, states mold perspectives of the past.

Memorializing sites regularly stimulate memory. Similarly, such market forces as "trauma tourism," corporate advertising, and trauma trinkets also influence how people reconstruct the past.[81] Attributable partly to such efforts, memory can be remarkably resilient. After recounting what it was like to work as a hat weaver as a child, a Japanese Peruvian woman exclaimed, "It's been eighty years, how can I remember that?"[82]

In lockstep with time, spatial transformations can as easily erase as preserve memories. By destroying or deindustrializing sites of collective memory like factories and mills, modernization can compound workers' sense of marginalization and exclusion. To counter that effect, when in 1998 a local factory closed after 167 years of production, youths in the Mexican community asked historian Mario Camarena Ocampo to train them in oral history techniques. As their parents and grandparents passed on and the factory was transformed into a different physical space, the youths feared the neighborhood's working-class identity, which continued to inspire their resistance, would be lost. They intended to use historical memories to legitimize their efforts to preserve the neighborhood's physical spaces.[83] As producers and consumers of oral history, they became more conscious of the past and how it could be harnessed to inspire their struggles.

Telling the Truth

Never intrinsic, the truth is a product of a dialogue between a speaker and an interlocutor who together establish the validity of statements in relation to their own perceptions and the people and material forces with whom they interact.[84] "While I cannot address this issue with any certainty, I am satisfied that the women who talked to me were telling me a truth, which reveals what was important *for them*," asserts Patai about her interviews with Brazilian women.[85] When he began to analyze the life history interviews he conducted with the Puerto Rican sugarcane worker Eustaquio Zayas Alvarado in 1953 and 1956, anthropologist Sidney Mintz realized he had "to distinguish between what seemed to be the objective truth and those aspects of what I was being told that were affected by the lens through which my friend was seeing his own past. . . . The best one can do is to try to be aware of one's perceptual limitations, as well as of those of the informant."[86]

Since interpreting research findings is contingent upon establishing their reliability and relevance, analyzing how and why people reconstruct the past as they do is further complicated when drawn from oral narratives intended as much to preserve culture, empower people, convey legitimacy, carve out autonomy, and provide roadmaps to the future as to recount the past. Mariana Mastrángelo, like her fellow Argentine historian Pozzi, has encouraged scholars to move beyond a preoccupation with fact, fiction, and truth to approach oral sources as windows into interviewees' experiences, values, sentiments, and feelings.[87] Necoechea similarly argues, "Veracity does not lie in the details of the story but in the values and ideas expressed that were collectively constructed."[88]

Comprehending local culture, narrative tropes, and epistemologies is essential for interpreting oral histories. A Kaqchikel elder's recollections about living under the Guatemalan dictator Manuel Estrada Cabrera (1898–1920) offers an opportunity to explore different levels of interpretation. Junlajuj Imox recalls:

> A long time ago Manuel Estrada Cabrera was president and he would not let us go to school. He also did not provide food or clothing to prisoners or men in the barracks; they had to walk around barefoot and that really hurt. He really punished people. He came here once . . . and punished people here. He set off bombs and killed people and animals but he survived. He did this quite a bit, but he was never killed in battles. Twenty-two years he was president, two more and he would have been king. . . . But he was overthrown in 1920; that is when slavery ended for our people. Before that, people would hide from *ladinos* and *ladinas* because they made you work without pay. You had to transport goods long distances and never get paid—exploitation. They also liked to call you *indio* and *ixto*. . . . Cabrera really made our people suffer. Nineteen-twenty is an important date because slavery ended for us. Before that, *ladinos* treated us badly.[89]

As is often true in oral accounts, the narrator personifies the government. Although Estrada Cabrera did not personally prevent Mayas from going to school or withhold food or clothing, Junlajuj Imox attributes those acts to him. His account illustrates Estrada Cabrera's tyranny and explains how racism—manifestations of which include the pejorative terms *indio* and *ixto*—disadvantaged Mayas economically and socially. Twice Junlajuj Imox describes forced labor mechanisms as slavery. Even though those systems continued into the second half of the twentieth century, he insists 1920 marks a clear break from excessive exploitation. Reflecting Maya epistemologies, he suggests the seamless continuum between human and animal life as he laments the loss of both. Understood in the context of the Maya counting system based on twenty, Junlajuj Imox's comment about Estrada Cabrera becoming king if he had ruled further into his next *b'ak'tun* (twenty-year period, according to Maya calendrics) evokes images of ancient Maya kings whose rule extended for many years because of their seeming immortality, just as Estrada Cabrera "was never killed in battles."

A number of details complicate analysis of this evocative account. His description of conscription in the military evokes suffering and exploitation, but as evidenced in oral histories, archival records, and photographs, Mayas generally ambulated barefoot, so why did Junlajuj Imox identify doing so in the military as particularly painful? Although the archives betray no record of Estrada Cabrera ever arriving in Junlajuj Imox's town, the claim that he did personalizes the narrative. Junlajuj Imox may be conflating Estrada Cabrera with his successor, Ubico, who regularly traveled to remote highland villages. Far from exhaustive, these observations demonstrate the richness and complexity of oral histories.

Scholars seldom cull all the interpretive potential from oral narratives; rather, they marshal the most salient points for their arguments and analyses. In an example of scholarly treatment that plumbs interpretive depths, historian Heidi Tinsman did not doubt the veracity of workers' accounts of a landowner who sold donated goods intended for them; she was more interested in narrators' outrage at their employer's greed, which was real whether or not the particular incident occurred.[90] Such "alternative meanings" serve as "counterpoints of clarification" to her analysis of archival and newspaper records.[91] Based on her broader understanding of class relations in rural Chile, Tinsman saw through the truth to meaning in oral histories. Since memories at best offer partial truths, the goal is not necessarily to discover the truth but to understand the meanings stories convey.

Since some Afro-Latin Americans, indigenous people, and other Latin Americans do not necessarily conceive of truth in ways that resonate with academic notions, one of the greatest challenges in oral history research is aligning local epistemologies and methodologies with the requirements of evidence in the academy. Historian Florencia Mallon argues, "Given the distinct nature of oral tradition and oral history as a performative medium based on imparting knowledge and wisdom gained through direct personal experience or connection, the rules of evidence associated with scientific method are less relevant or applicable."[92] Rather than sacrificing methodological rigor, scholars corroborate oral sources to the extent possible and analyze empirical information that is not verifiable. When scholars carefully approach the content of their interviews, Pozzi insists, there is no contradiction between oral history and academic history.[93] Conceding an emphasis on factual accuracy does not discount the insights oral history offers about what the past and present mean to people.[94] The further back into the past one goes, the less likely oral testimonies will be accurate factually. Interviewees are also more likely to remember greater detail about recent events than more distant ones. When going beyond an individual's lifetime, researchers are generally most interested in perspectives about the past. Like Mallon, James encourages scholars to focus on the "fidelity to meaning rather than to criteria of strict accuracy associated with information."[95]

Even if narrators did not directly experience events, let alone recall them accurately, those reconstructions are as important as what really happened. When other sources demonstrate that certain oral accounts are factually false, they may remain psychologically true. Since people act upon imagined pasts, untrue beliefs can acquire great power.[96] To unpack the meaning in oral histories, Portelli's distinction between life *stories* and *life* stories is helpful:

> We may insist that these stories are true—these people exist, and they relate events that actually happened—and, therefore, interviews allow us to glimpse actual experience (life). Or we may work with the assumption we are dealing with verbal artifacts (stories) shaped by narrator's self

perception, by encounter with interviewer, and by interviewer's perception and interpretation of them and their words.[97]

Both types of information are valuable; recognizing their unique characteristics is crucial to interpreting them.

The same methods archival historians employ to test the accuracy of written sources are useful for interrogating oral histories; among these are monitoring a source's internal consistency, confirming evidence against other sources, and considering details in broader historical contexts and biases. In some ways, the task of verification is easier with oral than written sources. Concerns such as forgery, the author's motives, and the source's social purpose are easily reconciled in the interview. Any evidence that can only be traced to one source demands corroboration. Though versions of an event will invariably differ, thereby enriching its description, a number of references to the same event help to establish its veracity. If a particular assertion cannot be verified, scholars note as much. Respect for the witness does not forgo the quest for veracity.

Multiple audiences and the social purpose of oral histories mitigate the potential for egregious lies or mistakes. Only when they emerge from a recognizable and plausible past are the lessons, strategies, and reformulations in oral histories credible and relevant. Gross exaggerations undermine oral histories' usefulness as practical solutions to contemporary challenges. Narrators' realities guard against hyperbole as well. In his research with banana plantation workers in Ecuador, historian Steve Striffler notes, "Most people eagerly recounted the histories of their political activities and organizations, but few were nostalgic about past struggles and almost no one overstated the implications of their successes."[98]

In addition to the analytical narrative that drives scholarly work in its many forms, scholars have gained invaluable insights by exploring oral histories' linguistic and literary structures. Absences can be instructive. Working with politicians who he assumed obscured their real intentions, Boesten noticed that interviewees refrained from disparaging the Constitutional Court and thereby conveyed the respect it enjoyed in Colombia.[99] Inaccuracies, omissions, misrepresentations, lies, and hyperbole likewise can indicate important realities and suggest what certain aspects of the past signify for the storyteller. Aware that the revolution portrayed gays as counterrevolutionaries and that critiques of official homophobia shaped Cuban homosexuals' identities and experiences, researchers with the Cuban Voices project realized that some interviewees deployed hyperbole for political and narrative effect.[100] William Cutler points out that recognizing inaccuracies can be fruitful: "If the researcher can identify them, especially those resulting from dishonesty or reticence, he can profit handsomely, for sometimes they provide an important avenue of insight into the respondent's state of mind."[101] When fabrications and mistakes are collective, they provide openings into the meaning and significance of events. Myths can reveal, inform, and transmit history.[102] Stern approaches collective inaccuracies as emblematic memory that "draws out the great truths" of a social experience and allows individuals to frame their own experiences and knowledge within a coherent collective narrative.[103] More than what people did or observed, we learn what they wanted or hoped to do or to observe, what they thought they were doing or observing, and how they understand those experiences.[104] Often marked by a flexibility that affords the coexistence of conflicting narratives, such wrong histories compel us to rethink the ways we interpret the past.

Offering alternative histories, memory entrepreneurs consciously advance a certain interpretation of the past with political ends in mind. Jelin contends that they "seek social recognition and political legitimacy of *one* (their own) interpretation or narrative of the past."[105] Juan Colín Padilla is one such storyteller. Faced with national discourse that portrayed railroad workers as lazy, drunken, inept troublemakers, Colín countered that railway workers' diligence and sacrifice were crucial to Mexico's economic development. The true standard bearers of the revolution, they represented all that was admirable about Mexico.[106] As scholars establish historical accuracy to the extent possible, they draw upon life story methodologies to explore "the truth of telling versus the telling of truth."[107] Often lies reveal more truth than do facts. "The importance of oral testimony may lie not in its adherence to fact, but rather in its divergence from it, as imagination, symbolism, and desire emerge," asserts Portelli.[108]

Amid romantic recollections, accurate descriptions still can be mined. As he explores how the past and present forge workers' memories of the United Fruit Company (UFCO), which operated in parts of Latin America, Striffler highlights concrete accounts that reveal their experiences. Ecuadoran workers who likened their pre–UFCO labor on cacao plantations to slavery had particularly fond memories of working for UFCO. Looking back through the more recent past when the provision of such basic services as electricity, water, and housing deteriorated as their costs increased, other workers portrayed the UFCO banana plantation as a paradise. Such glowing accounts belie most depictions of UFCO working conditions, but Striffler warns against dismissing them as nostalgia. UFCO employees received subsidized meat, milk, rice, and health care and earned wages four times those of their counterparts. Compared to other rural Ecuadorans in the 1950s and even in the 1990s, when he conducted his study, UFCO workers lived well, and they knew it. "One had to work hard and long. . . . But most recognized the benefits," recalls a former laborer.[109]

Individual narratives reveal complex and often conflicting memories. One of the founders of a Rio de Janeiro community association presented himself as a self-made man and someone who benefited from his social network.[110] Similarly, a Chilean miner insisted he was both a company loyalist and a militant union leader.[111] Instead of reconciling incongruous perceptions, scholars try to understand their meanings. Oral history reveals how individuals negotiate distinct identities. In narratives that explore her multiple roles,

Doña María discusses herself as a mother, wife, union organizer, Peronist, meatpacker, and political leader.[112] For James, the challenge of interpreting oral histories is precisely what makes them such valuable sources: "Oral testimony is more messy, more paradoxical, more contradiction-laden, and perhaps, because of this, more faithful to the complexity of working-class lives and working-class memory."[113] When landless Argentines harnessed solidarity to occupy and organize urban settlements in Quilmes, they suppressed opposition and conflict among themselves. Because opposing tactics could embolden future social movements, such contradictory and even hypocritical approaches did not necessarily undermine the landless movement or discredit its historical narratives.[114]

The magical and miraculous aspects of oral histories in Latin America pose another interpretive challenge. People buried alive in Guatemala, living in holes and breathing through reeds to avoid detection in El Salvador, and men who would not die in both countries push the boundaries of credulity. At times archival materials corroborate such stories, but often they can only be verified against other oral sources. Even without verification, scholars need not suppress fantastic accounts but rather contextualize them and take care not to attribute more significance to them than storytellers intend.

For many people, history and myth operate on a continuum. Some oral narratives are informed as much by myth, legend, hearsay, and rumor as they are by history, eyewitness accounts, and facts. Without ignoring their economic and political marginality, indigenous groups in the Amazon and the Andes seamlessly combine history, myth, and legend to maintain some superiority over their oppressors; some South American aborigines articulate accounts that suggest they are authors of their own subordination. By affording themselves control over their own situations, they carve out some autonomy. Even as myths distort reality, narratives that concurrently convey submission and resistance reflect power relations.[115] Failing to notice the mythic elements in historical testimonies or dismissing them outright limits scholars' ability to interpret the meanings of oral histories.

Silences

What one group of descendants of escaped slaves remembered was as calculated as what they forgot. The Surinamese storytellers elided the capture and forced labor of an eighteenth-century leader and highlighted his military victories; eschewing accounts of his victimhood underscored his heroics. Such recollections bolstered their history of resistance and autonomy in the face of attempts by "whitefolks" to enslave them.[116] In addition to the practical aspect of avoiding being overwhelmed by the vast detail of their experiences, interviewees use forgetting to modify their stories; by erasing certain aspects of the past, they highlight others. Communities and nations collectively perform the same process with events they prefer to forget. Because of the humiliating result of the 1982 Malvinas War, its Argentine veterans were largely forgotten and their role in the nation's past elided. Frequently, omissions are attributable to security, shame, effective storytelling, the fog of unimportance, deception, or some combination of these.

Though they often are interrelated, forgetting and silence are distinct processes. Silence can be a powerful card to play. Among some indigenous groups, silence is encouraged and appropriate, particularly when interacting with outsiders.[117] Creating memory involves creating silence.[118] Since secrets can maintain memories and facilitate historical narratives unaccounted for in other sources, some raconteurs feign ignorance to mask knowledge.[119] To deflect the state's attention, subordinates often use what Scott calls "hidden transcripts" to build oppositional cultures based on defiance and inversion without overtly confronting or challenging authorities.[120] In his description of Mexicans' traditional silences as a series of masks, Mexican Nobel Prize laureate Octavio Paz offers an evocative image of silence. Because it shields layers of meaning, silence can be strategic. Asked by a foreign researcher if she knew about gays being sent to labor camps in the 1960s, a Cuban woman emphatically declared, "No. We know nothing about that."[121] Cubans who refrain from critical commentary may be motivated as much by fear of recrimination as by the knowledge that detractors often use such critiques to discredit the revolution itself.[122] Not necessarily an absence or void, silence is often palpably present. Jelin explains, "Oblivion . . . is the presence of that absence, the representation of something that is no longer there, that has been erased, silenced, or denied."[123] Silence and secrets can have a formidable presence in narratives.

After developing familiarity with individuals and communities, researchers can begin to recognize and explore the significance of silences.[124] The goal is not to uncover secrets, as interviewers should respect interviewees' privacy, but rather to understand how people reconstruct the past in ways that serve them. By using Sarhuino artists' depictions of the struggle with Sendero Luminoso rebels to evoke narratives about the war, González came to understand not only what Peruvians remember and forget but why they do so. For Sarhuinos, silence maintained stability and peace, however uneasy, in a town where people were pitted against each other during the conflict.[125]

When those who committed atrocities retain powerful positions, their very presence imposes silences. "Here it is impossible to say what happens. Those men have kept the old evil guarded and hidden away. Here there is no freedom to speak, only to endure," explains a K'iche' survivor of Guatemala's civil war.[126] In an indication of how public discourse and functions are often as much about silencing as remembering, the Guatemalan military organized a public festival in which soldiers dressed up as clowns and disparaged and ridiculed refugees and others displaced by the war to reorganize "the collective memory of what happened during the conflict."[127] In a similar manifestation of silencing, a group of local power brokers held their dance festival right outside the Catholic church and blared mariachi music so the congregation could not hear the priest during Mass.[128] Some attempts to silence are explicit. In a comment aimed at institutionalizing reconciliation after a brutal civil war, the lieutenant governor of Uchuraccay, Peru, reminded locals, "There is no reason to maintain the history and words of our elders."[129] Such mandates speak to the importance of collecting oral histories.

During military rule, forgetting was a survival strategy. Argentine concentration camp survivor Pilar Calveiro notes, "When a militant is captured he not only pretends not to know, he authentically forgets: he forgets the information that may put other people in danger. . . . He has lost the capacity to remember precise information, especially having to do with names and addresses. This is a recurring pattern among survivors."[130]

Solidarity informs other types of intentional silences. "Many things happened that I can't say or let you record, because I don't feel like talking about it, and even less about a woman. If I can, I cover up a woman's faults with my skirt," explains Doña María when James asked about the time a rich and allegedly "loose" woman defeated her in the election for a national deputy post.[131] Although class, ethnicity, race, sexuality, and personal rivalries can undermine female solidarity, some women defend their gender by refusing to sully portrayals of other women. Such silence is an antidote to patriarchal privileges.

In a manifestation of how silences can communicate as much as words, what is left out of narratives can be as important as what is included in them. One omission helped Levenson understand the significance of Guatemalan union leader Marcos Antonio Figueroa's account of his abduction. After describing his detention, Figueroa explains that prior to his release, his kidnappers asked him and Roberto, a leader who was kidnapped with Figueroa, if they had eaten anything since they had been abducted:

> We said no, and yes we'd like something. Roberto told them I had an ulcer, and they said, "Don't worry, we'll get milk," which they did. And since we were tied up, they fed us with their own hands, putting the milk to my lips to drink, and we all sat together for a few moments eating. I will never forget this, the detectives, accustomed to kill and to maim, consoling someone with an ulcer. Humans have many aspects, and if we take advantage of the good ones, make them coherent, we can advance further than we know.[132]

Although he does not mention it, Figueroa was badly beaten during his captivity. Omitting his beating from the narrative helped Figueroa to save "the world for himself" and transform "terror and fear into renewed courage and faith in humanity," asserts Levenson.[133]

Shame, too, discourages full disclosure. Although Costa Rican union leaders and communists committed electoral fraud before the 1948 civil war, few admitted to it when interviewed years later. "In a country where liberty and the purity of suffrage are sacred, it is natural that today one is embarrassed to admit they participated in fraud in the past," Acuña observes.[134] He attributes the same motivations to "the absence of anarchy in their memories." An accepted version of the past can contradict personal experiences and cause some participants to deny or reject their own recollections.[135]

Silences can compel researchers to confront their own assumptions. When a team of Cuban and British scholars interviewed a man who alluded to homosexual relations but did not identify himself as gay, they disagreed on whether they should refer to him as homosexual. As their research progressed, they learned how complex and contested sexual identity was in Cuba—complexities that neither archival sources nor official histories captured.[136]

Interpreting through Gender and Patriarchy

Close listening and careful interpretation are contingent upon considering how internal (interviewee's) and external (society's) forces influence oral histories. Patriarchy and gender affect and are affected by economic structures, ideologies, religion, race, sexual orientation, nationality, and a host of other factors. Structures and discourse often determine the type of knowledge to which people believe they have access. Because they associate the right to speak with schooling and literacy, many poor and working-class women are reluctant to share their stories.[137] For Afro-Latin American, indigenous, and other women who do not speak the dominant language, their monolingualism compounds alienation emanating from their illiteracy and lack of formal education. Families' decisions not to send their daughters to school were informed by and reverberated throughout political systems that discouraged women's participation. Even women who were politically active have tended to minimize their contributions and thus discount their agency.[138]

Born into cultures and nations that privileged masculinity, many Latin American women had only limited, if any, access to public or professional positions of power. The extent to which such exclusions influence how women view the past, their role in it, and their ability to articulate history can be discerned in the narratives of Cuban women who recount the past through "male-defined" memory.[139] When gender imbalances permeate public conversation—as evident in communities that consider men more appropriate political actors than women and expect the latter to refrain from speaking with outsiders—men's voices are privileged and heard over women's.

Like dominant discourses, popular rhetoric can perpetuate elisions. During their oral history workshop in Oaxaca, Zapotecs and Mixtecs who were already well aware of how national histories erased them from the past discovered that their own telling of history "erases the experience of most people in the community."[140] While an emphasis on the collective over the individual in historical narratives has contributed to that erasure, gendered power structures influence how people recount the past as well.

Despite speaking from subordinate positions in patriarchal societies, female interviewees do not necessarily emphasize gender marginalization. Interviewed by a team of oral historians from Latin America as part of a project about political militancy, female activists did not introduce themes related to gender, much less the oppression of or discrimination against women.[141]

Often negotiating the liminal space between modernity and tradition, women and their distinct realities and positions tend to disappear in dominant male and nationalist discourse.[142] In some cases, information about women can more easily be gleaned from men. For example, since women seldom talk about extramarital affairs in interviews, such dalliances are largely discerned through men's narratives when they speak about their affairs or their partners who are married to or involved with others. Although difficult to corroborate, such hearsay provides valuable information and insight into other lines of inquiry.[143] In her study of Argentina's Dirty War, performance studies scholar Diane Taylor asserts, "Female subjects are forever linguistically absent and unrepresentable. Women who attempt to represent themselves . . . are condemned. . . . In a discursive system in which women are unrepresentable as subjects, representation seems, by definition, to be male self-representation."[144] When women break out of these confines, the cost of not conforming—being powerful and authoritative—is often ostracism and isolation.

As powerful and symbiotic as they are, patriarchal structures, discourses, and relations do not overdetermine female identities, experiences, or perspectives. At times tragedy and other circumstances invert gender power. Comprising the majority of survivors of Pinochet's dictatorship in southern Chile, women reformulated historical representations by determining whose perspectives and experiences informed oral histories.[145] Women deploy dominant discourse to their advantage and use their own narratives to chart less oppressive futures. More optimistic than Taylor, historian Luisa Passerini argues that women's life histories are "a means of expressing problems of identity in the context of a social order oppressive of women, but also of transmitting awareness of oppression and sense of otherness, and hence directing oneself to current and future changes."[146] Through oral narratives, women create and sustain their own accounts that may adhere to, contradict, or ignore their communities' and nations' historical narratives. "When women themselves speak about their position . . . the reference points shift radically. In Menchú's story, Indian women are not the long-suffering, quiet martyrs or repositories of culture they are in men's stories," observes Mallon.[147] As representational spaces that link women's identities to the community, nation, and world, women's counterhistories reveal how they think about the past.[148] When marginalized people articulate their own histories, conventional cultural concepts break down. Indeed, their ability to be heard is often predicated on breaking conventions. Since Argentine women who worked in meat-processing plants "did not have the appropriate language" to convey their histories to Lobato, they transformed their working-class experiences and knowledge and "reconfigured the usual notions" in their interviews.[149] How people tell their stories is often as revelatory as the content therein.

As manifestations of multiple dominant and countervailing gendered forces, masculinity and femininity affect how people remember the past. In turn, oral histories reveal how men and women reconstitute gender. One Chilean campesino's story of standing his ground against an armed *patrón* demonstrates that courage and pride were crucial to working-class manliness.[150] Another man's story about his wife attending a strike meeting with him portrays a sense of emasculation: "She was the only woman out of ten people. They just stared at me, looked evilly at each other and asked if I always needed my *señora* to put my pants on."[151] Masculinity could be emboldened or deflated with single acts and comments.

Because their ways of knowing can differ, women and men often recount history distinctly.[152] Disadvantages in one arena can open up expertise in another. In oral history interviews, women tend to talk about private life more than men do.[153] Jelin's assertion that women "remember within the framework of family relationships" can be attributed to an enduring division between the activities of men and women and bias introduced by interviewers who are more likely to ask women than men about child care, family life, and contraception.[154] Unlike men, who often recount the past from an individual viewpoint, women do not necessarily place themselves at the center of their historical narratives. Jelin contends that women "slip into narratives that are apparently centered on others" and talk of the past as a collective endeavor.[155] Female narrators generally put less emphasis on action than male narrators. For Russian Nobel laureate Svetlana Alexievich, that tendency is complemented by attention to emotions: "Women tell things in more interesting ways. They live with more feeling. They observe themselves and their lives. Men are more impressed with action. For them, the sequence of events is more important."[156] In her study of fascism in Italy, Passerini notes that women recounted stories of rebellion as allegories of their struggle against oppression and discrimination, not as descriptions of activities in which they actually engaged.[157] While men proudly frame their fights as part of their quest for justice and political change, few female perpetrators are forthcoming about violence.[158]

Gender distinctions also emerge in narratives recounted by political prisoners. In Rebekah Park's research in Argentina, men tended to emphasize historical events and resistance, and women focused more on specific encounters and acts of solidarity. Women worried more about others, while men were more concerned about the political situation beyond the prison walls.[159] Although women are more likely to narrate their experiences of political repression and violence as direct or indirect victims, for some of the same reasons that gender-based violence is underreported in the criminal record, few incidents of domestic violence surface in oral histories.[160] The theoretical underpinnings of these and other gender differences point to distinct definitions of self in men and women partly in response to how the social order influences them.

Diverse historical reconstructions by men and women also are attributable to their distinct goals and worldviews. Among migrants to São Paulo, male landowners from Minas Gerais were nostalgic about their rural lives because they had lost access to land when they left, while female migrants appreciated the educational and employment opportunities the city afforded their children. Those opportunities informed generational differences among women. First-generation migrants were tied to the home and "did not earn anything," reports a woman born in 1954. Women born to migrant families emphasized the labor market and their professional activities as direct results of their mothers' visions for them.[161]

In rural people's recollections about Chile's agrarian reform that began in the 1950s and culminated in the early 1970s, oral histories similarly diverge along gender lines. Convinced that it enhanced their families' lives, men celebrated their improved financial standing. "I made enough money to put shoes on the children and to buy her cloth [for sewing]. She didn't need to go into town. . . . In town there is too much danger of [a man] having the cap pulled over his eyes [being sexually deceived]," explains one husband. His wife, Rosa Saá, remembers that time differently: "Of course it was nice to have the house and to have more money, lots of money! But really, I tell you, life for me got harder, not easier. . . . I could have taken [the bus] to town, but my husband wouldn't hear about it. He wanted me in the house. . . . Sometimes I would get so mad I would just leave. 'To

Figure 5.3 Women preparing empanadas in Patagual, Chile, ca. 1991

Photograph by David Carey Jr.

do my job I must go to town,' I would say . . . but that always started a fight."[162] Rosa's and her husband's perspectives suggest that men had a more approving assessment of agrarian reform than women, who were "far more ambivalent about . . . [its] costs and consequences."[163] Although women did not challenge patriarchy outright, they navigated gender relations and activism in ways that defined women as important contributors irrespective of their relationships with men.

Since men took a long view of Chile's agrarian reform, its dismantlement with the 1973 coup meant that event represented a greater rupture in men's than women's oral histories. Excluded from much of the agrarian reform process, women focused their narratives on the period after 1973, when their political roles in public such as protesting the dictatorship and economic roles in private such as supporting their families as widows expanded. Men's increased income and autonomy during the intensified agrarian reform of the early 1970s gave them a sense of empowerment; women's increased activism and responsibility in the face of state violence thereafter emboldened them. As survivors who kept memories of military torture and execution alive, women became symbols of human rights and reparations.[164]

Differences in how men and women recount the past do not obscure the diversity of historical epistemologies and methods among women. Class, ethnicity, race, religion, sexuality, and other identities contribute to the content and form of women's historical narratives. In his study of two women in Mexico City, Necoechea argues that it is not merely their different income levels and employment experiences that determine the distinct ways they recount the past but also "different modes of cultural appropriation."[165] Class differences affected how they experienced, processed, and understood events either as direct participants or as witnesses.[166]

Like archival documents, oral histories only approximate past events, relations, and experiences. The limitations inherent in historical sources makes cross-checking and interrogating them vital and a transparent process crucial. Whether oral, archival, visual, material, or otherwise, windows into the past are clouded and truncated. Personal experiences, perceptions of the past, collective historical constructions, and larger political, economic, social, and cultural forces at play at the time of the events and at the time of the telling bear upon interviewees' recollections and scholars' biases. Knowing storytellers' backgrounds and goals is essential for interpreting their narratives.

Oral histories offer insight into the contested manner by which some facets of the past but not others become history. As raconteurs forget some aspects and intentionally omit others, silence guides historical narratives. As narrators try to make sense of their personal histories and relate them to the broader contexts in which they live and have lived, ambiguities and tensions abound.

Notes

1. The epigraph is from Portelli, *Death of Luigi Trastulli*, 50. I liberally borrow this definition of history from Stephen Jay Gould's conceptualization of science in *Time's Arrow* and *Mismeasure of Man*.
2. Cabrera Garcia and Scaramal, "Saber e cultura na família rural."
3. Schwarzstein, "Oral History in Latin America," 421 (quote); Schwarzstein, "La historia oral en América Latina," 42; Olivera de Bonfil, "Treinta años de historia oral en México," 78–9.
4. Cáceres Q., "¿Historia oral o fuentes orales?," 22.
5. Sarlo, *Tiempo pasado*; Pozzi, "Historia oral," 7; Schwarzstein, "Oral History in Latin America," 423.
6. Acuña Ortega, "Fuentes orales e historia obrera," 68; Acuña Ortega, "Cuestiones de memoria popular."
7. Barrientos, "Texturas, políticas y fisuras," 54.
8. Similarly, even as her "admiration for the campesinos of Oaxaca and Veracruz" deepened, Soto Laveaga sought to "maintain an analytical view." See *Jungle Laboratories*, 17.
9. La Serna, *Corner of the Living*, 13–14.
10. Ibid., 14–15.
11. Rappaport, *Politics of Memory*, 200.
12. Rappaport and Ramos Pacho, "Collaboration and Historical Writing," 126.
13. D. Carey, *Engendering Mayan History*; D. Carey, *Our Elders Teach Us*.
14. Hill, "Introduction: Myth and History," 7.
15. Hamilton, *Sexual Revolutions in Cuba*, 4, 83, 86, 130 (quote).
16. Necoechea Gracia, "El análisis en la historia oral," 73, 75; Camarena and Necoechea Gracia, "Continuidad, ruptura y ciclo," 57.
17. Hill and Wright, "Time, Narrative, and Ritual."
18. D. Carey, *Engendering Mayan History*, 52–6, 158–71.
19. Lajuj K'at, oral history interview by the author, April 4, 2005.
20. D. Carey, "Democracy Born in Violence."
21. Barrientos, "Narración, mujeres y memoria en el sur de Chile," 165; Hamilton, *Sexual Revolutions in Cuba*, 4.
22. Adleson, Camarena, and Iparraguirre, "Historia social y testimonios orales," 43–4; Necoechea Gracia, "El análisis en la historia oral," 82–3.
23. Necoechea Gracia, "El análisis en la historia oral," 73.
24. James, *Doña María's Story*, 228.
25. B. Allen, "Story in Oral History," 606.
26. Kab'lajuj Tijax, oral history interview by author, April 7, 1998.
27. Pozzi and Schneider, *Combatiendo al capital*; Berrotarán and Pozzi, *Estudios inconformistas*.
28. Levenson-Estrada, *Trade Unionists against Terror*.
29. James, *Doña María's Story*, 161–8; Levenson-Estrada, *Trade Unionists against Terror*; Striffler, *In the Shadows of State and Capital*.
30. Acuña Ortega, "Fuentes orales e historia obrera," 65.
31. James, *Doña María's Story*, 140.
32. Rappaport and Ramos Pacho, "Collaboration and Historical Writing."
33. Lewis, *La Vida*; Lewis, *Children of Sánchez*.
34. Burgos-Debray, *I, Rigoberta Menchú*.
35. In Wilkie, "Introduction."

Interpretation and Memory

36 Stoll, *Rigoberta Menchú*. For debates about Menchú's account and Burgos-Debray's role in it, see Arias, *Rigoberta Menchú Controversy*; Grandin, *Who Is Rigoberta Menchú?*
37 Lobato, "Voces subalternas de la memoria," 151.
38 Behar, *Translated Woman*, 14, 302.
39 Stern, *Battling for Hearts and Minds*, 5.
40 Rappaport, *Politics of Memory*, 12, 16; La Serna, *Corner of the Living*, 15; D. Carey, *Our Elders Teach Us*.
41 Price, *First-Time*, 158.
42 In Cowles, "Liars' Club."
43 Schwarzstein, "Memorializing Effervescence," 18.
44 Barrientos, "Texturas, políticas y fisuras," 48–9.
45 Taussig, *Shamanism, Colonialism*, 392.
46 In Hamilton, *Sexual Revolutions in Cuba*, 104.
47 Portelli, *Death of Luigi Trastulli*.
48 Gould and Lauria-Santiago, *To Rise in Darkness*, 271.
49 Abercrombie, *Pathways of Memory and Power*, 117.
50 Alegre, *Railroad Radicals in Cold War Mexico*, 59, 62–3.
51 Starn, *Nightwatch*, 82–5 (quote 85).
52 Popular Memory Group, "Popular Memory," 223–6.
53 Padilla Ramos, "Diagnosis 'Suspicious Yellow Fever.'"
54 Necoechea Gracia, "El análisis en la historia oral," 77–8.
55 Necoechea Gracia, "Custom and History," 121.
56 See especially Guzmán's films *Nostalgia for the Light* (2010) and *Chile, la memoria obstinada* (1997).
57 Stern, *Remembering Pinochet's Chile*, 147–8.
58 Yates, "Memoryscape," 60.
59 Dore, "Foreword," x.
60 Menand, "Elvis Oracle," 87.
61 Compare, for example, Grieb, *Guatemalan Caudillo*; Forster, *Time of Freedom*; D. Carey, *Our Elders Teach Us*.
62 In Dary, *Relatos de los antiguos*, 61.
63 D. Carey, *Our Elders Teach Us*, 195–219.
64 Gould and Lauria-Santiago, *To Rise in Darkness*, 242.
65 Taussig, "Violence and Resistance in the Americas," 24.
66 Gould and Lauria-Santiago, *To Rise in Darkness*, 243; D. Carey, "Democracy Born in Violence."
67 Turits, *Foundations of Despotism*, 207. Trujillo ruled as a military strongman from 1930 to 1961 and only officially served as president in 1930–38 and 1942–52.
68 Ibid., 208.
69 Kaplan, *Taking Back the Streets*, 181.
70 Farnsworth-Alvear, *Dulcinea in the Factory*, 3.
71 Necoechea Gracia, "Los contextos del recuerdo."
72 James, *Doña María's Story*, 223.
73 E. Basso, *Last Cannibals*, xii, 23, 36.
74 Schwarzstein, "Memorializing Effervescence," 18.
75 In Ferguson, "Judging Memory," 21.
76 Nora, "Between Memory and History," 18.
77 Jelin, *State Repression and the Labors of Memory*, 2; Falla, *Negreaba de zopilotes*.
78 Stern, *Remembering Pinochet's Chile*, 200n2.

79 Jelin and Kaufman, "Layers of Memories."
80 In Bolender, *Voices from the Other Side*, 43.
81 Bilbija and Payne, *Accounting for Violence*, 99.
82 Iwao Ueunten, "Japanese Latin American Internment," 100.
83 Camarena Ocampo, "Oral History and Consciousness."
84 Habermas, *Reason and the Rationalization of Society*, 8–26.
85 Patai, *Brazilian Women Speak*, 18 (emphasis in original).
86 Mintz, *Worker in the Cane*, 1.
87 Mastrángelo, "'Mi abuela cantaba Bandiera Rossa'"; Pozzi, "¿Quién hizo el mundo?"
88 Necoechea Gracia, "'Mi mamá me platicó,'" 5.
89 Junlajuj Imox, oral history interview with the author, September 15, 1998.
90 Tinsman, *Partners in Conflict*, 52.
91 Ibid., 17–18.
92 Mallon, "Introduction," 14.
93 Pozzi, "Oral History in Latin America."
94 Cruikshank, "Oral History, Narrative Strategies," 13; Stern, *Remembering Pinochet's Chile*, 231–2.
95 James, *Doña María's Story*, 136.
96 Montagu, *Race, Science, and Humanity*, iii.
97 Portelli, *Death of Luigi Trastulli*.
98 Striffler, *In the Shadows of State and Capital*, 17.
99 Boesten, "When Tintos Break Ice," 5.
100 Dore, "Foreword," xviii; Hamilton, *Sexual Revolutions in Cuba*, 153.
101 Cutler, "Accuracy in Oral History Interviewing," 104.
102 Samuel and Thompson, *Myths We Live By*.
103 Stern, *Battling for Hearts and Minds*, 4–5 (quote p. 5); Stern, *Remembering Pinochet's Chile*, 68, 105–7.
104 Portelli, *Death of Luigi Trastulli*, 15.
105 Jelin, *State Repression and the Labors of Memory*, 33.
106 Alegre, *Railroad Radicals in Cold War Mexico*, 94
107 G. Frank, "Anthropology and Individual Lives," 145.
108 Portelli, *Death of Luigi Trastulli*, 51.
109 In Striffler, *In the Shadows of State and Capital*, 48.
110 Alvito, "À sombra do jequitibá."
111 Klubock, "Working-Class Masculinity," 453.
112 James, *Doña María's Story*.
113 Ibid., 242.
114 Vommaro, "Territorios, organizaciones sociales y migraciones"; Vommaro, "Las organizaciones sociales en la Argentina contemporánea."
115 Hill, *Rethinking History and Myth*.
116 Price, *First-Time*, 94.
117 Plank, "What Silence Means," 3–4; K. Basso, "'To Give Up on Words,'" 214, 225–7.
118 Stern, *Remembering Pinochet's Chile*.
119 O. González, *Unveiling Secrets of War in the Peruvian Andes*, 8–9.
120 Scott, *Domination and the Arts of Resistance*.
121 In Hamilton, *Sexual Revolutions in Cuba*, 143.
122 Ibid., 143–4.
123 Jelin, *State Repression and the Labors of Memory*, 17.

134 Interpretation and Memory

124 For a fine example of extracting meaning from silences, see Passerini's *Fascism in Popular Memory*.
125 O. González, *Unveiling Secrets of War in the Peruvian Andes*, 10.
126 In M. González, "Man Who Brought Danger to the Village," 329.
127 Ibid., 335.
128 Ibid., 333–4.
129 In Pino, "Uchuraccay," 28.
130 Calveiro, *Poder y desaparición*, 106.
131 James, *Doña María's Story*, 190.
132 In Levenson-Estrada, *Trade Unionists against Terror*, 164.
133 Ibid., 164.
134 Acuña Ortega, "Fuentes orales e historia obrera," 68.
135 Pozzi and Schneider, "Memoria y socialismo," 99.
136 Hamilton, *Sexual Revolutions in Cuba*, 21.
137 Lobato, "Voces subalternas de la memoria," 149.
138 Pasquali, Ríos, and Viano, "Culturas militantes," 114–15; Grandin, *Last Colonial Massacre*, 139; D. Carey, *Engendering Mayan History*, 177–206.
139 Hamilton, *Sexual Revolutions in Cuba*, 55–6.
140 Necoechea Gracia, "Custom and History," 123 (quote); Necoechea Gracia, *Después de vivir un siglo*, 103–28.
141 Pensado Leglise, "Memorias de la experiencia política de cinco mujeres," 221.
142 Spivak, "Can the Subaltern Speak?"; Prakash, "Subaltern Studies as Postcolonial Criticism"; Chatterjee, *Nationalist Thought and the Colonial World*, 39–43.
143 Hamilton, *Sexual Revolutions in Cuba*, 22, 78–80, 113–41.
144 Taylor, *Disappearing Acts*, 88–9.
145 Barrientos, "Texturas, políticas y fisuras," 51–3, 55.
146 Passerini, *Fascism in Popular Memory*, 28.
147 Mallon, "Constructing *Mestizaje* in Latin America," 178.
148 Pasquali, "Mujeres y militantes."
149 Lobato, "Voces subalternas de la memoria," 157.
150 Tinsman, *Partners in Conflict*, 110.
151 Ibid., 117.
152 Pensado Leglise and Correa Ethegaray, "Historia oral de un barrio," 186–7; Thompson and Burchardt, *Our Common History*; James, *Doña María's Story*, 179–80.
153 Lucena, "Mobilidade social," 210; Hamilton, *Sexual Revolutions in Cuba*, 78–9.
154 Jelin, *State Repression and the Labors of Memory*, 83 (quote); Hamilton, *Sexual Revolutions in Cuba*, 78–80.
155 Jelin, *State Repression and the Labors of Memory*, 83.
156 In M. Green, "Memory Keeper," 37 (quote); Portelli, *Death of Luigi Trastulli*, 134–5; Johnstone, *Stories, Community, and Place*, 66–76.
157 Passerini, *Fascism in Popular Memory*, 27–8.
158 To cite one example, female insurgents in Argentina are reluctant to highlight their violent histories; Diana, *Mujeres guerrilleras*.
159 Park, "Remembering Resistance, Forgetting Torture."
160 Jelin, *State Repression and the Labors of Memory*, 84; D. Carey, *I Ask for Justice*, 153–90.
161 Lucena, "Mobilidade social," 213.
162 In Tinsman, *Partners in Conflict*, 186–7.
163 Ibid., 18.

164 Barrientos, "Texturas, políticas y fisuras," 51–3; Barrientos, "Narración, mujeres y memoria en el sur de Chile," 175–7.
165 Necoechea Gracia, "'Mi mamá me platicó,'" 13.
166 Ibid., 14.

Suggested Readings

Borland, Katherine. "'That's Not What I Said': Interpretative Conflict in Oral Narrative Research." In *The Oral History Reader*, edited by Robert Perks and Alistair Thomson, 310–21. 2nd edition. New York: Routledge, 2006.

Cano Sánchez, Beatriz. "El mensaje de los silencios." In *Historia y testimonios orales*, edited by Cuauhtémoc Velasco, 171–9. Mexico City: Instituto Nacional de Antropología e Historia, 1996.

Field, Sean. "Imagining Communities: Memory, Loss, and Resilience in Post-Apartheid Cape Town." In *Oral History and Public Memories*, edited by Paula Hamilton and Linda Shopes, 107–24. Philadelphia: Temple University Press, 2008.

Freud, Alexander. "Toward an Ethics of Silence? Negotiating Off-the-Record Events and Identity in Oral History." In *Oral History off the Record: Toward an Ethnography of Practice*, edited by Ann Sheftel and Stacey Zembrzycki, 223–38. New York: Palgrave Macmillan, 2013.

Hamilton, Paula, and Linda Shopes. *Oral History and Public Memories*. Philadelphia: Temple University Press, 2008.

Jaworski, Adam, ed. *Silence: Interdisciplinary Perspectives*. Berlin: Mouton de Gruyter, 1997.

Leydesdorff, Selma, Luisa Passerini, and Paul Thompson, eds. *International Yearbook of Oral History and Life Stories*. Vol. 4: *Gender and Memory*. New York: Oxford University Press, 1996.

Necoechea Gracia, Gerardo. *Después de vivir un siglo: ensayos de historia oral*. Mexico City: Instituto Nacional de Antropología e Historia, 2005.

———. "El análisis en la historia oral." In *Cuéntame cómo fue: introducción a la historia oral*, edited by Gerardo Necoechea Gracia and Pablo Pozzi, 73–83. Buenos Aires: Imago Mundi, 2008.

Passerini, Luisa. "Memories between Silence and Oblivion." In *Contested Pasts: The Politics of Memory*, edited by Katharine Hodgkins and Susannah Radstone, 238–54. New York: Routledge, 2003.

———. "Work Ideology and Consensus under Italian Fascism." *History Workshop* 8 (1979): 82–108.

Passerini, Luisa, and Polymeris Vogus, eds. *Gender in the Production of History*. Fiesole, Italy: Department of History and Civilization, European University Institute, 1999.

Patai, Daphne. *Historia oral, feminismo e politica*. São Paulo: Letra e Voz, 2010.

Ritchie, Donald. Chapter 4 of *Doing Oral History: Using Interviews to Uncover the Past and Preserve It for the Future*. 2nd edition. New York: Oxford University Press, 2003.

Ruiz-Funes, Concepción, and Enriqueta Tuñón. "Historia oral. Creación e interpretación de fuentes en los estudios de la mujer." In *Historia y testimonios orales*, edited by Cuauhtémoc Velasco, 191–7. Mexico City: INAH, 1996.

Sider, Gerald, and Gavin Smith, eds. *Between History and Histories: The Making of Silences and Commemorations*. Toronto: Toronto University Press, 1997.

6   Topical Oral History

Despite fundamental differences, the major branches of oral history—topical and life history—have much in common. Although scholars often draw from both, I address the two approaches separately to underscore the importance and richness of each. Oral life history constructs narratives around an individual's life and experiences in relation to larger historical forces, and topical oral history generally frames a study around a particular event, theme, process, or temporal period and only makes incidental reference to interviewees' personal life stories. While personal anecdotes and individual experiences enrich topical oral history, they are generally subordinate to the broader theme.

Dynamics of power, resistance, and acquiescence permeate the lives of people at different socioeconomic levels. Illuminating subjectivities and agency, oral histories from women, ethnic minorities, the poor and working classes, gays and lesbians, and other marginalized groups fill in gaps and correct misconceptions in hegemonic historical narratives. In turn, pointed questions with elites can inform an understanding of why specific policies were pursued and not others. To explore the complex relations between government, economics, and religion, scholars have asked politicians, presidents, business leaders, bishops, and other elites how they viewed their respective roles in their nations' development. Without ignoring larger trends, scholars contextualize individual recollections of ordinary and extraordinary experiences lost to broad historical brushstrokes. Focusing on the interrelated identities of class, sexuality, gender, and ethnicity illuminates how scholars move from analyzing individual interviews to explaining larger processes and forces.

The power and politics of oral history can be discerned in the stakes for determining which versions of the past become authoritative. While studying the 1932 massacre, Salvadoran research assistant Reynaldo Patriz stressed the importance of unofficial narratives, particularly from survivors. By pointing out the legitimacy of land reform and the innocence of bystanders caught in the crossfire, survivors' stories counteract military leaders' and conservative politicians' claims that the victims were communist insurgents.[1] To understand the trajectory of state violence, many survivors deploy oral history.[2] As peripheral perspectives countervail hegemonic histories, national narratives become more representative. By referring to victims of Argentina's Dirty War as *hijos* and *hijas* (sons and daughters) to dispute the military's portrayal of them as communists and terrorists, the Madres de la Plaza de Mayo garnered international support that helped to depose the military dictatorship.[3] Popular idiom can dislodge political discourse.

Through oral history, scholars have demonstrated how oppression and violence have pervaded governments from presidents and dictators to midlevel bureaucrats and local authorities; many officials abused their power with the backing of military and other state-sanctioned security forces. By approaching place as a lens through which to conduct research, researchers have revealed how tenuous financial stability and material comfort can be in mutable patterns of state rule. Rather than pursuing an exhaustive exploration, highlighting a few fruitful areas of study demonstrates the rich products and possibilities of topical oral history.

Politics and Violence

Attaining power through armed intervention, many military elites ruled through authoritarian governments. Latin American military leaders often took pride in their unique approaches to rule and military strategy. General Ramón Camps explains,

> In Argentina we first received French influence and then North American, and we tried them out separately as well as in combinations, drawing out ideas from both. . . . So it went until the moment arrived in which we reached our maturity and applied our own doctrine, which definitely permitted us to win the victory in Argentina against armed subversion.[4]

After interviewing relatives of the disappeared in Chile, Argentina, El Salvador, and Guatemala who kept referring to the national security doctrine to explain repression and frame their resistance, Schirmer decided to interview military officials who adhered to that doctrine: "To understand the actions of a repressive State toward its citizens, especially toward the women I was studying, I needed to speak with high-ranking military officers."[5] Through those interviews, Schirmer reveals the rationale and progenitors of the Guatemalan military's infamous *frijoles o fusiles* (beans or bullets) program and officers' tendency to deploy the latter more than the former.[6] Interviews with the former Argentine dictator Jorge Rafael Videla (1976–81), who in 2008 admitted to ordering the murder of some seven thousand to eight thousand people, similarly disclosed how military governments suppressed dissent and maintained a culture of fear.[7] Perspectives of political and military elites and their supporters offer insights into how authoritarian rule was forged, justified, and practiced.

Whether living under military or civilian rule, those subjected to state terror expose authorities' strategies. Survivors of the 1968 Tlatelolco massacre in Mexico City describe the insidious nature of state surveillance. María Alicia Medrano recalls the confusion amid the shooting:

> I was about to go downstairs again, because I had spied some girl friends of mine down on the esplanade. But the boy took me by the arm and very solicitously helped me up the stairs. I was touched by this courageous behavior on the part of yet another student here, and went upstairs with him. . . . Many hours later, I discovered that my escort was one of the assassins guarding the stairway so that none of the CNH [Consejo Nacional de Huelga (National Strike Committee)] people would escape.[8]

Since the government continues to deny and obscure its involvement, oral accounts remain some of the most vital sources for understanding that massacre.

Even as authoritarian governments unleashed death squads, at times violence was internecine and locally instigated. Peeling back the layers of violence in Latin America reveals how social conflict could turn fatal when, for example, neighbors denounced rivals to military officials or death squads. Victims' innocence was a central theme in oral histories about the aftermath of the 1973 military coup in Chile. One *chilena* recounts,

> These people were campesinos who did not harm anyone, the military came because don Américo called them and sold out our families, but there were no guerrillas here; they invented them. . . . [A]fter killing people [in a neighboring community] the planes came and bombed everything. One did not dare leave the house for fear that the planes would return and the helicopters would land again in the soccer field. We were all traumatized [*espirituados*] by that; one could not see a plane without being scared to death.[9]

Guatemalan survivors similarly concede that conflicts that predated state terror precipitated violence.[10]

Enjoyed by the highest-ranking military officers in many Latin American nations until recently, impunity has deep roots throughout the region. By refusing to accept responsibility for their charges, let alone for their own crimes, mid-level military officers helped to institutionalize impunity. The lack of accountability and civility that permeated the military from the ground up created the conditions whereby terror, torture, rape, and murder seemed reasonable.[11] While courts in Guatemala and elsewhere recently have prosecuted high-profile human rights violators, local communities frequently have turned to lynching to counteract impunity.

In the wake of state violence punctuated by local treachery, building peaceful societies is challenging. "My father was denounced by a brother, my uncle, whom I have not spoken to since. My uncle was jealous of my father because our family was doing well. When my father disappeared and my mom was all alone, my uncle took all our things, our animals, etc.," bemoans a *chileno*.[12] Decades after Pinochet's rule, local military collaborators and informants like this man's uncle struggle with their consciences and ostracism. Many agents who justified violence as a political means to eradicate perceived threats—communism, socialism, insurgency—suffer from the trauma of having tortured and executed people.[13] By orchestrating terror as part of their rule, military governments traumatized victims and perpetrators alike.

Without a deep understanding of survivors' thoughts, motives, and feelings, the reconstruction of traumatic pasts remains incomplete.[14] A Guatemalan survivor articulates how encompassing trauma can be: "My heart hurts a lot because you don't know when they're going to kill you, when they're going to come to take you away. . . . No, we're not hungry anymore because when you feel you're going to die, you don't have any desire to eat."[15] Recalling what it was like to organize a movement during a time when death squads harassed, beat, tortured, and killed leaders, a Guatemalan trade unionist explains why he persisted: "You question yourself, whether you call life one thing which is not life, and whether you prefer to be a human being for a short time or a vegetable for a long time. You know that by choosing to be a human being for a short time you point the way for others to live as humans."[16]

As with all history, traumatic memories can hold dramatically different lessons for people. Insisting that agitating for land and rights resulted in death, a Salvadoran survivor of the 1932 massacre warned his son not to get involved in social movements. In contrast, the survivor's nephew embraced political mobilization in the 1970s because to his mind its regional character would allow it to succeed where the local uprising that led to the 1932 massacre had failed.[17] Tragically, the Salvadoran military's murder of civilians in the 1980s proved the survivor's interpretation to be more accurate than his nephew's.

No matter its origins—state-sponsored, parastatal, insurgent, random, domestic, sexual, structural—violence marginalizes victims. Recurrent patterns of trauma are devastating for victims of domestic violence. The judicial record of women who accused their husbands of gender-based violence offers a broad historical context; oral histories offer a window into the psychological trauma that accompanied physical trauma.[18] By deepening our understanding of individual trauma, oral histories make written sources more intelligible. Just as powerful *patrones* and their sons in urban areas raped domestic workers, plantation and hacienda owners took advantage of poor rural women. A Salvadoran woman whose father was killed in the 1932 massacre recalls that the *hacendado* Gabino Mata "brought about the massacre in order to keep for himself the young women and the land."[19] Revealing how sexual violence perpetuated class oppression, the offspring of rapists remained subordinated even when their fathers recognized them. A man born in 1932 recounts,

> My grandmother was a servant for Gabino Mata. My mother used to visit her at the hacienda. So then I was born. Three years later, my mother died. Then my grandmother started to take me to the hacienda so *don* Gabino could get to know me. He embraced me and told me that I was his child and he gave me his name. When I was ten years old, my grandmother died and I was left alone. Then I was sent to *don* Gabino's hacienda to work cutting trees. My father remembered me, you know. He embraced me, 'My son, my son!' But I came there barefoot and I left barefoot.[20]

Rife with the complexities of honor, legitimacy, bloodlines, and inheritance, his account adds poignancy to histories of landowner abuse and exploitation.

In contrast to the victims who were impoverished by political and violent turmoil, those who enjoyed privileged positions often weathered economic crises. One director of a private girls' school and mother of five who was desperate to feed her children recalled the period with little rancor. While other *chilenas* waited in line for basic foodstuffs that never came, she benefited from a storeowner who hid milk, rice, sugar, and other goods for his regular customers.[21]

Some elites allied with or otherwise benefited from military dictatorships; others were persecuted and exiled for their opposition. Oral histories from the latter reveal how the experience of exile impacted people's worldviews and sense of belonging.[22] Since her father was a politician with close ties to Brazilian president João Belchior Marques Goulart (1961–64), Flávia Schilling's family fled to Uruguay after the 1964 military coup deposed him, when she was eleven years old. As she grew up and studied in Uruguay, Schilling first became involved in the student movement and then quit school to dedicate herself full time to political activism. Far from glorifying her experience, however, she came to resent it:

> Clandestineness is your social death, it is a situation that even now I do not like to talk about, because it is a time without social life, a blank time, an empty space. It is so useless, so brutal. . . . Realistically clandestineness is a terrible moment, because you do not do anything, you just hide, you do not exist.[23]

For others, political activism was a source of pride. "When I finished high school I had big expectations, as a young person, to become a professional and fill my pockets with money and get a pretty girl, but after I caught the revolutionary fever . . . I became obsessed," explains a former Colombian student leader.[24] "What would have become of me if I . . . had been a good student, studied hard, been responsible, all of that?" he asks rhetorically, suggesting that he was content to have skirted a conventional life "by embracing service to the community over career goals."[25]

Refusing to succumb to fascist rule in Uruguay, Argentina, and Brazil, political elites clandestinely met, organized, and strategized.[26] Argentine leader Deolindo Felipe Bittel explains, "The first thing we had to do was bury the dead, heal the injured, and recruit to see what we had left."[27] Determined to reinstate constitutional rule and democracy "without demagogy," party leaders set aside their political ideologies and united in opposition to the military dictatorship.[28] When the military coup and ensuing dictatorship in Uruguay (1973–84) ousted politicians, banned political activity, and disappeared political leaders, party leaders adapted and positioned themselves to regain political power. Rather than refrain from political plotting, when politicians fall from power, "socializing becomes political"; birthdays, tributes, and other festivities are excuses "to get together, debate, and design action plans."[29] According to the Uruguayan soccer player-turned-historian Gerardo Caetano, political parties that survived repressive rule demonstrated that "everything was possible."[30] Their resilience offered hope to battered civilians. Even the armed forces recognized how crucial political parties were to institutionalizing the government.[31] Given the dearth of archival information about wartime clandestine activity, oral history interviews with political elites are crucial for understanding transitions from authoritarian to democratic rule and how elites reposition themselves without official power.[32]

With such dramatic ruptures, halcyon recollections of predictatorial politics are understandable. As the head of the government's union and labor department and enjoying direct access to the president, Clodesmidt Riani lauded Brazilian President Goulart for "being close to the workers." Ninety-three when he was interviewed, Riani described Goulart as a "simple and modest man."[33] Looking back on the period, former student leaders similarly praised Goulart's reformist projects. For Riani, the military coup was devastating not only personally, as one of the first public officials to be arrested, but also for working-class people who would wait a long time before they had another advocate at the presidential level.[34]

Some memories of despotic regimes favorably portray pasts that historians have depicted as oppressive and exploitative. Rather than discount the sense of fear that permeated the dictatorial rule of Trujillo in the Dominican Republic and Ubico in Guatemala, many elders in those societies contextualize it as one aspect of the respective state's increased intervention in their lives. Like Ubico, who enhanced the legitimacy of his rule with his travel to and investment in rural communities, Trujillo increased the state's presence in people's lives in ways that ushered in material progress without dismissing rural values. The construction of roads, canals, and irrigation systems generally improved people's lives. Turits argues, "Because many of the state's demands and interventions were framed in terms of peasants' own values—*respeto*, patriarchal social relations, customary rights to land—they were widely perceived as legitimate among the popular ruling classes."[35]

The violence that marked their regimes notwithstanding, Ubico and Trujillo established social order and a sense of security.[36] Guatemalan and Dominican elders alike insist they "slept with the [front] door wide open," or without one at all.[37] A Dominican interviewee explains, "The early years of Trujillo was when confidence and liberty developed . . . with the exception of opinions and words that is, not those. . . . But you could go anywhere without qualms or fear.'"[38] Despite the loss of civil liberties, a combination of responding to local concerns and maintaining the rule of law appealed to rural people.

Lest such recollections of fascist regimes seem Pollyannaish, oral histories contain evidence of resistance. In response to the Trujillo regime's compulsory latrine construction law, one peasant observes, "No one ever likes to be forced to do something even if it's for one's own good."[39] Yet even seen through the eyes of those who despised aspects of his rule, Trujillo remained a hallowed leader in many peasants' calculations, like this one's: "As bad as he may have been, as much of a killer and a totalitarian as he may have been, he had his good part."[40]

Fleeing Nazi Germany, a group of Jewish immigrants emphasizes Trujillo's benevolence, though for very different reasons. "No one wanted us. He was the only one who took us in," recalls an emigrant to Sosúa, a Dominican agricultural settlement.[41] The US refusal to admit Jewish refugees punctuated Trujillo's gesture. Eager to deflect international attention from the Dominican military's massacre of fifteen thousand unarmed Haitians in 1937, Trujillo welcomed Jewish refugees in 1938. Although the island nation offered security and equality, the 750 refugees were cautious about their dealings with Trujillo, participating in requisite civic duties but mainly trying to remain invisible. Elie Topf notes, "We could criticize the regime any time we wanted, so long as we did it in German."[42] As ambivalent as the Jewish refugees were about Trujillo, they generally agreed with the sentiment that "Sosúa served its purpose. It saved lives."[43] In an example of how scholars critically assess interviewees' narratives, historian Allen Wells acknowledges the Sosúa settlers' debt to Trujillo but criticizes "their willful ignorance of the dictatorship's seamier side."[44]

Rural people and refugees are not the only ones whose memories cast a favorable light on dictators. In Santiago, perspectives of Pinochet's regime ranged from praise to condemnation.[45] Peruvians likewise articulate diverse reactions to ex-president Alberto Fujimori (1990–2000) and the Shining Path. Rural villages that enjoyed fair and functioning local political and judicial processes resisted the Shining Path's attempt to overthrow authority, while towns whose judicial and political officials were corrupt and exploitative welcomed the Maoist guerrilla group's violent tactics.[46] Local conditions more than ideology or tactics informed how Peruvian peasants responded to outside intervention. For some Latin Americans, a certain level of despotism among their leaders is inevitable. One woman praised a Mexican politician because he was "less despotic" than his counterparts.[47]

Popular Culture

Popular culture has catalyzed social movements. Influenced by Hollywood and rock and roll, Mexico City youths came to define themselves as a group with interests that diverged from the nation's conventional customs and culture. A Mexican who came of age during the 1950s and 1960s recalls,

> Young people started to get together, be more of a group, to talk more about their own interests and worries, their own views on life. And then more gangs sprang up, and there were the films with James Dean and Marlon Brando, and *Rebel without a Cause* became famous and everyone wore jeans. This happened a lot in certain neighborhoods and high schools and the university. . . . [T]hen when it came our time, it had sharpened because there was rock and roll and Elvis Presley and all that.[48]

Among the norms Mexican youths flouted were gender and sexuality. As men grew their hair, women cut theirs; converging clothing styles further blurred gender distinctions.[49]

Almost by definition, popular culture contrasts with and often contests state power. When concerts increasingly morphed into wild affairs, authorities came to see music as a threat. "The government began to realize that [the clubs] were a hazard, that rock 'n' roll had gone from being something healthy to something unhealthy and noxious. People took advantage of [rock] as a pretext for their *desmadres* and sexual exploits—screwing in the bathroom and that whole scene," asserts Los Rebeldes del Rock band member Johnny Laboriel.[50] The Mexican government closed down cafes, but rock culture spread.

Embracing countervailing cultural markers allowed Mexican youth to shape images of *lo mexicano* (being Mexican) in ways that contravened state discourse and ideology. A woman explains,

> We used to go to school in huaraches, which was considered extraordinary. . . . It allowed you to identify yourself with a culture that you considered more authentic, not a copy of something else . . . [b]ecause people in the countryside still use huaraches. So it was like wearing your credo and going against the majority of people in the city, who were imitating gringos."[51]

Ironically, the very footwear choice she heralds as affirming indigenous and rural cultures and contrasting gringo influences also was associated with US hippies.

Some participants knew little about the politics that enveloped them. In his early teens during the Mexican student movement, a man recalls,

> I was very young and did not have any clear sense of political reality, but I supported the youth, the students. This was because [President Gustavo] Díaz Ordaz [1964–70] was a shithead, as were all the police. . . . [T]hey were a bunch of shithead moralists. I didn't understand much about the movement except that they were from the UNAM [national university], that they were students and youth, and that they listened to rock.[52]

If the Mexico City PHO collections are any indication, widespread support for the student movement was as much inspired by the personal connections of "people who had sons and daughters in the university" as by any political leanings.[53]

In addition to contesting hegemonic forces, popular culture catapulted careers. Known for their athleticism, soccer players tapped into that prowess to become union leaders.[54] An Argentine worker suggests a connection between striving for idealistic goals and heroism in a sport loved by millions: "We did not want cultural oligarchy, but rather a nation with culture, where everyone had access. . . . [W]hen here there was a world-class soccer player, there were people, there were hundreds who had played soccer since their childhood."[55] So powerful was soccer success that it could supersede politics. Asked about the soccer player-turned-politician Felix Stradella, a rural worker explains,

> He does not win because he is a communist, but rather in spite of it. . . . [W]hen we found out that Stradella had won, we were not surprised because he was very popular. He was a very good football player, and besides a fine person and a communist, but he just as well might have been a conservative, he would have been elected as well.[56]

Privileged positions in one realm can lead to authoritative ones in another. Conversely, women's exclusion from playing sports, except for volleyball, in male-dominated mining communities hindered their ability to become union and political leaders.[57]

Lived Architecture

Framing their studies around place, scholars have deployed oral history to understand how people came to perceive their own possibilities, achievements, and plights.[58] By focusing on a housing complex in Mexico City, one PHO project reveals how the economic crisis of the 1980s that precipitated the shift from tenancy to ownership affected residents. State-subsidized housing facilitated a high quality of life for the middle-class state employees who lived there. As Mexico sought to portray itself as a modern nation in the

Figure 6.1 A middle-class family, Cuernavaca, Mexico, 1990

Photograph by David Carey Jr.

late 1940s and 1950s, oral histories of federal employees and other individuals indicate that they secured housing despite building administrators' repeated refusals to process their applications. Their narratives reveal that patron–client relationships were crucial to achieving personal goals amid the rules and regulations that authorities hoped would institutionalize order and accountability.[59] Mundane topics can often yield penetrating insights.

Throughout much of the twentieth century, the dominant Partido Revolucionario Institucional sought to maintain the loyalty or at least acquiescence of Mexicans by connecting them to its revolutionary project. In many ways, the Miguel Aleman housing complex was a successful manifestation of that project. From 1950 to 1980, the Mexican Instituto de Seguridad y Servicios Sociales de los Trabajadores del Estado (Institute of Social Security and Services for State Employees) managed the complex. With a crew that was available twenty-four hours a day, the housing administration took care of all repairs and upkeep. Waxing nostalgic about rent control, state-sponsored social and cultural activities, hot water, a sports club, child care, and other benefits, residents recall the era as a "golden age."[60] One resident considered it "a privileged social life."[61] Such benefits had costs, however. Instead of developing self-sufficient citizens, the government had created reliant subjects. "We were immersed in a culture of dependence. . . . We were children of the government," conceded an inhabitant.[62] Similarly evoking perceptions of patronage, another occupant spoke of a shared "vision that our father government gives us everything, and if you fought for something it was to press father government to give us things."[63]

Evident in the state-sponsored social gatherings, common social spaces—soccer pitches, pool, gardens, courtyards—and residents' shared experiences as federal employees that helped to create strong social networks, the same conditions that limited individuals' self-sufficiency facilitated a sense of community.[64] A resident explains,

> A cultural, social, and even political identity begins to emerge. . . . [I]t was natural. You have state employees all with a particular way of seeing life, with levels of income, education and culture that are not very different, more or less homogenous. . . . If you talk to any of the residents you will find they have more or less the same views about life, the same attitudes about problems. Then there is an identity and that is why many of the neighbors speak proudly of being residents of this housing unit.[65]

While interviewees extolled the benefits of solidarity, they also revealed how gender relations developed among middle-class families in the housing complex. Faced with an older brother who sought to limit her mobility under the pretense of protecting her, Alejandra was fortunate her mother supported her right to make her own decisions. In response, her brother resorted to violence. When he punched Alejandra and knocked her down, she fought back: "I overcame my fear and I would just throw myself against him as best I could. In this way you learn to fight like a male."[66] Evading possessive brothers and territorial men was one of the responses to gendered subjectivities that fostered girls' camaraderie in the complex. They fought among themselves, but they also pooled their strategies and looked out for each other. In doing so, they expanded their autonomy.

Among young men in the housing complex, geography and territory fomented confidence. Male youths organized and reconstituted their masculinity within the spaces they inhabited. One explains, "We had our own youth gangs and then there were some in Actipan [a nearby neighborhood], so they fought one another, you know, for whatever reason. . . . [W]hen that happened, then all of us would stick together in solidarity. At other times . . . each group defended its own space."[67] Such conceptions of space were decidedly male; given the restrictions on their mobility, young women were more interested in breaking boundaries than maintaining them.

When the government transformed residents from tenants to owners by privatizing the Miguel Aleman complex in 1981, their lack of self-reliance became problematic. Without financial support or outside management, residents were compelled to solve their quotidian problems. The issues were both structural (the buildings and facilities had aged and needed more regular maintenance) and demographic (many of the original resident had retired, and their modest pensions meant they could contribute little to association dues and fees). As a result, buildings and grounds fell into disrepair. Distrust and apathy replaced solidarity and camaraderie as their quality of life deteriorated. "Each one is out for himself and we cannot carry on in harmony inside or outside our apartment," a resident says.[68] As the social contract dissolved, residents struggled to facilitate a smooth transition to ownership; a few disavowed it.

Residents' criticism of the government ranged from a sense of abandonment to the lack of preparation that one questions:

> Now that this is in our hands we may turn it into something great, but like everything else, we have to work hard. Above all we need organization and creativity. The [government agency] did not leave us with any experience there, so we can't even get organized. We now have to start a process of planning, when the [agency] should have done all that. The old administration should have started meeting with us a year before leaving, because they had the moral authority. Today it's an uphill battle.[69]

Suggesting that successful transitions were contingent upon state support, the autonomous organizations that best addressed their buildings' needs were those that received aid from the government. The occupant owners of one building pooled their resources to address water issues, garbage collection, elevator maintenance, and painting. So bad was the conflict and payment default in other buildings that some maintenance companies resigned from their projects.[70] Anger informed many people's nostalgia: "Of course people were upset, pissed off, and they wished the [government] had not abandoned the place, that things would be as they were."[71] Precipitated by an economic crisis, the Mexican government's decision to implement such neoliberal economic strategies as privatizing state-owned enterprises dramatically altered the lives of those who previously had enjoyed the state's largesse. In light of such a stark contrast, it is hardly surprising that residents harkened back to an idealized past.

Socioeconomic Class

Like the Mexican middle-class oral histories, many working-class accounts intersperse instances of solidarity in narratives about conflict. Given their subordinate positions, working-class people often recall interactions in which they contested or capitulated to authority.[72] To understand their movement, Argentine scholars conducted oral history interviews with *piqueteros* (picketers) who blocked traffic to protest the neoliberal economic reforms of the 1990s that increased poverty and unemployment. The scholars' goal was to inject alienated voices into the national debate, as María Marta Aversa and Graciela Browarnik explain: "There was talk of pauperism but not of the poor, of unemployment but not of the unemployed, of exclusion but not of the excluded."[73] For *piqueteros*, the street was one aspect of their lives they could control, even if only fleetingly before police came to remove their barriers. The 1990s *piqueteros'* sense of being menaced by authorities and subjugated in public spaces echoes that of an Argentine interviewee of a much earlier generation who recalled working-class people having to maintain "an obstinate silence" in the 1930s:

> You felt you didn't have rights to anything, everything seemed to be a favour they did for you through the church or some charity. . . . Another thing I remember about the thirties is that I always felt strange when I went to the city, downtown Buenos Aires—like you didn't belong there, which was stupid but you felt that they were looking down on you, that you weren't dressed right. The police there threatened you like animals.[74]

Complex in its constitution and behavior, the Argentine working class enjoyed considerable sway but also adhered to the status quo at different points in the twentieth century.[75] Like many histories from the margins, working-class testimonies often tack between agency and acquiescence.

In an example of how oral histories reveal exploitation that otherwise might remain obscure, survivors of the 1932 massacre in El Salvador explain how dire conditions reinforced their poverty. With her children starving, a woman asked a neighbor for yucca; he replied that "he would be glad to give her yucca, but in exchange for the legal papers of ownership to her land. And so for a few pieces of yucca her property passed to his hands."[76] Even meticulous land records would be unlikely to capture the catalyst for that expropriation, which reverberated through the woman's family for generations.

Despite the tendency for workers to highlight confrontations with superiors, oral histories also reveal the potential for workplace symbiosis. As demanding as their seamstress labor was, women who worked at the INTECO factory in Patagonia in the 1970s came to identify with it. When a military patrol came looking for a worker accused of being an insurgent, the manager stalled the military boss in his office and had the worker evacuated in a private car and given money for his escape.[77] During a time when the military disappeared thousands of people, such acts went a long way in cementing relations between workers and management. Female workers also appreciated the factory's concession to let them work nine-hour shifts and forgo the half-day Saturdays so they would have more time to do their domestic chores and be with their families.

Complex and often contentious, intraclass relations are readily discernible through oral histories. A shop-floor ethos could motivate workers, as a Chilean miner recalls: "Among the workers there was a certain competitiveness that made them, well, 'I'm *agallado* (strong, brave, clever, enterprising)

because I can carry so much. I worked this much, I advanced that much. . . . '
[T]here are workers . . . who are truly animals for work."[78] Another observes,

> That's what makes the miners different, you see? For their form of being at work, for their system of work and what the atmosphere there is like. Traditionally the miner has always distinguished himself for being a *roto chorro* (cool *roto*), like we say, *un roto macanudo* (first-rate *roto*) . . . *un hombre sobresaliente* (a distinctive man/a man who stands out) because . . . earning money at work makes him different, makes him be seen in a different way.[79]

Such pride in work allowed miners to appropriate the pejorative term *roto* (broken one) and imbue it with diligence, self-respect, and masculinity.[80]

A shared class position did not ensure solidarity, however. A supporter of land reform considers detractors traitors: "They didn't want [expropriations] because they were accommodated, taken care of by the *patrón*, and felt their situation was just a little bit better than everybody else's."[81] Looking back on Allende's overthrow, the reversal of agrarian reform, and the retrenchment of workers' rights during Pinochet's dictatorship, some rural workers criticized the reform: "It was crazy! . . . We had a decent relationship with the *patrón*—he was so scared of the Communists that he gave into almost everything we wanted. . . . Sure, I would have liked to have been my own boss, too, [but they] weren't thinking with their heads."[82] Such differences fueled animosity. A former Chilean union officer observes, "The conflict wasn't so much with the *patrón*, but between us . . . [a] hate among us, a hate among [union and political] leaders so strong—a deadly, deadly hate."[83]

At times, rank-and-file members' motives and perceptions provide detailed insights that contradict contemporary portrayals of labor movements. As she listened to former industrial workers recall their demands to dismiss abusive superiors and ensure "good treatment," Farnsworth-Alvear observed that Colombian strikers did not frame their struggle as one between capital and labor. Contemporary newspaper accounts failed to convey that nuance because journalists who focused their reporting on demands for higher wages did not appreciate the significance of the emotional claim shared by workers who had been abused by supervisors. Abstract analysis frequently fades into the background as personal struggles come to light in people's memories.[84] "We didn't fight because it was in style. I fought because I was poor and had no chance to go to school, and that either kills you from hunger or kills you from ignorance," confides a Guatemalan.[85]

In the absence of documentary evidence from workers' perspectives, oral history can be a crucial corrective to extant sources' distortions. Unemployed, landless, and struggling to support themselves and their families, Ecuadorans living on the southern coast invaded the UFCO's Tenguel hacienda in March 1962. Convinced that Cuban communists coordinated the movement, contemporary journalists claimed workers shot pistols, threw

Molotov cocktails, and dynamited the superintendent's house. Such reports contrast sharply with accounts of participants who remember a relatively peaceful and orderly expropriation of the plantation. Even as he concedes that what really happened may never be clear, Striffler argues, "Newspaper accounts probably tell us more about growing urban middle-class fears of communism and the peasantry than they do about the invasion of the hacienda."[86] All sources are subjective; by introducing biases of those who otherwise remain on the margins of history, oral history can interrogate archival materials and official histories.

While some individuals and groups eschewed ideology, others embraced it. Indicating how diverse activists' experiences were, some credited the Communist Party with educating them. An Argentine woman explains, "If you do not have theoretical and philosophical elements, [you] just [have] loose ideas that fail to offer a solution to the problem."[87] The potential for righting social injustices compelled many women to dedicate their lives to the party, another says: "Days and nights we were involved in the work of organizing laborers and making them understand that the organization helps them more than any other thing."[88] By bringing her child to meetings with her, an Argentine woman balanced work, activism, and motherhood, which was especially difficult because "during that time the work was clandestine."[89] At times, activism and motherhood seemed at odds. Maria, a member of the Ejército Revolucionario del Pueblo (People's Revolutionary Army), notes that her struggle "on behalf of the next generation" compelled her to expose her young daughter to dangerous situations.[90] Union members had to be careful because "in each meeting, there were spies . . . [who] would put you on a black list because you were a communist."[91]

For some, charisma more than social conditions or ideology catalyzed their participation. A Cuban proclaims, "If Fidel is a Communist, so am I."[92] Affiliation was often more personal than political. At times it was not political at all. Flummoxed by the accusation that he was a communist, an Argentine labor activist responds, "Bolsheviks? But how? I was always a Peronist. . . . I never got involved in politics."[93]

Even in organizations defined by particular ideologies, participants did not necessarily share motives or inspiration. Within Argentina's Communist Party, militants and Trotskyites understood and approached their political activism differently. While militants' disdain for theory was a manifestation of their "anti-intellectual humility," Trotskyites' pride in their knowledge of scientific socialism was an indication of their pride in intellectual acumen.[94] Even as they expressed frustration and a sense of loss, insurgents framed their involvement as "the best moment of their lives."[95] "I have a lot of pain and a lot of pride in my soul. . . . I do not regret anything. . . . I ache for the fallen, I miss the disappeared, and I am saddened by those who do not know how to rescue their own past of dignity and struggle. But I am sure that . . . with our struggle, our efforts and with our sacrifice we showed the way," reflects an insurgent.[96]

In Chile, oral history research has revealed how urban groups became politicized.[97] Conducting interviews shortly before the 1973 coup, historian Peter Winn heard from workers who, acting upon Allende's promise to empower them, socialized their workplaces, which destabilized the government.[98] "We have to break the laws if we want a workers' government in the future. If we are not able to pass over this legal wall that the reactionaries have built, we will never be able to do anything because there is no law that favors the workers. In order to achieve justice, we have to go beyond the limits of the law," explains one worker to development studies scholar Cristóbal Kay.[99] For workers, a sense of euphoria and empowerment permeated the short-lived socialist government.

Detractors point out that the benefits were short lived. "No one knew how to take advantage of the opportunity, they were all well here, they had nice things in their homes, and they bought various changes of clothes and shoes during the year. They became so comfortable that they threw things away when they broke, they did not fix them. There in the ravine they threw boots, clothes, shoes. Afterwards, when everything ended, they went down to collect their things anew," explains one woman.[100] With estate owners hosting open-bar barbecues for military officials and local police to celebrate the day's detentions, laborers were worse off after the 1973 coup.[101]

Sexuality Struggles

From comparative studies of sexual rights movements to social and cultural histories of lesbians and gays, scholars are using oral histories to reframe historical reconstructions to include gay and lesbian perspectives.[102] Oral history research also has revealed how heterosexual behavior has been reinforced. To underscore the importance of masculinity and heterosexuality in railway work and culture, for example, railroad workers in Puebla, Mexico, forced a colleague they presumed to be gay to dance with women while they laughed at him.[103] Oppositional responses such as poor Argentine gays' and "transvestites'" development of the term *putez* to signify sexual diversity seldom gained widespread support.[104] Even in Brazil, where conceptualizing sexuality on a continuum facilitated and was fostered by the social mixture of straight and gay men, sexual permissiveness on a scale rarely found in other nations in the Americas did not necessarily translate into broad social acceptance of homosexuality.[105] "There was a group of a half dozen middle-class boys who . . . attacked people for the simple fact that they had an effeminate appearance," recalls one Brazilian.[106] At times, violence escalated to murder.[107] Faced with possible prosecution if discovered, gays and lesbians in Cuba and Brazil kept their parties quiet so as not to draw the attention of neighbors who might call the police and complain of "immoral" behavior.[108]

Familial rejection was particularly painful. "The comments began when I was ten years old," recalls an interviewee who says his father never accepted him. "And people made fun of me! . . . And [they] said, my God, your son is gay and everything. And from there on I understood that my dad was ignorant. Then he . . . threw me out of the house."[109] Regardless of whether families were supportive, gay and transgender individuals faced pressure to conform to heterosexuality and gender norms in public schools where teachers encouraged effeminate boys to be more masculine. When gays reported being victims of violence, the Brazilian police refused to record the crimes, let alone help them.[110] As a Cuban man living with AIDS explains, gays in Cuba have faced similar challenges: "We don't have a place [to go]. We don't have anything. So the police don't treat us as people, they treat us as homosexuals. So they send you to the station where they charge you."[111] When men appropriated cafes or restaurants as gay hangouts, proprietors often ran them off. The combination of police and public persecution compelled many men to suppress their sexuality in certain contexts.[112] "I am gay outside the [factory] gate. From the moment I walk in the gate, I'll act like a man. I'll work and I will show that I have ability," Márcio declares.[113] Like female laborers in male-dominated industries, gays often had to outperform their colleagues to prove their worth.

For some, persecution contravened perceptions of liberty and equality. Yolanda, a Cuban lesbian who came from a working-class family and was a university student in the 1960s, recalls her devastating disillusionment:

> Imagine what it meant for a young person who's there in that glorious and ethical moment of the Revolution, which was freedom, which was a marvel. . . . The arrival of the Revolution, for us, imagine it, was like a fairy tale. . . . But women [lesbians] were purged . . . You see discrimination. And this Cuban culture, there's a very homophobic culture. . . . That was my moment of discrimination, against homosexuality. It was very cruel being at the university, suddenly saying to someone, "So where's María? I haven't seen her for a week." And they say, "Ah, but didn't you know? María was kicked out." That, for a young person—I say it and admit it and at some point I'm going to write it down. For me that was traumatic.[114]

In her narrative, Yolanda suggests that she avoided persecution because she dressed a "certain way," while friends who appeared and acted butch were targeted. The same was true for men; a young man who plucked his eyebrows was exiled from Cuba. Even for those who were not gay, the regime's and society's homophobia contributed to their political disenchantment. So prevalent was gay denigration that one straight Cuban was "totally surprised by the friendship and affection that he got from those guys who were homosexuals."[115]

At times persecution emboldened homosexual subcultures. Dubbing themselves Putos Peronistas (Peronist Faggots), a group of men responded to their double oppression of poverty and homosexuality with activism. Inspired by "the desire of changing things," a gay activist explains, "I fell in love with the capacity for struggle, the magic, the protection given by Peronism."[116] Since homophobia was institutionalized and pervasive, developing a thick skin was crucial.[117] "They make fun, make a joke, a sting. I try not to give importance to it. Because if I give importance to what people say, I would never leave the home," contends a young gay migrant.[118] The story of an Argentine who "was a beloved faggot in the 'hood' because . . . he helped the poor" demonstrates that some gays and lesbians were revered figures in their communities.[119]

Since sexuality is but one aspect of people's identities, tensions and violence among gay and lesbian populations are not surprising.[120] Class frequently divided gays. Interviewees like twenty-five-year-old Iara, who worked "cleaning other people's dirt," distinguish between their lives in poor townships and those of middle- and upper-class gays who live in wealthy Buenos Aires neighborhoods. So ostracized were poor transgender individuals that Ayala describes their place of refuge as being "marginalized."[121]

With its nightlife and concentrations of openly gay men, Rio de Janiero was attractive to many young men who moved there to escape expectations of heterosexual mores. Having experienced arduous physical labor in their rural communities, many appreciated the comparatively lighter workloads and modern conveniences cities offered.[122] By establishing alternative families, many gay men found strong social support networks in cities. "I arrived here all alone, and I felt the need to have a family here. People came to Rio crying out for a family," one explains.[123] Offering less fettered places to claim as their own, streets and beaches allowed men to circulate in gay communities without spending money. Compared to Cuba, where the police harassed, hit, and arrested gays who gathered in parks, squares, and on the streets, Rio de Janiero was welcoming. The combination of discrimination and Havana's severe housing shortage meant there were few places where gay men could have sex, while in a manifestation of how class shaped homosexual lives, middle-class and wealthy gays in Rio de Janiero enjoyed private intimacy.[124]

Through oral history research, scholars have studied how social and sexual relations have changed over time in ways that both challenged and adhered to gender conventions. As more men came to enjoy a fuller range of sexual practices in the 1970s, Brazilian conceptions of male homosexuality broadened from the 1950s-era dichotomy of partners being either active or passive in sexual acts.[125] Indicating the extent to which that distinction defined whether a man was considered gay, in Cuba a man could "defend his manliness by [actively] engaging in homosexual acts."[126] Although many maintained that dichotomy, by the 1960s, a new sexual identity emerged that resembled the more egalitarian approach among gay couples in the United States that dated to the 1930s and 1940s. By recognizing both partners as women, lesbians similarly downplayed dichotomous distinctions in their relationships.[127] Even as fluid identities slowly caught on, some men deployed the old dichotomy to distinguish themselves from gays.[128]

Shifting perceptions in one realm often were predicated upon the adherence to norms in another. Men who embraced broad definitions of masculinity frequently upheld gender codes of femininity; indeed, the latter facilitated the former. Some men had sex with men because their girlfriends were expected to remain virgins until marriage or were not interested in alternative forms of sex. "Some women didn't like to suck, didn't want to be [anally] penetrated. A *bicha* [faggot] had sex on her mind. She'd do anything. These men fell into their hands," explains an interviewee.[129] Although Brazilian men enjoyed increased sexual liberation, some social norms changed little.

In some countries, lesbian, gay, bisexual, transgender, and queer (and/or questioning; LGBTQ) communities have lost ground. In others, relations have improved. Born in 1922, one Cuban man recalls that during the 1970s, homosexuals were denied jobs, but "today, they're working."[130] Those who openly identified as homosexual were more ambiguous about how life had changed. "From what they tell me, gay people, years ago it was worse than now. . . . For being homosexual, for having a bit of powder on your face you were put in prison for years. Now it's got a bit better but it's still the same, practically the same because when they want to take you, for example, they take all the transvestites when they want," says a gay Cuban man born in 1970.[131] Narratives of progress often are peppered with accounts of oppression. Despite changes in domestic violence policy and legislation, the LGBTQ movement, and Brazilian nationalism during the twentieth century, cultural understandings about race, gender, and sexuality remain mired in inequality; blacks, women, and homosexuals continue to face discrimination.[132]

Gendered and Patriarchal Pasts

Similar to the way heterosexual norms discount homosexuality, masculine paradigms undermine gender parity. Official histories, school textbooks, and other historical narratives perpetuate patriarchal privileges by downplaying if not eliding women's contributions. In an example of oral histories capturing how men reconstitute their own positions of power, a refrigeration worker with political aspirations in Buenos Aires explains, "They forced me to give up my candidacy so that a man could occupy that position."[133] Sharing an urgent sense of political purpose based partly on an understanding that voices silenced facilitate oppression, feminist history and oral history frequently work in tandem. Marked by "dislocations, inversions, gender instability, and heterodox expressions," women's voices are as diverse as any other group's.[134] Brazilian and Chilean feminists' militancy inspired their newly minted feminist identities, while feminism failed to gain much traction among indigenous women in the Guatemalan highlands. Maya women's historical narratives portray racism and poverty as more formidable impediments than sexism to justice and equality.[135]

Regardless of whether they were part of broader movements, individual women often charted pioneering courses. Absent a collective women's movement, let alone much discussion about feminism, in 1929, Ecuador became one of the first Latin American countries to recognize female suffrage.[136] In a society that discouraged female autonomy, women were hardly passive observers. María Luisa Salazar, the director of the Colegio Normal Manuel Cañizares in the 1980s, explains how her mother became one of the first Ecuadorean women to study education:

> Before Eloy Alfaro became president [1895–1901, 1906–11], General Terán of the liberal army received help from my grandmother, a young widow with two daughters, when his troops stopped at her rural property in Patate. Eloy Alfaro heard of this and sent my grandmother a note to thank her and ask her to come to Quito. When she went, he told her: "A *colegio* is going to be opened and I want to give you the opportunity to educate your daughters. Women in the future will need to be educated; not just men, but women too." My grandmother looked frankly at her situation and decided to educate her daughters in the Normal [school], despite the recriminations of her conservative family: "You are going to lose everything, you are allying yourself with the liberals; if you are going to give your daughters a Godless education, then just say good-bye, we can no longer recognize you."[137]

Such painful advances did not necessarily guarantee autonomy, though. Because her husband wanted her to stay home, the interviewee's mother never taught. Even when mothers worked hard to create the conditions for their daughters' independence, their daughters' husbands and fathers often curtailed it.

Women's perspectives alter historical reconstructions. Confiding that their behavior led to the spread of syphilis, Mexican railroad workers waxed nostalgically about earning enough money to have extramarital affairs and father children by different women. Sexual prowess could bolster working-class men's reputations. When women complained about male infidelity, their husbands often beat them.[138] For working-class women, contracting sexually transmitted diseases was part of a broader problem. Suffering marked a shared femininity among many railroad workers' wives, who recalled going without food and other basic necessities while their husbands feted their mistresses. At the same time, some daughters exuded a sense of pride as railroad women.[139] The same forces that wreaked havoc in some women's lives buoyed the lives of others.

Discourses and images of masculinity cut many ways. By legitimating their sense of patriarchal authority over their wives and children, Trujillo's patriarchal social contract of protection in return for subservience and loyalty enhanced Dominican men's commitment to the regime.[140] As a result, many cast his regime in a soft light. Conversely, the regime's reinforcement of patriarchal relations and traditional gender roles led many women, like this interviewee, to be more critical than men: "Without the possibility of outside employment, women lived like slaves, since one had to take care of the household things, waiting on one's husband, but now no. Now there is more liberty."[141] Even as men enjoyed privileged positions vis-à-vis women during Trujillo's regime, at times his power eviscerated them. To honor the national patriarch and underscore the local patriarch's power, most Dominican peasants had an image of Trujillo in their homes. One read, "In this house, Trujillo is boss." An interviewee describes how "there were men who cried because of this plaque."[142] Sold at a price few rural workers could afford, the plaque affected middle-class and elite men more than poor patriarchs. When a member of the national guard complained about it, a neighbor asked him why he kept it. "Why don't you get rid of it, tough guy?" the guardsman bellowed.[143] Gender and class intersected in ways that could make privileged people feel as powerless as the poor.

Some aspects of gender permeated different socioeconomic levels. Independent of their class, women in São Paulo received social education that oriented them toward "good customs" and being respectful and obedient to their elders and spouses.[144] While each class seemed to have its own "feminine habitus," complementarity between husbands and wives favored the former.[145] Although class distinctions often faded during incarceration, gender distinctions remained stark. Brazilian female inmates established more egalitarian relationships and a sense of solidarity, but Brazilian male prisoners adhered to hierarchical social relations in which one alpha male was the "sheriff."[146]

Without oral histories, gendered topics such as sexual relations, sex work, abortion, and birth control are hard to address.[147] In his study of labor and social relations at a Chilean mine, historian Thomas Klubock used oral histories because the archives revealed little about work-crew relations or family life.[148] Folk customs and local knowledge about menstruation and other aspects of sexuality also fall largely outside the written record.[149] Save letters, diaries, and judicial records describing rape, sodomy, adultery, and divorce, sex also tends to be obscure in archival records, in which people's voices generally are refracted through the lens of scribes. Some rural Chilean women used sex to flee oppressive marital or parental relationships, while others describe sex with their husbands as coercive and lament the lack of birth control or planning.[150] One woman notes, "It was easier to give in than put up a fight since [objection] would put him in a bad state of mind, and he might be drunk. [Sex] is part of what a wife owes her husband even if it was something he enjoys much more than she."[151]

Such inherently unequal gender relations help explain why some women have opted out of marriage. "Why have a husband? I fed my own children. I didn't need a man telling me what to do, how to raise my children, how to

Figure 6.2 Two couples in Calle Larga, Chile, ca. 1991
Photograph by David Carey Jr.

serve him. Husbands are abusive, they take advantage, make you a servant. I didn't want it. Thank you, no. I run my life myself," insists a rural *chilena*.[152] Faced with the injustices and inequalities of patriarchy, many women pursued income-producing activities and/or landownership that afforded them autonomy. At the same time, marriage did not necessitate female subservience. In spite of their husbands' opposition, many Argentine women worked in industries typically associated with men, such as meat-processing plants. By succeeding in such masculine spaces, they attenuated gendered power that favored male employees.[153]

Even in seemingly traditional female roles, women broke gender conventions. The 1952 winner of the Argentine National Queen of Work contest explains, "This was not a beauty contest, it was [about] dignifying the female worker."[154] In a testament to her commitment to the working class, the 1974 *reina* declined offers to pursue a career in beauty and television. Promoting the working class motivated many contestants.[155]

By deploying gendered tropes and norms, women could advance their movements. Such was the case in standoffs between the Brazilian national police and rubber tappers. María Mendes recalls how she used her reputation as a well-known and respected woman to distract the police while they inspected her, thereby allowing her comrades to sneak bags containing arms past a checkpoint.[156] In an example of how women deployed gendered tropes to encourage sustainability, they analogized Brazil nut harvesting with breastfeeding to prove resources could be extracted without destroying the provider. "Rubber tappers who behaved as gardeners of the forest paid tribute to those mothers," notes Brazilian historian Marcos Montysuma.[157]

Women who threw their support behind strikes, occupations, and other protests often injected gendered discourse into contentious intraclass relations. "The women were stronger than the men. . . . They [told] men, 'Don't be hens, be men and stand up for your rights, for your family, like we are,'" a rural Chileno recalls admiringly.[158] Such prodding encouraged some men to be more radical, though they seldom applied their workplace struggles for justice to the home.

When told from women's perspectives, the effects of indigenous patriarchy come into focus. Couched in concerns about the loss of ethnicity, many Maya parents refused to allow their daughters to attend school, where they would be subjected to assimilationist pressures. "We are blind because we cannot speak, but I am not the only one. My whole generation was kept out of school so we all struggle to speak Spanish," notes a female elder.[159] Maya women's acute sense of how monolingualism handicaps them encourages a broad conceptualization of the structural conditions under which silencing operates. Historical silencing is active and deliberate.[160] Indigenous women's oral histories explode the misconception that indigenous knowledge systems are uniform. Alternating between pride in their perpetuation of cultural markers such as indigenous languages and clothing and frustration at their illiteracy and monolingualism, women who recalled being denied an education hinted at the complex and often contradictory corollaries of indigenous patriarchy.[161] Gender and ethnicity intertwined in ways that could both constrain and embolden women.

Neither submissive nor autonomous, women often lived in the liminal space between oppression and empowerment. On the Ecuadoran coast, women facilitated projects that led to the provision of such basic rights as potable water, education, and medicine, but they seldom assumed leadership roles. By the 1970s, they began to form their own organizations because, as one woman explains, "women played a key role in these struggles but the men dominated the organizations. So we formed our own organization. We wanted to remain part of the struggle for land but have an independent organization. This gave us some strength. . . . But the men remained in control."[162]

Without discounting the challenges of balancing domestic responsibilities and workplace demands, women pointed to the ways employment improved their lives. Regardless of their subordination in relation to their bosses and foremen, women coffee sorters in Veracruz, Mexico, generally were satisfied with their employment, especially the financial freedom it afforded them. Their leadership positions in the union and ability to secure better working conditions and wages buoyed their sense of empowerment.[163]

Even in scenarios where women's wage labor altered gender dynamics in the home, equality was elusive. Although Patagonian female factory workers' husbands did household chores, they never assumed domestic labor as their responsibility. Balancing home and work responsibilities was particularly stressful for single mothers. "One has that worry! How many times? One is working, and I did not know if they [her children] arrived safely or had been hurt," recounts a single mother.[164] With good reason, working women feared for their children's safety in their absence. Left unattended as their mother worked, an eight-year-old and her sister nearly drowned when a river swept them away.[165] Despite such dangers, most women appreciated the opportunity to balance workplace and domestic demands. Unlike *colombianas* who retired from industrial labor after they married or had children, neither life choice was an obstacle for Patagonian women at INTECO because the company integrated work and home life. Women also appreciated the lifelong friendships and sense of being valued that resulted from their factory work.[166]

Employment did not necessarily empower women in the home or society. Explaining that she worked irregularly on plantations because her husband's income was not enough to support the family, an Ecuadoran woman concedes that "the woman today has to work just for the family to survive. But we are not workers. Not like the men."[167] As women took on paid positions, some considered their contributions supplementary rather than primary and thus shied away from unions or other forms of activism.

Ethnic Expressions

Like gender, sexuality, and class, ethnicity shapes historical perspectives in ways that often compel narrators to recognize their subordination without discounting their agency. With their exclusion from national narratives that focus on European or mestizo identities and histories, indigenous people, Afro-Latin American, Asian-Latin American, and other groups share their histories among themselves; until recently, few historians had accessed those pasts. Ironically, assimilationist pressures frequently have countervailing effects. Working in tandem with the prestige afforded light-skinned society, national politics and economics marked by domination and exploitation often reinforce rather than dilute ethnic distinctions. Despite being subjected to forced relocations in the Amazon, Wakuénais do not portray themselves as passive victims of "white greed"; rather, they highlight their refusal to assimilate and ability to find refuge in remote areas. Political and economic elites dominated their nation and reaped its resources, but Wakuénais maintained autochthonous narratives and physical spaces.[168]

To embolden their autonomy, indigenous groups tack between rejecting and appropriating national discourse. Instead of recognizing themselves as "Indians," many indigenous people identify with their specific cultural and linguistic groups. In turn, draining its denigration, indigenous leaders have appropriated "Indian" to expand their representative power and distinguish themselves from nonindigenous nationals.

Among ethnic groups, manifestations of modernization have elicited diverse responses. While many marginalized peoples embraced education as a means to improve their lot, Mixtecs and Zapotecs approached it as a tool that could help stave off threats to their culture and customs. Educated indigenous youths who balanced personal ambitions with community obligations weighed the allure of progress against the responsibility to defend local traditions.[169] Ethnicity, education, and economic change often engendered contested individual and communal goals.

As charged as many race relations are, oral histories reveal how people have overcome differences. Set against a backdrop of endemic racism, Salvadoran union leaders' willingness to travel on foot to rural communities and eat, drink, and dance with indigenous workers went a long way in solidifying alliances. Indigenous informants who attended the gatherings as young children recall the festive air of uplifting and emotionally charged meetings that often morphed into fiestas, which facilitated "the emergence of a new form of cross-class sociability . . . [and] new identity as equals."[170] Although urban organizers did not advocate for indigenous issues, their antiracist stance hinted that their emancipatory agenda included indigenous rights, which in turn facilitated indigenous leaders' ability to assume leadership roles in the movement. Even indigenous militants who resented racism worked with poor *ladinos* from other towns to achieve their shared goals.

Racism cut many ways. According to a former Tela Railroad Company employee, the UFCO did not allow its foreign white employees to fraternize with black or Hispanic Central Americans. Since managers dismissed employees who had affairs with hired help, some employees kept their relationships with local women secret. Social relations in enclave communities likewise enforced racial purity. After a Scottish engineer began a relationship with a local woman of color, the white women made his life so miserable that the couple moved out of the compound. Workers also drew clear racial and linguistic lines. A West Indian domestic servant insisted she only worked for "English" employers; she refused to eat, let alone prepare Spanish food. Because they could speak and read English, West Indian servants enjoyed an advantage over their Hispanic counterparts.[171]

Initiated by immigration, racial distinctions imbued with national differences also marginalized people. While their reasons for migrating from Japan to Peru ranged from a thirst for adventure to escaping World War II, Japanese Peruvians shared the hardship of finding good employment and running businesses amid discrimination and violence such as the 1940 anti-Japanese riot in Lima and Callao that destroyed many Japanese businesses and homes. The extent to which the intersections of ethnic, national, and regional differences affected people's lives can be discerned within the Japanese-Peruvian community, where mainland Japanese ostracized those from the recently annexed island of Okinawa.[172]

For women, the syncretism of Japanese and Peruvian societies was both empowering and constraining. In contrast to the women who felt isolated in their new homes and excluded from male-dominated educational and professional opportunities, some women assumed important responsibilities in family businesses; a few embraced entrepreneurship. Though exceptional in her peripatetic nature, the experience of this mother of seven children is illuminating:

> When I arrived in Peru, I went directly to the Hacienda Villa and we began to raise chickens and pigs. . . . I moved to Miraflores and opened an ice cream shop, then I worked two years in my brother's store. I subsequently opened a bakery, closed it and converted it into a store selling chicken. . . . I also opened a public bathroom business where I worked for 5 years but since it didn't earn any money, I sold it and began working in the restaurant again.[173]

Breaking traditional gender roles, some Japanese Brazilian women similarly enjoyed upward mobility in São Paulo. After her husband's death, one woman's family urged her to return to Japan with her young child. Her decision to stay in São Paulo facilitated her success and her child's education.[174]

To mitigate their children's assimilation, Japanese Brazilians established their own schools. As the dream of returning home faded from reality

Figure 6.3 Japanese Peruvian men filing by armed military police. New Orleans, LA, ca. 1943.

Publication of photographs furnished by the National Archives Still Picture Branch

and Brazilian authorities sought to establish control over Japanese schools, immigrants established sports clubs and other cultural institutions to maintain their distinct identities. After World War II, however, some immigrant families forged new ways of being Japanese by integrating into Brazilian society.[175] Although they faced persecution and discrimination, Japanese Brazilians fared better than their counterparts elsewhere in Latin America.

Tragically, as Japanese Latin Americans came to establish themselves in their host countries and negotiate the challenges of their ethnic and national distinctions, US hysteria about foreigners from Axis nations extended beyond its borders. During World War II, the United States worked with twelve Latin American and Caribbean nations—among them the Dominican Republic, Haiti, Mexico, and Bolivia—to deport Latin American Germans, Italians, and Japanese and their descendants to US war camps. When their bank accounts were frozen and business and labor opportunities closed off, family members had little choice but to join their deported husbands and fathers. A former internee from Peru describes the events: "Grandfather . . . had gone fishing with his friends, and when he came back, he was caught by the police who were waiting for him at the entrance of the home. They took him to the police station. . . . After they took Grandfather, no one sold us flour. We had to close the bakery."[176] Upon arriving in the United States, deportees were stripped naked and sprayed with DDT. To steel themselves against such degrading experiences, Japanese Peruvians recreated their culture in the camps by carving *sanshins* (Okinawan banjo-like instruments) and making music boxes. In light of the many Japanese Peruvians who navigated assimilation in Peru by changing their names and refusing to teach their children Japanese, internees' reproduction of some aspects of their culture in the camps speaks to their sense of alienation there.[177]

Despite efforts to make the best of their plight and rebuild their lives after the war, Japanese Peruvians resented the way their incarceration derailed them. Augusto Kague shares why he continues to struggle for reparations:

> One cannot know what my life could have been, that is to say, my father had the idea that I would be a doctor, that I would study medicine, my brothers could have had a different destiny . . . but they took all those options away from us, not just us, they took away everything our families could have achieved, very intelligent and diligent people that could have been better off than what they are now.[178]

Since Peru refused to accept internees after the war, some children who only spoke Spanish were deported to Japan. Many of the three hundred Japanese Peruvians who fought to stay in the United States lived in poverty. Often restricted to menial labor, they had to learn yet another language, culture, and country. Mirroring the divisions among Japanese in Peru, once released, Japanese Latin Americans

Figure 6.4 Transfer to US internment camps. Italian, German, and Japanese residents of Latin America leave a temporary internment camp in the Panama Canal Zone to join their male relatives in US internment camps, April 7, 1942.

Courtesy of the San Francisco History Center, San Francisco Public Library

received little support from Japanese Americans. A former internee recounts his isolation: "When I was in high school [in Los Angeles], I had a Spanish accent. And being Okinawan [the discrimination] was double. So most of my friends were Latinos because they were much closer to us than the Nisei. The Nisei people . . . didn't want to have anything to do with us."[179]

As Japanese Peruvians' and Afro-Latin American testimonies suggest, some of the most bitter experiences with discrimination came from within their own ethnic groups. An oral history study of carnaval clubs reveals that some Afro-Brazilian clubs discriminated against darker-skinned members. Those clubs' short existence suggests the broader black community's censure of such behavior. Suggesting that discrimination at the intersections of race and class was more difficult to extricate, in the twenty-first century, Afro-Brazilians have continued to denigrate the oldest club, founded in 1917, because its members were mainly poor and working class. At the other end of the spectrum, prestigious clubs seldom allowed people who were not wealthy professionals to join.[180]

164 *Topical Oral History*

Although the themes touched upon here offer but a few examples of the crucial elements explored via topical oral history research, they demonstrate how perspectives that emerge from oral history interviews enrich not only our understanding of the past but also approaches to it. As people craft their own histories, broader historical narratives become more inclusive and compelling.

Notes

1. Gould and Lauria-Santiago, *To Rise in Darkness*, xi.
2. M. González, "Modernización capitalista," xiv; AVANCSO, *Se cambió el tiempo*, 15–334.
3. Bouvard, *Revolutionizing Motherhood*.
4. In Gasparini, *Montoneros*, 93. For similar pride in the Mexican military, see Camp, *Generals in the Palacio*, 167.
5. Schirmer, "Interviewing Military Officers," n.p.
6. Schirmer, *Guatemalan Military Project*.
7. Beato, *Disposición final*.
8. In Poniatowska, *Massacre in Mexico*, 220.
9. In Barrientos, "Narración, mujeres y memoria en el sur de Chile," 167.
10. M. González, "Man Who Brought Danger to the Village," 321.
11. Ibid., 319, 326–7.
12. In Barrientos, "Narración, mujeres y memoria en el sur de Chile," 169.
13. Huggins, Haritos-Fatouros, and Zimbardo, *Violence Workers*, 1–2; M. González, "Man Who Brought Danger to the Village," 328.
14. Levenson-Estrada, *Trade Unionists against Terror*, 2.
15. In M. González, "Man Who Brought Danger to the Village," 326.
16. In Levenson-Estrada, *Trade Unionists against Terror*, 3.
17. Gould and Lauria-Santiago, *To Rise in Darkness*.
18. D. Carey, *I Ask for Justice*, 153–81.
19. In Gould and Lauria-Santiago, *To Rise in Darkness*, 260.
20. Ibid.
21. Kaplan, *Taking Back the Streets*, 43.
22. Olivera Costa et al., *Memórias do exílio*.
23. In Araújo, "História oral, memória e reparação," 16.
24. In van Isschot, "Heart of Activism in Colombia," 244.
25. Ibid.
26. Dutrénit Bielous, *Diversidad partidaria y dictaduras*; Dutrénit Bielous, "Asuntos y temas partidarios," 151–6.
27. In Dutrénit Bielous, "Asuntos y temas partidarios," 152.
28. Ibid., 144, 158–61.
29. Dutrénit Bielous, "La memoria de los políticos," 88.
30. Caetano, "Prólogo," 12.
31. Dutrénit Bielous, "Del margen al centro del sistema político."
32. Dutrénit Bielous, *El maremoto militar*, 17–18, 20; Caetano, "Introducción general," 13–14, 16.
33. In Araújo, "História oral, memória e reparação," 12.
34. Ansaldi, "Continuidades y rupturas"; Araújo, "História oral, memória e reparação," 12.
35. Turits, *Foundations of Despotism*, 231.

36 Ibid., 212, 215–19, 223; D. Carey, *Our Elders Teach Us*, 195–219.
37 Turits, *Foundations of Despotism*, 211; D. Carey, *Our Elders Teach Us*, 206–11.
38 Turits, *Foundations of Despotism*, 210.
39 Ibid., 224.
40 Ibid., 227.
41 Wells, *Tropical Zion*, xix.
42 Ibid., 297.
43 Ibid., 339, 354 (quote).
44 Ibid., 208.
45 Stern, *Reckoning with Pinochet*; Stern, *Remembering Pinochet's Chile*.
46 La Serna, *Corner of the Living*, 9, 16–17.
47 Venegas Aguilera, "Cultura política y mujeres de sector popular," 133.
48 In Pensado Leglise, "Elements of Identity," 16.
49 Zolov, *Refried Elvis*, 105–7, 115.
50 Ibid., 99.
51 Ibid., 104.
52 Ibid., 123.
53 Necoechea Gracia, "From Favour to Right," 13.
54 Nash, *We Eat the Mines and the Mines Eat Us*, 107; Klubock, "Working-Class Masculinity," 454, 463n91; and *Contested Communities*, chapter 6.
55 In Lobato, *La vida en las fábricas*, 262.
56 In Mastrángelo, "'Mi abuela cantaba Bandiera Rossa,'" 7.
57 Nash, *We Eat the Mines and the Mines Eat Us*, 107.
58 Guimarães Neto, "Vira mundo, vira mundo"; "História, política e testemunho," 13; and "Espaços e tempos entrecruzados na história," 135–66.
59 Necoechea Gracia, "From Favour to Right"; Pensado Leglise, "Elements of Identity," 214.
60 Martínez Omaña, "Services, Management, and the Construction of Place," 6.
61 Ibid., 7.
62 Ibid., 8.
63 In Pensado Leglise, "Elements of Identity," 16.
64 Pensado Leglise, "Elements of Identity"; Martínez Omaña, "Services, Management, and the Construction of Place," 7.
65 In Pensado Leglise, "Elements of Identity," 16.
66 In Necoechea Gracia, "From Favour to Right," 13.
67 In Pensado Leglise, "Elements of Identity," 16.
68 In Martínez Omaña, "Services, Management, and the Construction of Place," 8.
69 In Pensado Leglise, "Elements of Identity," 17.
70 In Martínez Omaña, "Services, Management, and the Construction of Place," 8–9.
71 Ibid., 9.
72 Jelin and Vila, *Podría ser yo*, 171.
73 Aversa and Browarnik, "Herida profunda," 17.
74 In James, *Resistance and Integration*, 29.
75 Ibid., 103, 164, 257, 260.
76 Gould and Lauria-Santiago, *To Rise in Darkness*, xii.
77 Gatica, "Industrialización y proletarización," 136–7.
78 In Klubock, "Working-Class Masculinity," 441 (parentheses in original).
79 Ibid., 442.
80 Tinsman, *Partners in Conflict*, 40–1.

81 Ibid., 198.
82 Ibid., 259.
83 Ibid., 265.
84 Farnsworth-Alvear, *Dulcinea in the Factory*, 135–7. For a former Mexican railroad worker's critique of journalists, see Alegre, *Railroad Radicals in Cold War Mexico*, 165.
85 In Weld, *Paper Cadavers*, 154.
86 Striffler, *In the Shadows of State and Capital*, 97.
87 In Lobato, *Historia de las trabajadoras en la Argentina*, 255.
88 Ibid., 180.
89 Ibid.
90 Pozzi, "'En function de la nueva generación,'" 216.
91 In Lobato, *La vida en las fábricas*, 60.
92 In Hamilton, *Sexual Revolutions in Cuba*, 67.
93 In James, *Resistance and Integration*, 264.
94 Pozzi and Schneider, *Los setentistas*, 93.
95 Pozzi and Schneider, "Memoria y socialismo," 92.
96 Ibid., 100.
97 Garcés Durán, *Tomando su sitio*.
98 Winn, *Weavers of Revolution*.
99 Kay, "Agrarian Reform and the Class Struggle in Chile," 134.
100 In Barrientos, "Narración, mujeres y memoria en el sur de Chile," 173.
101 Barrientos, "'Y las enormes trilladoras vinieron,'" 129; Barrientos, "Narración, mujeres y memoria en el sur de Chile," 174.
102 Laverdi, "Vivencias urbanos de jóvenes muchachos homosexuales"; Dehesa, *Queering the Public Sphere in Mexico and Brazil*; J. Green, *Beyond Carnival*; Diez, *Politics of Gay Marriage in Latin America*; Encarnación, "Latin America's Gay Rights Revolution."
103 Alegre, *Railroad Radicals in Cold War Mexico*, 85.
104 Médica and Villegas, "A la vera de la Ruta 3." Since interviewees use the term transvestite, I adhere to their preference over the term transgender, which is the more common term in the United States.
105 Dehesa, *Queering the Public Sphere in Mexico and Brazil*, 20.
106 In J. Green, *Beyond Carnival*, 158–9.
107 Benjamin and Mendonça, *Benedita da Silva*, 96.
108 Hamilton, *Sexual Revolutions in Cuba*, 179; J. Green, *Beyond Carnival*, 183 (quote).
109 Laverdi, "Vivencias urbanos de jóvenes muchachos homosexuales," 128.
110 Médica and Villegas, "A la vera de la Ruta 3"; Laverdi, "Cidade, trabalho e homossexualidade vividos"; Laverdi, "Vivencias urbanos de jóvenes muchachos homosexuales," 131.
111 Hamilton, *Sexual Revolutions in Cuba*, 164, 178–9, 196 (quote).
112 J. Green, *Beyond Carnival*, 153; Laverdi, "Vivencias urbanos de jóvenes muchachos homosexuales," 132.
113 Laverdi, "Cidade, trabalho e homossexualidade vividos," 10.
114 In Hamilton, *Sexual Revolutions in Cuba*, 139–40.
115 Ibid., 73–4, 122 (quote), 138, 142, 145, 188.
116 In Médica and Villegas, "A la vera de la Ruta 3," 11.
117 Hamilton, *Sexual Revolutions in Cuba*, 178, 189.
118 In Laverdi, "Cidade, trabalho e homossexualidade vividos," 8.
119 Médica and Villegas, "A la vera de la Ruta 3," 9.
120 A. Allen, *Violence and Desire in Brazilian Lesbian Relationships*.

121 Médica and Villegas, "A la vera de la Ruta 3," 13.
122 Laverdi, "Vivencias urbanos de jóvenes muchachos homosexuales," 124–7, 133; J. Green, *Beyond Carnival*, 149–50.
123 In J. Green, *Beyond Carnival*, 178.
124 Ibid., 97, 153–9.
125 Ibid., 270.
126 Hamilton, *Sexual Revolutions in Cuba*, 120.
127 J. Green, *Beyond Carnival*, 7; Hamilton, *Sexual Revolutions in Cuba*, 187.
128 J. Green, *Beyond Carnival*, 7; Hamilton, *Sexual Revolutions in Cuba*, 161–2, 164, 169, 187.
129 In J. Green, *Beyond Carnival*, 187.
130 In Hamilton, *Sexual Revolutions in Cuba*, 125.
131 Ibid., 146–7. Reinaldo Arenas documents the persecution of gays under Castro's regime in *Antes que anochezca*.
132 Allen, *Violence and Desire in Brazilian Lesbian Relationships*.
133 In Lobato, *Historia de las trabajadoras en la Argentina*, 184.
134 Lobato, "Recordar, recuperar, conservar," 7.
135 Woitowicz and Pedro, "O movimento feminista durante a ditadura militar"; D. Carey, *Engendering Mayan History*.
136 Clark, *Gender, State, and Medicine in Highland Ecuador*, 22–3.
137 Ibid., 10.
138 Tinsman, *Partners in Conflict*, 65; Klubock, "Working-Class Masculinity," 448; Alegre, *Railroad Radicals in Cold War Mexico*, 78–9, 95.
139 Alegre, *Railroad Radicals in Cold War Mexico*, 83–4, 88, 95.
140 Turits, *Foundations of Despotism*, 219.
141 Ibid., 220.
142 Ibid., 229.
143 Ibid.
144 Siqueira de Souza Campos, "Mulheres de diferentes classes sociais em São Paulo," 185.
145 Ibid., 179–96.
146 Araújo, "História oral, memória e reparação," 15.
147 Stein, "La historia oral y la creación de los documentos históricos," 140.
148 Klubock, *Contested Communities*, 15.
149 Hamilton, *Sexual Revolutions in Cuba*, 84–5.
150 Tinsman, *Partners in Conflict*, 57, 75, 78.
151 Ibid., 58.
152 Ibid., 74.
153 Lobato, "Voces subalternas de la memoria," 151–3.
154 In Lobato, "Introducción," 10.
155 Lobato, Damilokou, and Tornay, "Las reinas del trabajo bajo el peronismo," 119; Crespo, "Madres, esposas, reinas," 171.
156 Montysuma, "Lecturas de género y medio ambiente," 172–3.
157 Ibid., 177.
158 In Tinsman, *Partners in Conflict*, 199.
159 Ixchipix, Interview by Ixk'at, June 29, 2001.
160 Trouillot, *Silencing the Past*, 48.
161 D. Carey, *Engendering Mayan History*, 177–206; Gould and Lauria-Santiago, *To Rise in Darkness*, 261.
162 In Striffler, *In the Shadows of State and Capital*, 189.

168 *Topical Oral History*

163 Fowler-Salamini, *Working Women, Entrepreneurs, and the Mexican Revolution*. For a similar phenomenon in Panama, see Camargo Ríos, "Rebeldía y perseverancia," 36–7.
164 In Gatica, "Industrialización y proletarización," 137.
165 Lobato, *La vida en las fábricas*, 126.
166 Gatica, "Industrialización y proletarización," 135, 139.
167 In Striffler, *In the Shadows of State and Capital*, 201.
168 Hill and Wright, "Time, Narrative, and Ritual."
169 Necoechea Gracia, *Después de vivir un siglo*, 217, 220.
170 Gould and Lauria-Santiago, *To Rise in Darkness*, 77, 79.
171 Harpelle, "White Zones," 317–19, 323, 327–8.
172 Iwao Ueunten, "Japanese Latin American Internment," 107, 109; Moore, "Gender and Japanese Immigrants to Peru," 22, 26–7; Kudo, "Preface to the Year 2000 Edition."
173 Moore, "Gender and Japanese Immigrants to Peru," 24–5.
174 Brito Fabri Demartini et al., "Dilemas da vivência em nova terra," 303–4.
175 Ibid.
176 In Iwao Ueunten, "Japanese Latin American Internment," 110.
177 Iwao Ueunten, "Japanese Latin American Internment"; Moore, "Gender and Japanese Immigrants to Peru"; Moore, "Los Nikkei internados durante la Segunda Guerra Mundial"; Hagihara and Shimizu, "Japanese Latin American Wartime and Redress Movement"; Higashide, *Adios to Tears*, 219.
178 Moore, "Los Nikkei internados durante la Segunda Guerra Mundial," 2. For more on the reparations effort, see Small's epilogue to *Adios to Tears*, 250–3.
179 In Iwao Ueunten, "Japanese Latin American Internment," 115.
180 Loner and Almeida Gill, "Clubes carnavaleros afrobrasileños en Pelotas."

Suggested Readings

Batinga de Mendonça, Fernando. *A outra banda da mulher: Encontros sobre a sexualidade feminina*. Rio de Janeiro: Codecri, 1981.

Duarte, Geni Rosa, Méri Frotshcer, and Robson Laverdi, eds. *Desplazamientos en Argentina y Brasil: Aproximaciones en el presente desde la historia oral*. Buenos Aires: Red Latinoamericana de Historia Oral, Imago Mundi, 2012.

Dutrénit Bielous, Silvia. *Diversidad partidaria y dictaduras: Argentina, Brasil y Uruguay*. Mexico City: Instituto Mora, 1996.

Garulli, Liliana, Liliana Caraballo, Naomi Charlier, and Mercedes Cafiero. *Nomeolvides. Memoria de la resistencia peronista*. 1955–1972. Buenos Aires: Editorial Biblos, 2000.

Mott, Luiz. *O lesbianismo no Brasil*. Porto Alegre, Brazil: Mercado Aberto, 1987.

Necoechea Gracia, Gerardo, and Patricia Pensado Leglise, eds. *Voltear el mundo de cabeza. Historias de la militancia de izquierda en América Latina*. Buenos Aires: Imago Mundi, 2011.

Parker, Richard. *Beneath the Equator: Cultures of Desire, Male Homosexuality, and Emerging Gay Communities in Brazil*. New York: Routledge, 1999.

Randall, Margaret. *Mujeres en revolución*. Mexico City: Siglo XXI Editores, 1974.

Torres Montenegro, Antonio, Geni Rosa Duarte, Marcos R. Freire Montysuma, Méri Frotscher, and Robson Laverdi, eds. *História oral, desigualdades e diferenças*. Recife, Brazil: Editora Universitária UFPE, 2012.

7 Oral Life History and *Testimonios*

Often defined as the merger of biography (as constructed by the interviewer) and autobiography (as guided by the interviewee), oral life history offers Latin Americans the opportunity to participate in crafting their stories. While the life-story technique encourages interviewees to narrate with little interruption or prodding from the interviewer, some oral life history practitioners are more assertive, at times challenging interviewees to reconsider certain assertions or to take their narratives in different directions.

Deployed for contemporary social science research, oral testimony also allows interviewees to articulate their perspectives. In Latin America, the type of oral testimony known as *testimonio* generally provides a venue for disenfranchised individuals who can represent larger groups in ways that reveal forms of oppression and physical, structural, or symbolic violence. Just as *testimonios* offer perspectives theretofore largely absent in public discourse, so too did early practitioners of oral life history seek to fill a knowledge gap.

Unlike their counterparts in the United States and Europe, Latin American elites tend to refrain from writing memoirs or autobiographies because of concerns about honor and perceptions of arrogance. The former president of Mexico Lázaro Cárdenas (1934–40) explains, "Political acts speak for themselves; any personal explanation of the 'how's or why's' behind such acts only appear to be a defense of such actions."[1] Mexican elites' early attempts to write about their political or personal pasts like the former Mexican minister of public education José Vasconcelos's autobiography were met with mixed if not biting reactions.[2] Oral life history affords elites the opportunity to tell their own stories without seeming arrogant; they can even demur and then politely respond to interviewers' questions. The presence of an interviewer is not merely a formality for Latin American elites, however. Indicating how crucial the interviewer is to accessing rich descriptions and reflections, the Mexican intellectual Daniel Cosío Villegas gave only a perfunctory account of his life when scholars at the Columbia University OHRO asked him to sit in a room alone and record his answers to their questions. When prompted by interviewers, however, he offered detailed accounts of his life and perspectives on the past.[3]

On the eve of military dictatorships in Latin America, some of the first oral archives were organized to gather life stories of public figures. Given Columbia University OHRO's early financial backing and training, the predominance of interviews with politicians, labor leaders, and elites at Argentina's Instituto Di Tella is not surprising. In 1975, four years after the creation of the Instituto Di Tella, the Getúlio Vargas Foundation in Brazil founded its own oral history program to interview politicians whose careers dated to the 1920s.[4] When elites describe recruitment and advancement in their careers, they allude to the intricacies of power and how leadership actually worked.[5]

While oral life histories of elites and middle-class professionals primed the nascent field in the region, since the early 1980s, scholars and activists increasingly have approached marginalized people as protagonists through *testimonios*. Written within a circumscribed tradition of indigenous orality and interpolated by the editor Burgos-Debray, Menchú's narrative about civil war and genocide in *I, Rigoberta Menchú* is an iconic and controversial *testimonio*.[6] By comparison, although James too constructed a version of his interviewee's story from hours of recordings to read like an autobiography, his dialogue with Argentine meatpacker María Roldán at various points in her narrative and his penetrating analysis of her story squarely situate his book in oral life history canon.[7]

Oral life history facilitates interviewees' ability to make sense of the ways their life stages have built upon each other. Instead of fitting their personal experiences into larger narratives, interviewees can articulate how their perceptions contradict, deviate from, or resonate with broad analyses of the past and present. Ordinary Latin Americans can illuminate underexplored topics and intersections of the mundane and extraordinary when afforded the narrative time and space to recount memories that span their lifetimes. Legitimized through corroboration, oral life history, oral testimony, and *testimonio* research contribute to more transparent and democratic societies.

The Long View

With its longitudinal approach, oral life history encourages interviewees to think about change over time. Looking back on the twentieth century in ways that challenge the Cuban Revolution's claim of social justice, for example, Reyita recalls that the gay community enjoyed greater freedom of expression, albeit during carnival and other fiestas, in Cuba prior to the 1959 revolution than after it.[8] Highlighting how life history explores the relation between "biographical time and socio-historical time," Argentine sociologist Jorge Balán finds the method particularly useful for understanding "problems related to individual and family life cycles (careers, migrations, family formation); other connections to social change . . . (urbanization, industrialization, revolutions); and . . . modifications introduced to . . . the life cycle of entire generations."[9] To underscore the junctures between biographical and sociohistorical time, Medea Benjamin and Maisa Mendonça include a timeline they title "Key Political Events in Brazil during Benedita da Silva's Life" at the end of the Afro-Brazilian activist-politician's account.[10] Such studies are crucial for comprehending how certain sectors of the population experience and shape significant structural changes through which they live.

Oral life histories are particularly valuable tools for exploring changes that might otherwise remain imperceptible. Complex and private, domestic relations can be difficult to access. As Mexican husbands gradually surrendered their role as sole income earners in their families over the course of the twentieth century, domestic relations changed. Less dependent on their husbands' salaries, many wives redefined their relationships to the home. Born in 1908 and having worked much of her life in a factory, one woman considered the factory her husband. In contrast, her contemporary Bladina said she was married to her home; she quit her job when she married because her husband enjoyed a comfortable salary. Women and men regularly negotiated the shifting foundations that undergirded gender relations.[11]

Like topical oral history, oral life history allows people who forged the past to contribute to its telling. That telling reflects the priorities and aspirations of raconteurs as well as the influence of societal forces upon them. Patai has recognized that her oral life history interviews with Brazilian women may have captured "intentional misrepresentation, self censorship, or unintentional replication of a given society's myths and cherished beliefs about the world, itself, or the roles that distinctive individuals or groups play."[12] In an open format, some raconteurs veer from convention. After realizing that the sixty-year-old Mexican Esperanza Hernández defied temporal, spatial, gender, and historical distinctions in her oral life story, Behar was compelled to look beyond the academic fields of anthropology and feminism to interpret her interviews. She allowed Hernández's "different ways of making sense" to guide the research and monograph.[13] By doing so, Behar stayed true to Hernández's notions of history and what makes a story worth telling.

Often tinged with recollections of inequality and discrimination, oral life histories contain kernels of empowerment and autonomy that explode portrayals of hapless, passive victims. When asked about her Argentine city of Berisso, a female worker insists, "It is the city of emigrants. It has not been a whim of destiny; it is because the immigrant raised Berisso. They raised it and they will continue to raise it. . . . Of that I am certain."[14] Even more emphatically, one of her counterparts declares, "We have never been vanquished . . . [or] dominated from any point of view."[15] By presenting marginalized people as protagonists, oral histories expose how shallow the category of "oppressed" can be; workers become central to factories, the disenfranchised disrupt politics, and rural farmhands influence the fate of agrarian reform.

When they recount achievements unfulfilled or dreams denied, however, some raconteurs point to their own limitations as representations of larger problems. "A woman of my caliber, this isn't to boast, but of my caliber there were many in the country, women of the packing plants especially, hard workers, capable of doing great good and of struggling for their workmates, women who should have made it as deputies, as senators, as mayors, very capable women, but they never got that chance," laments Doña María.[16] Reflecting on the Perón period, another worker surmises that legislation to protect workers and rein in the power of meat-processing companies never materialized "because it did not align with the interests of the capitalists. . . . [S]till they dominated everything."[17]

A palpable sense of alienation often marks tales of exploitation and discrimination. As da Silva explains, marginalization could be all encompassing: "My body did not belong to me by any means. Not my body, nor my house, nor anything. The police would arrive, hit me, and mess up my food. I lived in a place that did not ever appear on the city map!"[18] With their strategies for securing and maintaining labor, many elites dehumanized workers from a young age. A Mexican elder recalls how early-twentieth-century landowners in the Yucatán ensured that they had a steady supply of labor: "They gave kids rum when they were very young; then, when they reached their tenth birthday, they wanted to drink but didn't have the money. The landowner was there to lend it, and that's how they came by many of their servants."[19] With so many tales of abuse, disdain for elites is not surprising. A Chilean domestic worker subjected to abuse asks, "Who treats another person like that? Their fancy things made them the real animals."[20]

Like life histories, myths, folktales, songs, and other genres convey historical and contemporary issues. Wilkie has found that leaders seeking to direct the destinies of their nations frequently employed legends to do so.[21] Besides inspiring social movements, songs recreate the past by accessing illiterate people's perspectives and practices.[22] At times they challenge literary discourse. Such was the case in Mexico, where folk songs and oral histories of *braceros* (migrant manual laborers) countered disparaging writings about them.[23] Through their respective analyses of songs, anecdotes, and oral histories, both Mastrángelo and Pozzi have identified a common culture or sense among left-leaning, working-class people characterized by a resistance to capitalism and corrupt governments and by a struggle for equality reflecting a mentality of "us" (workers) versus "them" (the rich, police, military).[24] Pozzi approaches working-class culture "as a mobilizing element, as a worldview, and as an articulation of a specific class action."[25] Those elements invariably affect how people narrate the past and their life stories.

To underscore the "fictions of self-representation" that result when raconteurs impose "an ordered past . . . upon a disordered life,"[26] Behar called her work with Hernández "a life story rather than a life history."[27] That distinction allowed her to explore how Hernández both lived in the past and crafted a personal history related to that past. Similarly exploring the space between fiction and history, Marjorie Becker recorded oral histories to create what she imagined to be women's perspectives. Instead of taking women's words verbatim, she developed composite quotes based on her interviews. Of the Cárdenas presidency, she writes,

> Something changed when Cárdenas was elected. It seemed like both the church and the government believed that we women mattered. And they each offered us something—the Church with the cult of La Purísima, the government inviting us out of our homes for [women's] *liga* [league] meetings. It might seem small, but to us, it was an invitation to take what they offered, and then to ask for more.[28]

Although she invented the quote, Becker argues that it captures the collective memory of women in Michoacán. In some ways, fiction can more closely approximate the past than narratives constrained by empiricism, but few scholars veer so far from empirical evidence in their analyses. Nonetheless, Becker's methodology underscores the constructed nature of oral histories.

Instead of approaching the relation between fiction and history from the scholarly end, Latin American novelists and short story writers like Agustín Yáñez, Juan José Arreola, Gabriel García Márquez, and Juan Rulfo have used oral histories and oral tradition to inform their writings. By approaching fiction as epitomized oral history, they have earned widespread acclaim. To cite the most famous example, each generation of the Buendía family at the center of García Márquez's *Cien años de soledad* (1967) is bound to the ones that preceded it. Through seven generations, García Márquez explores Colombia's past from early-nineteenth-century Liberal efforts to break free from colonial influences to such subsequent manifestations of modernity as railways, automobiles, and cinema. The Thousand Days War (1899–1902) and the Colombian military's massacre of protesting UFCO workers (in 1928)—real events fictionalized in the novel—reveal dark sides of nation formation. By mixing fact and fiction, García Márquez explores the complex relation between truth and memory. To erase memories of the 1928 massacre, a US administrator for the fruit company conjures a whirlwind. In a reflection of the way oral history infuses his novel, García Márquez highlights how both remembering and forgetting influence the past and its telling.

Many scholars analyze the creative nature of oral accounts. Through oral life history research, Wilkie has recognized the ways socioeconomic position and status shape people's narratives. He argues that leaders distinguish themselves from others and justify their actions and privileges through their own narrative form, which he calls "elitelore." As a field of inquiry and a theory, elitelore is an attempt to explain how elites create their own discourse and truths to develop a base of unquestioning followers. Instead of focusing solely on the most powerful people, Wilkie contends that elites at all levels of society deploy elitelore to craft narratives about the past that validate their own exploits and ideas.[29] By endowing certain episodes with symbolic significance, raconteurs create myths to advance their agendas.

They also regularly revise their life histories to fabricate their own ontology.[30]

Since justifications for leaders' decisions and feats often require "the building of myths and self deception," analyzing those interviews through the lens of elitelore is helpful.[31] Like many of their charges, leaders seldom have time to reflect upon, let alone research the complex world in which they live, so their worldviews and understandings of the past are not necessarily based on the "truth," contends Wilkie. The 1958–1959 strikes and the Mexican state's violent response to them threatened the newly elected president Adolfo López Mateos's legitimacy and rule (1958–64), yet Mexican labor leader Fidel Velázquez (1900–97), whose authority also was undermined by the events, denied that there was any strife or even instability during those years when he was asked about them in 1964.[32]

Some elites consciously engage in myth-making. When the twenty-nine-year-old Chilean minister of the economy Fernando Flores assumed his post in 1972, he sought to buoy his sway by soliciting an honorary degree from a university and gaining acceptance into a scientific society or club.[33] In light of the diversity of elites' positions, contested views of the past are not surprising. Perspectives of a Socialist Party leader and an air force general whom Pinochet dismissed contrast sharply with those of the dictator.[34] Given leaders' tendency toward self-delusion, Wilkie encourages researchers to challenge elites' perceptions of the past. As a counterpoint to Latin American leaders' reluctance to write their own memoirs, collaborative oral life history research with elites has found fertile ground in Latin America.[35]

Economic Elites

In contrast to well-known political leaders like Fidel Castro (1959–2008), Latin American business leaders have garnered little international attention or interest compared to their counterparts in the United States, Europe, and Japan. Afraid that a lack of knowledge about business history in his country and other areas of Latin America handicapped future business leaders, Chilean shipping magnate Sven von Appen approached business historian Geoffrey Jones. Well versed in the history of such multinational companies based in the United States and Europe as General Motors, Coca-Cola, and Apple, Jones and his Harvard colleagues wanted to learn how business leaders in emerging markets created and managed businesses. Launched with a pilot project in Argentina and Chile, as of January 2016, Creating Emerging Markets housed more than seventy interviews with entrepreneurs, forty-three of whom were from Latin America. In an indication of the organizers' interests and gender power in Latin American business, only two of the Latin American interviewees were female: Argentine businesswoman Amalia Lacroze de Fortabat and the Brazilian businesswoman Luiza Helena Trajano.

Aware that many Latin American business leaders were reared in tumultuous times, interviewers began with questions like one asked of Peruvian businessman Tony Custer: "I would like to take you back to your infancy and [ask] that you recount where you were born, what your family environment/setting was like in your first years."[36] Jelin similarly uses oral life history to explore how occupational life cycles coincided (or not) with broader phenomena of historical change to better understand the contributions and challenges of entrepreneurs. While she focuses on working-class people in that study, oral life history methods equally elucidate how the trajectories of economic elites altered and were altered by larger forces.[37]

With their expertise in navigating shifting regulatory terrains and volatile domestic economies and politics, Latin American business leaders have much to teach their counterparts worldwide who face unpredictable economic, political, and social situations. Brazil and other nations that long were considered economically unstable and underdeveloped emerged as international economic leaders in the early twenty-first century. Yet by the mid-2010s, their financial situation again became precarious. Such rapidly changing realities make capturing the expertise and experiences of Latin American business leaders crucial to forging sustainable and successful business models. Living and working through tumultuous times, many leaders point to their adaptability and willingness to accept risk. "You immediately assumed a greater level of responsibility than you thought you could handle," explains Brazilian business leader Paulo Cunha about working at Petrobas, the national petroleum corporation.[38]

Although some elites enjoyed close ties and mutually beneficial relations with military dictatorships in ways that implicated them in human rights abuses, many industry leaders who emerged during times of democratic transition pledged their commitment to social justice in its various forms. Lacroze de Fortabat remarks, "I feel a great social responsibility for all I have been given, and I believe it's my obligation to give it back."[39] Cognizant of the histories of neocolonialism, exploitation, and military terror that marked many Latin American lives, some Latin American business leaders reflected on how sharply their own privilege contrasts with the marginalization of so many others. Jones points out that one of the common threads to emerge from the interviews in Latin America and other emerging economies is business leaders' sense of social and environmental responsibility.[40]

The dramatic reconstitution of Argentine viticulture offers an example of what can be learned by interviewing successful business leaders. Considered a staple by most European immigrants, Argentine wine was characterized by its high alcohol content, heavy color, and viscosity rather than taste. Most consumers diluted wine with water and ice to economize. With the emphasis on mass consumption, quality seldom emerged as a priority. "Giving a bottle of wine was an insult," explains Argentine historian Adolfo Cueto.[41] When Argentina's domestic market shifted to beer and other alcoholic drinks in the 1960s and 1970s, wine producers faced a crisis.[42] Many responded by hiring foreign wine experts and investing in technology and quality controls such as oak barrels for aging. Instead of mass production, vineyards shifted to produce diverse high-quality wines. By the 1990s, Argentine wines had gained an international reputation for excellence.

A crucial component of their success was marketing. Claiming he "invented the idea of publicity" for Argentine wines, the head of one of the country's largest wineries, Nicolás Catena, said wine producers jettisoned working-class associations of wine to portray it as an elite beverage.[43] By deploying what he called "emotional publicity" to tap into special moments in people's everyday lives, Catena and his counterparts heightened awareness of the impeccable quality of their products. Recognizing women's crucial role in the consumption of wine, they explicitly addressed gender in advertisements and developed specific brands for romantics; others were aimed at social climbers and anarchists.[44] Upwardly mobile middle-class Mexicans who shifted from *pulque* to beer as their alcoholic drink of choice are another manifestation of Latin American alcohol entrepreneurs' success in relating their products to prestige and power.[45] Social mobility was tied to conspicuous consumption.

By combining social science insights with humanities-based discursive concepts, historian Lowell Gudmundson explores the entrepreneurship behind another conspicuously consumed beverage: Costa Rican coffee. In interviews with coffee cooperative members and technicians, agronomists, and extension agents that he and Costa Rican scholar Wilson Picado conducted, Gudmundson demonstrates how small-scale farmers and coffee cooperatives made Costa Rican coffee competitive internationally without relying on political patronage. Although their rise was supported by the Banco Nacional and closely connected to a political party after the 1948 civil war, co-op members and technicians attributed their success to a combination of technical knowledge and understanding of local land and labor issues.[46]

Vignettes from the sole female co-op representative reveal the incredibly challenging road one woman took to becoming a salesperson in a co-op; Gudmundson uses her recollections to demonstrate how gender power discouraged women. He moves beyond a local study about the coffee co-op's political and social context to understanding how the green revolution, dwarf-variety coffee bushes, and new cultivation schemes facilitated the product's success in world markets in the mid-1970s. By outperforming private processors and eschewing political clientelism, co-ops fortified Costa Rica's economy and democracy.

Given that wealth, privilege, and access to resources tend to perpetuate themselves across generations, Garay contextualizes her interviews with the Mexican architect Mario Pani within his family and history more broadly. Born in 1911, Pani was reared in revolution. His father and uncle held political posts during the revolution (1910–17) and its consolidation thereafter. As was true in other nations, Mexican entrepreneurs and business elites frequently enjoyed close relations with powerful politicians. Pani could not help but be a product of his family's role in politics and particularly his father's positions as the Mexican consul in Milan and Paris.[47]

Pani returned to Mexico in 1934 after completing his degree in architecture at the École des Beaux Arts at a time when his counterparts were deciding whether to endorse the state and its vision of the revolution or part with authorities and protest the state's failure to live up to the revolution's goals. Architects may have sided with the disenfranchised, but their clients invariably were elites. Complicating the delicate negotiations of class and politics, architects were striving to introduce modernist strands of their trade—primarily functionalism—to Mexico by the 1930s. In a context whereby socialists regarded architecture as a technical engineering field rather than an art, a classification Pani considered "absurd," Pani's education at the Paris School of Fine Arts was considered elitist.[48]

While they afforded him opportunities few of his countrymen enjoyed, Pani's family, travel, and education disadvantaged him in many circles. His genealogy associated him with the old, corrupt regime, his stint in Europe linked him to foreigners, and his architectural training cast him as an antiquated Frenchman. Overcoming those obstacles figures prominently in his life history. To advance his career and leave his mark on his profession, Pani sought to synthesize Mexican traditions with international modernist influences.[49]

As urbanization increased throughout the twentieth century, particularly in Mexico City, one of the most pressing problems was providing affordable housing for working- and middle-class people. In the midst of efforts to expand the nation's industrial development and domestic market, architects and government officials alike sought to solve the housing crisis. That confluence of forces created the opportunity for architecture and business to work together. While influencing architectural style, Pani cultivated a new clientele and demand for his skills. In addition to reasserting architecture as an art form, Pani addressed social justice issues with large-scale urban housing projects. Art and revolutionary promises dovetailed as the masses came to occupy spaces marked by "comfort, quality of life, and beauty."[50]

Religious Sway

Given its import throughout Latin America's history, religion—like business—has been surprisingly understudied by means of oral history. If the insights and richness from oral history studies of religion are any indication, the topic promises to be fruitful. Just as oral testimonies explore traditions, rituals, and legends pertaining to religious norms and moral values, oral life histories reveal how a commitment to helping others inspired many Latin Americans' religious vows.[51] A Mexican bishop recalls his formation as a child: "One day the priest invited me to accompany him on his visit to rural areas, which I did. I had many conversations with rural people and I learned to understand their problems. It occurred to me that this would be a wonderful occupation, doing what the priest was doing on these visits."[52]

Partly attributable to liberation theology—a movement within the Catholic Church to accompany and empower the poor and oppressed—some priests understood their vocation to be political as well as religious. A Colombian priest who was born in 1923 and ordained in 1946 describes this calling: "The Church, although this is not its principal function, must exercise a role of leadership. Then we find that one comes up against existing structures, which see one as an enemy because one speaks of the needs of the peasant, even saying that they have to be better paid for their work—better salaries."[53]

For many lay Latin Americans, liberation theology was a welcome break from the past. Da Silva has observed that "liberation theology is very different from the mainstream Catholic Church, which cooperated for many centuries with the system that repressed blacks, indigenous people, and women. The church hierarchy worked hand in glove with the state, especially during the military dictatorship, when it was complicit with the government's gross violation of human rights."[54]

Motivated by a desire to improve people's lives, many missionaries arrived with ideas about Latin America that were little grounded in reality.[55] Through his dozens of interviews with priests from the United States and Europe who emigrated to Brazil in the 1950s and 1960s, Brazilian historian

Figure 7.1 Father Gerardo Papen in rural Chile, ca. 1991. As concerned with enriching material as spiritual lives, many priests like Papen sought to alleviate poverty.

Photograph by David Carey Jr.

Antonio Torres Montenegro came to understand the mindset of men who arrived in Latin America determined to bring about religious and political change and "save that pueblo from the 'darkness of backwardness.'"[56] Dutch priest Lambertus Bogaard explains, "The idea we had in Holland of Brazil was of a completely backward country. When I disembarked in Recife, I was surprised by all the buildings. I thought I was going to encounter especially Indians and poor and backward blacks, but it was exactly the contrary."[57] Convinced they needed to educate rather than collaborate in the Cold War context, Catholic priests arrived to battle Protestantism, Spiritualism, and communism. While many ultimately embraced a collaborative approach, Bogaard laments that some priests never understood that they could not simply "impose their ideas."[58] Those who broke out of that neocolonial mindset attributed their change of heart to their relationships with laity. Such sympathies suggest why, after the 1964 coup, the Brazilian military accused some clergy of being communists.[59]

Even before liberation theologians confronted the military, progressive priests butted up against conservative bishops who were content to maintain the status quo. In the 1950s, the Belgian priest Joseph Comblin set his sights on working abroad because he considered the European Catholic Church decadent and moribund. When Pope Pius XII called for northern European and US priests to work in Latin America, Comblin embraced the opportunity. Predisposed to critiquing structures of power in the Catholic Church, Comblin distanced himself from the colonialist aspects of his mission.[60]

Challenging the religious hegemony of the Catholic Church in Latin America, evangelical religions have come to play increasingly influential roles in politics and society, most notably in Guatemala and Brazil. Through oral life history, Mintz learned how a Puerto Rican couple raised Catholic converted to Pentecostalism in the 1950s. In a rural society where most people were nominally Catholic but had not been baptized or received Communion, Mintz explores the appeal of Pentecostalism. Both Taso and his wife, Elisabeth, were attracted to Pentecostal services' curative powers. After witnessing several people recover from inoperable tumors, Elisabeth's health improved, too: "I also used to feel many small illnesses that I have not felt ever again, thanks God. I believe this too was accomplished through prayer. . . . Because I took no medicine, I did nothing, and even so the illness I had has left me."[61] Taso recovered from a childhood condition, though he did not convert until weeks later. No longer fighting with each other, they recognized a change in their behavior—particularly the curbing of Elisabeth's jealousy, tantrums, and fits of rage. Convinced there were more efficacious ways than violence for resolving problems, Taso explains how the Bible served as a defense mechanism:

> If any person would come to me concerning my membership, the only thing I would have to do is put Scriptures before him—why it is that I came to join and testimony as to why I am as I am [in the church]. And

if he were a little mistaken, I would explain my reasons. So I can't fall into a quarrel now.[62]

Recollecting her childhood, Elisabeth hints at why evangelical religions' insistence on temperance has attracted many converts, particularly women: "My father used to take me and my brothers Mariano and Salvador to the Evangelical church. . . . But afterward he lost his faith. He gave up religion. And then he began to drink. Under the influence of liquor, he gave my mother a bad life."[63] Conveying conversion as "one of the most important experiences in the man's life," Mintz reveals how evangelical religions slowly gained traction in predominantly Catholic areas.[64] Over time, many of the couple's twelve children also joined the church.

A highly individual experience, conversion does not necessitate blind faith. Her mother practiced Umbanda, a traditional Brazilian religion grounded in Catholicism and African religions, but da Silva rejected religion growing up. Twenty-six years old and in search of "inner peace and . . . a way to cope with things that were out of my control," she joined an evangelical Protestant church.[65] Before she left that church twenty years later to marry her second husband, da Silva was critical of its conservative discourse and policies, particularly those concerning gender and sexuality: "In the Evangelical Church, many people continue to think that women should keep quiet and submit themselves unconditionally to the will of men. These ideas serve to reinforce prejudices that already exist in society."[66] Da Silva attributes her liberal viewpoints to the tremendous diversity in her family, which includes "prostitutes and homosexuals."[67] Even amid conservative majorities, liberal ideas flourished.

Evangelical faiths were not the first to disrupt the Catholic Church's sway. Dating to the colonial era, the coexistence of Catholicism and indigenous and African religions resulted in hybrid faiths. Innovative projects have revealed how religious syncretism permeates the mundane and secular. In some Oaxacan communities, people relate their labor to the divine. Insisting that gods are the creators, weavers attribute their skills, knowledge, and resources to gods and patron saints. Some weavers say designs come to them in dreams. One interviewee explains that palms are "a gift from the pre-Hispanic gods and even from the Christian god."[68] For palm weavers, that sacred product marks their lives, as enumerated by an interviewee:

> For many centuries [the palm] has been present when a man is born, in his childhood games, in his work, in the roof of his home and in the *petate* [mat] in which he is wrapped when he dies and is deposited forever in the bosom of mother earth, and one can say 'the blessed palm' of Palm Sunday or of huaraches of the deceased will transport them to eternity.[69]

Generally associated with rural indigenous inhabitants, huaraches exemplify the syncretism of palms that help those who follow Christianity, indigenous religions, or some combination thereof.

Scholars are beginning to study the ways religion influences memory and historical narratives. Among rural inhabitants of Ayacucho, Peru, oral histories reflected their indigenous worldviews and their interpretations of local evangelical religions. The interplay between recently introduced religious concepts and their long-standing knowledge and epistemologies helped them to make sense of Sendero Luminoso and other violence to which they were subjected in the late twentieth century.[70] As one example of the ways religion and spirituality affect how people perceive the past, a local leader in Uchuraccay uses religious references to frame the violence and exile to which his community was subjected:

> We have suffered these years as Adam and Eve did when they were expelled from Eden. And like that . . . we should work together, and reconcile ourselves with the Lord's love. And in this way, the Lord will bless us. . . . Just as he took from Job, he blessed him a thousand times over. . . . We are going to live as Christians, not like before, rather as one sole Christian [community].[71]

Peruvian historian Ponciano del Pino points out that evangelical discourse and particularly the term *hermano* (brother) facilitate efforts to recreate new communities from the ashes of violence and exile. In the aftermath of the

Figure 7.2 Indigenous vendor in Cuzco, Peru, 1992

Photograph by David Carey Jr.

civil war, 40 percent of the population of the eight returning communities had become evangelical by the mid-1990s; such shifts undoubtedly shape collective memories and community histories. For converts, their evangelical faith helped them to move beyond past horrors to hopeful futures.[72]

From Catholicism and evangelical sects to indigenous and African faiths, Latin American religions often affect political and social relations. Although many Latin Americans are comfortable with the extent to which religion and politics are intertwined, some are not. When asked about politicians' use of religion, Vicky, a political activist from Ciudad Juárez, remarks, "It is not good that they talk about religion because . . . our *señor* [president] Benito Juárez [1858–72] separated them. . . . . It is not good because there are many people who do not practice the same religion, but they have the same ideology. One thing is religion and another is politics."[73]

Dictating Difference and Discrimination

In an extreme manifestation of the separation of church and state, Castro all but dissolved the Catholic Church. To understand the effects of that and other countervailing initiatives, scholars increasingly deployed oral life history research in Cuba. Adept at controlling—even dominating—a conversation, Castro highlighted the revolution's successes by expounding on issues ranging from his childhood to foreign policy and state–party relations.[74] When journalist Lee Lockwood interviewed him in 1965 and published his findings two years later, he tapped into a deep thirst for knowledge about Castro, particularly among college students. Responding to pointed questions with answers that presented the revolution in its most attractive light, Castro demonstrated how interviewees can control interviews as much as interviewers do. Lockwood concedes that an interview with Castro was "more like an extended lecture with occasional questions."[75] While he celebrated the success of the literacy and public health campaigns, Castro avoided acknowledging the disappointing results of housing and other initiatives. Understanding the power brokers and state institutions that interpolate people's lives is crucial to reconstructing the past.

In turn, life histories provided a venue whereby Cubans of different backgrounds could critique the regime. In contrast to narratives by members of the Communist Party, many counterrevolutionaries have highlighted the regime's weaknesses, failings, and injustices in their analyses of the island's religious, political, labor, and social relations.[76]

Memoirs and *testimonios* produced by Cubans, including exiles, further depict Cuba's past and present.[77] An activist who opposed the regimes of both Fulgencio Batista (1940–44, 1952–59) and Castro, Ana Rodríguez was imprisoned at the age of twenty for nearly two decades. Her experience in Cuba's "reeducation program" reveals the revolutionary regime's repression: "You signed a confession of your sins against the Revolution, implicating others to prove your sincerity; with other prisoners, you went to 'self-criticism' sessions where Ministry officials organized you into psychological paddle lines; and you performed slave labor to show your gratitude for the whole process."[78]

Castro extolled the virtues and success of socialized medicine, but a former sex worker explains that access to health care remained gendered and restricted. If a pregnant woman was not accompanied by a friend of the doctor, "he wouldn't have dared to take the risk" of performing an abortion.[79] As sexual education advanced in Cuba, abortions were no longer an underground procedure, but even into the 1980s, many doctors refused to perform them. "With abortion I believe it is a manifestation of *machismo*. All too often our doctors consider a girl who gets pregnant to be 'easy,' and punish her by denying the operation," observes the sexologist Monika Krause, who encouraged doctors to advise teenage girls to have abortions.[80]

Concerns about premarital sex led to extreme measures. When male and female volunteers were at a literacy campaign training camp at Varadero beach in 1961, officials separated girls and boys. One woman recalls:

> We were strictly segregated from the boys. . . . One day . . . [we] were all taken to the movies and a net was hung in the auditorium between the boys' side and the girls'! That created a lot of tension. . . . The boys tore down the net and rushed over to us. Immediately the supervisors gathered the girls together and made us file out, double-time.[81]

As authorities sought to limit sexual encounters, the revolutionary government tacitly condoned them. When Lockwood asked if the revolutionary government had not closed *posadas* (rooms rented for sex) as promised because they responded to a privation created by the housing shortage, Castro replied, "Closing them makes no sense . . . because they satisfy a social need."[82] Carefully crafting his narrative, Castro avoided addressing the housing crisis that compelled many Havana residents to live with extended families in cramped and dilapidated conditions. He also skirted a reality that contradicted revolutionary leaders' claims that foreigners drove the sex industry; after the revolution, business increased for Cuban sex workers.[83]

Further limiting women's options and mobility on the island, machismo overlapped with racism in ways that portrayed women as prey. Any time white girls went out with or even in the vicinity of black men, middle-class parents were convinced they would get pregnant: "One goes out and two come back," they feared.[84] Growing up in rural Cuba in the 1920s, one woman recalls how much black men terrified her: "At night I covered my head with the bedsheets in fear, and I often had bad dreams."[85]

Subjected to racism, poor Latin Americans of color articulate their experiences and perspectives in ways that reveal the complexities of discrimination. Claiming that capitalism was the source of racism, Castro and other Cuban leaders insisted the socialist revolution would eradicate it, and thus they discouraged Cubans from identifying by race. Yet even as Reyita contends that she "prevail[ed] over discrimination," accounts of her *mulata* mother denigrating her because of her dark skin, coupled with her anecdotes detailing how employment and educational opportunities favored people with lighter skin, reveal that racism remains a pernicious force on the island.[86] Being black could cost people their jobs. One Cuban official admitted that when the Habana Libre hotel laid off dozens of black workers in 1994, racism more than management's reference to efficiency and service motivated the cuts.[87] When Reyita wanted to pursue an education, relatives and neighbors exclaimed, "That *negrita* has gone crazy."[88]

As was true for many indigenous and Afro-Latin Americans, the combination of poverty and racism undercut black Cubans' ability to succeed. Reyita points out that "the fundamental problem in Cuba is not just being black, but being poor."[89] Simultaneously celebrating her race and recognizing its disadvantages, Reyita further notes, "It goes without saying, now, that I love my race, that I'm proud to be black, but in those days, marrying white was vital."[90] The ability to do so was gendered. A black Cuban born in 1922 explained that he almost had to leave town when people learned of his secret relationship with a white girl.[91] Forty-six years younger, another black man confirms such hostilities: "A black man with a blonde? That was a scandal."[92] As blacks moved about Cuba, whites often considered them a threat. In response to migrants from eastern Cuba arriving in Havana, a white professional complains, "These *negros orientales* [blacks from the east] are taking over."[93]

Testimonio and Truth Telling

Testimonio literature and contestations of it have a long history in Latin America. Critiqued for its lax methodology, one of the first such efforts was Mexican anthropologist Ricardo Pozas's *Juan Pérez Jolote* (1952). Born in San Juan Chamula, the Tzotzil-speaking Pérez was swept up in the Mexican Revolution as a boy when he ran away from an abusive father; he later returned to his Chamula roots in highland Chiapas. Similarly situated in the *testimonio* tradition, Esteban Montejo's account of slavery in Cuba as told to Miguel Barnet was published in 1966. Although the author's and narrator's voices often become indistinguishable, *The Autobiography of a Runaway Slave* enriches historical understandings of race relations in Cuba and Latin America more broadly.

In 1972, Roque Dalton published *Miguel Mármol*, which he based on that Salvadoran revolutionary leader's recollections. By exploring the entirety of his life and how it intertwined with broader historical forces, *Miguel Mármol* more closely resembles oral life history than recent *testimonio* literature or post–civil war human rights *testimonios* in Argentina, Peru, and Guatemala that generally consist of oral evidence that is fragmented and aimed at specifics. By the 1990s, *testimonio* literature came to be defined by the use of a marginalized person's voice that reflects a broader collective experience to speak against power, exploitation, and abuse. In an indication of its often overtly political nature, Beverley characterizes *testimonio* as "the voice of the body in pain, of the disappeared."[94] As true for Pozas's, Barnet's, and Dalton's accounts as for more recent publications, *testimonios* demand a critical read that considers how historical context, political interests, and other factors affect the texts.

Initiated by Stoll's book *Rigoberta Menchú and the Story of All Poor Guatemalans*, debate about Menchú's 1982 *testimonio* attracted international attention, partly because questioning the veracity of her account challenged her 1992 Nobel Peace Prize. Stoll insists that Menchú lied about witnessing her brother's death and about never having attended school, but he adds, "There is no doubt about [her] most important points: that a dictatorship massacred thousands of indigenous peasants, that the victims included half of Rigoberta's immediate family, that she fled to Mexico to save her life, and that she joined a revolutionary movement to liberate her country."[95] More alarmingly, Stoll implicates the Left for "using Rigoberta's story to justify continuing a war at the expense of peasants who did not support it."[96] When scholars and activists uncritically accepted Menchú's portrayal of indigenous people railing against the government, they perpetuated a myth that encouraged the military to increasingly target indigenous people as enemies of the state, Stoll contends. Pointing out that subsequent evidence, particularly the Guatemalan Catholic Church's study, contradicted Stoll's argument, Grandin counters that Menchú's *testimonio* helped nonmilitant insurgents push for peace through a forceful promotion of indigenous identity and rights.[97]

In his quest to disprove particular interpretations of Guatemalan history, Stoll presents oral accounts from Ixil Mayas in northern Quiche that contradict Menchú's *testimonio*. For Stoll, the two most important discrepancies are that the Ixil residents he interviewed considered both guerrillas and the military their enemies, not just the latter, as Menchú purported. Second, he argues that the socioeconomic conditions leading up to the most intense violence were not characterized by threats to their land and livelihood by *ladinos*, as Menchú contends, but rather Ixils' attempts to expand their political and economic power.[98] Although Stoll raises some important questions about the nature and power of *testimonios*, he fails to apply the same meticulous methodology to his research that he demands from Menchú's account: he does not sufficiently corroborate his evidence against other oral and written accounts.[99] Relying almost exclusively on oral testimony from participants and survivors, both the Catholic Church and United Nations concluded that the military was responsible for more than 90 percent of the human rights abuses during Guatemala's thirty-six-year civil war.[100] In addition to affirming Menchú's interpretation of the war, the Catholic Church's report and analysis pointed to the war's broader historical and structural conditions such as racism and poverty that dated to the colonial era.

Though a comprehensive exploration of them is beyond the scope of this book, the heated debates among scholars often obscured the perils of using oral narratives or any source as fact without corroborating evidence. Contextualizing narratives and their elisions is also crucial. Increasingly aware of her position as a spokesperson against a violent regime, Menchú refrained from mentioning the Belgian school she attended in Guatemala City to protect the Catholic nuns working there from the military government's reprisals.[101] Other departures from full disclosure or accurate portrayals have antecedents in native texts dating to the colonial period.[102] Indicative of Maya oral traditions that blend fact and fiction, one Maya storyteller has explained that Maya see things that other ethnic groups do not.[103] To explain that her descriptions blur distinctions between her experience and that of Mayas more broadly, Menchú begins her *testimonio* by asserting, "I'd like to stress that it's not only *my* life, it's also the testimony of my people."[104] Although few interviewees are as explicit as Menchú, scholars are wise to pay close attention to the tension between collective and individual stories when working with oral life history and other oral evidence. Mintz aptly captures the dialectic between the individual and collective in oral life history in commenting on the husband of the Pentecostal couple:

> Taso conveys to the reader in an individual way the collective experience of a conquered people. What happened to him happened in the broadest terms to his society as well. . . . [H]is experiences . . . are embodied in, and embody, the history of his society. In this way, Taso emerges as a historical figure; . . . he becomes powerfully representative of his culture and his time, without being either ordinary or typical.[105]

Such storytelling traits suggest why assumptions about the truth of oral accounts are fundamental.

Even as they came to Menchú's defense and buffered aspects of her account with evidence of their own, her distortions raised problems for scholars and activists. Underscoring that dishonesty destroys trust, Patai argues that Menchú's lies undermine her credibility. Building "her reputation at least in part on falsehoods" reminds human rights activists "that their witnesses are apt to deceive them," Patai observes, and diminishes "the public's humane responses to repression and privation."[106] Keenly aware of varying versions of and approaches to truth, some interviewees formulate their accounts accordingly. As a torture survivor speaking about the Dirty War, Argentine writer and activist Nora Strejelivich felt she had to meet "the expectations readers or listeners have regarding what truth means and how it should be invoked."[107]

In addition to *testimonios*, some of the most compelling studies of such state violence as civil war, genocide, and torture are based on survivors' oral testimonies.[108] As the debates surrounding Menchú's account have demanded closer scrutiny of the truth in the telling—Pisani and Jemio encourage interviewers to maintain a "thoughtful and critical posture vis-à-vis a tale of horror"—oral history research and *testimonio* literature remain crucial to reconstructing human rights abuses and convicting their perpetrators.[109]

Arrested, tortured, and raped in the aftermath of the Chilean coup, Ayress sneaked her story out with a prisoner who was being exiled. Publicizing her ordeal while it was still happening probably saved her life. After she was released, she continued to tell her story in Chile, Mexico, Cuba, Germany, and Italy to call attention to authoritarian governments' human rights abuses. When Chileans voted to end the dictatorship in 1988, Ayress used her story to decry human rights abuses more broadly and to buttress efforts to try Pinochet for crimes against humanity. Each time she detailed the atrocities committed against her, Ayress "reversed the shame, turning it back on the Chilean dictatorship where it belonged."[110] By reweaving her traumatic story with contemporary political issues, she ensured that her account would maintain its powerful political resistance.

As examples of topical oral history and oral life history attest, these two approaches can overlap in fruitful ways. Dedicating discussion to each one is intended to highlight the insights and innovation of each rather than to suggest a sharp dichotomy between them. A good example of combining topical oral history with oral life history is Mexican filmmaker and scholar Alejandro Pelayo Rangel's book *La generación de la crisis*. By using oral history interviews with actors and other "principal collaborators" to frame his more in-depth life history interviews with fourteen director-producers, Pelayo explores the complex course of cinema during Mexico's economic crisis in the 1980s. By juxtaposing those accounts with contemporary critics' reviews of the fourteen films, Pelayo demonstrates that although budgets were modest, the independent filmmakers enjoyed "creative freedom that was reflected in formal and thematic audacity."[111] Captivated by how power shapes individual and collective lives, Pelayo underscores in an interview the importance of taking the long view when reflecting on the past:

> I emerge from my formation. Fundamentally, I am a lawyer; I studied Law, afterwards I . . . earned a Masters in Administration . . . and in general I have been indirectly in contact with politics and I like to read about power.
>
> I believe that power is an elastic mechanism that moves many things, everything that we are living in Mexico this year I believe has to do with power, with the loss of power, the empty spaces.[112]

Wrapping his diverse developmental experiences around his fascination with power, Pelayo highlights the synergy of different types of oral history. Combining oral history, archival research, and movie stills, Pelayo underscores how an economic crisis that all but destroyed the private- and state-supported movie industry stimulated a new generation of independent filmmakers who reshaped Mexican cinema.[113]

Like Pelayo, other scholars have used different types of oral evidence to contextualize their findings and interpretations. By using formal, semistructured interviews and informal conversations, Stern has developed his concepts of memory knots and memory as a closed box to frame his analysis of Chileans' different recollections of Pinochet's dictatorship. Throughout his research, interviewees could convey the stories they wanted to tell about the past while he redirected the exchanges toward memories of dictatorship and their reverberations when possible.[114] Facilitating a process whereby interviewees can relate their life experiences to specific issues or events helps researchers contextualize the significance of their findings beyond the immediate questions and individuals at hand.

Notes

1 In Wilkie, *Elitelore*.
2 Vasconcelos, *Mexican Ulysses*.
3 Wilkie and Wilkie, *Frente a la Revolución Mexicana*, vol. 1: *Intelectuales: Luis Chávez Orozco, Daniel Cosío Villegas, José Muñoz Cota, Jesús Silva Herzog*, 119–222; Rodríguez Castañeda, Castañón, and Flores Magón, *Daniel Cosío Villegas*.
4 FGV, and Programa de Historia Oral, *Catálogo de departamentos*; Schwarzstein, "Oral History in Latin America."
5 Camp, *Making of a Government*; Camp, *Mexico's Mandarins*; Levine, *Religion and Politics in Latin America*.
6 Burgos-Debray, *I, Rigoberta Menchú*.
7 James, *Doña María's Story*. Similarly based on interviews, popular social histories fall between *testimonios* and oral history. See, for example, Meyer, *Testimonios para la historia del cine mexicano*; Alonso et al., *Palabras del exilio*.
8 Reyes Castillo Bueno, *Reyita*; Arenas, *Antes que anochezca*.
9 Balán, "Introducción," 11.
10 Benjamin and Mendonça, *Benedita da Silva*, 205–6.
11 Necoechea Gracia, *Después de vivir un siglo*, 129–88, 218–19.
12 Patai, *Brazilian Women Speak*, 18.
13 Behar, *Translated Woman*, 270.
14 In Lobato, *La vida en las fábricas*, 57.
15 Ibid.
16 In James, *Doña María's Story*, 211.
17 In Lobato, *La vida en las fábricas*, 281.
18 In Pensado Leglise, "Memorias de la experiencia política de cinco mujeres," 225.
19 In Wells and Joseph, *Summer of Discontent*, 209.
20 In Tinsman, *Partners in Conflict*, 42.
21 Wilkie, *Elitelore*.
22 Pozzi, "Consignas, historia y oralidad"; McPherson, "Artful Resistance." Dance too conveys history and stimulates its retelling, see, for example, Hinojosa, *In This Body*, 173.
23 Herrera-Sobek, *Bracero Experience*, 13–128.
24 Mastrángelo, "'Mi abuela cantaba Bandiera Rossa'"; Pozzi, "¿Quién hizo el mundo?"
25 Pozzi, "Historia oral," 4.
26 Titan, "The Life Story," 290.

Oral Life History and Testimonios 189

27 Behar, "Rage and Redemption," 224–5.
28 Becker, "Though It Seemed a Lie," 65. For an exploration of the relationship between history and fiction, see Pérez Arce, "De la historia oral a la historia escrita," 203–6.
29 Wilkie, "Introduction."
30 Hankiss, "Ontologies of the Self," 204.
31 Wilkie, "Introduction."
32 Ibid., part 4.
33 Medina, *Cybernetic Revolutionaries*, 152.
34 Politzer, *Altamirano*; Politzer, *Fear in Chile*; Varas, *Gustavo Leigh*; Correa and Subercaseaux, *Ego sum Pinochet*.
35 Dutrénit Bielous, "Presentación," 12.
36 In Custer, oral history interview.
37 Jelin, "Secuencias ocupacionales y cambio estructural," 190–1.
38 Cunha, oral history interview.
39 Lacroze de Fortabat, oral history interview.
40 Hanna, "Building Histories of Emerging Economies."
41 In Stein, "Essence and Identity," 219.
42 Perone, *Identidad o masificación*; Stein, "Essence and Identity."
43 In Stein, "Essence and Identity," 220.
44 Ibid., 222.
45 Necoechea Gracia, *Después de vivir un siglo*, 215.
46 Gudmundson, "On Green Revolutions and Golden Beans."
47 Garay, *Mario Pani*; Camp, *Entrepreneurs and Politics in Twentieth-Century Mexico*.
48 Garay, *Mario Pani*, 45 (quote); Garay, "Un ensayo de contextualización histórica," 87–90.
49 Garay, "Un ensayo de contextualización histórica," 92–4; Garay, *Mario Pani*.
50 Garay, "Un ensayo de contextualización histórica," 96.
51 Adleson, Camarena, and Iparraguirre, "Historia social y testimonios orales," 40.
52 In Camp, *Crossing Swords*, 144.
53 In Levine, *Religion and Politics in Latin America*, 128.
54 In Benjamin and Mendonça, *Benedita da Silva*, 88.
55 Sobrino, *The Principle of Mercy*, 1–11.
56 Torres Montenegro, "Dominación cultural y memoria," 162.
57 Ibid.
58 Ibid., 163.
59 Ibid., 163–4.
60 Ibid., 164–6.
61 In Mintz, *Worker in the Cane*, 237.
62 Ibid., 227.
63 Ibid., 229.
64 Ibid., 8.
65 In Benjamin and Mendonça, *Benedita da Silva*, 88.
66 Ibid., 98.
67 Ibid., 97.
68 Camarena and Necoechea Gracia, "Continuidad, ruptura y ciclo," 59.
69 Ibid., 60.
70 Pino, "Uchuraccay."
71 Ibid., 13.
72 Ibid., 17–18.
73 Venegas Aguilera, "Cultura política y mujeres de sector popular," 138.

74 See, for example, Castro and Ramonet, *Fidel Castro*; Castro and Bretto, *Fidel y la Religión*; Mankiewicz and Jones, *With Fidel*.
75 Lockwood, *Castro's Cuba*, 78.
76 Reyes Castillo Bueno, *Reyita*; Pavón Tamayo and Vázquez Tamargo, *Días de combate*; Lewis, Lewis, and Rigdon, *Living the Revolution*.
77 Ferrara, *Memorias*; Suárez Núñez, *El gran culpable*; Casuso, *Cuba and Castro*; Urrutia Lleo, *Fidel Castro and Company*; Pardo Llada, *Memoria de la Sierra Maestra*; Oltuski, *Vida campesina*.
78 Rodríguez and Garvin, *Diary of a Survivor*, 228–9.
79 In Lewis, Lewis, and Rigdon, *Living the Revolution*, 2: 277.
80 In Smith and Padula, *Sex and Revolution*, 76.
81 In Lewis, Lewis, and Rigdon, *Living the Revolution*, 2: 67–8.
82 In Lockwood, *Castro's Cuba*, 123.
83 Lewis, Lewis, and Rigdon, *Living the Revolution*, 2: 277.
84 Ibid., 66.
85 Ibid., 366.
86 Reyes Castillo Bueno, *Reyita*, 29.
87 Fuente, *Nation for All*, 321.
88 Reyes Castillo Bueno, *Reyita*, 58.
89 Ibid., 72.
90 Ibid., 59.
91 Hamilton, *Sexual Revolutions in Cuba*, 209–10.
92 Ibid., 212.
93 Fuente, *Nation for All*, 327.
94 Beverley, "The Real Thing," 281.
95 Stoll, *Rigoberta Menchú*, vii.
96 Ibid., 241.
97 Grandin, *Who Is Rigoberta Menchú?*, viii, 16–18; CEH, *Guatemala, memoria del silencio*.
98 Stoll, *Rigoberta Menchú*, 8–9.
99 Grandin, *Who Is Rigoberta Menchú?*, 15–16; Sanford, *Buried Secrets*, 81.
100 ODHAG, *Guatemala*; CEH, *Guatemala, memoria del silencio*, conclusion, part 2, notes 108–23.
101 Grandin, *Who Is Rigoberta Menchú?*, 18.
102 Lovell and Lutz, "Primacy of Larger Truths."
103 Sexton and Rodríguez, *Dog Who Spoke*.
104 In Burgos-Debray, *I, Rigoberta Menchú*, 1 (emphasis in original).
105 Mintz, "Sensation of Moving," 792.
106 Patai, "Whose Truth?," 279–80.
107 Strejelivich, "Testimony," 701.
108 See, for example, Falla, *Masacres en la selva*; Montejo, *Testimony*.
109 Pisani and Jemio, "El proceso de construcción del Archivo Testimonial," 18.
110 Kaplan, "Reversing the Shame," 187.
111 Pelayo Rangel, *La generación de la crisis*, 20.
112 In Medrano Platas, *Quince directores del cine mexicano*, 41.
113 Pelayo Rangel, *La generación de la crisis*.
114 Stern, *Remembering Pinochet's Chile*, 227, 230–1.

Suggested Readings

Alterman Blay, Eva. "Histórias de vida: problemas metodológicos de investigação e análise." *Cadernos* (Centro de Estudios Rurais e Urbanos, São Paulo) 19 (1984): 115–16.

Álvarez Bautista, Víctor. *Mis memorias*. Interviewed by Rafael Rodríguez Castañeda. Guanajuato, Mexico: Sayer Lack Mexicana, 2008.

Fulchiron, Amandine, Olga Alicia Paz, and Angélica López. *Tejidos que lleva el alma: Memoria de las mujeres mayas sobrevivientes de violación sexual durante el conflicto armado*. Guatemala City: Equipo de Estudios Comunitarios y Acción Psicosocial, Unión Nacional de Mujeres Guatemaltecas, and F&G Editores, 2009.

Gómez Pérez, María, Diane L. Rus, and Xalik Guzmán, eds. *Ta jlok'ta chobtik ta k'u'il: Slo'il Maruch Komes Peres, jun antz ch'abtej ta jolob ta San Juan Chamula, ta sikil oxil, Chiapas/ Bordando milpas: Testimonio de María Gómez Pérez una tejedora chamula de los Altos de Chiapas*. San Cristóbal de las Casas, Mexico: Taller Tzoltzil de Instituto de Asesoría Antropológica para la Región Maya, 1990.

James, Daniel. *Doña María's Story: Life History, Memory, and Political Identity*. Durham, NC: Duke University Press, 2000.

Lewis, Oscar. *Pedro Martínez: A Mexican Peasant and His Family*. New York: Random House, 1964.

———. *La Vida: A Puerto Rican Family in the Culture of Poverty—San Juan and New York*. New York: Random House, 1965.

Nash, June. *I Spent My Life in the Mines: The Story of Juan Rojas, Bolivian Tin Miner*. New York: Columbia University Press, 1992.

Reuque Paillalef, Rosa Isolde. *When a Flower Is Reborn: The Life and Times of a Mapuche Feminist*. Edited and translated by Florencia E. Mallon. Durham, NC: Duke University Press, 2002.

Reyes Castillo Bueno, María de los. *Reyita: The Life of a Black Cuban Woman in the Twentieth Century*. Translated by Anne McClean. Durham, NC: Duke University Press, 2000.

Wilkie, James W. *Elitelore*. Los Angeles: University of California, Latin American Center, 1973.

Conclusion
Oral History in Twenty-First-Century Latin America

By the turn of the twenty-first century, oral history in Latin America enjoyed firm grounding as many nations stabilized their democratic traditions and institutions. As researchers seek to understand the impact of deepening democracies, oral history interviews with entrepreneurs, bureaucrats, authorities, politicians, and professionals reveal their roles, responsibilities, and influence. At the same time, oral history remains a powerful tool for revealing how subjectivity is both socially constructed and historically contingent. Pozzi celebrates its ability "to discern the subjectivity of the great masses, the workers, and *el pueblo*."[1] Evident in the ways feminists, Jews, and laborers have collected and analyzed oral histories to expose the historical roots and challenge the contemporary tools of patriarchy, anti-Semitism, and workplace exploitation, oral history continues to be both a means and an end.[2] Illuminating what people value and how they think, oral histories do more than recount the past; they help people understand change and enable them to strategically reinvent and reposition themselves in the present.

In a region where national contexts range from peaceful stability to violent insecurity, scholars ply their trades in diverse ways. In some countries, leftist governments have won elections; in others, governments have embraced neoliberal economics and conservative politics. In a few cases such as parts of Mexico and the Northern Triangle—Guatemala, Honduras, and El Salvador—violence characterizes daily life. The phenomena of femicide (killing of women because they are women) and *juvencidio* (killing of youths because they are young) in Mexico and Guatemala are manifestations of extreme violence that have reached epidemic proportions. While some practitioners pursue projects that steer clear of politics or sensitive issues, others like Torres Montenegro consider their work crucial to ensuring that governments committed to social justice "do not fail and create opportunities for a new round of governments of the right to spring forth."[3] Such activist approaches can overdetermine oral history research and scholarship in ways that are difficult to perceive. Acknowledging those and other influences, researchers strive for transparency regarding their motives and perspectives to facilitate audiences' capacity to critique the scholarship.

As scholars bring their expertise and methods to bear on questions of inequality and exploitation, some recognize oral history as a methodology that can facilitate healing, justice, and democracy. For countries whose national narratives primarily follow the trajectory of elites and tend to legitimate vastly unequal wealth and resource distribution, oral history can buttress the region's ongoing process of democracy by allowing broader representations of the past and analyses of the present.[4] For Necoechea, the "utopic intention of not solely understanding but rather transforming the world" inspires oral history in Latin America.[5] "If the individual recognizes that their personal history is a tributary in the course of history, they can also recognize that they are capable of changing their course," he explains.[6]

Through oral history, interviewees can take ownership of their past and lives. In Latin America's postconflict societies, oral history allows survivors to construct their own stories whether they resonate with or challenge discourses of reconciliation that seek to establish a single healing narrative about horrific pasts. Breaking free from narratives of collective victimization permits individuals to cast themselves as protagonists instead of victims.[7] Multiple contrasting narratives about the past can encourage inclusive national debates that are critical for strengthening democratic societies. By showcasing how even illiterate people who may not speak the national language are not without history, oral history enables scholars to move beyond treating marginalized people as hapless and passive or elites as omnipotent and self-serving; the complexities of power, resistance, and acquiescence come to life in interviewees' words.

In Latin America as in many parts of the world, understanding the recent past is contingent upon oral sources. This is especially true in postcolonial societies where a large number of people are illiterate and where storytelling remains an important means of transmitting knowledge. As communities come to agreement about what stories best convey the past and guide them in the present, narratives are adapted to contemporary circumstances. Those negotiations demonstrate that oral history is a process rather than a product.

Orality and Writing

Tensions between orality and writing pervade oral history and affect the study of many regions of the world. For years, oral history was relegated to the margins of the historical profession. Historian William McNeill observes, "One of the problems has been the historical profession's resistance to history that is not based in primary texts. We have an enormous fixation on what seems to me to be the naïve idea that truth resides in what somebody wrote sometime in the past. If it's not written down, it isn't true. And that's absurd."[8] In an indication of the power of privileging written over oral sources, even those with a keen understanding of the necessity and validity of orality sometimes discount it. "I started to see the archives as a possibility, as a way to tell future generations that this [violent repression] happened—not just because some person here or there said so, but because there is now documentary proof of how it took place," confides a former insurgent whose very safety during the Guatemalan civil war depended upon not leaving a paper trail of his activities.[9]

Since war discourages the creation of some documents and restricts access to others, oral sources are vital for studying those pasts. Explaining how the Guatemalan guerrilla group Fuerzas Armadas Rebeldes (FAR, Armed Rebel Forces) drafted laws to maintain control over their members and to avoid military infiltration during the civil war, a FAR commander reveals why much information about violent conflicts can only be obtained orally: "This has not been written/recorded anywhere."[10] If security dictated that even laws not be documented, then little else was. Dutrénit Bielous explains, "Clandestine and semilegal activities do not favor the sustained production of newspapers or documents."[11] In contrast, such state entities of terror as the military and police documented their strategies, procedures, and exploits. But officials either restricted access to those papers or denied their existence. For example, Guatemalan authorities had denied the existence of the Archivo Histórico de la Policía Nacional (AHPH, Guatemalan National Police Archive) until investigators from the Human Rights Ombudsman Office stumbled upon it while inspecting a rat-infested munitions depot in downtown Guatemala City on July 5, 2005. With the majority of the some 80 million pages pertaining to Guatemala's civil war, the archive houses the largest collection of secret state documents in Latin America.[12] Official denial of those materials fueled Guatemalan conservatives' criticisms that the nation's human rights reports were baseless because their findings were grounded in oral testimony rather than documentary evidence. The integrity and legitimacy of the field of oral history has never been more important.

Besides attempts to occlude archival evidence of the past, political and military elites advance narratives that contest those of former insurgents, survivors, bystanders, and other participants and observers—many of whom are semiliterate or illiterate. Oral histories are one of the few sources and methods that can counterbalance such hegemonic discourse. Argentine historian Liliana Barela argues that "oral history techniques are . . . often the only manner . . . [for] examining periods of dictatorial governments."[13]

Even without state duplicity, archival materials disappear at an alarming rate in Latin America. Compared to those in the United States and western Europe, Latin American archives often are vulnerable and technologically handicapped. Scarce resources and dire needs often limit the elevation of archival preservation as a national priority. At times documents are lost or incorrectly filed and as good as lost; some government entities destroy official records because they do not have the space, personnel, or inclination to maintain them. Humidity and other challenging environmental conditions have resulted in documents being damaged or destroyed by mold, insects, or rodents. In turn, the trappings of modernization like telephones, email, and texting have diminished the proverbial paper trail.

Like written sources, oral histories are incomplete and biased; scholars examine them critically even as they form personal relationships with raconteurs. French historian Roland Mousnier's observations about archival sources resonate with oral histories:

> There are facts, even important ones, of which contemporaries are unaware, others that they prefer not to admit or confess to, and others again that are so basic that they seem commonplace to such a degree that contemporaries do not take the trouble to describe them, and they come to our notice only through a few words dropped in passing in some document. The historian's task is to bring out these forms of social behavior by analyzing a substantial number of accounts.[14]

What makes many of the archival accounts to which Mousnier refers similar to oral history is that verbal exchanges frequently prompted them. From evidence of miracles in the colonial period to criminal litigation in the modern era, scribes and notaries recorded information conveyed to them orally. Witnesses testified to what they experienced and saw. Although the relationship between the interviewer and the interviewee is entirely different, oral testimony in contemporary courts of law has much in common with oral history. Curated, combed, and elicited by leading questions, testimonies in colonial Latin American courts tend to be expansive, thanks to less confining rules of evidence and recording. With their exalted, Solomonic roles in colonial Mexico, judges frequently welcomed hearsay and circumstantial oral evidence as they sought to render justice.[15] In many ways, oral accounts are represented in archival documents.

Unlike that in the United States and Europe, writing does not necessarily reign supreme over verbal communication in Latin America. To cite a few examples, many Afro-Surinamese privilege spoken truth because written histories can be stolen; in highland Guatemala, magistrates often give more weight to witnesses' testimonies than to legal documents.[16] Orality and literacy are not always at odds, though; often they work in tandem. Some individuals and communities consult historical and legal documents, ethnographic studies, and transcripts to enrich or clarify their oral histories.[17] With an eye toward teaching younger generations about the civil war, ex-insurgents-turned-archivists at the AHPH hired university students who had only vague if any memories of the civil war. Tapping into the synergy of written and spoken accounts, the students learned not only from documents but also from activist-archivists who had participated in the civil war.[18] By the mid-1980s, Mexican historian Antonio García de León had demonstrated how oral histories could be used in unison with archival materials to develop methodologically innovative and analytically sophisticated studies of the past. Instead of using oral histories to complement archival materials, he approached them as coeval sources that together produced lucid historical insights.[19] A dialogic relation between oral and written sources produces rich historical analysis.[20]

Even when archives are secure, organized, and accessible, they still have large gaps that oral histories can fill in ways that can complement, correct, or complicate official histories. Reflecting on his research in Mexico, Camp notes that conducting interviews with elites "within an authoritarian system . . . meant gathering information that was never published, while at the same time, getting at documents and printed information that was essentially unavailable or unknown to the public."[21] In Burma, where archival lacunae and shortcomings mirror those in Latin America, historian Manday Sadan finds that oral history illuminates "events for which no written sources are available or accessible."[22] By creating sources with people whose voices were distorted or absent in the archives, oral histories offer a window into otherwise inaccessible perspectives and experiences. In a manifestation of the way oral accounts contribute to a more accurate, broader-based history, scholars use them to read between the lines of and better interpret archival documents.[23] Documents describe events, movements, and trends; oral history offers the potential to understand what these happenings meant to people. By putting lived experiences at the center of historical narratives, oral history provides access to the undocumented things of life such as fantasy, desire, emotion, and intimate details that are often lost to the broader brush of history.

When Schwarzstein and Pablo Yankelevich wanted to understand radical reform at the Universidad de Buenos Aires, they interviewed "protagonists of the history of the institution: authorities, teachers, graduates, staff and students with the idea to elucidate distinct aspects of university life that written sources do not provide."[24] They used a "multiplicity of voices" to complicate portrayals of a homogeneous and collectively shared process that emerges from reading "resolutions and decrees."[25] Demonstrating how politics could undermine education, interviewees who attended the university in the early 1950s recalled that *peronismo* deadened professors.[26] After the 1955 military coup, students and faculty sought to create a new university. Yet even as many looked back on what they considered a golden era, some felt they had failed to institutionalize their success: "Thirty years later, what can we show? A university in a worse state than when we had received it in 1955. What frustration!"[27]

The most compelling historical scholarship interrogates and cross-references oral, written, visual, and other sources to offer analysis that spans the individual and community to the national and international levels. A fine-grained tool, oral history also can capture large-scale developments such as the expanding interconnectedness in the Americas. Histories that take as their focus gender, ethnicity, sexuality, class, and other identities often uncover phenomena that cut across neat temporal and causal categories and compel scholars to rethink long-standing periodizations, chronologies, and interpretations.

Promising Directions

In Latin American oral historiography, various topics remain largely unexplored. A few of the dim voices in this book hint at areas that will benefit from oral history research: the histories of many Afro- and Asian-Latin

American and some indigenous groups have received little scholarly attention. Besides deepening understandings of transitions to democracy, oral history interviews with mid-level functionaries and bureaucrats are poised to reveal the inner workings of neoliberal economic reforms and how power works at intermediate levels such as the way low-level assistants can disrupt or facilitate hegemonic functions. The criminal justice system, particularly incarceration, is another area ripe for oral history research.

As diverse in its application as archival history, oral history goes beyond contributions to the well-worn fields of political, social, intellectual, cultural, and economic history to such burgeoning areas as environmental and borderlands history.[28] A Brazilian automotive worker describes learning how larger forces affected his life: "I was raised in extreme poverty. I mean shoeless and lacking everything, mainly hungry due to . . . well, when they cut down the trees in that area the rains left—I discovered years later that rain disappeared because they had cut down the forest—and, well, it became a very arid zone, very arid."[29] His insight into the connections between poverty, deforestation, drought, and ecological devastation reveals his perceptions of and relationship with the natural world. Evidenced by the elevated status forests, water, and other natural resources have in Afro-Brazilian, Afro-Caribbean, and indigenous memories, oral traditions similarly contain environmental perspectives.[30]

With studies of migration and borders, oral history informs understandings of the permeability and international influence of nation-states. Often catalyzed by economic and political forces, migration is richly portrayed through immigrants' voices.[31] As early as the mid-1950s, members of the Community Service Agency in San Jose, California, responded to the complaint of a migrant domestic worker who alleged that she was being held against her will by her employers. The archives do not divulge the abuse she endured.[32] Contemporary oral history and oral testimony of Latin American immigrants has revealed the trials of the trail, exploitation by employers, and resilience of migrant laborers. Living in border cities made Mexicans and Mexican Americans targets of US policies on public health and other issues. From 1917 into the 1920s, border officials forced Mexicans and Mexican Americans—but not Anglo-Americans—to strip, bathe, and wait while their clothes were cleaned and dried. A longtime resident of El Paso, Texas, decades later still bitterly recalled her sense of alienation in the city she considered her own: "They disinfected us as if we were some kind of animals that were bringing germs."[33]

For many immigrants and their families, ambiguity has marked their lives. Born to Mexican parents and raised in a US border city in the 1930s and 1940s, Leonard Pacheco describes himself as "being neither/nor."[34] Although Anglo friends did not invite him to parties, he felt more comfortable with them than with Mexican relatives in town. His dark complexion made living in a border town difficult, but it became an asset when he moved to Kentucky, where girls who would never speak to blacks were attracted to his "Spanish" phenotype. Place reconstitutes race in ways that range from oppression to redemption. Passing as another ethnic group helped some Mexicans avoid violence. Enraged about Pancho Villa's March 1916 raid of Columbus, New Mexico, a mob in El Paso sought retribution by attacking Mexican residents of their own city. To escape that fate, Maurio Cordero convinced them he was African American.[35]

In another indication of its transnational potential, oral history research has illuminated the development, consequences, and perceptions of changing US foreign policy in Latin America. A collection of oral histories with eight of the previous nine US ambassadors to Mexico reveals the challenges of addressing bilateral trade and the political agendas of two governments. In the middle of some of the most important negotiations in the hemisphere, US ambassadors were painfully aware they had little authority.[36]

By revealing how local phenomena precipitate national transitions, oral histories complicate our understandings of the impact of US interventions. Because the Frente Sandinista de Liberación Nacional (FSLN, or Sandinistas) expropriated Nicaraguan highland peasants' land to form cooperatives, forced them to sell their surpluses at low prices and buy what they needed at high prices, removed their children to indoctrinate them in lowland schools, criticized Catholicism, instituted a socialist government, and abused members of their communities, many of the highlanders defied the new government. Some began to resist the FSLN even before it overthrew the dictator Anastasio Somoza Debayle in 1979.[37] The role of the US CIA and US military aid notwithstanding, such ethnic and geographic divisions in Nicaraguan civil society contributed to the downfall of the Sandinista Revolution by 1990.

Studies of medicine, health, and disease have benefited from oral history with research that has elucidated ways ethnicity and class influence how people perceive, practice, and pursue health care. By deploying oral history to explore how people experience illness, health care, and public health programs, scholars have demonstrated that the sick and those subjected to state interventions contribute to medical practices and knowledge. For the state, health clinics have offered a venue for acculturating rural residents. Class often has determined the success of such efforts; working-class indigenous people continued to consider traditional medicine viable, while many middle-class indigenous people deemed it superstitious and backward. Embracing notions of modern medicine did not necessarily change people's habits, however. Born in 1908 and employed at a factory most of her life, Altagracia regarded access to a hospital in her Mexican *colonia* an important achievement, but she did not trust its efficacy, so she still practiced medicine her mother taught her.[38] Besides influencing health care preferences, class also largely determined access to health care. Convinced she contracted typhus from soldiers returning from the Chaco War in the 1930s, one Bolivian woman believed she only survived the disease because her godfather was a doctor at a private clinic, so she was attended there instead of the La Paz municipal hospital.[39] Among the scholars who have charted innovative approaches to studying how health care and its provision have changed over time, Anna Beatriz de Sá Almeida and her colleagues use oral histories to show how politics condition the performance of Brazilian medical professionals.[40] By interviewing Mexican scientists, wild yam gatherers, and brokers to craft a counternarrative to the most common history of the Pill that celebrates US contributions and knowledge, Soto Laveaga demonstrates how oral histories can offer more inclusive and accurate accounts of the development and production of contraceptives and medications more broadly.[41]

As demonstrated in documentary films like *Cicatriz de la memoria* that mix interviews and other kinds of utterances with visual images, some of the most exciting oral history projects have been at the frontiers of different media and technology. The Colombian human rights organization Asociación Minga's Galleries of Memory explore how oral histories can inform art. After asking questions and listening to civil war survivors' stories, artists created images and symbols that formed the basis of public art installations.[42]

In another innovative study that explores the interplay of words and images, Mexican historian Alberto del Castillo Troncoso analyzes the reflections of the photographers who covered the 1968 student movement. The head of the photography department at the Mexican daily *El Universal*, Daniel Soto explained how the military and government sought to control media access and publications. When the military illegally occupied the City University, they took photojournalists on a tour that included what they alleged to be student protestors' decommissioned Molotov cocktails. When authorities refused to allow the journalists to leave, Soto sneaked his film out to a colleague. After the October 2, 1968, student massacre, government authorities demanded that any documents or images pertaining to the massacre be surrendered to them. By refusing to comply, Soto preserved a counternarrative to the state's claims that the students were pawns of communist subversives.[43]

Like Soto, many photojournalists advanced the cause of popular movements as they covered them. Reflecting upon his coverage of the 1958 railroad strikes, independent photographer Rodrigo Moya came to see the unrest in 1968 as part of a longer historical pattern of protest against an authoritarian regime.[44] Suggesting the power of text and images, Castillo argues that their photographs and words "converted the old 'ruffians' and 'terrorists' into founding heroes and martyrs of Mexican democracy."[45]

Computers and other technologies that employ words and images also altered political and economic fates. To understand how cybernetics, the study of control and communication, and Salvador Allende's socialist government influenced each other, Medina interviewed political elites as well as scientists, designers, engineers, technologists, and others who attempted to create a computer system to manage Chile's economy via Project Cybersyn (1971–1973). Their perspectives contributed to understanding the historical and social contingencies of technology and its interplay with politics. At times, technological challenges have bridged political divides. A textile plant manager who opposed Allende's socialist agenda was "difficult to deal with, [but] . . . when it came to the more technical aspects, he could work quite openly," explains his Chilean supervisor.[46]

For those involved in the project, the work was rewarding, demanding, and intense. With its communication network and command center, Project Cybersyn helped the Allende government survive a nationwide trucker strike in October 1972. An employee in the energy sector says, "I remember that a message would arrive from the presidential palace saying that in this community there was no kerosene or natural gas, or gasoline. We would look and say, 'But why? We sent a truck there.'"[47] Alerted to the problem, he and his colleagues could solve it. Without that information, the project stumbled. Explaining that some employees failed to send data when requested, Isaquino Benadof says the problem was "not the technology, it was not the computer, it was the people."[48] Just as political revolution spurred this technological innovation, political devolution doomed it. Referring to the forces that took over in the September 1973 coup, the young cabinet member Fernando Flores knew Project Cybersyn's limits: "If they are trying to kill you, the concept [of cybernetics] is worthless."[49]

Revolutionizing Oral History Digitally

Since the mid-1990s, the digital revolution has radically altered how oral history practitioners conduct, disseminate, and interpret their research. One emerging area poised to make exciting inroads in Latin America is the interpretation of oral history metadata made possible through the digitization of audio and visual interviews and transcripts. For enormous volumes of recordings, artificial intelligence can emulate the thinking processes of researchers to narrow search fields. Thanks to advanced indexing, cross-referencing, and cataloguing tools, audio and video recordings and transcripts are searchable by terms. In addition to making recordings more accessible, sophisticated search tools facilitate comparisons across oral history collections and other primary source materials.

Working across a variety of content management systems, metadata synchronizers allow scholars to mine thousands of interviews for specific themes, patterns, or content. Borrowing from linguistics, scholars can explore patterns of term and phrase usage and formation within and among interviews. Some software can locate emotional intensity and body language as easily as if it were searching for names or places. What makes the digital revolution as it relates to video and audio media so exciting is that the challenges related to fully realizing their potential are less technical than intellectual. Researchers continue to create innovative ways to analyze and conceptualize the content and aurality of oral history recordings and collections. Digital technology is transforming how people remember and recount the past.[50]

Improved access and interactivity are encouraging increased engagement by users who may not otherwise be inclined to explore oral history or visit archives. Some oral history centers have taken advantage of their online presence to educate interested visitors on oral history methodology. Younger generations' tendency to engage more with audio and visual media than literary sources may help oral history recover its aurality as users become more likely to listen to and watch interviews than to read transcripts.[51] The dramatic effect of hearing voices immediately makes the allure of the Internet all the more powerful. Researchers' preference for transcripts may dwindle as browsing and exporting interviews become less cumbersome.

The digital revolution undergirds oral history's democratic aspirations. Researchers, scholars, and archivists no longer serve as gatekeepers for oral history presentations and interpretations when people can create their own meanings from oral history materials by accessing their own themes by way of searchable recordings and analyzing the results. For those who embrace these technologies, oral history materials may increasingly encourage dialogic explorations and interpretations. Internationally inclusive sharing and interpretation of historical memories through the Internet may facilitate new approaches to and understandings of oral history and memory. Frisch concludes, "New digital tools and the rich landscape of practice they define may become powerful resources in restoring one of the original appeals of oral history—to open new dimensions of understanding and engagement through the broadly inclusive sharing and interrogation of memory."[52]

As scholars expand their experience by adhering to the framework and parameters of oral history research, they increasingly can trust their instincts regarding process and interpretation. Open-minded listening—with interviewees, research assistants, and informants—and a commitment to collaboration are crucial to designing and carrying out research projects that benefit scholars, participants, and host communities and countries. Such decolonizing approaches and outcomes are particularly imperative in Latin America and other regions where nations that have been subjected to oftentimes violent colonial and neocolonial forces continue to strive for more just, equitable, and peaceful societies.

Notes

1 Pozzi, "Historia oral," 6, 9.
2 Sebe Bom Meihy, "Radicalization of Oral History," 35.
3 Torres Montenegro, "Dominación cultural y memoria," 156–7.
4 Pozzi, "Oral History in Argentina and the IOHA."
5 Necoechea Gracia, "¿Existe una historia oral latinoamericana?," 3.
6 Necoechea Gracia, *Después de vivir un siglo*, 12.
7 Araújo, "História oral, memória e reparação," 1; Pozzi, "Historia oral," 9.
8 In McNeill and McNeill, "Interview," 15.
9 In Weld, *Paper Cadavers*, 153.

10 In Posocco, *Secrecy and Insurgency*, 164.
11 Dutrénit Bielous, *El maremoto militar*, 20.
12 Weld, *Paper Cadavers*.
13 Barela, "Oral History."
14 Mousnier, *Peasant Uprisings*, 15.
15 Taylor, *Drinking, Homicide and Rebellion*; Taylor, *Theater of a Thousand Wonders*.
16 Price, *First-Time*; Dabb et al., "Land Divided without Clear Titles," 125–6.
17 Sherzer, "Kuna and Columbus," 903–4; Rappaport, *Politics of Memory*.
18 Weld, "Dignifying the *Guerrillero*," 48.
19 García de León, *Resistencia y utopía*; García de León, *Ejército de ciegos*.
20 For an astute examination of the benefits and challenges of the dialogical method, see Mallon, *Courage Tastes of Blood*, 14–17.
21 Camp, email, January 5, 2016.
22 Sadan, *Learning to Listen*, 8.
23 American Historical Association, "'Bárbaros' in the Archive."
24 Plate, Schwarzstein, and Yankelevich, *Historia de la Universidad de Buenos Aires*, i.
25 Schwarzstein and Yankelevich, *Historia oral y fuentes escritas*, 22.
26 Pozzi and Schneider, "Memoria y socialismo"; Schwarzstein and Yankelevich, *Historia oral y fuentes escritas*, 12, 14 (quote).
27 In Schwarzstein and Yankelevich, *Historia oral y fuentes escritas*, 21.
28 See for example, Soluri, *Banana Cultures*; M. Carey, *In the Shadow of Melting Glaciers*.
29 In Mastrángelo, "'Mi abuela cantaba Bandiera Rossa.'"
30 Leinhard, *O mar e o mato*, 20; Necoechea Gracia, "El análisis en la historia oral," 78; Camarena and Necoechea Gracia, "Continuidad, ruptura y ciclo," 59.
31 Davis, *Mexican Voices / American Dreams*; Morrison and Zabusky, *American Mosaic*; Gamio, *Mexican Immigrant*; P. Taylor, *Mexican Labor in the United States*.
32 Schmidt Camacho, "Ciudadana X," 283.
33 In Sanchéz, *Becoming Mexican American*, 56.
34 In Martínez, *Border People*, 260–1.
35 Mauricio Cordero Transcript, 41, Institute of Oral History collection, University of Texas-El Paso as cited in Mckiernan-González, *Fevered Measures*, 335n79.
36 Estévez, *U.S. Ambassadors to Mexico*.
37 Brown, *Real Contra War*.
38 Necoechea Gracia, *Después de vivir un siglo*, 215–16.
39 Zulawski, *Unequal Cures*, 75–6.
40 Sá Almeida, Fonseca, and Hamilton, "Os sanitaristas," 323.
41 Soto Laveaga, *Jungle Laboratories*.
42 Pizzato, "Language of Public Memory."
43 Castillo Troncoso, "Palabra de fotógrafo," 49–51.
44 Ibid., 57.
45 Ibid.
46 In Medina, *Cybernetic Revolutionaries*, 131.
47 Ibid., 149–50.
48 Ibid., 190.
49 Ibid., 153.
50 Thomson, "Four Paradigm Transformations in Oral History"; Frisch, "Oral History and the Digital Revolution," 106.
51 Frisch, "Oral History and the Digital Revolution."
52 Ibid., 114.

Suggested Readings

Boyd, Douglas, ed. "Oral History in the Digital Age." Special Issue of *Oral History Review* 40, no. 1 (2013): i–iii.

Gluck, Sherna Berger, Donald A. Ritchie, and Bret Eynon, "Reflections on Oral History in the New Millennium: Roundtable Comments." *Oral History Review* 26, no. 2 (1999): 1–27.

Institute of Museum and Library Services. Oral History in the Digital Age. http://ohda.matrix.msu.edu/.

Larson, Mary A. "Potential, Potential, Potential: The Marriage of Oral History and the World Wide Web." *Journal of American History* 88, no. 2 (2001): 596–603.

Bibliography

Archives

Archivo de la Palabra. Instituto Nacional de Antropología e Historia (INAH), Mexico City.
Creating Emerging Markets. Harvard Business History Initiative, Oral History Collection, Baker Library Historical Collections, Harvard Business School, Boston. http://www.hbs.edu/businesshistory/emerging-markets/Pages/default.aspx/.
Internet Archive. https://archive.org/.
K'iche' Maya. Oral History Project. Latin American and Iberian Studies, University of New Mexico, Albuquerque. http://laii.unm.edu/kiche/index.php/.
Open Archives Initiative. https://www.openarchives.org/.
University of Texas, El Paso (UTEP). Oral History Collection. http://digitalcommons.utep.edu/interviews/.
University of Texas Libraries. http://www.lib.utexas.edu/voces/index.html/.
Voces: Giving Voice to the American Latino Experience. Oral History Project Website. University of Texas, Austin. http://www.lib.utexas.edu/voces/index.html.

Primary Sources

Author's note: Due to the continued political volatility and recurrent human rights abuses in Guatemala, I have preserved the anonymity of Maya interviewees. I use pseudonyms derived from the Maya calendar. Female informants can be recognized by the "Ix" prefix to their one-word names. Male names have two words. Except for one interview by the research assistant Ixk'at, I performed all interviews. Unless otherwise noted, all interviews were conducted in Kaqchikel.

Alegre, Robert. Personal communication with the author, October 21, 2015.
B'eleje' Imox. Interviews by the author, September 7 and November 30, 1997; January 11 and August 1, 1998, San Juan Comalapa, Guatemala.
Camp, Roderic Ai. Email correspondence with the author, March 29, 2015, and January 5, 2016.
Crafts, Lydia. Personal conversation with the author, Baltimore, MD, February 16, 2016.
Cunha, Paolo. Oral History Interview by Ricardo Reisen de Pinho. July 3, 2013. São Paulo, Brazil. http://www.hbs.edu/businesshistory/emerging-markets/pages/profile-detail.aspx?profile=pcunha.
Custer, Felipe Antonio. Oral History Interview by Andrea Lluch, Lima, June 12, 2013. http://www.hbs.edu/businesshistory/emerging-markets/pages/profile-detail.aspx?profile=fantoniocuster.

Ixaq'. Oral history interview by the author, June 21, 2001, San Juan Comalapa, Guatemala.
Ixchipix. Oral history interview by Ixk'at, June 29, 2001, Paquixic, San Juan Comalapa, Guatemala.
Ixkate'. Oral history interview by the author, June 6, 2001, San Juan Comalapa, Guatemala.
Ixq'anil. Oral history interview by the author, May 5, 1998, San Juan Comalapa, Guatemala.
Jones, Geoffrey. Email correspondence with the author, July 31 and August 1, 2014.
Junlajuj Imox. Oral history interview with the author, September 15, 1998, San Juan Comalapa, Guatemala.
Kab'lajuj Tijax. Oral history interview by author, April 7, 1998, San Juan Comalapa, Guatemala.
Lacroze de Fortabat, Amalia. Oral History Interview by Andrea Lluch. May 12, 2008, New York. http://www.hbs.edu/businesshistory/emerging-markets/pages/profile-detail.aspx?profile=alacrozedefortabat.
Lajuj K'at. Oral history interview by the author, April 4, 2005, San Juan Comalapa, Guatemala.
Maxwell, Judith. Email correspondence with the author, February 15, 2015.
Schmidt, Elizabeth. Email correspondence with the author, May 23, 2015.
Torres, Gabriela. Personal conversation with the author, Wheaton College, Norton, MA, November 8, 2013.
Wolfe, Justin. Personal conversation with the author, American Historical Association Annual Conference, Boston, MA, January 7, 2011.

Secondary Sources

Abercrombie, Thomas. *Pathways of Memory and Power: Ethnography and History among an Andean People*. Madison: University of Wisconsin Press, 1998.
Acuña Ortega, Víctor Hugo. "Cuestiones de memoria popular e historia social." In *Memoria y cultura popular costarricense: selección de ponencias y comentarios presentados al primer encuentro sobre Memoria Colectiva y Cultura Popular Costarricense. Celebrado en San José el dieciocho y diecinueve de octubre de 1985*, 45–52. Compiled by Patricia Badilla Gómez. San José, Costa Rica: Centro Nacional de Acción Pastoral, 1986.
———. "Fuentes orales e historia obrera: el caso de los zapateros en Costa Rica." In *Cuéntame cómo fue*, edited by Necoechea Gracia and Pablo Pozzi, 63–71.
Adleson, Steven Lief, Mario Camarena, and Hilda Iparraguirre. "Historia social y testimonios orales." In *Cuéntame cómo fue*, edited by Necoechea Gracia and Pablo Pozzi, 37–44.
Aguila, Gabriela, and Cristina Viano. "Las voces del conflicto: En defensa de la historia oral." In *Historiografía y memoria colectiva. Tiempos y territorios*, edited by Cristina Godoy, 243–54. Buenos Aires: Miño y Dávila, 2002.
Alberti, Verena. *Manual de história oral*. Rio de Janeiro: Edita Fundação Getúlio Vargas, 2004.
Alegre, Robert. *Railroad Radicals in Cold War Mexico: Gender, Class, and Memory*. Lincoln: University of Nebraska Press, 2014.
Allen, Andrea Stevenson. *Violence and Desire in Brazilian Lesbian Relationships*. New York: Palgrave Macmillan, 2015.
Allen, Barbara. "Story in Oral History: Clues to Historical Consciousness." *Journal of American History* 79, no. 2 (September 1992): 606–11.

206 Bibliography

Alonso, María Soledad, María Luisa Capella, Eduardo Casar, Matilde Mantecón, Dolores Plá, Concepción Ruiz-Funes, and Enriqueta Tuñón, with coordination by Eugenia Meyer. *Palabras del exilio: contribución a la historia de los refugiados españoles en México*. Vol. 1. Mexico City: Instituto Nacional de Antropología y Historia, Secretaría de Educación Pública, Librería Madero, 1980.

Alvarado, Elvia. *Don't be Afraid Gringo: A Honduran Woman Speaks from the Heart*. Edited by Medea Benjamin. New York: Harper Perennial, 1987.

Alvito, Marcos. "À sombra do jequitibá." In *História oral, desigualdades e diferenças*, edited by Antonio Torres Montenegro, Geni Rosa Duarte, Marcos F. Freire Montysuma, Méri Frotscher, and Robson Laverdi, 117–39. Recife, Brazil: Editora Universitária UFPE, 2012.

American Association of University Professors (AAUP). *Research on Human Subjects: Academic Freedom and the Institutional Review Board*. Washington, DC: AAUP, 2006. http://www.aaup.org/AAUP/comm/rep/A/humansubs.htm.

American Historical Association. "'Bárbaros' in the Archive: Sources and Methods for the Study of Autonomous Indigenous Peoples in South America." Panel 120, American Historical Association Annual Conference, January 8, 2016, Atlanta, GA.

American Psychological Association. *Ethical Principles of Psychologists and Code of Conduct*. Washington, DC: ca. 2010. http://www.apa.org/ethics/code/.

Anderson, Kathyryn, and Dana C. Jack. "Learning to Listen: Interview Techniques and Analyses." In *Women's Words: The Feminist Practice of Oral History*, edited by Sherna Berger Gluck and Daphne Patai, 11–26. New York: Routledge, 1991.

Ansaldi, Waldo. "Continuidades y rupturas en un sistema de partidos políticos en situación de dictadura: Brasil, 1964–1985." In *Diversidad partidaria y dictaduras: Argentina, Brasil y Uruguay*, edited by Silvia Dutrénit Bielous, 89–234.

Araújo, Maria Paula. "História oral, memória e reparação: Reflexões sobre a importância do testemunho na superação de contextos de violência política." *Oral History Forum / Forum d'histoire orale* 32 (2012). Special issue of *Oral History in Latin America / Historia Oral en América Latina*, edited by Pablo Pozzi et al.

Araújo, Maria Paula, and Myrian Sepúlveda. "História, memoria e esquecimento: Implicações políticas." *Revista Crítica de Ciéncias Sociais* 79 (December 2007): 95–111.

Arenas, Reinaldo. *Antes que anochezca: autbiografía*. Barcelona: Tusquets Editories, 2001.

Arias, Arturo, ed. *The Rigoberta Menchú Controversy*. Minneapolis: University of Minnesota Press, 2001.

Asociación para el Avance de las Ciencias Sociales en Guatemala (AVANCSO). *Se cambió el tiempo*. 2 vols. Guatemala City: AVANCSO, 2002.

Atkinson, Robert. *The Gift of Stories*. Westport, CT: Bergin and Garvey, 1995.

———. *The Life Story Interview*. Thousand Oaks, CA: Sage, 1998.

Auyero, Javier. *Poor People's Politics: Peronist Survival Networks and the Legacy of Evita*. Durham, NC: Duke University Press, 2001.

Aversa, María Marta, and Graciela Browarnik. "Herida profunda. Los piqueteros: una mirada desde la historia." *El Politólogo* 3, no. 1 (Spring 2002): 17–18.

Balán, Jorge. "Introducción." In *Las historias de vida en ciencias sociales: teoría y técnica*, edited by Jorge Balán, 7–15. Buenos Aires: Ediciones Nueva Visión, 1974.

Barela, Liliana. "Oral History: Past, Present, and Future. The Guadalajara Conference." *Face to Face* 17, no. 1 (July 8, 2014). http://www.iohanet.org/face-to-face-12/.

Barnet, Miguel. *The Autobiography of a Runaway Slave*. Willimantic, CT: Curbstone Press, 1994.

Barrientos, Claudio Javier. "Narración, mujeres y memoria en el sur de Chile." *Actuel Marx/Intervenciones* 4 (2005): 163–77.

———. "Texturas, políticas y fisuras de memorias campesinas: fragmentos para una contraescritura de la historia reciente en Chile." *Revista de Estudios Latinoamericanos* 1, no. 1 (2009): 43–57.

———. "Y las enormes trilladoras vinieron [. . .] a llevarse la calma: Neltume, Liquiñe y Chihuío, tres escenarios de la construcción cultural de la memoria y la violencia en el sur de Chile." In *Luchas locales, comunidades e identidades*, edited by Elizabeth Jelin and Ponciano del Pino, 107–41. Madrid/Buenos Aires: Siglo XXI Editores, 2003.

Barrios de Chungara, Domitila, with Moema Viezzer. *Let Me Speak: Testimony of Domitila, a Woman of the Bolivian Mines*. New York: Monthly Review Press, 1978.

Basso, Ellen. *The Last Cannibals: A South American Oral History*. Austin: University of Texas Press, 1995.

Basso, Keith H. "To Give Up on Words: Silence in Western Apache Culture." *Journal of Anthropology* 26, no. 3 (1970): 213–30.

Bauman, Richard. *Story, Performance, and Event: Contextualized Studies of Oral Narratives*. Cambridge: Cambridge University Press, 1986.

———. "Verbal Art as Performance." *American Anthropologist* 77, no. 2 (1975): 290–311.

Beato, Ceferino. *Disposición final: la confesión de Videla sobre los desaparecidos*. Buenos Aires: Editorial Sudamericana, 2012.

Becker, Marjorie. "Though It Seemed a Lie, the Women (Even the Shy One) Danced on the Pulpit That Night: What Mexicans Made of the Revolutionaries among Them, 1934–1940, *The Most Languid, Untold Pleasure*." *Rethinking History* 16, no. 1 (2012): 59–70.

Behar, Ruth. "Rage and Redemption: Reading the Life Story of a Mexican Marketing Woman." *Feminist Studies* 16, no. 2 (1990): 223–58.

———. *Translated Woman: Crossing the Border with Esperanza's Story*. Boston: Beacon Press, 1993.

Benjamin, Medea, and Maisa Mendonça. *Benedita da Silva: An Afro-Brazilian Woman's Story of Politics and Love*. Oakland, CA: Institute for Food and Development Policy, 1997.

Berrotarán, Patricia M., and Pablo Pozzi. *Estudios inconformistas sobre la clase obrera Argentina: 1955–1989*. Buenos Aires: Letra Buena, 1994.

Beverley, John. "The Real Thing." In *The Real Thing: Testimonial Discourse and Latin America*, edited by George M. Gugelberger, 266–86. Durham, NC: Duke University Press, 1996.

Bibliographic Center of the Institute of Contemporary Jewry, Hebrew University of Jerusalem. *Oral History of Contemporary Jewry: An Annotated Catalogue*. New York: Garland, 1990.

Bilbija, Ksenija, and Leigh Payne, eds. *Accounting for Violence: Marketing Memory in Latin America*. Durham, NC: Duke University Press, 2011.

Blee, Kathleen. *Women of the Klan: Racism and Gender in the 1920s*. Berkeley: University of California Press, 2008.

Bodnar, John, Roger Simon, and Michael P. Weber. *Lives of Their Own: Blacks, Italians, and Poles in Pittsburgh, 1900–1960*. Urbana: University of Illinois Press, 1982.

Boesten, Jan. "When Tintos Break Ice: Elite Interviews in Colombia." *LASA Forum* 45, no. 2 (2014): 3–5.

Bolender, Keith. *Voices from the Other Side: An Oral History of Terrorism against Cuba*. New York: Pluto Press, 2010.

Bouvard, Marguerite Guzman. *Revolutionizing Motherhood: The Mothers of the Plaza de Mayo*. Wilmington, DE: Scholarly Resources Books, 1994.

Brecher, Jeremy. "A Report on Doing History from Down Below: The Brass Workers History Project." In *Presenting the Past: Essays on History and the Public*, edited by Roy Rosenzweig, Susan Porter Benson, and Stephen Brier, 267–80. Philadelphia: Temple University Press, 1986.

Briggs, Laura. *Reproducing Empire: Race, Sex, Science, and U.S. Imperialism in Puerto Rico*. Berkeley: University of California Press, 2002.

Brito Fabri Demartini de, Zeila, Gilmar Santana, Maria Helena Lara Netto, Odila Carvalho Reis, and Valéria Barbosa Magalhães. "Dilemas da vivência em nova terra: A educação, o lazer e o consumo cultural entre japoneses em São Paulo na 1ª metade deste sécolo." In *(Re)Introduzindo a história oral no Brasil*, edited by Sebe Bom Meihy, 296–305.

Brown, Cecil H. "Hieroglyphic Literacy in Ancient Mayaland: Inferences from Linguistic Data." *Current Anthropology* 32, no. 4 (August–October 1991): 489–96.

Brown, George P. "Oral History in Brazil off to an Encouraging Start." *Oral History Review* 4 (1976): 53–5.

Brown, Timothy C. *The Real Contra War: Highlander Peasant Resistance in Nicaragua*. Norman: University of Oklahoma, 2001.

Bruey, Alison J. "I Don't Like to Ask Names, and I Never Remember Anything: Narratives of Violence, Resistance, and Justice in Poblaciones of Gran Santiago, 1973–2013." Paper presented at the American Historical Association Annual Conference, January 4, 2015, New York.

Burgos-Debray, Elisabeth, ed. *Me llamo Rigoberta Menchú y así me nació la conciencia*. Barcelona: Editorial Argos Vergara, 1983. Translated by Ann Wright as *I, Rigoberta Menchú: An Indian Woman in Guatemala*. London: Verso, 1984.

Cabrera Garcia, Olga, and Eliesse Scaramal. "Saber e cultura na família rural." In *(Re)Introduzindo a história oral no Brasil*, edited by Sebe Bom Meihy, 197–205.

Cáceres Q., Gonzalo. "¿Historia oral o Fuentes orales para la investigacion historica? Algunas reflexiones sobre la situacion Chilena." *Solar Estudios Latinoamericanos: revista de la Sociedad Latinoamericana de Estudios sobre América Latina y el Caribe (Sección Chilena)* 3 (1993): 20–4.

Caetano, Gerardo. "Introducción general." In *Diversidad partidaria y dictaduras: Argentina, Brasil y Uruguay*, edited by Dutrénit Bielous, 13–23.

———. "Prólogo." In *El maremoto militar y el archipiélago partidario. Testimonios para la historia reciente de los partidos politicos uruguayos*, edited by Dutrénit Bielous, 9–14. Montevideo: Productora Editorial, 1994.

Calveiro, Pilar. *Poder y desaparición: los campos de concentración en Argentina*. Buenos Aires: Ediciones Colihue, 1995.

Camarena, Mario, and Gerardo Necoechea Gracia. "Continuidad, ruptura y ciclo en la historia oral." In *Cuéntame cómo fue*, edited by Necoechea Gracia and Pablo Pozzi, 55–62.

Camarena Ocampo, Mario. "Oral History and Consciousness." *Journal of the International Oral History Association* 2, no. 2 (2003): 6–7.

Camargo Ríos, Marcela. "Past Conferences and Oral History in Panama." *Face to Face* 17, no. 1 (July 8, 2014). http://www.iohanet.org/face-to-face-12/.

———. "Rebeldía y perseverancia en el sindicalista Perseverando Bernal." In *Caminos de historia y memoria en América Latina*, edited by Necoechea Gracia and Torres Montenegro, 27–41.

Camp, Roderic Ai. *Crossing Swords: Politics and Religion in Mexico*. New York: Oxford University Press, 1997.

———. *Entrepreneurs and Politics in Twentieth-Century Mexico*. New York: Oxford University Press, 1989.

———. *Generals in the Palacio: The Military in Modern Mexico*. New York: Oxford University Press, 1992.

———. *The Making of a Government: Political Leaders in Modern Mexico*. Tucson: University of Arizona Press, 1984.

———. *Mexico's Leaders: Their Education and Recruitment*. Tucson: University of Arizona Press, 1980.

———. *Mexico's Mandarins: Crafting a Power Elite for the Twenty-First Century*. Berkeley: University of California Press, 2002.

Cano Sánchez, Beatriz. "El mensaje de los silencios." In *Historia y testimonios orales*, edited by Cuauhtémoc Velasco, 171–9.

Carey, David Jr. "A Democracy Born in Violence: Maya Perceptions of the 1944 Patzicía Massacre and the 1954 Coup." In *After the Coup: An Ethnographic Reframing of Guatemala 1954*, edited by Timothy J. Smith and Abigail E. Adams, 73–98. Champaign: University of Illinois Press, 2011.

———. *Engendering Mayan History: Kaqchikel Women as Conduits and Agents of the Past, 1875–1970*. New York: Routledge, 2006.

———. *I Ask for Justice: Maya Women, Dictators, and Crime in Guatemala, 1898–1944*. Austin: University of Texas Press, 2013.

———. *Ojer taq tzijob'äl kichin ri Kaqchikela' Winaqi'*. Guatemala City: Q'anilsa Ediciones, 2004.

———. *Our Elders Teach Us: Maya-Kaqchikel Historical Perspectives. Xkib'ij kan qate' qatata'*. Tuscaloosa: University of Alabama Press, 2001.

———. "Symbiotic Research in the Humanities and Social Sciences: A Utilitarian Argument for Ethical Scholarship." *Thought & Action* 19, no. 1 (Summer 2003): 99–114.

Carey, David Jr., and Robert Atkinson, eds. *Latino Voices in New England*. Albany: State University of New York Press, 2009.

Carey, David Jr., and Walter Little. "Reclaiming the Nation through Public Murals: Maya Resistance and the Reinterpretation of History." *Radical History Review* 106 (Winter 2010): 5–26.

Carey, Mark. *In the Shadow of Melting Glaciers: Climate Change and Andean Society*. New York: Oxford University Press, 2010.

Carlsen, Robert. *The War for the Heart and Soul of a Highland Maya Town*. Austin: University of Texas Press, 1997.

Castaneda, Ingrid. "Fighting the 'Insatiable Octopus': Revolutionary Nationalism and the Enclave, 1944–1954." Paper presented at the American Historical Association Annual Conference, January 9, 2016, Atlanta, GA.

Castañeda, Mario. "De memoria y justicia." *Plaza Pública*, June 19, 2011. http://www.plazapublica.com.gt/content/de-memoria-y-justicia.

Castillo Troncoso, Alberto del. "Palabra de fotógrafo. Testimonios del movimiento estudiantil de 1968 en México." In *Caminos de historia y memoria en América Latina*, edited by Necoechea Gracia and Torres Montenegro, 43–58.

Castro, Fidel, and Frei Betto. *Fidel y la religión: conversaciones con Frei Betto sobre el marxismo y la teología de liberación*. Havana: Ocean Sur, 2006.

Castro, Fidel, and Ignacio Ramonet. *Fidel Castro; My Life; A Spoken Autobiography*. New York: Charles Scribner's Sons, 2009.

Casuso, Teresa. *Cuba and Castro*. New York: Random House, 1961.

Celiberti, Lilian, and Lucy Garrido. *Mi habitación, mi celda*. Montevideo: Arca, 1989.

Chakrabarty, Dipesh. "Postcoloniality and the Artifice of History: Who Speaks for 'Indian' Pasts?" *Representations* 37 (1992): 1–26.

Chatterjee, Partha. *Nationalist Thought and the Colonial World: A Derivative Discourse*. London: Zed Books, 1986.

Cieza de León, Pedro. *Parte primera de la crónica del Perú*. Madrid: Dastin, 2000 [1553].

Clark, A. Kim. *Gender, State, and Medicine in Highland Ecuador: Modernizing Women, Modernizing the State, 1895–1950*. Pittsburgh, PA: University of Pittsburgh Press, 2012.

Clifford, James, and George Marcus. *Writing Culture: The Poetics and Politics of Ethnography*. Berkeley: University of California Press, 1986.

Coffee, Mary. *How a Revolutionary Art Became Official Culture: Murals, Museums, and the Mexican State*. Durham, NC: Duke University Press, 2012.

Coiolarro, Noemí. *Pájaros sin luz. Testimonios de mujeres de desaparecidos*. Buenos Aires: Planeta, 2000.

Comisión Nacional de Verdad y Reconciliación. *Informe de la Comisión Nacional de Verdad y Reconciliación*. 3 vols. Santiago, Chile: Ministerio Secretaría General del Gobierno, 1991.

Comisión para el Esclarecimiento Histórico (CEH). *Guatemala, memoria del silencio*. 12 vols. Guatemala City: CEH, 1999. http://www.iom.int/seguridad-fronteriza/lit/land/cap2_2.pdf.

Correa, Raquel, and Elizabeth Subercaseaux. *Ego sum Pinochet*. Santiago, Chile: Zig-Zag, 1989.

Cowles, Gregory. "The Liars' Club: Is There Such a Thing as a Reliable Memoir?" *New York Times*, October 25, 2015: 20–21.

Crandon-Malamud, Libbet. *From the Fat of Our Souls: Social Change, Political Process, and Medical Pluralism in Bolivia*. Berkeley: University of California Press, 1993.

Crespo, Edda Lía. "Madres, esposas, reinas . . . Petróleo, mujeres y nacionalismo en Comodoro Rivadavia durante los años del primer peronismo." In *Cuando las mujeres reinaban: belleza, virtud y poder en la Argentina del siglo XX*, edited by Mirta Zaida Lobato, 55–62. Buenos Aires: Biblos, 2005.

Cruikshank, Julie. "Oral History, Narrative Strategies, and Native American Historiography: Perspectives from the Yukon Territory, Canada." In *Clearing a Path: Theorizing the Past in Native American Studies*, edited by Nancy Shoemaker, 3–27. New York: Routledge, 2002.

Cubilié, Ann. *Women Witnessing Terror*. New York: Fordham University Press, 2005.

Cutler, William III. "Accuracy in Oral History Interviewing." In *Oral History: An Interdisciplinary Anthology*, edited by David K. Dunaway and Willa K. Baum, 99–106. New York: Routledge, 1984.

Dabb, Curtis W., James H. McDonald, John P. Hawkins, and Walter Randolph Adams. "A Land Divided without Clear Titles: The Clash of Communal and Individual Land Claims in Nahualá and Santa Catarina Ixtahuacán." In *Crisis of Governance in Maya Guatemala: Indigenous Responses to a Failing State*, edited by John P. Hawkins, James H. McDonald, and Walter Randolph Adams, 115–48. Norman: University of Oklahoma Press, 2013.

Dalton, Roque. *Miguel Mármol*. Translated by Kathleen Ross and Richard Schaff. Willimantic, CT: Curbstone Press, 1982.

Dary, Claudia. *Relatos de los antiguos: estudios de la tradición oral de Comalapa, Chimaltenango*. Guatemala City: Universidad de San Carlos de Guatemala, 1992.

Davis, Marilyn P. *Mexican Voices/American Dreams: An Oral History of Mexican Immigration to the United States*. New York: Holt, 1990.

Dehesa, Rafael de la. *Queering the Public Sphere in Mexico and Brazil: Sexual Rights Movements in Emerging Democracies*. Durham, NC: Duke University Press, 2010.

Desling, Riet. "Issues of Land and Sovereignty: The Uneasy Relationship between Chile and Rapa Nui." In *Decolonizing Native Histories: Collaboration, Knowledge, and Language in the Americas*, edited by Florencia Mallon, 54–78. Durham, NC: Duke University Press, 2011.

Detwiler, Louise, and Janis Breckenridge, eds. *Pushing the Boundaries of Latin American Testimony: Meta-Morphoses and Migrations.* New York: Palgrave Macmillan, 2012.

Diana, Marta. *Mujeres guerrilleras. La militancia de los setenta en el testimonio de sus protagonistas femeninas.* Buenos Aires: Planeta, 1996.

Diez, Jordy. *The Politics of Gay Marriage in Latin America: Argentina, Chile, and Mexico.* New York: Cambridge University Press, 2015.

Dore, Elizabeth. "Foreword: Cuban Voices." In *Sexual Revolutions in Cuba: Passion, Politics, and Memory,* by Carrie Hamilton, vii–xi. Chapel Hill: University of North Carolina Press, 2012.

Duarte, Geni Rosa, Méri Frotscher, and Robson Laverdi, eds. *Desplazamientos en Argentina y Brasil: aproximaciones en el presente desde la historia oral.* Buenos Aires: Red Latinoamericana de Historia Oral, Imago Mundi, 2012.

Dunaway, David, and Willa Baum, eds. *Oral History: An Interdisciplinary Anthology.* 2nd edition. London: Altamira Press, 1996.

Dutrénit Bielous, Silvia. "Asuntos y temas partidarios en la memoria de las elites radical y peronista." In *A viente años del golpe. Con memoria democrática,* edited by Hugo Quiroga y César Teach, 143–67. Rosario, Argentina: Homo Sapiens, 1996.

———. "Del margen al centro del sistema político: los partidos uruguayos durante la dictadura." In *Diversidad partidaria y dictaduras: Argentina, Brasil y Uruguay,* edited by Dutrénit Bielous, 235–317.

———, ed. *Diversidad partidaria y dictaduras: Argentina, Brasil y Uruguay.* Mexico City: Instituto Mora, 1996.

———. *El maremoto militar y el archipiélago partidario. Testimonios para la historia reciente de los partidos políticos uruguayos.* Montevideo: Productora Editorial, 1994.

———. "La memoria de los políticos: sobre la pérdida y la recuperación de su estelaridad." In *Cuéntame cómo fue,* edited by Necoechea Gracia and Pablo Pozzi, 85–90.

———. "Presentación." In *Diversidad partidaria y dictaduras: Argentina, Brasil y Uruguay,* edited by Dutrénit Bielous, 9–12.

Encarnación, Omar G. "Latin America's Gay Rights Revolution." *Journal of Democracy* 22, no. 2 (April 2011): 104–18.

Esquit, Edgar. *La superación del indígena: la política de la modernización entre las élites indígenas de Comalapa, siglo XX.* Guatemala City: Instituto de Estudios Interétnicos, Universidad de San Carlos, 2010.

Esquit, Edgar, and Héctor Concoha. "Anthropologists in the Archives, Historians in 'the Field'." Presentation, Guatemalan Scholars Network Conference, July 11, 2013, Antigua, Guatemala.

Estévez, Dolia. *U.S. Ambassadors to Mexico: The Relationship through Their Eyes.* Washington, DC: Woodrow Wilson International Center for Scholars, 2013.

Evans, George Ewart. *Tools of Their Trade: An Oral History of Men at Work.* New York: Taplinger, 1970.

Evaristo Wenceslau, Marina. "Afimação e resistência—História oral de vida: O índio kayowá—Suicídio pelo tekohá." In *(Re)Introduzindo a história oral no Brasil,* edited by Sebe Bom Meihy, 217–22.

Falla, Ricardo. *Masacres en la selva: Ixcán, Guatemala (1975–1982).* Guatemala: Editorial Universitaria de Guatemala, 1992.

———. *Negreaba de zopilotes: masacre y sobrevivencia; Finca San Francisco, Nentón, Guatemala (1871–2010).* Guatemala City: Instituto AVANCSO, 2011.

Farnsworth-Alvear, Ann. *Dulcinea in the Factory: Myths, Morals, Men, and Women in Colombia's Industrial Experiment, 1905–1960.* Durham, NC: Duke University Press, 2000.

Felman, Shoshana, and Dori Laub. *Testimony: Crises of Witnessing in Literature, Psychoanalysis, and History*. New York: Routledge, 1991.
Ferguson, Sam. "Judging Memory." *LASA Forum* 44, no. 3 (Summer 2013): 21–3.
Fernandez, Nadine T. *Revolutionizing Romance: Interracial Couples in Contemporary Cuba*. New Brunswick, NJ: Rutgers University Press, 2010.
Ferrara, Orestes. *Memorias: una mirada sobre tres siglos*. Madrid: Ediciones Universal, 1975.
Finnegan, Ruth. "A Note on Oral Tradition and Historical Evidence." *History and Theory* 9 (1970): 195–201.
Forster, Cindy. *The Time of Freedom: Campesino Workers in Guatemala's October Revolution*. Pittsburgh, PA: University of Pittsburgh Press, 2001.
Fowler-Salamini, Heather. *Working Women, Entrepreneurs, and the Mexican Revolution: The Coffee Culture of Córdoba, Veracruz*. Lincoln: University of Nebraska Press, 2013.
Frank, Geyla. "Anthropology and Individual Lives: The Story of Life History and the History of Life Story." *American Anthropologist* 97, no. 1 (1995): 145–8.
Frank, Joceline. "A Woman's Journey: From Ecuador to L.A." Film Review. *Los Angeles Times*, November 20, 1989. http://articles.latimes.com/1989-11-20/entertainment/ca-93_1_culture-shock.
Freire, Paulo. *Pedagogy of the Oppressed*. Translated by Myra Bergman Ramos. New York: Herder and Herder, 1970.
Freire Montysuma, Marcos Fábio. "Um encontro com as fontes em História Oral." *Estudos Ibero Americanos* (Pontifícia Católica Universidade do Rio Grande do Sul, Brazil) 32, no. 1 (2006): 117–25.
———. *See also* Montysuma, Marcos.
Friedrich, Paul. *The Princes of Naranja*. Austin: University of Texas Press, 1987.
Frisch, Michael. "Oral History and the Digital Revolution: Toward a Post-Documentary Sensibility." In *The Oral History Reader*, edited by Robert Perks and Alistair Thomson, 102–14. 2nd edition. New York: Routledge, 2006.
———. *A Shared Authority: Essays on the Craft and Meaning of Oral and Public History*. Albany: State University of New York, 1990.
Frotscher, Meri, and Alexander Freund. "Conference Report: 5th Biennial Conference of the Brazilian Oral History Association's South Section in Marechal Candido Rondon, Paraná, 25–28 May 2009." *Oral History Forum* 29 (2009): 2–6.
Fuente, Alejandro de la. *A Nation for All: Race, Inequality, and Politics in Twentieth-Century Cuba*. Chapel Hill: University of North Carolina Press, 2001.
Fundação Getúlio Vargas (FGV), and Programa de História Oral. *Catálogo de departamentos, Centro de Pesquisa e Documentação de História Contemporânea do Brasil, Instituto de Direito Público e Ciências Políticas*. Rio de Janeiro: FGV, 1981.
Gamio, Manuel. *The Mexican Immigrant: His Life Story*. Chicago: University of Chicago Press, 1931.
Garay, Graciela de. "Another Turn of Screw." *Journal of the International Oral History Association* 2, no. 2 (2003): 14–15.
———. "La entrevista de historia oral: ¿Monólogo o conversación?" *Revista Electrónica de Investigación Educativa* 1, no. 1 (1999): 1–9. http://redie.uabc.mx/vol1no1/contenido-garay.html.
———. *Mario Pani: investigación y entrevistas. Historial oral de la Ciudad de México: testimonios de sus arquitectos, 1940–1990*. Mexico City: Consejo Nacional para la Cultura y las Artes, Instituto Mora, 2000.
———. "Un ensayo de contextualización histórica para entender una vida professional. Mario Pani, ejemplo mexicano de arquitecto moderno (1911–1993)." In *Caminos de*

historia y memoria en América Latina, edited by Necoechea Gracia and Torres Montenegro, 83–96.

Garcés Durán, Mario. *Recreando el pasado: guía metodológica para le memoria y la historia social*. Santiago, Chile: Educación y comunicaciones, 2002. http://www.ongeco.cl/wp-content/uploads/2015/04/Guia_metodologica_Recreando_el_pasado.pdf.

———. *Tomando su sitio: el movimiento de pobladores de Santiago, 1957–1970*. Santiago, Chile: Ediciones LOM, 2002.

Garcés Durán, Mario, Beatriz Ríos Etcheverry, and Hanny Suckel Ayala. *Voces de identidad: propuesta metodológica para la recuperación de la historia oral*. Santiago, Chile: Centro de Investigación y Desarrollo de la Educación, Educación y Comunicaciones, Corporación Privada de Desarrollo Social, and Fondo para el Desarrollo de la Cultura y las Artes, 1993.

Garcés Durán, Mario, and Sebastián Leiva. *El golpe en La Legua. Los caminos de la historia y memoria*. Santiago, Chile: Ediciones LOM, 2005.

García de León, Antonio. *Ejército de ciegos, Testimonios de la guerra chiapaneca entre carrancistas y rebeldes, 1914–1920*. Mexico City: Ediciones Toledo, 1991.

———. *Resistencia y utopia. Memorial de agravios y crónicas de revueltas y profecías acaecidas en la provincial de Chiapas durantes los últimos quinientos años de su historia*. Mexico City: Ediciones Era, 2002.

García Márquez, Gabriel. *Cien años de soledad*. Buenos Aires: Editorial Sudamericana, 1967.

Garulli, Liliana. "Oral History and Peronista Resistance." *Journal of the International Oral History Association* 2, no. 2 (June 2003): 10–2.

Gasparini, Juan. *Montoneros: final de cuentas*. Buenos Aires: Puntosur Editores, 1988.

Gatica, Mónica. "Industrialización y proletarización: las trabajadoras de INTECO en Trelew." In *Mujeres en palabras de mujeres*, edited by Edda Lía Crespo and Myriam Susana González, 131–41. Rawson, Argentina: Fondo Editorial Provincial, Secrétaria de Cultura del Chubut, 2009.

Gelman, Juan, and Mara La Madrid. *Ni el flaco perdón de Dios. Hijos de desaparecidos*. Buenos Aires: Planeta, 1997.

Gil, Carlos. *Hope and Frustration: Interviews with Leaders of Mexico's Political Opposition*. Wilmington, DE: Scholarly Resources Books, 1992.

Gluck, Sherna. "What's So Special about Women? Women's Oral History." *Frontiers: Journal of Women's Studies* 2, no. 1 (Summer 1977): 3–13.

Gluck, Sherna Berger, and Daphne Patai. "Introduction." In *Women's Words: The Feminist Practice of Oral History*, edited by Sherna Berger Gluck and Daphne Patai, 1–5.

———, eds. *Women's Words: The Feminist Practice of Oral History*. New York: Routledge, 1991.

González, Matilde. "The Man Who Brought Danger to the Village: Representations of the Armed Conflict in Guatemala from a Local Perspective." *Journal of Southern African Studies* 26, no. 2 (2000): 317–35.

———. "Modernización capitalista, racismo y violencia en Guatemala (1810–1930)." PhD diss., Colegio de México, 2009.

González, Olga M. *Unveiling Secrets of War in the Peruvian Andes*. Chicago: University of Chicago Press, 2011.

Gossen, Gary. "Chamula Genres of Verbal Behavior." In *Toward New Perspectives in Folklore*, edited by Américo Paredes and Richard Bauman, 145–67. Austin: University of Texas Press, 1972.

———. "To Speak with a Heated Heart: Chamula Canons of Style and Good Performance." In *Explorations in the Ethnography of Speaking*, edited by Richard Bauman and Joel Sherzer, 389–413. New York: Cambridge University Press, 1974.

Gould, Jeffrey, and Carlos Henríquez Consalvi, dirs. *1932: Scars of Memory (Cicatriz de la memoria)*. New York: First Run/Icarus Films, 2002. Film, 53 min.

Gould, Jeffrey, and Aldo Lauria-Santiago. *To Rise in Darkness: Revolution, Repression, and Memory in El Salvador*. Durham, NC: Duke University Press, 2008.

Gould, Stephen Jay. *The Mismeasure of Man*. New York: W. W. Norton, 1996.

———. *Time's Arrow, Time's Cycle: Myth and Metaphor in the Discovery of Geological Time*. Cambridge, MA: Harvard University Press, 1988.

Grandin, Greg. *The Last Colonial Massacre: Latin America in the Cold War*. Chicago: University of Chicago Press, 2004.

———. *Who Is Rigoberta Menchú?* New York: Verso Books, 2011.

Grandin, Greg, and Thomas Miller Klubock. "Editors' Introduction." In *Truth Commissions: State Terror, History, and Memory*, edited by Greg Grandin and Thomas Miller Klubock. Special issue of *Radical History Review* 97 (2007): 1–10.

Green, James. *Beyond Carnival: Male Homosexuality in Twentieth-Century Brazil*. Chicago: University of Chicago Press, 1999.

Green, Masha. "The Memory Keeper: The Oral Histories of Russia's New Nobel Laureate." *New Yorker*, October 26, 2015, 36–41.

Grieb, Kenneth. *Guatemalan Caudillo: The Regime of Jorge Ubico, Guatemala 1931–1944*. Athens: Ohio University Press, 1979.

Grupo de Investigaciones Agrarias. *Vida y palabra campesina*. 5 vols. Santiago, Chile: Grupo de Investigaciones Agrarias, 1986–88.

Gudmundson, Lowell. "On Green Revolutions and Golden Beans: Memories and Metaphors of Costa Rican Coffee Co-Op Founders." *Agricultural History* 88, no. 4 (2014): 538–65.

Guimarães Neto, Regina Beatriz. "Espaços e tempos entrecruzados na história: Práticas de pesquisa e escrita." In *História: Cultura e sentimiento. Outras histórias do Brasil*, edited by Antonio Torres Montenegro, António Paulo Rezende, Regina Beatria Guimarães Neto, Isabel Cristina Martins Guillen, Flávio Wenstein Teixeira, and Leny Caselli Anzai, 135–66. Recife and Cuiabá, Brazil: Editora Universitária Universidade Federal de Pernambuco and Editora Universitária Universidade Federal de Mato Grosso, 2008.

———. "História, política e testemunho: Violência e trabalho na Amazônia Brasileira. A narrativa oral da presidenta do Sindicato dos Trabalhadores Rurais de Confresa—Mato Grosso, Aparecida Barbosa da Silva." *História Oral: Revista da Associação Brasileira de História Oral* 13 (2010): 53–86.

———. "Vira mundo, vira mundo: Trajetórias nômades as cidades na Amazônia." *Projeto História: Revista do Programa de Estudos Pós-Graduados em História e do Departamento de História, São Paulo* 27 (2003): 49–69.

Gutiérrez, Ana. *Se necesita muchacha*. Mexico City: Fondo de Cultura Económica, 1983.

Gutiérrez Alea, Tomás, and Juan Carlos Tabio, dirs. *Fresa y chocolate*. Havana: Instituto Cubano del Arte e Industria Cinematograficos, 1993. Film, 110 min.

Guzmán, Patricio. *Chile, la memoria obstinada*. New York: Icarus Films, 1997.

———. *Nostalgia for the Light*. New York: Icarus Films, 2010. Film, 90 min.

Habermas, Jürgen. *Reason and the Rationalization of Society: Vol. 1 of the Theory of Communicative Action*. Boston: Beacon Press, 1984.

Hagihara, Ayako, and Grace Shimizu. "The Japanese Latin American Wartime and Redress Movement." *Amerasia* 28, no. 2 (2002): 203–16.

Hale, Sondra. "Feminist Method, Process, and Self-Criticism: Interviewing Sudanese Women." In *Women's Words: The Feminist Practice of Oral History*, edited by Sherna Berger Gluck and Daphne Patai, 121–36.

Hall, Jacquelyn Dowd. "You Must Remember This: Autobiography as Social Critique." *Journal of American History* 85, no. 2 (1998): 439–41.

Hamilton, Carrie. *Sexual Revolutions in Cuba: Passion, Politics, and Memory*. Chapel Hill: University of North Carolina Press, 2012.

Hankiss, Agnes. "Ontologies of the Self: On the Mythological Rearranging of One's Life-History." In *Biography and Society: The Life History Approach in the Social Sciences*, edited by Daniel Bertaux, 203–9. Oakland, CA: Sage, 1981.

Hanna, Julia. "Building Histories of Emerging Economies One Interview at a Time." *Working Knowledge* (Harvard Business School), May 28, 2014. http://hbswk.hbs.edu/item/building-histories-of-emerging-economies-one-interview-at-a-time.

Harpelle, Ronald. "White Zones: American Enclave Communities of Central America." In *Blacks and Blackness in Central America: Between Race and Place*, edited by Lowell Gudmundson and Justin Wolfe, 307–33. Durham, NC: Duke University Press, 2010.

Heilburn, Carolyn, and Catharine Stimpson. "Theories of Feminist Criticism: A Dialogue." In *Feminist Literary Criticism*, edited by Josephine Donovan, 61–73. Lexington: University of Kentucky Press, 1975.

Hendrickson, Carol. *Weaving Identities: Construction of Dress and Self in a Highland Guatemalan Town*. Austin: University of Texas Press, 1995.

Herrera-Sobek, Maria. *The Bracero Experience: Elitelore versus Folklore*. Los Angeles: UCLA Latin American Center Publications, 1979.

Higashide, Seiichi. *Adios to Tears: The Memoirs of a Japanese-Peruvian Internee in U.S. Concentration Camps*. Seattle: University of Washington Press, 2009.

Hill, Jonathan D. "Introduction: Myth and History." In *Rethinking History and Myth*, edited by Jonathan D. Hill, 1–17.

———, ed. *Rethinking History and Myth: Indigenous South American Perspectives on the Past*. Urbana: University of Illinois Press, 1988.

Hill, Jonathan D., and Robin M. Wright. "Time, Narrative, and Ritual: Historical Interpretations from an Amazonian Society." In *Rethinking History and Myth*, edited by Jonathan D. Hill, 78–105.

Hinojosa, Servando Z. *In This Body: Kaqchikel Maya and the Grounding of Spirit*. Albuquerque: University of New Mexico Press, 2016.

Hook, Elizabeth Snyder. "Awakening from War: History, Trauma, and Testimony in the Work of Heinrich Böll." In *The Work of Memory: New Directions in the Study of German Society and Culture*, edited by Alon Confino and Peter Fritzche, 136–53. Urbana: University of Illinois Press, 2002.

Horton, Myles, with Judith Kohl and Herbert Kohl. *The Long Haul: An Autobiography*. New York: Doubleday, 1990.

Hostnig, Rainer, and Luis Vásquez Vicente, eds. *Nab'ab'l Qtanam: la memoria colectiva del pueblo mam de Quetzaltenango*. Quetzaltenango, Guatemala: Centro de Capacitación e Investigación Campesina, 1994.

Huggins, Martha, Mika Haritos-Fatouros, and Philip Zimbardo. *Violence Workers: Police Torturers and Murderers Reconstruct Brazilian Atrocities*. Berkeley: University of California Press, 2002.

Hymes, Dell. *In Vain I Tried to Tell You: Essays in Native American Ethnopoetics*. Philadelphia: University of Pennsylvania Press, 1981.

Iacovetta, Franca. "Post-Modern Ethnography, Historical Materialism, and Decentering the (Male) Authorial Voice: A Feminist Conversation." *Histoire Sociale/Social History* 32, no. 64 (November 1999): 275–93.

Iglesia Guatemalteca en el Exilio. *Nosotros conocemos nuestra historia: 500 años de resistencia indígena, negra y popular.* Guatemala City: Iglesia Guatemalteca en el Exilio, 1992.

Instituto de Estudio del Sandinismo. *Y se armó la runga–! Testimonios de la insurrección popular sandinista en Masaya.* Managua: Editorial Nueva Europa, 1982.

Instituto Nacional de Antropología y Historia (INAH). *Catálogo del Archivo de la Palabra.* Mexico City: INAH, 1977.

Iwao Ueunten, Wesley. "Japanese Latin American Internment from an Okinawan Perspective." *Social Process in Hawai'i* 42 (2007): 97–120.

Jaksíc, Iván. "Oral History in the Americas." *Journal of American History* 79, no. 2 (September 1992): 590–600.

James, Daniel. *Doña María's Story: Life History, Memory, and Political Identity.* Durham, NC: Duke University Press, 2000.

———. *Resistance and Integration: Peronism and the Argentine Working Class, 1946–1976.* Cambridge: Cambridge University Press, 1994.

Jelin, Elizabeth. "Secuencias ocupacionales y cambio estructural: historias de trabajadores por cuenta propia." In *Las historias de vida en ciencias sociales: teoría y técnica*, edited by Jorge Balán, 175–92. Buenos Aires: Ediciones Nueva Visión, 1974.

———. *State Repression and the Labors of Memory.* Minneapolis: University of Minnesota Press, 2003.

Jelin, Elizabeth, and Susana G. Kaufman. "Layers of Memories: Twenty Years after in Argentina." In *The Politics of War Memory and Commemoration*, edited by T. G. Ashplant, Graham Dawson, and Michael Roper, 89–110. New York: Routledge, 2000.

Jelin, Elizabeth, and Pablo Vila, with photos by Alicia D'Amico. *Podría ser yo: los sectores populares urbanos en imagen y palabra.* Buenos Aires: Ediciones de la Flor, Centro de Estudios de Estado y Sociedad, 1987.

Johnstone, Barbara. *Stories, Community, and Place: Narratives from Middle America.* Bloomington: Indiana University Press, 1990.

Julião, Francisco. *Cambão—The Yoke: The Hidden Face of Brazil.* Middlesex, England: Penguin, 1972.

Kaplan, Temma. "Reversing the Shame and Gendering the Memory." *Signs* 28, no. 1 (2002): 184–91.

———. *Taking Back the Streets: Women, Youth, and Direct Democracy.* Berkeley: University of California Press, 2003.

Kay, Cristóbal. "Agrarian Reform and the Class Struggle in Chile." *Latin American Perspectives* 18 (1978): 133–5.

Kennedy, Elizabeth Lapovsky, and Madeline D. Davis. *Boots of Leather, Slippers of Gold: The History of a Lesbian Community.* New York: Penguin, 1993.

Kerr, Daniel. "Allan Nevins Is Not My Grandfather: The Roots of Radical Oral History Practice in the United States." *Oral History Review* 43, no. 2 (Summer/Fall 2016): 367–91.

———. "We Know What the Problem Is: Using Oral History to Develop Collaborative Analysis of Homelessness from the Bottom Up." *Oral History Review* 30, no. 1 (Winter–Spring, 2003): 27–45.

Klubock, Thomas Miller. *Contested Communities: Class, Gender, and Politics in Chile's El Teniente Copper Mine, 1904–1951.* Durham, NC: Duke University Press, 1998.

———. "Working-Class Masculinity, Middle-Class Morality, and Labor Politics in the Chilean Mines." *Journal of Social History* 3, no. 2 (1996): 435–63.

Kudo, Elsa H. "Preface to the Year 2000 Edition." In *Adios to Tears: The Memoirs of a Japanese-Peruvian Internee in U.S. Concentration Camps*, edited by Seiichi Higashide, 3–6. Seattle: University of Washington Press, 2000.

Kurasaw, Fuyuki. "A Message in a Bottle: Bearing Witness as a Mode of Ethico-Political Practice." *Theory, Culture, and Society* 26, no. 1 (2009): 95–114.

LaCapra, Dominick. *History and Memory after Auschwitz*. Ithaca, NY: Cornell University Press, 1998.

Landsman, Gail. *Sovereignty and Symbol: Indian-White Conflict at Ganienkeh*. Albuquerque: University of New Mexico Press, 1988.

La Serna, Miguel. *The Corner of the Living: Ayacucho on the Eve of the Shining Path Insurgency*. Chapel Hill: University of North Carolina Press, 2012.

Laverdi, Robson. "Cidade, trabalho e homossexualidade vividos: Por uma história oral da alteridade gay em pequenas cidades no Brasil." In *Oral History in Latin America/Historia Oral en América Latina*, edited by Pablo Pozzi et al.

———. "Vivencias urbanos de jóvenes muchachos homosexuales en el interior de Brasil: alteridades en y por la historia oral." In *Caminos de historia y memoria en América Latina*, edited by Necoechea Gracia and Torres Montenegro, 117–37.

Leinhard, Martín. *O mar e o mato: Histórias da escravidão (Congo-Angola, Brasil, Caribe)*. Salvador, Brazil: Editora da Federal Universidade Federal da Bahia/Centro de Estudos Afro-Orientais, 1998.

Levenson, Deborah. *Adios Niño: The Gangs of Guatemala City and the Politics of Death*. Durham, NC: Duke University Press, 2013.

Levenson-Estrada, Deborah. *Trade Unionists against Terror: Guatemala City, 1954–1985*. Chapel Hill: University of North Carolina Press, 1994.

Levine, Daniel. *Religion and Politics in Latin America: The Catholic Church in Venezuela and Colombia*. Princeton, NJ: Princeton University Press, 1981.

Lewis, Oscar. *The Children of Sánchez: Autobiography of a Mexican Family*. New York: Random House, 1961.

———. *La Vida: A Puerto Rican Family in the Culture of Poverty—San Juan and New York*. New York: Random House, 1966.

Lewis, Oscar, Ruth M. Lewis, and Susan M. Ridgon. *Living the Revolution: An Oral History of Contemporary Cuba*. 3 vols. Urbana: University of Illinois Press, 1977–78.

Linde, Charlotte. *Life Stories: The Creation of Coherence*. Oxford: Oxford University Press, 1993.

Lobato, Mirta Zaida. *Historia de las trabajadoras en la Argentina (1869–1960)*. Buenos Aires: Edhasa, 2007.

———. "Introducción." In *Cuando las mujeres reinaban: belleza, virtud y poder en la Argentina del siglo XX*, edited by Mirta Zaida Lobato, 9–18. Buenos Aires: Biblos, 2005.

———. *La vida en las fábricas. Trabajo, protesta y conflicto en una comunidad obrera, Berisso, (1904–1970)*. Buenos Aires: Entrepasados/Prometeo Libros, 2001.

———. "Recordar, recuperar, conservar palabras e imágenes de mujeres: la construcción de un archivo en Argentina." *Voces Recobradas: Revistas de Historia Oral* 5, no. 13 (2002): 8–11.

———. "Voces subalternas de la memoria." *Mora, Revista del Instituto Interdisciplinaria de Estudios de Género* 7 (2001): 149–57.

Lobato, Mirta Zaida, María Damilokou, and Lizel Tornay. "Las reinas del trabajo bajo el peronismo." In *Cuando las mujeres reinaban: belleza, virtud y poder en la Argentina del siglo XX*, edited by Mirta Zaida Lobato, 77–120. Buenos Aires: Biblos, 2005.

Lockwood, Lee. *Castro's Cuba, Cuba's Fidel: An American Journalist's Inside Look at Today's Cuba in Text and Picture*. New York: Vintage Books, 1967.

Loner, Beatriz Ana, and Lorena Almeida Gill. "Clubes carnavaleros afrobrasileños en Pelotas: la emoria más allá de la samba." In *Oral History in Latin America/Historia Oral en América Latina*, edited by Pablo Pozzi et al.

Lovell, George. *A Beauty That Hurts: Life and Death in Guatemala*. Austin: University of Texas Press, 2000.

Lovell, George W., and Christopher H. Lutz. "The Primacy of Larger Truths: Rigoberta Menchú and the Tradition of Native Testimony in Guatemala." In *The Rigoberta Menchú Controversy*, edited by Arturo Arias, 171–97. Minneapolis: University of Minnesota Press, 2001.

Loveman, Brian, and Elizabeth Lira. "Truth, Justice, Reconciliation, and Impunity as Historical Themes: Chile, 1814–2006." In *Truth Commissions: State Terror, History, and Memory*, edited by Greg Grandin and Thomas Miller Klubock. Special issue of *Radical History Review* 97 (2007): 43–76.

Lucena, Célia. "Mobilidade social: Histórias de família e variedades de gênero." In *(Re) Introduzindo a história oral no Brasil*, edited by Sebe Bom Meihy, 206–16.

Lynd, Alice, and Robert Staughton Lynd, eds. *Rank and File: Personal Histories by Working-Class Organizers*. Boston: Beacon Press, 1973.

Mallon, Florencia E. "Conclusion." In *Decolonizing Native Histories: Collaboration, Knowledge, and Language in the Americas*, edited by Florencia E. Mallon, 219–20. Durham, NC: Duke University Press, 2012.

———. "Constructing *Mestizaje* in Latin America: Authenticity, Marginality, and Gender in the Claiming of Ethnic Identities." *Journal of Latin American Anthropology* 2, no. 1 (1996): 170–81.

———. *Courage Tastes of Blood: The Mapuche Community of Nicolás Ailío and the Chilean State, 1906–2001*. Durham, NC: Duke University Press, 2005.

———. "Editor's Introduction." In *When a Flower Is Reborn: The Life and Times of a Mapuche Feminist*. By Rosa Isolde Reuque Paillalef, edited by Florencia E. Mallon, 1–33. Durham, NC: Duke University Press, 2002.

———. "Introduction: Decolonizing Knowledge, Language, and Narrative." In *Decolonizing Native Histories: Collaboration, Knowledge, and Language in the America*, edited by Florencia E. Mallon, 1–19. Durham, NC: Duke University Press, 2012.

Mankiewicz, Frank, and Kirby Jones. *With Fidel: A Portrait of Castro and Cuba*. Chicago: Playboy Press, 1975.

Marcus, George, and Michael M. J. Fischer. *Anthropology as Cultural Critique: An Experimental Moment in the Human Sciences*. Chicago: University of Chicago Press, 1986.

Martínez, Oscar J. *Border People: Life and Society in the U.S.-Mexican Borderlands*. Tucson: University of Arizona Press, 1994.

Martínez Omaña, María Concepción. "Oral History, a Political Resource for Public Action." *Journal of the International Oral History Association* 2, no. 2 (June 2003): 12–13.

———. "Services, Management, and the Construction of Place." *Oral History Association of Australia Journal* 25 (2003): 6–9.

Mason, Elizabeth B., and Louis M. Starr. *The Oral History Collection of Colombia University*. New York: Oral History and Research Office, Columbia University, 1973.

Mastrángelo, Mariana. "Mi abuela cantaba Bandiera Rossa y La Internacional e iba a misa todos los días. Política y cultura izquierdista en Argentino." In *Oral History in Latin America/Historia Oral en América Latina*, edited by Pablo Pozzi et al.

Matters, Marion. *Oral History Cataloging Manual*. Chicago: Society of American Archivists, 1995.

Maxwell, Judith. "Three Tales—Two and a Half Linguistic Systems." Paper presented at the American Anthropological Association Conference, November 1986, Philadelphia.

McAlister, Carlotta. "A Headlong Rush into the Future: Violence and Revolution in a Guatemalan Indigenous Village." In *A Century of Revolution: Insurgent and Counterinsurgent Violence during Latin America's Long Cold War*, edited by Greg Grandin and Gilbert Joseph, 276–308. Durham, NC: Duke University Press, 2010.

McCoy, Donald. "University of Kansas Oral History Project in Costa Rica." *LASA Newsletter* 4 (March 1973): 36–7.

Mckiernan-González, John. *Fevered Measures: Public Health and Race at the Texas-Mexico Border, 1848–1942*. Durham, NC: Duke University Press, 2012.

McNeill, J. R., and William H. McNeill. "Interview by Donald A. Yerxa." *Historically Speaking* 4, no. 2 (November 2002): 13–15.

McPherson, Alan. "Artful Resistance: Song, Literature, and Representations of U.S. Occupations in Nicaragua and Hispaniola." *Latin Americanist* 56, no. 2 (June 2012): 93–117.

Médica, Gerardo, and Viviana Villegas. "A la vera de la Ruta 3 'la gloriosa doble P'. Una aproximación a los 'putos peronistas' de La Matanza." In *Oral History in Latin America/Historia Oral en América Latina*, edited by Pablo Pozzi et al.

Medina, Eden. *Cybernetic Revolutionaries: Technology and Politics in Allende's Chile*. Cambridge, MA: MIT Press, 2014.

Medrano Platas, Alejandro. *Quince directores del cine mexicano*. Mexico City: Plaza y Valdez, 1999.

Menand, Louis. "Bad Comma: Lynne Truss's Strange Grammar." *New Yorker*, June 28, 2004, 102–5.

———. "The Elvis Oracle: Did Anyone Invent Rock and Roll?" *New Yorker*, November 16, 2015, 80–7.

Menchú, Rigoberta. *Crossing Borders*. London: Verso, 1998.

Meyer, Eugenia. "Documenting the Earthquake of 1985 in Mexico City." *Oral History Review* 16 (Spring 1988): 1–5.

———. "El Archivo de la Palabra: hacia una historia de masas." *Antropología e Historia* (Boletín del INAH) 3, no. 23 (July–September 1978): 3–5.

———. "Oral History in Mexico and the Caribbean." In *Oral History: An Interdisciplinary Anthology*, edited by David K. Dunaway and Willa K. Baum, 343–50. 2nd edition. New York: Altamira Press, 1996.

———. "Oral History in Mexico and Latin America." *Oral History Review* 4 (1976): 56–61.

———. "Recuperando, recordando, denunciando, custodiando la memoria del pasado puesto al día. Historia oral en Latinoamérica y el Caribe." *Historia y Fuente Oral* 5 (1991): 139–44.

———, ed. *Testimonios para la historia del cine Mexicano*. Vol. 4. Mexico City: Instituto Nacional de Antropología y Historia, ca. 1975.

Meyer, Eugenia, and Alicia Olivera de Bonfil. "La historia oral: origen, metodología, desarrollo y perspectivas." *Historia Mexicana* 21 (October–December 1971): 372–87.

Millar, Gearoid. "Assessing Local Experience of Truth-Telling in Sierra Leone: Getting to 'Why' through a Qualitative Case Study Analysis." *International Journal of Transitional Justice* 4, no. 3 (2010): 477–96.

Miloslavich Tupac, Diana. "Women in Peru: A History of Struggle and Courage." In *The Autobiography of María Elena Moyano: The Life and Death of a Peruvian Activist*, edited by Diana Miloslavich Tupac, 3–22. Gainesville: University Press of Florida, 2000.

Mintz, Sidney. "The Sensation of Moving, While Standing Still." *American Ethnologist* 16, no. 4 (1989): 786–96.

———. *Worker in the Cane: A Puerto Rican Life History*. New Haven, CT: Yale University Press, 1960.

Mondloch, James. *K'iche' Maya Oral History Project*. Albuquerque: Latin American and Iberian Institute, University of New Mexico. http://laii.unm.edu/kiche/index.php.

Montagu, Ashley. *Race, Science, and Humanity*. New York: Van Nostrand Reinhold, 1963.

Montejo, Victor. *Testimony: Death of a Guatemalan Village*. Willimantic, CT: Curbstone Press, 1987.

Montysuma, Marcos. "Lecturas de género y medio ambiente a través de los recuerdos y experiencias de las mujeres de Xapuri-Acre (1964–2006)." In *Caminos de historia y memoria en América Latina*, edited by Gerardo Necoechea Gracia and Antonio Torres, 167–80.

———. *See also* Freire Montysuma, Marcos Fabio.

Moore, Stephanie. "Gender and Japanese Immigrants to Peru, 1899 through World War II." Working Papers, University of California History Workshop. 2010. http://escholarship.org/uc/item/0g06x8z0.

———. "Los Nikkei internados durante la Segunda Guerra Mundial: la larga lucha por una reparación justa." *Discover Nikkei*, December 4, 2007. http://www.discovernikkei.org/en/journal/2007/12/4/nikkei-internados/.

Moreiras, Alberto. "The Aura of Testimonio." In *The Real Thing: Testimonial Discourse and Latin America*, edited by George M. Gugelberger, 194–224. Durham, NC: Duke University Press, 1996.

Morrison, Joan, and Charlotte Fox Zabusky, eds. *American Mosaic: The Immigrant Experience in the Words of Those Who Lived It*. New York: Dutton, 1980.

Mousnier, Roland. *Peasant Uprisings in Seventeenth-Century France, Russia, and China*. Translated by Brian Pearce. New York: Harper and Row, 1970.

Myerhoff, Barbara. *Remembered Lives: The Work of Ritual, Storytelling, and Growing Older*. Ann Arbor: University of Michigan Press, 1992.

Nash, June. *We Eat the Mines and the Mines Eat Us: Dependency and Exploitation in Bolivian Tin Mines*. New York: Columbia University Press, 1979.

Necoechea Gracia, Gerardo. "Custom and History: Teaching Oral History in the Community Museums Project of Oaxaca, Mexico." *Radical History Review* 65 (1996): 124–8.

———. *Después de vivir un siglo: ensayos de historia oral*. Mexico City: Instituto Nacional de Antropología e Historia, 2005.

———. "Editorial." *Words and Silences* 2, no. 1 (2003): 1–3.

———. "El análisis en la historia oral." In *Cuéntame cómo fue*, edited by Necoechea Gracia and Pablo Pozzi, 73–83.

———. "¿Existe una historia oral latinoamericana?" In *Caminos de historia y memoria en América Latina*, edited by Necoechea Gracia and Torres Montenegro, 1–4.

———. "From Favour to Right: Two Generations View Their Living Space in Mexico City." *Oral History Association of Australia Journal* 25 (2003): 10–14.

———. "Los contextos del recuerdo y la historia oral." In *Caminos de historia y memoria en América Latina*, edited by Necoechea Gracia and Torres Montenegro, 181–90.

———. "Mi mamá me platicó: punto de vista e historia reciente." In *Oral History in Latin America/Historia Oral en América Latina*, edited by Pablo Pozzi et al.

Necoechea Gracia, Gerardo, and Patricia Pensado Leglise, eds. *Voltear el mundo de cabeza. Historias de la militancia de izquierda en América Latina*. Buenos Aires: Imago Mundi, 2011.

Necoechea Gracia, Gerardo, and Antonio Torres Montenegro, eds. *Caminos de historia y memoria en América Latina*. Buenos Aires: Imago Mundi/Red Latinoamericana de Historia Oral, 2011.

Necoechea Gracia, Gerardo, and Pablo Pozzi, eds. *Cuéntame cómo fue. Introducción a la historia oral*. Buenos Aires: Imago Mundi, 2008.

Neira Samarez, Hugo. *Huillca, habla un campesino peruano*. Havana: Premio Testimonio Casa de las Americas, 1979.

Nora, Pierre. "Between Memory and History: Les Lieux de Mémoire." *Representations* 26 (1989): 7–25.

Oakley, Ann. "Interviewing Women: A Contradiction in Terms." In *Doing Feminist Research*, edited by Helen Roberts, 30–61. London, Boston, Henley: Routlege & Kegan Paul, 1981.

Oficina de Derechos Humanos del Arzobispado de Guatemala (ODHAG). Guatemala: Nunca Más. Informe de *Proyecto Interdiocesano de Recuperación de la Memoria Histórica. 4 volumes*. Guatemala City: ODHAG *La memoria tiene la palabra: sistemización del Proyecto Interdiocesano de Recuperación de la Memoria Histórica*. Guatemala City: ODHAG, 2007.

Olivera Costa, Albertina, Maria Teresa de Porciuncula Moraes, Norma Marzola, and Valentina da Rocha Lima. *Memórias do exílio, depoimentos*. Vol. 2. Rio de Janeiro: Paz e Terra, 1980.

Olivera de Bonfil, Alicia. "Treinta años de historia oral en México: revisión, aportes y tendencias." In *Historia y testimonios orales*, edited by Cuauhtémoc Velasco, 73–90.

Oltuski, Enrique. *Vida Campesina: My Life in the Cuban Revolution*. New York: Wiley, 2002.

Oral History Association. Principles and Best Practices: Principles for Oral History and Best Practices for Oral History. Carlisle, PA. 2009. http://www.oralhistory.org/about/principles-and-practices/.

Padilla Ramos, Raquel. "Diagnosis 'Suspicious Yellow Fever': Yaquis among Medical Doctors and Health Authorities in Yucatan, 1900–1911." Paper presented at the American Historical Association Annual Conference, January 8, 2016, Atlanta.

Pádua Bosi, Antonio de, Davi Félix Schreiner, Rinaldo José Varussa, and Robson Laverdi. "Trabalho e movimentos sociais." *Tempos Históricos* 8 (2006): 309–18.

Park, Rebekah. "Remembering Resistance, Forgetting Torture: *Compromiso* and Gender in Former Political Prisoners' Oral History Narrative in Post-Dictatorial Argentina." *History of Communism in Europe* 4, no. 4 (2013): 87–111.

Pardo Llada, José. *Memoria de la Sierra Maestra*. Havana: Editorial Tierra Nueva, 1960.

Pasquali, Laura. "Mujeres y militantes. Un acercamiento a las organizaciones armadas revolucionarias desde la historia oral." *Zona Franca* (Centro de Estudios Interdisciplinarios sobre las Mujeres) 13, no. 14 (May 2005): 122–39.

Pasquali, Laura, Guillermo Ríos, and Cristina Viano. "Culturas militantes." In *Cuéntame cómo fue*, edited by Necoechea Gracia and Pozzi, 109–16.

Passerini, Luisa. *Fascism in Popular Memory: The Cultural Experience of the Turin Working Class*. Cambridge, England: Cambridge University Press, 1987.

Patai, Daphne. *Brazilian Women Speak: Contemporary Life Stories*. New Brunswick, NJ: Rutgers University Press, 1988.

———. "Ethical Problems of Personal Narratives, or, Who Should Eat the Last Piece of Cake." *International Journal of Oral History* 8 (February 1987): 5–27.

———. "U.S. Academics and Third World Women: Is Ethical Research Possible?" In *Women's Words: The Feminist Practice of Oral History*, edited by Sherna Berger Gluck and Daphne Patai, 137–53.

———. "Whose Truth? Iconicity and Accuracy in the World of Testimonial Literature." In *The Rigoberta Menchú Controversy*, edited by Arturo Arias, 270–87. Minneapolis: University of Minnesota Press, 2001.

Pavón Tamayo, Luis, and Asya Vázquez Tamargo. *Días de combate*. Havana: La Habana Instituto del Libro, 1970.

Pelayo Rangel, Alejandro. *La generación de la crisis. El cine independiente mexicano de los años ochenta*. Mexico City: Instituto Mexicano de Cinematografía, Consejo Nacional para la Cultura y las Artes, 2012.

Pensado Leglise, María Patricia. "Elements of Identity in a Modern Community." *Oral History Association of Australia Journal* 25 (2003): 15–17.

———. "Memorias de la experiencia política de cinco mujeres latinoamericanas de izquierda." In *Caminos de historia y memoria en América Latina*, edited by Necoechea Gracia and Torres Montenegro, 217–28.

———. "The Reach of Oral History: The Case of San Pedro de los Pinos." *Journal of the International Oral History Association* 2, no. 2 (2003): 7–8.

Pensado Leglise, María Patricia, and Leonor Correa Ethegaray. "Historia oral de un barrio de la ciudad de México: Mixcoac." In *Historia y testimonios orales*, edited by Cuauhtémoc Velasco, 183–90.

Pérez Arce, Francisco. "De la historia oral a la historia escrita. Las posibilidades de la memoria." In *Historia y testimonios orales*, edited by Cuauhtémoc Velasco, 199–209.

Perks, Robert, and Alistair Thomson, eds. *The Oral History Reader*. 2nd edition. New York: Routledge, 2006.

Perone, Jorge Aldo. *Identidad o masificación: Una encrucijada en la industria vitivinícola Argentina*. Mendoza, Argentina: Facultad de Ciencias Económicas, Universidad Nacional de Cuyo, 1985.

Petrich, Perla. *Memoria de mi pueblo: Santa Catarina Palopó*. Guatemala City: Instituto de Relaciones Internacionales para la Paz Publicaciones, 1992.

Pino, Ponciano del. "Uchuraccay: memoria y representación de la violencia política en los Andes." In *Luchas locales, comunidades e identidades*, edited by Elizabeth Jelin and Ponciano del Pino, 11–62. Madrid/Buenos Aires: Siglos XXI Editores, 2003.

Pisani, Alejandra, and Ana Jemio. "El proceso de construcción del Archivo Testimonial sobre el Operativo Independencia y la dictadura militar en Famaillá." In *Oral History in Latin America/Historia Oral en América Latina*, edited by Pablo Pozzi et al.

Pizzato, J. Luke. "The Language of Public Memory: La Asociación Minga and the Authentic Image of the Victim." *ReVista: Harvard Review of Latin America* 13, no. 1 (Fall 2013): 38–40.

Pla Brugat, Dolores. "Algo acerca de archivos de historia oral." In *Historia y testimonios orales*, edited by Cuauhtémoc Velasco, 91–102.

Plank, Gary A. "What Silence Means for Educators of American Indian Children." *Journal of American Indian Education* 34, no. 1 (1994): 3–19.

Plate, Leonor, Dora Schwarzstein, and Pablo Yankelevich. *Historia de la Universidad de Buenos Aires, Bibliografía*. Buenos Aires: Editorial Universitaria de Buenos Aires, 1990.

Politzer, Patricia. *Altamirano*. Buenos Aires: Grupo Editorial Zeta/Santiago, Chile: Ediciones Melquíades, 1989.

———. *Fear in Chile: Lives under Pinochet*. New York: Pantheon Books, 1989.

Poniatowska, Elena. "The Earthquake." *Oral History Review* 16 (Spring 1988): 7–20.

———. *Massacre in Mexico*. Translated by Helen R. Lane. Columbia: University of Missouri Press, 1992.

Popular Memory Group. "Popular Memory: Theory, Politics, Method." In *Making Histories: Studies in History-Writing and Politics*, edited by Richard Johnson, Gregor McLennan, Bill Schwarz, and David Sutton, 205–52. Minneapolis: University of Minnesota Press, 1982.

Portelli, Alessandro. "Apresentação." In *Historia oral, possibilidades e procedimientos*, edited by Sónia Maria de Freitas, 9–14. São Paulo: Humanitas/Imprensa Oficial SP, 2002.

———. *The Battle of Valle Giulia: Oral History and the Art of Dialogue*. Madison: University of Wisconsin Press, 1997.

———. *The Death of Luigi Trastulli and Other Stories: Form and Meaning in Oral History*. Albany: State University of New York Press, 1991.

Posocco, Sylvia. *Secrecy and Insurgency: Socialities and Knowledge Practices in Guatemala*. Tuscaloosa: University of Alabama Press, 2014.

Power, Margaret. *Right-Wing Women in Chile: Feminine Power and the Struggle against Allende, 1964–1973*. College Station: Pennsylvania State University Press, 2002.

Pozas, Ricardo. *Juan Pérez Jolote: Biografía de un Tzotzil*. Mexico City: Fondo de Cultura Económica, 1952.

Pozzi, Pablo. "Consignas, historia y oralidad: los cánticos en las movilizaciones Argentinas." In *Caminos de historia y memoria en América Latina*, edited by Necoechea Gracia and Torres Montenegro, 245–59.

———. "'En function de la nueva generación', una mujer del ERP." In *Voltear el mundo de cabeza*, edited by Necoechea Gracia and María Patricia Pensado Leglise, 201–29.

———. "Historia oral: repensar la historia." In *Cuéntame cómo fue*, edited by Necoechea Gracia and Pablo Pozzi, 3–9.

———. "Oral History in Argentina and the IOHA." *Face to Face* 17, no. 1 (July 8, 2014). http://www.iohanet.org/face-to-face-12/.

———. "Oral History in Latin America." *Oral History Forum/Forum d'histoire orale* 32 (2012). Special issue of *Oral History in Latin America/Historia Oral en América Latina*, edited by Pablo Pozzi et al. http://www.oralhistoryforum.ca/index.php/ohf/issue/view/42.

———. "¿Quién hizo el mundo? Fuentes orales y política en la cultura de los obreros argentinos." *Oral History in Latin America/Historia Oral en América Latina*. Special issue of *Oral History Forum/Forum d'histoire orale* 32 (2012), edited by Pablo Pozzi et al.

Pozzi, Pablo, Alexander Freund, Gerardo Necoechea Gracia, and Robson Laverdi, eds. *Oral History in Latin America/Historia Oral en América Latina*. Special issue of *Oral History Forum/Forum d'histoire orale* 32 (2012). http://www.oralhistoryforum.ca/index.php/ohf/issue/view/42.

Pozzi, Pablo, and Alejandro M. Schneider. *Combatiendo al capital: crisis y recomposición de la clase obrera Argentina (1983–1993)*. Buenos Aires: El Bloque Editorial, 1994.

———. *Los setentistas: izquierda y clase obrera*. Buenos Aires: Editorial de Universitaria de Buenos Aires, 2000.

———. "Memoria y socialismo." In *Cuéntame cómo fue*, edited by Necoechea Gracia and Pablo Pozzi, 91–107.

Prakash, Gyan. "Subaltern Studies as Postcolonial Criticism." *American Historical Review* 99, no. 5 (December 1994): 1475–90.

Prelorán, Jorge, Mabel Prelorán, and Zulay Saravino. *Zulay, Facing the Twenty-First Century*. Documentary film, 110 minutes. Hollywood, CA: Advanced Digital Services, 1992 [1989].

Price, Richard. *First-Time: The Historical Vision of an African American People*. Chicago: University of Chicago Press, 2002.

Quinney, Valerie. "Childhood in a Southern Mill Village." *International Journal of Oral History* 3, no. 3 (November 1982): 167–92.

Ramos, Alcida. "Indian Voices: Contact Experienced and Expressed." In *Rethinking History and Myth*, edited by Jonathan D. Hill, 214–34.

Rappaport, Joanne. *Cumbe Reborn: An Andean Ethnography of History*. Chicago: University of Chicago Press, 1994.

———. *The Politics of Memory: Native Historical Interpretation in the Colombian Andes*. Durham, NC: Duke University Press, 1998.

Rappaport, Joanne, and Abelardo Ramos Pacho. "Collaboration and Historical Writing: Challenges for the Indigenous-Academic Dialogue." In *Decolonizing Native Histories: Collaboration, Knowledge, and Language in the Americas*, edited by Florencia E. Mallon, 122–43, Durham, NC: Duke University Press, 2012.

Rasnake, Roger. "Images of Resistance to Colonial Domination." In *Rethinking History and Myth: Indigenous South American Perspectives on the Past*, edited by Jonathan D. Hill, 136–56.

Recovery of History Memory Project (REHMI). *Guatemala Never Again!* Maryknoll, NY: Orbis Books, 1999.

Reuda, Salvador, and Alicia Olivera. "La historia oral. Su importancia en la investigación histórica contemporánea." *Boletín del Centro de Estudios de la Revolución Mexicana. Lázaro Cárdenas* 3, no. 3 (1980): 74–83.

Reuque Paillalef, Rosa Isolde. *When a Flower Is Reborn: The Life and Times of a Mapuche Feminist*. Edited and Translated by Florencia Mallon. Durham, NC: Duke University Press, 2002.

Reyes Castillo Bueno, María de los. *Reyita: The Life of a Black Cuban Woman in the Twentieth Century*. Translated by Anne McClean. Durham, NC: Duke University Press, 2000.

Richardson, Laurel. "Narrative and Sociology." *Journal of Contemporary Ethnography* 2, no. 1 (1990): 117–35.

Rieff, David. "After the Caudillo." *New York Times*, November 18, 2007: 50.

Rigney, Ann. "Reconciliation and Remembering: (How) Does It Work?" *Memory Studies* 5, no. 3 (2012): 251–8.

Ritchie, Donald. *Doing Oral History: Using Interviews to Uncover the Past and Preserve It for the Future*. 2nd edition. New York: Oxford University Press, 2003.

———. "www.oralhistory.infinity." *Oral History Review* 26, no. 2 (Summer–Autumn 1999): 9–16.

Rodríguez, Ana, and Glenn Garvin. *Diary of a Survivor: Nineteen Years in a Cuban Women's Prison*. New York: St. Martin's Press, 1995.

Rodríguez Castañeda, Rafael, Adolfo Castañón, and Diego Flores Magón, eds. *Daniel Cosío Villegas: un protagonista de la etapa constructive de la Revolución Mexicana—Entrevistas de James W. Wilkie y Edna Monzón Wilkie [en 1964–1965]*. Mexico City: Colegio de México, 2011.

Ruiz-Funes, Concepción, and Enriqueta Tuñón. "Historia oral. Creación e interpretación de Fuentes en los estudios de la mujer." In *Historia y testimonios orales*, 191–7.

Rus, Jan, and Diane L. Rus. "The Taller Tzotzil of Chiapas, Mexico: A Native Language Publishing Project, 1985–2002." In *Decolonizing Native Histories: Collaboration, Knowledge, and Language in the Americas*, edited by Florencia E. Mallon, 144–74. Durham, NC: Duke University Press, 2012.

Sá Almeida, Anna Beatriz de, Cristina Fonseca, and Wanda Hamilton. "Os sanitaristas e a institucionalização da saúde pública no Brasil (1930–1970)." In *(Re)Introduzindo a história oral no Brasil*, edited by Sebe Bom Meihy, 319–24.
Sadan, Manday. *Learning to Listen: A Manual for Oral History Projects*. New York: Open Society Foundations, 2008. https://www.opensocietyfoundations.org/publications/learning-listen-manual-oral-history-projects.
Sahagún, Bernadino de. *Historia General de las cosas de Nueva España*. Barcelona: Linkgua Ediciones, 2009 [1577].
Salgado Andrade, Eva. "Epilogue: One Year Later." *Oral History Review* 16 (Spring 1988): 21–31.
Samuel, Raphael, and Paul Thompson, eds. *The Myths We Live By*. New York: Routledge, 1990.
Sanchéz, George. *Becoming Mexican American: Ethnicity, Culture, and Identity in Chicano Los Angeles, 1900–1945*. New York: Oxford University Press, 1994.
Sanford, Victoria. *Buried Secrets: Truth and Human Rights in Guatemala*. New York: Palgrave Macmillan, 2003.
Sarlo, Beatriz. *Tiempo pasado: cultura de la memoria y giro subjetivo. Una discusión*. Buenos Aires: Siglo Veintiuno Editores, 2007.
Scarry, Elaine. *The Body of Pain: The Making and Unmaking of the World*. Oxford, England: Oxford University Press, 1987.
Scheper-Hughes, Nancy. *Saints, Scholars, and Schizophrenics: Mental Illness in Rural Ireland*. Berkeley: University of California Press, 1982.
Schirmer, Jennifer. *The Guatemalan Military Project: A Violence Called Democracy*. Philadelphia: University of Pennsylvania Press, 1998.
———. "Interviewing Military Officers: A Woman Researcher's Perspective." *ReVista: Harvard Review of Latin America* (Winter 1998). http://revista.drclas.harvard.edu/book/export/html/322651.
Schmidt Camacho, Alicia. "Ciudadana X: Gender Violence and the Denationalization of Women's Rights in Ciudad Juarez, Mexico." *New Centennial Review* 5, no. 1 (2005): 255–92.
Schreiner, Davi Félix. "Memórias da luta pela terra: De sem-terra migrantes ás ocupações coletivas." *Espaço Plural* 10, no. 20 (2009): 94–102.
Schwarzstein, Dora. "Historia oral, memoria e historias traumáticas." *Historia Oral* 4 (2001): 73–85.
———. "La historia oral en América Latina." *Historia y Fuente Oral* 14 (1994): 39–50.
———. "Memorializing Effervescence." *Journal of the International Oral History Association* 2, no. 2 (June 2003): 17–24.
———. "Oral History in Latin America." In *Oral History: An Interdisciplinary Anthology*, edited by David K. Dunaway and Willa K. Baum, 418–24. 2nd edition. New York: Altamira Press, 1996.
———. "Tendencias y temáticas de la historia oral en la Argentina." *Entrepasados: Revista de Historia* 9 (1995): 51–61.
Schwarzstein, Dora, and Pablo Yankelevich. *Historia oral y fuentes escritas en la historia de una institucion: La Universidad de Buenos Aires, 1955–1966*. Buenos Aires: Centro de Estudios de Estado y Sociedad, 1996.
Scott, James C. *Domination and the Arts of Resistance: Hidden Transcripts*. New Haven, CT: Yale University Press, 1990.

———. *Weapons of the Weak: Everyday Forms of Peasant Resistance.* New Haven, CT: Yale University Press, 1985.

Sebe Bom Meihy, José Carlos. "História oral: Um *locus* disciplinar federativo." In *(Re) Introduzindo a história oral no Brasil*, edited by Sebe Bom Meihy, 48–55.

———. "The Radicalization of Oral History." *Words and Silences* 2, no. 1 (2003): 31–41.

———, ed. *(Re)Introduzindo a história oral no Brasil.* São Paulo: Xamã, 1996.

———. "(Re)Introduzindo a história oral no Brasil." In *(Re)Introduzindo a história oral no Brasil*, edited by Sebe Bom Meihy, 1–10.

Sexton, James D., and Fredy Rodríguez, eds. and trans. *The Dog Who Spoke and More Mayan Folktales. El perro que habló y más cuentos mayas.* Stories told by Pedro Cholotío and Alberto Barreno. Norman: University of Oklahoma Press, 2010.

Sherzer, Joel. "The Kuna and Columbus: Encounters and Confrontations of Discourse." *American Anthropologist* 96, no. 4 (1994): 902–24.

———. "Namakke, Sunmakke, Kormakke: Three Types of Cuna Speech Events." In *Explorations in the Ethnography of Speaking*, edited by Richard Bauman and Joel Sherzer, 263–82. New York: Cambridge University Press, 1974.

———. "Strategies in Text and Context: The Hot Pepper Story." In *Recovering the Word: Essays on Native American Literature*, edited by Brian Swann and Arnold Krupat, 151–97. Berkeley: University of California Press, 1987.

Shopes, Linda. "Oral History and Community Involvement: The Baltimore Neighborhood Heritage Project." In *Presenting the Past: Essays on History and the Public*, edited by Roy Rosenzweig, Susan Porter Benson, and Stephen Brier, 249–66. Philadelphia: Temple University Press, 1986.

Siqueira de Souza Campos, Maria Christina. "Mulheres de diferentes classes sociais em São Paulo: A família e a penetração no mercado de trabalho." In *(Re)Introduzindo a história oral no Brasil*, edited by Sebe Bom Meihy, 179–96.

Sklodowska, Elzbieta. *Testimonio hispanoamericano: historia, teoría, poetíca.* New York: Peter Lang, 1992.

Slim, Hugo, and Paul Thompson. *Listening for a Change: Oral Testimony and Development.* London: Panos, 1993.

Small, Julie. Epilogue to *Adios to Tears: The Memoirs of a Japanese-Peruvian Internee in U.S. Concentration Camps*, edited by Seiichi Higashide, 249–53. Seattle: University of Washington Press, 2000.

Smith, Linda Tuhiwai. *Decolonizing Methodologies: Research and Indigenous People.* New York: Zed Books, 1999.

Smith, Lois M., and Fred Padula. *Sex and Revolution: Women in Socialist Cuba.* New York: Oxford University Press, 1996.

Los Socios de la Unión Tierra Tzotzil. *Lo'il sventa k'u cha'al la jmankutik jpinkatkutik Kipaltik: la historia de como compramos nuestra finca.* Edited and Translated by Salvador Guzmán López and Jan Rus. San Cristóbal de las Casas, Mexico: El Taller Tzotzil, Instituto de Asesoría Antropológica para la Región Maya, 1990.

Sobrino, Jon. *The Principle of Mercy: Taking the Crucified People from the Cross.* Maryknoll, NY: Orbis Books, 1994.

Solomon, Frank, and George L. Urioste, trans. *The Huarochiri Manuscript: A Testament of Ancient and Colonial Andean Religion.* Austin: University of Texas Press, 1991.

Soluri, John. *Banana Cultures: Agriculture, Consumption, and Environmental Change in Honduras and the United States.* Austin: University of Texas Press, 2006.

Sommer, Barbara W., and Mary Kay Quinlan. *The Oral History Manual.* 2nd edition. Lanham, MD: Altamira Press, 2009.

Soto Laveaga, Gabriela. *Jungle Laboratories: Mexican Peasants, National Projects, and the Making of the Pill*. Durham, NC: Duke University Press, 2009.

Spivak, Gayatri Chakravorty. "Can the Subaltern Speak?" In *Colonial Discourse and Post-Colonial Theory: A Reader*, edited by Patrick Williams and Laura Chrisman, 66–111. New York: Columbia University Press, 1994.

Stacey, Judith. "Can There be a Feminist Ethnography?" In *Women's Words: The Feminist Practice of Oral History*, edited by Sherna Berger Gluck and Daphne Patai, 111–19.

Starn, Orin. *Nightwatch: The Politics of Protest in the Andes*. Durham, NC: Duke University Press, 1999.

Stein, Steve. "Essence and Identity: Transformations in Argentine Wine, 1880–2010." In *Alcohol in Latin America: A Social and Cultural History*, edited by Gretchen Pierce and Áurea Toxqui, 210–41. Tucson: University of Arizona Press, 2014.

———. "La historia oral y la creación de los documentos históricos." *Universitas Humanística* 15, no. 26 (July–December 1986): 135–40.

Stephen, Lynn. *¡Zapata Lives! History and Cultural Politics in Southern Mexico*. Berkeley: University of California Press, 2002.

Stephenson, Marcia. "Forging an Indigenous Counterpublic Sphere: The Taller de Historia Oral Andina in Bolivia." *Latin American Research Review* 37, no. 2 (2002): 99–118.

Stern, Steve. *Battling for Hearts and Minds: Memory Struggles in Pinochet's Chile, 1973–1988*. Durham, NC: Duke University Press, 2006.

———. *Reckoning with Pinochet: The Memory Question in Democratic Chile, 1989–2006*. Durham, NC: Duke University Press, 2010.

———. *Remembering Pinochet's Chile: On the Eve of London 1998*. Durham, NC: Duke University Press, 2004.

Stockwell, Jill. "The Country That Doesn't Want to Heal Itself: The Burdens of History, Affect, and Women's Memories in Post-Dictatorial Argentina." *International Journal of Conflict and Violence* 8, no. 1 (2014): 30–44.

Stoll, David. *Rigoberta Menchú and the Story of All Poor Guatemalans*. Boulder, CO: Westview Press, 1999.

Strejelivich, Nora. "Testimony: Beyond the Language of Truth." *Human Rights Quarterly* 23, no. 3 (2006): 701–13.

Striffler, Steve. *In the Shadows of State and Capital: The United Fruit Company, Popular Struggle, and Agrarian Restructuring in Ecuador, 1900–1995*. Durham, NC: Duke University Press, 2001.

Suárez Núñez, José. *El gran culpable: ¿Cómo 12 guerrilleros aniquilaron a 45.000 soldados?* Caracas, 1963.

Sullivan, Paul. *Unfinished Conversations: Mayas and Foreigners between Two Wars*. New York: Alfred A. Knopf, 1989.

Taller de Historia Oral Andina (THOA). Taller de Historia Oral Andina (Oral Andean History Workshop)–Bolivia. December 19, 2002. http://www.comminit.com/democracy-governance/content/taller-de-historia-oral-andina-oral-andean-history-workshop-bolivia.

Tate, Winifred. *Counting the Dead: The Culture and Politics of Human Rights Activism in Colombia*. Berkeley: University of California Press, 2007.

Taussig, Michael. *Shamanism, Colonialism, and the Wild Man: A Study in Terror and Healing*. Chicago: University of Chicago Press, 1987.

———. "Violence and Resistance in the Americas: The Legacy of Conquest." In *Challenging the Field: Vol. 2 of Twenty Years of the Journal of Historical Sociology*, edited by Yoke-Sum Wong and Derek Sayer, 7–24. Hoboken, NJ: Wiley-Blackwell, 2009.

Taylor, Diane. *Disappearing Acts: Spectacles of Gender and Nationalism in Argentina's 'Dirty War'*. Durham, NC: Duke University Press, 1997.

Taylor, Paul S. *Mexican Labor in the United States.* 2 vols. New York: Arno Press and New York Times, 1970.

Taylor, William. *Drinking, Homicide, and Rebellion in Colonial Mexican Villages.* Stanford, CA: Stanford University Press, 1979.

———. *Theater of a Thousand Wonders: A History of Miraculous Images and Shrines in New Spain.* New York: Cambridge University Press, 2016.

Tedlock, Dennis. *Finding the Center: Narrative Poetry of the Zuni Indians.* Lincoln: University of Nebraska Press, 1978.

———, trans. *Popol Vuh: The Definitive Edition of the Mayan Book of the Dawn of Life and the Glories of Gods and Kings.* New York: Touchstone, 1996.

———. *Spoken Word and the Work of Interpretation.* Philadelphia: University of Pennsylvania Press, 1983.

Thompson, Paul. *The Voice of the Past: Oral History.* 3rd edition. Oxford: Oxford University Press, 2000.

Thompson, Paul, and Natasha Burchardt, eds. *Our Common History: The Transformation of Europe.* Atlantic Highlands, NJ: Humanities Press, 1982.

Thomson, Alistair. "Four Paradigm Transformations in Oral History." *Oral History Review* 34, no. 1 (2007): 49–70.

Tinsman, Heidi. "A Paradigm of Our Own: Joan Scott in Latin American History." *American Historical Review* 113, no. 5 (2008): 1357–74.

———. *Partners in Conflict: The Politics of Gender, Sexuality, and Labor in the Chilean Agrarian Reform, 1950–1973.* Durham, NC: Duke University Press, 2014.

Titan, Jeff Todd. "The Life Story." *Journal of American Folklore* 93 (July/September, 1980): 276–92.

Torres Montenegro, Antonio. "Dominación cultural y memoria, otras historias." In *Caminos de historia y memoria en América Latina,* edited by Necoechea Gracia and Torres Montenegro, 155–66.

Tracy, Ramsey. "Mayan Interpretations of Time and History: Mediating the Past to Understand the Present." Paper presented at Latin American Studies Association Conference, May 26, 2012, San Francisco, CA.

Trouillot, Michel-Rolph. *Silencing the Past: Power and the Production of History.* Boston: Beacon Press, 1995.

Tula, Maria Teresa. *Hear My Testimony: María Teresa Tula, Human Rights Activist of El Salvador.* Edited by Lynn Stephen. Boston: South End Press, 1994.

Turits, Richard Lee. *Foundations of Despotism: Peasants, the Trujillo Regime, and Modernity in Dominican History.* Stanford, CA: Stanford University Press, 2003.

Urban, Greg. *Discourse Centered Approach to Culture: Native South American Myths and Rituals.* Austin: University of Texas Press, 1991.

Urrutia Lleo, Manuel. *Fidel Castro and Company, Inc.* New York: F. A. Praeger, 1984.

Van Isschot, Luis. "The Heart of Activism in Colombia: Reflections on Activism and Oral History Research in a Conflict Area." In *Oral History off the Record: Toward an Ethnography of Practice,* edited by Ann Sheftel and Stacey Zembrzycki, 239–53. New York: Palgrave Macmillan, 2013.

Vansina, Jan. *Living with Africa.* Madison: University of Wisconsin Press, 1994.

———. *Oral Tradition as History.* Madison: University of Wisconsin Press, 1985.

Varas, Florencia. *Gustavo Leigh: El general disidente.* Santiago, Chile: Editorial Aconcagua, 1979.

Vasconcelos, José. *A Mexican Ulysses: An Autobiography.* Translated and abridged by W. Rex Crawford. Bloomington: University of Indiana Press, 1936.

Vásquez, Juan Gabriel. *The Sound of Things Falling*. New York: Riverhead Books, 2013.
Velasco, Cuauhtémoc, ed. *Historia y testimonios orales*. Mexico City: Instituto Nacional de Antropología e Historia, 1996.
Venegas Aguilera, Lilia. "Cultura política y mujeres de sector popular: Ciudad Juárez entre 1983 y 1986." In *Historia y testimonios orales*, edited by Cuauhtémoc Velasco, 123–40.
Viano, Cristina. "Historia reciente e historia oral. Algunas reflexiones sobre un derrotero inseparable en la historiografía argentina actual." In *Caminos de historia y memoria en América Latina*, edited by Necoechea Gracia and Torres Montenegro, 277–88.
Vicaría de Solidaridad. *Chile, la memoria prohibida*. Santiago, Chile: Vicaría de Solidaridad, 1989.
———. *¿Donde están?* Santiago, Chile: Vicaría de Solidaridad, 1979.
Vommaro, Pablo. "Las organizaciones sociales en la Argentina contemporánea: un acercamiento desde la historia oral." *Voces Recobradas* 32, no. 1 (2012): 60–7.
———. "Territorios, organizaciones sociales y migraciones: las experiencias de las tomas de tierras y los astentamientos de 1981 en Quilmes." *Espaço Plural* 10, no. 20 (2009): 81–93.
Wankar (Ramiro Reynaga). *Tawantinsuyu: cinco siglos de guerra qheswaymara contra España*. Mexico City: Nuevo Imagen, 1981.
Warren, Kay. *Symbolism of Subordination: Indian Identity in a Guatemalan Town*. Austin: University of Texas Press, 1989.
Weld, Kirsten A. "Dignifying the *Guerrillero*, Not the Assassin: Rewriting a History of Criminal Subversion in Postwar Guatemala." *Radical History Review* 113 (Spring 2012): 35–53.
———. *Paper Cadavers: The Archives of Dictatorship in Guatemala*. Durham, NC: Duke University Press, 2014.
Wells, Allen. *Tropical Zion: General Trujillo, FDR, and the Jews of Sosúa*. Durham, NC: Duke University Press, 2009.
Wells, Allen, and Gilbert M. Joseph. *Summer of Discontent, Seasons of Upheaval: Elite Politics and Rural Insurgency in Yucatán, 1876–1915*. Stanford, CA: Stanford University Press.
Wilkie, James W. *Elitelore*. Los Angeles: UCLA Latin American Center, 1996.
———. "Introduction: The Scope of Elitelore (Elitelore at Forty Five)." In *Elitelore Varieties: 17 Views in World Context*, edited by James W. Wilkie, David E. Lorey, and Olga M. Lazín, 1–31. Los Angeles: Elitelore Books, 2012. http://elitelore.org/articles/Introduction_The_Scope_of_Elitelore.pdf.
———. "Postulates of the Oral History Center for Latin America." *Journal of Library History* 2 (January 1967): 45–55.
Wilkie, James W., and Edna Monzón Wilkie, eds. *Frente a la Revolución Mexicana: 17 protagonistas de la etapa constructiva: entrevistas de historial oral*. 4 vols. Mexico City: Universidad Autónoma Metropolitana, 1995–2004.
———. *México visto en el siglo XX*. Mexico City: Instituto Mexicano de Investigaciones Económicas, 1969.
Wilkinson, Daniel. *Silence on the Mountain: Stories of Terror, Betrayal, and Forgetting in Guatemala*. Durham, NC: Duke University Press, 2012.
Winn, Peter. "Oral History and the Factory Study: New Approaches to Labor History." *Latin American Research Review* 14, no. 2 (1979): 130–40.
———. *Weavers of Revolution: The Yarur Workers and Chile's Road to Socialism*. New York: Oxford University Press, 1986.

Woitowicz, Karina Janz, and Joana Maria Pedro. "O movimento feminista durante a ditadura militar no Brasil e no Chile: Conjugando as lutas pela democracia política com o direito ao corpo." *Espaco Plural* 10, no. 21 (2nd Semester 2009): 43–55.

Yates, Pamela. "Memoryscape." *ReVista: Harvard Review of Latin America* 13, no. 1 (Fall 2013): 58–61.

Yool Gómez, Juan, and Juan Kaqjay. *Tzijonik kan qate' qatata'*. Guatemala City: Universidad Rafael Landivar, 1990.

Yow, Valerie Raleigh. *Recording Oral History: A Guide for Humanities and Social Sciences*. 2nd edition. Lanham, MD: Altamira Press, 2005.

Zinn, Howard. *SNCC: The New Abolitionists*. Boston: Beacon Press, 1964.

Zolov, Eric. *Refried Elvis: The Rise of Mexican Counterculture*. Berkeley: University of California Press, 1999.

Zulawski, Ann. *Unequal Cures: Public Health and Political Change in Bolivia, 1900–1950*. Durham, NC: Duke University Press, 2007.

Index

Note: Page number in *italics* indicate figures.

Abercrombie, Thomas 112
abstracts of interviews 48–9, 50
academic imperialism 77
activism 84–7, 140–1
Acuña Ortega, Victor Hugo 21, 39, 110, 125–6
Adams, Gerry 83
Adleson, Steven Lief 94
advocacy and oral history projects 86–7
Afro-Brazilians 163, 172, 197
Afro-Latin Americans: discrimination against 61, 163; *historia patria* and 67–8; histories of 159; interview techniques and 38; orality and 6, 80; poverty of 184; Saramakas 111, 123; truth and 120; women and language 126
AHPH (Archivo Histórico de la Policía Nacional, Guatemala) 194, 195
Alegre, Robert 30, 37
Alexievich, Svetlana 128
Allen, Barbara 109
American Historical Association, ethical guidelines of 76
amnesia, historical 117
analysis of oral histories 20; *see also* interpretation of oral history
Anderson, Kathryn 42
anonymity 22, 23, 61, 82
anthropology and oral history 13; *see also* ethnography and oral history; *specific anthropologists and ethnographers*
Araújo, Maria Paula 5
Arbenz, Jacobo 108
architecture, lived 144–7
archival collections: access to 60–2; example of 56; identifying repositories 57–60; in Latin America 194; rules on protecting identity of human subjects and 82–3; storage and maintenance 62–3; supporting materials 63–5
Archivo Histórico de la Policía Nacional (AHPH, Guatemala) 194, 195
Argentina: Asociación de Historia Oral de la República Argentina 12; Dirty War in 24, 44, 61, 117, 127, 137, 186; gays and lesbians in 152–3; Instituto Di Tella 10, 170; *piqueteros'* accounts from 147–8; repositories in 58; viticulture in 175–6
audio recordings 47, 68, 200–1
authorial relations 78–82
authoritarian regimes, accounts of 113, 115–16; *see also* Pinochet, Augusto; Trujillo, Rafael; Ubico, Jorge
Auyero, Javier 13
Aversa, María Marta 147
Ayress, Nieves 44, 78, 187

Bachelet, Michelle 70, 117
Balán, Jorge 170
Bancroft, Hubert Howe 7–8
Barela, Liliana 194
Barnet, Miguel 184
Barros Arana, Diego 6
Bauman, Richard 99
Becker, Marjorie 172–3
Behar, Ruth 110–11, 171, 172
Benjamin, Medea 170–1
Bergen, Jonas 7
Beverley, John 81, 185
biases in scholarship 106–7
Blee, Kathleen 20
body language and nonverbal communication 92–4

Boesten, Jan 24, 37–8, 121
Bolivia, Taller de Historia Aral Andina 96–7
borderlands history 197–8
Brazil: Amnesty Caravan program 70–1; Amnesty Committee of Justice Department 5; gays and lesbians in 153; Getúlio Vargas Foundation 8–9, 170; Japanese in 161–2; oral history projects in 9, 10, 58
Browarnik, Graciela 147
Bruey, Alison 35
budget for research projects 23–4
Burgos-Debray, Elizabeth 81, 110, 170
business in oral life history 174–7

Cabrera Garcia, Olga 105
Cabrera y Quintero, Cayetano 6
Caetano, Gerardo 141
Calveiro, Pilar 125
Camarena Ocampo, Mario 118
Camargo Ríos, Marcela 12, 30
Camp, Rod 36, 38, 45, 48, 65, 196
Cano Sánchez, Beatriz 40, 92
Cárdenas, Lázaro 169, 173
Castañeda, Mario 86
Castillo Troncoso, Alberto del 199
Castro, Fidel 82, 182, 183
Catholic Church in Latin America 177–80
Chile: agrarian reform in 129–30, 149; military coup in 138–9; oral history projects in 10; Project Cybersyn 199–200; *see also* Pinochet, Augusto
chronology in reconstruction of past 107–9
Cicatriz de la memoria (documentary film) 66, 67, 87, 199
Cieza de León, Pedro 6
civil war: in Colombia 39, 111, 199; crimes associated with 83–4; in El Salvador 5; in Guatemala 34, *40*, 45, 68, 86, 90, 124, 194, 195; in Ireland 83; in Peru 113, 125, 181–2; *testimonio* and 184–7; *see also* truth and reconciliation commissions
class: middle-class accounts 144–7, *145*; in oral life history 173–4; in topical oral history 147–51; *see also* working-class accounts
Coca-Cola union members 101
collaboration: on dissemination of research materials 65–8; ethical relations and 75, 76–8; on interpretation 110; on research projects 20–1; transnational 12
collective inaccuracies 121–2
collective in oral life history 186
Colombia 39, 111, 199; *see also* Cumbales
communication across cultures: body language and nonverbal cues 92–4; language and 90–2; overview of 90, 101–2; performance 98–101; translations 94–8
Communist Party, accounts of 150
community: as absent audience to interviews 100–1; in development of research projects 20–1
Consalvi, Carlos Henríquez 66
Cosío Villegas, Daniel 169
Costa Rica, coffee from 176
courts, testimony in 195
Creating Emerging Markets Oral History Collection 64, 174–5
critical theory 20
Cuba: gays and lesbians in 152, 153, 154; oral history projects in 11, 82; oral life history research in 182–4
Cueto, Adolfo 175
cultural context and interpretation of oral histories 118–19; *see also* communication across cultures
Cumbales 77, 80, 86
Cutler, William 121

Dalton, Roque 184
Dary, Claudia 113
da Silva, Benedita 172, 178, 180
decolonizing: dissemination 66; interpretation 110; research and scholarship 20–1, 28–9, 67, 75, 76–9, 201
Dehesa, Rafael de la 37
del Pino, Ponciano 181
digital revolution and oral history 200–1
discrimination, accounts of 162–3, 172
dissemination 60, 65–8
domestic/gender-based violence 128, 139, 154
Dominican Republic 142; *see also* Trujillo, Rafael
Dore, Elizabeth 37
Duarte, Geni Rosa 65
Dutrénit Bielous, Silvia 34, 194

Ecuador 149–50, 155
Edelman, Gerald 111

elitelore 173, 174
elites: economic, oral life histories of 169–70, 173–7; memoirs or autobiographies of 169; oral histories of 7–8, 9
El Salvador 5, 115, 148; *see also Cicatriz de la memoria*
environmental history 197
Esquit, Edgar 41, 97
Estrada Cabrera, Manuel 119
ethical concerns: collaboration and 76–8; in developing nations 76; overview of 75; protection of identity of interviewees 82–4; when preparing for projects 76
ethnicity in topical oral history 159–64
ethnography and oral history 45–7, *46*, 99
evangelical religion 179–80, 181–2
Evaristo Wenceslau, Marina 90
evidence, corroborating, for oral narratives 185–6
exile, accounts of 140
eye contact 93

Falla, Ricardo 68
Farnsworth-Alvear, Ann 13–14, 42, 100, 116, 149
female interviewees 28–9, 100
femininity 1, 116, 128, 154, 155
Fernandez, Nadine 95–6
fiction, as epitomized oral history 183
fieldwork 22, 46–7
Florencia, Francisco de 6
following up 48
forgetting 112, 123–6; *see also* memory; silences
Frank, Benis 106
Freire, Paulo xi, xii, 8
Frisch, Michael 66–7, 75, 81, 106, 201
Fujimori, Alberto 113, 142

Garay, Graciela de 83, 176
García de León, Antonio 195
García Márquez, Gabriel 173
Garulli, Liliana 33
gays and lesbians *see* sexual identity
gender: in Cuba 183; interpretation through 126–30; in Mexican housing complex 146; in topical oral history 154–9; violence and 128, 139, 154; *see also* femininity; masculinity; women
Gerardi Conedera, Juan José 69

Gómez, Juan Yool 67
González, Olga 39, 124
Gossen, Gary 99
Goulart, João Belchior Marques 140, 141
Gould, Jeffrey 24, 25, 66, 115
Grandin, Greg 69
group interviews 35–6
Guatemala: Archivo Histórico de la Policía Nacional (AHPH) 194, 195; civil war in 34, *40*, 45, 68, 86, 90, 124, 194, 195; Ixil Maya of 185; K'iche' Maya of 5, 86, 124; *see also* Kaqchikel Maya
Gudmundson, Lowell 176
Guzmán, Patricio 112
Guzmán López, Salvador 65

Haiti, language in 91
Hamilton, Carrie 98–9
Hankiss, Agnes 173–4
historia patria narratives 68
Historia y Fuente Oral (journal) 12
historical preservation grants 59
historicity, aspects of 5
history: interpretation of 105; myth as on continuum with 123; of oral history 6–12; writing, views of 80
Horton, Myles xi, xii, 8
housing in Mexico 144–7, *145*, 177
Huggins, Martha 2, 84
human rights abuses: Catholic Church and 178; ethical issues and 83–4; forgetting 117; *historia patria* and 68; industry leaders and 175; Meyer on 4; by military officers 138, 185; oral history and 10, 11, 69–71, 186–7, 194; scholar-activists and 84–5; trauma and 43–5

images and oral history 199
indigenous languages, disparagement of 91, 96; *see also* Maya languages and Spanish
indigenous voices in oral history 5, 159–64, 196–7; *see also specific indigenous groups*
inequality in interviewer-interviewee relations 78–82
informant-influenced approaches 20–1
informed consent 23, 32, 47–8, 82
institutional review boards (IRBs) 22–3, 82–3
Instituto Mora Programa de Historia Oral (Mexico City) 85, 86

Instituto Nacional de Antropología e Historia (Mexico) 10, 58, 63–4
Instituto Torcuato Di Tella 57
interclass relations, accounts of 120, 148–9, 151
interdisciplinary nature of oral history 13–14
International Oral History Association 12
Internet Archive digital library 62
interpretation of oral history: through gender and patriarchy 126–30; memory and 111–13, 115–18; overview of 105–6; silences 123–6; transparency of 106–11; truth, telling 118–23
interviewees: control of interviews by 182; dissemination of recordings or transcripts to 65; female 28–9, 100; imposing perspectives on 85; meeting with 29–30; paying 31; protecting identity of 82–4; rapport with 30–1, 32; repaying and reciprocating time of 78; sampling and recruiting 25–8, 27; working with 24–5
interviewing techniques: cross-examination 34; cultural context 36, 38; examples of 33–4; group interviews 35–6; introduction 33; political context 37–9; preparation 36–7; questions 37–8; rapport, building 32–3; technology and 34–5; visual aids 39–41, *40*, *41*
interviews: abstracts and summaries of 48–9, 50; as co-constructed 79, 81; community as audience to 100–1; as contested processes 80; reflexivity in 110; rights to and ownership of 81–2; timing of 106; transcriptions of 49–50; *see also* interviewees; interviewing techniques
IRBs (institutional review boards) 22–3, 82–3
Ireland, civil war in 83
Isschot, Luis van 79
Ixil Maya 185

Jack, Dana C. 42
Jaksíc, Iván 3, 9
James, Daniel 33, 34, 39, 40, 80, 81, 110, 116, 120, 123, 125, 170
Japanese Brazilians 161–2
Japanese Peruvians 160–1, *161*, 162–3
Jelin, Elizabeth 67, 122, 124, 128, 175
Jemio, Ana 26, 31, 44–5, 56, 61, 85, 186–7

Jewish refugees in Dominican Republic 142
Jones, Geoffrey 174, 175
Journal for Multimedia History 68
Julião, Francisco 81–2

Kaplan, Temma 78, 116
Kaqchikel Maya: collaboration with 28–9; Dary and 113; Esquit and 97; interviews with 41, 45–6, 57, 109; life among 107; performance and 98; sharing of findings with 65, 75, 77–8, 79; watershed events and 21, 108, 118–19
Kaqjay, Juan 67
Kay, Cristóbal 151
Kennedy, Elizabeth 48
Kerr, Dan 37
K'iche' Maya 5, 86, 124; *see also* Menchú, Rigoberta
K'iche' Maya Oral History Project 64
Klubock, Thomas 69, 156

labor movements, accounts of 149–51, 160
ladinos 65, 119, 160, 185
language: body language 92–4; power and 90–2; of publication 65, 77, 79; translations of 94–8
La Serna, Miguel 41, 107
Latin America, map of 7
lesbians *see* sexual identity
Levenson, Deborah 39, 76, 101, 125
Lewis, Oscar 9, 56, 82, 110
liberation theology 178
life history interview methodology 33
life-story technique *see* oral life history
listening skills and tools 42–3
literacy/illiteracy 117, 195
Lobato, Marta Zaida 58–9, 110, 127
locations for interviews 31–2
Lockwood, Lee 182, 183
Lovell, George 96
Lynd, Alice 8
Lynd, Staughton 8

McNeill, William 193
Mallon, Florencia 21, 120, 127
marginalization and language 91
marginalized perspectives in oral history 1, 8–9
Mármol, Miguel 184
Martínez, Maximiliano Hernández 115
Martínez Omaña, María Concepción 86

masculinity 116, 126, 128, 146, 149, 151, 154, 155–6
Mastrángelo, Mariana 118, 172
Maya ceremony, author at 17, *18*
Maya languages and Spanish 91, 97; *see also* Kaqchikel Maya; K'iche' Maya; Tzotzil language
Mbilinyi, Marjorie 85
medicine, health, and disease research 198–9
Medina, Eden 27, 199
memoirs 11, 14, 169, 174, 182
memory: analyzing past and 111–13; buried xiii–xiv; chronological time and 107–8; forgetting and 123–6; language and 91–2; religion and 181
men *see* gender; masculinity; patriarchy
Menand, Louis 92, 113
Menchú, Rigoberta 80, 81, 91, 170, 185–6
Mendonça, Maisa 170–1
metadaya synchronizers 200
Mexico: housing in 144–7, *145*, 177; Instituto Nacional de Antropología e Historia 10, 58, 63–4; oral history projects in 2, 10–11, 42, 57–8, 118, 130; Programa de Historia Oral 10–11, 57–8; student movement in 144; Tlatelolco massacre in 138; *see also* Mixtecs; Tzotzil language; Zapotecs
Meyer, Eugenia 2, 4, 9, 10, 11, 42, 63
middle-class accounts 144–7, *145*
military elites 137, 138
Mintz, Sidney 118, 179, 180, 186
Mitre, Bartolomé 6
Mixtecs 37, 85–6, 94–5, 126, 160
Mondloch, James 64
Montejo, Esteban 184
Montysuma, Marcos 158
monuments, public 117–18
Moreiras, Alberto 79
Mousnier, Roland 195
murals *39*, 39–41, 45, 66, 101
myth, as on continuum with history 123

Necoechea Gracia, Gerardo 2, 4, 37, 42, 68, 84, 85–6, 94–5, 118, 130, 193
Nevins, Allan 7
Nicaragua 37, 198
nonelites, oral histories of 8–9
nonverbal communication 92–4
Nora, Pierre 117
Northern Ireland, oral history project in 83

Oakley, Ann 34, 38, 76
Office of Human Research Protections 22–3
oppressor perspectives in oral history 1–2
oral history: buried memory and xiii–xiv; constructed nature of 105, 173; definition of 2–3; digital revolution and 200–1; first wave of projects in Latin America 105; history of 6–12; interdisciplinary nature of 13–14; as learning experience xi–xii; as means and end xii–xiii; scholarship in field of 3; in twenty-first century 192–3; uses of, in Latin America 1–2, 8–9; *see also* interpretation of oral history; oral life history; politics of oral history; techniques of oral history; topical oral history
Oral History Association 8, 76
oral history collections, creation of 19–20
Oral History Research Office, Columbia University 10, 57, 170
orality and writing, tensions between 193–6
oral life history: in Cuba 182–4; of economic elites 173–7; longitudinal approach of 170–4; overview of 2, 136, 169–70; religion and 177–82; techniques of 17, 19
oral testimony 2, 4–5
ownership of interviews 81–2

Pandolfi, Dulce 70–1
Park, Rebekah 128
Pasquali, Laura 33, 43
Passerini, Luisa 127, 128
Patagonia, INTECO factory in 148, 158–9
Patai, Daphne 76–7, 78, 85, 118, 171, 186
patriarchy 126–30, 154–9
Patriz, Reynaldo 24, 25, 136
patterns of narrative organization 109
Patzicía, Guatemala, massacre in 108
Paz, Octavio 124
Pelayo Rangel, Alejandro 187
Pérez Jolote, Juan 184
performance and storytelling 98–101
Peru: civil war in 113, 125, 181–2; Japanese in 160–1, *161*, 162; oral history projects in 10
Picado, Wilson 176
Pinochet, Augusto: Ayress and 187; dictatorship of 10, 35, 44, 112, 149; massacre under 93; oral histories of life

under 45, 46; perspectives on 142, 174, 188; TRC after 69; victims/survivors of 70, 127, 139
Pisani, Alejandra 26, 31, 44–5, 56, 61, 85, 186–7
politics and religion 178
politics of oral history: overview of 3–6; scholar-activists and 84–7; topical oral history and 137–43; versions of past and 136–7
Poniatowska, Elena 2, 20
Popol Wuj 5
popular culture and state power 143–4
Portelli, Alessandro 4, 20, 76, 77, 99, 101, 108, 120–1
Posocco, Silvia 79
postconflict nations, rebuilding of 5, 69–71
Power, Margaret 39
power interviewer-interviewee relations 78–82
Pozas, Ricardo 184
Pozzi, Pablo 4, 23, 38, 68, 78, 84, 120, 172, 192
Prelorán, Jorge 66
Prelorán, Mabel 66
Price, Richard 111
Programa de Historia Oral (Mexico) 10–11, 57–8
protection of informants 82–4
psychology and oral history 13
public schools, dissemination in 65

Quechua 66, 86, 96
questions, neutral, open-ended 37
quota sampling 26

racial identity 96, 197–8
racism 160, 183–4
Rainer, Hostig 67
Ramos Pacho, Abelardo 20, 21, 107
Rapa Nui 99, 101
rape, accounts of 139–40
Rappaport, Joanne 21, 28, 77, 107
Rasnake, Roger 86
reciprocal manipulation 79; *see also* power interviewer-interviewee relations
reconstruction of past, understanding 107–9
recruiting interviewees 25–8, 27
Red Latinoamericana de Historia Oral 12
reflexivity in interview process 110
regional differences in oral history 4

Regional Oral History Center, University of California, Berkeley 7
religion in oral life history 177–82
repositories 57–63
research assistants, working with 24, 25
research projects: defining 19–22; directions for 196–200; vetting 22–4
resistance, accounts of 33, 101, 123, 142, 172
Rettig, Raúl 69
Reyes Castillo Bueno, María de los 80
Riani, Clodesmidt 141
Ríos Montt, José Efraín 5
Ritchie, Donald 45, 63
Rodríguez, Ana 182–3
Ruiz-Funes, Concepción 29
Rus, Diane 92
Rus, Jan 65, 92

Sá Almeida, Anna Beatriz de 199
Sadan, Manday 196
Sahagún, Bernadino de 6
sampling techniques 25–7
Sanford, Victoria 39, 70
Saramakas 111, 123
Sarlo, Beatriz 105–6
Scaramal, Eliesse 105
Scheper-Hughes, Nancy 76
Schilling, Flávia 1, 140
Schirmer, Jennifer 33, 137
scholar-activists 84–7
Schwarzstein, Dora 19, 43–4, 105, 111, 117, 196
Scott, James 79, 124
Sebe Bom Meihy, José Carlos 14, 84
semistructured interviews 33
sexual identity 96, 151–4
Shining Path (Sendero Luminoso) 113, 142, 181
silences: historical 158; interpretation of 123–6; listening for 42–3
Silva, Hélio 10
Siqueira de Souza Campos, Maria Christina 29
social context of oral histories 110–11
social justice 9, 11, 78, 109, 150, 175; *see also* truth and reconciliation commissions
social location method 26
socioeconomic class *see* class; working-class accounts
sociology and oral history 13
Soto Laveaga, Gabriela 27, 61, 199

spatial conceptions in reconstruction of past 108
spatial transformations and memory 118
Stacey, Judith 30
Starn, Orin 24, 29
state power and popular culture 143–4
state terror, accounts of 138–9, 194
Stephen, Lynn 77, 85
Stern, Steve 26, 35, 45, 46, 93, 111, 112, 122, 188
Stoll, David 110, 185
storytelling, performative aspects of 98–101
Strejelivich, Nora 186
Striffler, Steve 121, 122, 150
structured forgetting 112
subjectivity and oral history 80, 105, 110, 192
Sullivan, Paul 98
summaries of interviews 48–9
supporting materials 63–5

Taller de Historia Aral Andina (Bolivia) 96–7
Tate, Winifred 30, 39
Taussig, Michael 111, 115
Taylor, Diane 127
techniques of oral history: defining project, informant group, and interviewees 19–22; ethnography 45–7, *46*; interviewing 32–41; listening 42–3; overview of 17, 19; relationships with interviewees 25–32; technology 47; transcribing interviews 49–50; traumatic topics 43–5; vetting research projects 22–4; working with research assistants and interviewees 24–5; wrapping up interviews 47–9
technology: digital 64, 200–1; interviewing techniques and 34–5, 47; recordings 47, 68, 92, 200–1; storage and maintenance of materials and 62–3
testimonio literature: marginalized people and 170; overview of 9–10, 169; power imbalances and 79; truth telling and 184–8
theory, organic development of 20–1
Thompson, Paul 26, 28
timing of interviews 106
Tinsman, Heidi 120
topical oral history: ethnicity and 159–64; gender and patriarchy and 154–9; lived architecture and 144–7; oral life history and 187–8; overview of 2, 19, 136–7; politics, violence, and 137–43; popular culture and 143–4; sexuality struggles and 151–4; socioeconomic class and 147–51
Torres Montenegro, Antonio 178–9, 192
transcriptions of interviews 49–50
translations 94–8
transnational collaborations 12
transparency of interpretation of oral history 106–11
trauma, recounting 43–5, 93, 139–40
Trouillot, Michel-Rolph 60
Trujillo, Rafael 115, *116*, 141–2, 155–6
truth, telling 118–23, 184–8
truth and reconciliation commissions (TRCs) 4, 68–71, 113
Tuñón, Enriqueta 29
Turits, Richard 115, 141–2
Tzotzil language 65, 92, 184

Ubico, Jorge 113, *114*, 119, 141
United Fruit Company (UFCO) 122, 149, 160, 173
United States (US): foreign policy in Latin America 106, 198; oral history in 7–8, 37, 45; universities in, as repositories 57
universal sampling 26–7
Uruguay 1, 141

Vansina, Jan 99
Vásquez, Juan Gabriel 36
Vasquez Vicente, Luis 67
Velázquez, Fidel 174
verification of oral histories 121
vetting research projects 22–4
Viano, Cristina 85
Videla, Jorge Rafael 137
video recordings 47, 92, 200–1
Vieira de Souza, Jessie Jane 1
Vila, Pablo 67
violence: domestic/gender-based 128, 139, 154; in Latin America 1–2, 125, 137–43, 192
visual aids 39–41, *40*, *41*
Voces oral history project, University of Texas at Austin 64–5

Wakuénais 80, 108, 159
Wankar (Ramiro Reynaga) 77
Weld, Kirsten 32, 82
Wells, Allen 142

Wilkie, Edna 9, 34, 35–6
Wilkie, James 9, 34, 35–6, 81, 172, 173, 174
Wilkinson, Daniel 90
Winn, Peter 151
Wolfe, Justin 37
women: dominant narratives of 100; education of 126, 158; employment of 158–9; as interviewees 28–9, 100; *see also* femininity; gender
working-class accounts 147–51, 172

World War II internment camps 162–3, *163*
writing and orality, tensions between 193–6
writing history, views of 80
Wyschogrod, Edith 70

Yankelevich, Pablo 196
Yow, Valerie 26

Zapotecs 37, 85–6, 94–5, 126, 160